The Politics of Imagining Asia

The Politics of Imagining Asia

WANG HUI

Edited by Theodore Huters

Harvard University Press
Cambridge, Massachusetts, and London, England
2011

Copyright © 2011 by the President and Fellows of Harvard College
All rights reserved
Printed in the United States of America

Library of Congress Cataloging-in-Publication Data
Wang, Hui.
    The politics of imagining Asia / Wang Hui ; edited by Theodore Huters.
      p. cm.
    Includes bibliographical references and index.
    ISBN 978-0-674-05519-3 (alk. paper)
    1. East Asia—Civilization.   2. Civilization, Modern.   3. Comparative civilization.   4. Historiography—Political aspects—East Asia.   5. East Asia—Relations—Western countries.   6. Western countries—Relations—East Asia.   I. Huters, Theodore.   II. Title.
  DS509.3.W28   2011
  950.072—dc22   2010036508

Contents

Introduction ... 1
by Theodore Huters

1 The Politics of Imagining Asia ... 10
Translated by Matthew A. Hale

2 How to Explain "China" and Its "Modernity":
Rethinking *The Rise of Modern Chinese Thought* ... 63
Translated by Wang Yang

3 Local Forms, Vernacular Dialects, and the
War of Resistance against Japan:
The "National Forms" Debate ... 95
Translated by Chris Berry

4 The "Tibetan Question" East and West:
Orientalism, Regional Ethnic Autonomy, and the
Politics of Dignity ... 136
Translated by Theodore Huters

5 Okinawa and Two Dramatic Changes to the
Regional Order ... 228
Translated by Zhang Yongle

6 Weber and the Question of Chinese Modernity   264
Translated by Theodore Huters

Notes   309

Credits   347

Index   349

The Politics of Imagining Asia

Introduction

BY THEODORE HUTERS

Writing some forty-five years ago in his Introduction to Benjamin Schwartz's landmark monograph on the late Qing Dynasty intellectual and translator Yan Fu, the scholar of American history Louis Hartz transcended the conventional wisdom of the China field of his generation—and, indeed, of generations to come—when he commented that "it is the genius of the foreign critic to bring to the surface aspects of thought implicit in the life of the nation he studies, but explicit for him because of the contrasts supplied by his own culture. It is the shock of self-discovery which makes Halévy interesting to the English, Tocqueville to the Americans."[1] While Hartz is here focusing strictly on Yan Fu's interpretations of modern Western thought, it must be said that what occasioned Yan's intellectual peregrinations was his overwhelming concern with the desperate predicament facing China following its defeat by Japan in 1895, precisely the moment he began his writing career, at the somewhat ripe age of 42. In the writings gathered here, Wang Hui is similarly concerned with China and its future, and his point of entry is also invariably through the ways in which China discursively interacts with Europe and its ideas, resulting in a similarly "exotic" look at the West, particularly at the ways in which it relates to and treats China and the larger Asia, of which that country forms such a key part. It is to be hoped that a similar "shock of self-discovery" for the Western reader will follow upon reading Wang Hui's analysis and comments on the ways in which Western scholars have conceptualized Asia.

Somewhat different from the previous two collections of Wang Hui's work that have been published in English—both of which concentrate on contemporary Chinese social and political problems[2]—the work gathered here, while certainly cognizant of the pressing questions of the day, is focused more on historical issues and on how the questions of today and the perception of them have evolved through the collisions of different historical models. The inquiry centers on Asia, and particularly on China as the largest signifier in its premodern order. For all that Wang Hui is intent upon the analysis and self-definition of the Chinese situation, however, the real leitmotif of these essays is a profound dissatisfaction with the imported Western discourses that have been used to characterize and analyze China for most of the past century. In this he is merely one of the first, most prominent, as well as the most systematically rigorous of contemporary Chinese intellectuals who engage in this critique. The most obvious source of discontent these scholars share is with the ordinary Western ways of conceiving the Chinese past and how it is connected to the evolution of modern China. These essays offer a sample of Wang Hui's ongoing efforts to delineate a different vision of Chinese history, one that is not set exclusively in the Western conceptual framework that has dominated most Western and recent Chinese thinking about Chinese history and its legacy.[3]

In a sense, Wang Hui is working Paul Cohen's vein of "discovering history in China"[4] by tracing out indigenous strands of thought and notions of causation, but Wang quite consciously seeks to escape the binary of an exclusively Western or Chinese perspective, moving beyond the narration of historical event to a new analysis of the discursive patterns that structure historical understanding. He explicitly works to expose the inadequacies of analytical standards that were originally developed to measure European history, when brought to the evaluation of China. Throughout his work, also, is the awareness that in much of the scholarship produced, even in modern China, these standards convey a vision of a China always behind and lacking in the prerequisites for becoming the agent of its own historical progress. Such perspectives produce an "Asia [that] has neither history nor the historical conditions or impetus for producing modernity" ("The Politics of Imagining Asia," p. 18). While the last thing Wang Hui intends to do is place China in an intellectual ghetto sanitized of all contact with foreign ideas, he does seek to deconstruct these categories of European origin and put them in suspension, in the hope that new ways of looking at China in particular and Asia in general, as well as their situations in the world, will emerge.

More specifically, if one had to nominate the theme running through the essays here that best illustrates this historical distortion, it would be how the China that Wang Hui examines fits neither into the nation-state system imposed on the world as a result of the rise of the West after the eighteenth century, nor into the concept of a traditional, agrarian empire, the definition of which precludes, in its very design, the capacity for self-conscious participation in the making of its own modern history. Indeed, it is in this context that he develops the notion of "nation-state logic" or "nationalist knowledge" to characterize the whole mind-set of the modern West, and thus, alas, of most of the modern world. Wang sees this as a pattern of rigid definitions of how states should function, ineluctably based on the state-making process that swept over Western Europe in the eighteenth and nineteenth centuries. It is thus an equally rigid set of exclusions, in which "late-comer" states are essentially deprived of agency, the only option available to them being to follow in the footsteps of Europe and the United States.

In a number of the essays, Wang explicitly shows how nation-state logic worked in the growth and development of the Japanese empire in the decades after the 1868 Meiji Restoration, but there is a largely unstated subtext here in which Wang expresses his fear that China, too, has moved in this direction, particularly in the post-1979 period, in which the Chinese state has fully embraced a capitalist path of development. His writing makes it abundantly clear that this is not the path Wang Hui would have chosen, and it is not too much to say that the thread uniting his entire oeuvre is his attempt to develop the possibility of an alternative modernity, one based on the rich possibilities existing in the complex historical practice of the East Asian region that has been studiously ignored in the scholarly apparatus built on the basis of a system of nation-states. He is aware, however, of the dangers involved in simply inverting the binary: "If one proceeds on the premise of a binary of tribute versus treaty, or empire versus state, to attack such Eurocentric ideas by merely inverting the relations between the terms, the complexity of historical relations within Asia will in all likelihood be oversimplified." It would be much better, then, "to say that this 'Asia'—neither starting point nor end, neither self-sufficient subject nor subordinate object—provides the moment to reconstruct 'world history.' If we need to rectify mistakes in theories of 'Asia,' we must also reexamine the notion of Europe. As we correct the errors in the idea of Asia, we must also reexamine the idea of Europe" ("Politics of Imagining Asia," pp. 57, 58). Wang Hui's concerns, then, extend beyond China and Asia to an ambition to rethink world history as a whole as something other than a triumphant procession of ascendant Western social, economic, and political models.

In the first essay in the collection, "The Politics of Imagining Asia," Wang Hui sets out his views of the historical complexity of Asia and the process by which that diversity has been written into obscurity by the "nationalist knowledge" that accompanied the expansionism of capitalism and the modern imperialism brought into being in its wake. His analysis is at once historical, cultural, and profoundly political in that he sees political awareness as an inevitable component of any thinking that both enables and obliges flexibility of interpretation. It is here that he sets out his perception of the complexity of East Asian history, and how it cannot be fit into the discursive frames that have hitherto been used to describe it. The binary between empire and nation-state is the principal locus of his attack, as he shows how neither category can do justice to the relationships between premodern states in the region nor to the internal complexity of each polity. His analysis here must be sharply distinguished from the neoliberal ideology embodied in the "Washington Consensus," which, while it constantly talked of and seemed to assume the demise of nationalism, envisioned such nationalism being replaced only by a homogeneous, market-based transnational society, where meaningful diversity cannot exist, except perhaps in university departments of ethnic studies. Wang sums up this inquiry with a question: "In an era in which the nation-state has become the dominant political structure, will the traditional Asian experiences of various types of communication, coexistence, and institutions provide possibilities with which to overcome the internal and external dilemmas brought about by the nation-state system?" ("Politics of Imagining Asia," p. 60).

This inquiry continues in the volume's second essay, "How to Explain 'China' and Its 'Modernity': Rethinking *The Rise of Modern Chinese Thought*," originally the preface to the second edition of Wang Hui's epochal 2004 tetralogy of that name, a comprehensive journey through the history of Chinese thought, searching out potential sources for alternative modernities.[5] The essay included here takes a close look at three of the major questions raised in the book as a whole: (1) the problem of the nation-state versus empire; (2) a look at two different visions of traditional Chinese state administration, the centralized bureaucracy versus decentralized enfeoffment, and how these two concepts were used to debate statecraft and ideology in premodern China; and (3) the differentiation between rites/music and institutions, things that were held to have been unified in ancient China, and how the split between them figured in later discussion of statecraft. It is significant that the latter two points could be easily dismissed as parochial concerns of the old empire, with little relevance to the present, but Wang Hui carefully brings each of them into focus and points out their enduring discursive force. He looks at them in the context of the complications they engender in developing notions of historical rupture or continuity as well as how they function in the context of "the propensity of the times *(shishi)*," a concept enabling dynamic elasticity to new implementations of ideas from the past. The net result is a powerful argument for the importance of liberating the historical world of thought from its position as a mere object of observation and transforming it into a perspective from which we can reflect upon and differently conceive our modern world.

The collection's final essay, "Weber and the Question of Chinese Modernity," offers a unique theoretical perspective on Western views of China through a detailed comparison between Max Weber's perception of European modernity and his analysis of Chinese society. Not content simply to rehearse the many empirical errors Weber made in his characterizations of

Chinese society—the sources available to him in European languages in the 1910s were, after all, vastly inadequate to the task he set himself—Wang Hui instead develops a key insight based on the pervasive view of modern European scholarship of Weber as a skeptic of the overarching rationality characteristic of European modernity. It is in this sense that contemporary Western scholarship views the German sociologist as the forerunner of such critical insights of Foucault's as "'since the beginning of the nineteenth century, [politics] stubbornly persists in seeing in the immense domain of practice only the epiphany of a triumphant reason, or in deciphering in it only the historico-transcendental destination of the West.'"[6] As Wang argues, however, the contrast between Weber's views on the position of rationality in Europe and in China could not be stronger, as the oppressive rationality produced in modern Europe is treated in Weber's late writings on China as precisely that which the country lacks and which prevents it from developing into a modern state. Here Wang Hui differs significantly with most critics of Weber's work on China, who rarely question the inconsistencies in the latter's theory of modernity but rather develop the easy critique of empirical error. In Wang's view of Weber's treatment of China, rationality completely loses the negative overtones he detects in Europe and becomes the country's positive Other. In other words, Wang points out a gaping inconsistency in Weber that calls into question the latter's entire perception and critique of modernity.

It might perhaps be fair to say that Wang's essay on Weber does not grasp the nettle of trying to adduce ways in which traditional Chinese society and state effectively dealt with the issues Weber accuses it of failing to be able to surmount, but Wang Hui's is a profoundly tactful sort of deconstruction—breaking down preexisting discourses on China rather than trying to rush in with new solutions. His ultimate concern is to show the damage done by Weber's homogenization of world history within the universal rubric of rationalization: "My question is . . . how the concept of rationalization has been employed for all societies and for all historical junctures as a conceptual and theoretical principle, how it has organized and regulated our view of social and cultural history, and how it has managed to align all historical data within a seamless theoretical discourse" ("Weber and the Question," p. 281).

The essay on language, "Local Forms, Vernacular Dialects, and the War of Resistance against Japan: The 'National Forms' Debate," shows

Wang Hui's concern with maintaining what he sees as the rich diversity within Chinese culture and its polity, something particularly evident when he takes a highly critical stance against the efforts of the May Fourth New Culture movement's efforts at "nation-state" standardization. The essay also shows, however, the nation-state and its ideology at work in undermining that diversity by revealing how an urban-based national language ultimately won the day in modern China. Of particular interest is the story that for all the radical reformist awareness of the need to include local dialect within any sort of revolutionary new culture, the needs of the nation-state turned out to be impossible to resist. As Wang concludes the essay: "In the quest for setting up a modern nation-state, a general national language and artistic forms that transcended the local were always among the most important means for building cultural unity. Between the old and the new, the urban and the rural, the modern and the folk, the nation and class, local culture could not garner an autonomous theoretical basis" ("Local Forms, p. 135).

"The 'Tibetan Question' East and West—Orientalism, Regional Ethnic Autonomy, and the Politics of Dignity," the fourth and by far the longest article in the set, will also be the most difficult for Western readers to accept, if only for the reasons that Wang Hui sets out so clearly in the essay itself—the long history of the mythologizing of Tibet in the West has raised the stakes in the discussion of its status, and rendered rational analysis or even measured discussion difficult. His careful historical exposition of the ways in which nineteenth-century British imperialism shattered the fragile yet flexible relationships among the Himalayan nations should at least serve to complicate calcified views. Beyond that, however, the Wilsonian sense of national self-determination is so firmly engrained in the modern Western way of seeing things—a way of seeing things that Wang Hui would regard as dominated by "nation-state logic"—that it is all but impossible for us to envision alternative ways of peoples living together. Events in the former Yugoslavia and the response to them have shown this to be true even for modern Europe. Clearly, as the recent conflicts in both Tibet and Xinjiang have shown, the carefully crafted Chinese policies of local autonomy that Wang Hui describes in his essay have encountered extreme turbulence, with the polarization between the Han and the indigenous populations of these border lands only becoming worse in recent years, something he frankly admits. He places the blame, however, on the globalization of the Chinese economy after 1979, and the concomitant expansion of economic and social inequality. The issue of just how much the changes in China since that time have brought "nation-state logic" to the fore and captured Chinese attitudes and politics toward places like Tibet and Xinjiang, however, is a specter hovering over the essay, giving it its at once urgent and pessimistic charge.

"Okinawa and Two Dramatic Changes to the Regional Order" yet again tries to dismantle "nation-state logic" and show possible alternatives to the seemingly intractable problems of the current world order. Wang Hui does this by providing a meticulous detailing of how the "tribute system" worked vis-à-vis the old Ryukyuan kingdom and its transformation into relationships characteristic of the modern nation-state, resulting in a significant decrease in autonomy for the smaller nations involved. He again stresses that the "meaning of all such work lies in establishing a new horizon for reflection and critique, and conceiving of new types of regional-global relationships and the rules for them" ("Okinawa," p. 243), a refrain running throughout the collection—Wang Hui is intent upon bringing up alternative models from the past as a way of developing alternatives, rather than some simple return to earlier practices.

Taken as a whole, Wang Hui's work profoundly challenges the reader—the thinking is complicated and not afraid of abstraction, the train of thought at times seems to meander, the writing often verges on the baroque, and the ideas quite deliberately take issue with wide swaths of received wisdom. There has been, over the course of the last century in many quarters in Western academia and journalism, an unrelenting critique of modern China based on China's perceived failure to adhere to models generated by the Western social sciences.[7] Wang's work contests this, and is marked throughout by a struggle for discursive equality—the right to critique ideas from the West on an equal footing with Western theorists—and Wang explores a rich range of historical differences between China and the West as the point of departure in this quest. This has been, and will be for some time to come, an uphill climb. Highly ramified Western networks of academic theorizing have developed in tandem with the economic success of Euro-American capitalism over the past two and a half centuries, whereas critical scholarship in China, on the other hand, is just beginning, and the determination to challenge Western models of historical development got under way even later.

Whether dealing with the problem of the nation-state versus the multinational empire or any of the other crucial issues that come within his purview, Wang Hui constantly seeks to provide us with new ways of envisioning possibility. In contrast to a binary view of history that obliged us either to view China as evolving toward modernity on the Euro-American model or remain permanently stuck in the same static holding pattern, Wang points ways out of such sterile dilemmas. If, as he notes, we simply put all data into frameworks developed from European historical practice, "we lose the internal historical perspective of the period [we are examining] and the opportunity to rethink our own knowledge, beliefs, and worldviews from this perspective" ("How to Explain 'China' and Its 'Modernity,'" p. 67). The possibility to place ourselves in radically different historical times and places and to achieve real understanding of them is the "shock of self-discovery" Wang Hui offers us.

1

The Politics of Imagining Asia

Introduction: The Background Conditions for "Imagining the New Asia"

The idea of "New Empire" that has reemerged during the "war on terror" follows naturally on the heels of the concept of neoliberal globalization—the former uses the violence, crises, and social disintegration caused by the globalization process as pretexts to reconstruct a military and political "New Empire." The latter seeks to restructure various social traditions according to such neoliberal market principles as legal systems focused on private property, the state's withdrawal from the economic sphere, and the transnationalization of productive, commercial, and financial systems. These two apparently different notions work in concert to knit together military alliances, organizations of economic association, and international political institutions in the construction of a total order

---

Translated by Matthew A. Hale

at all levels—political, economic, cultural, and military. This new order may, therefore, be called a "neoliberal empire/imperialism."

In his article "Why Europe Needs a Constitution," Jürgen Habermas argues the necessity for Europe to organize its nation-states into a unified political community so as to uphold the European social model and its modern achievements. In order to defend the European way of life represented by social security and welfare, democracy, and freedom, Habermas proposes three major tasks in the construction of a "post-national democracy": to form a European civil society, to build a Europe-wide political public sphere, and to create a political culture in which all citizens of the European Union would be able to share as well as establish a unified constitution via a popular referendum. Thus would Europe apply to itself "as a whole, 'the logic of the circular creation of state and society that shaped the modern history of European countries.'"[1] A Europe formed according to these three principles would resemble a superstate or an empire—its component societies would to a certain extent retain their own, distinctive features and autonomy, even as they would have integrated standing institutions to carry out governmental functions, including a unified parliamentary and legal system, supported and safeguarded by a historically formed civic political culture and social order.

Corresponding to the development and crises of Europe's unification is a twofold process taking place in Asia. On the one hand, there is the concentration and expansion of a new kind of power network with the United States at its core. For instance, in the Afghan War, Asian countries have actively participated in the U.S.-centered war alliance for their own particular economic or political interests. On the other hand, there has been a strengthening of Asian regional cooperation following the 1997 financial crisis: in June 2001, China, Russia, Kazakhstan, Tajikistan, Kyrgyzstan, and, slightly later, Uzbekistan founded the Shanghai Cooperation Organization (the "Shanghai Six"), and in November 2001, China came to an agreement with the ten countries of ASEAN that within ten years it would sign a free-trade agreement with the group. This plan rapidly expanded from "10 plus 1" to "10 plus 3" (ASEAN plus China, Japan, and Korea), and eventually to "10 plus 6'" (ASEAN plus China, Japan, Korea, India, Australia, and New Zealand). A Japanese media organization published a commentary saying that "if the unification of Asia accelerates . . . the sense of distance between Japan and China will disappear naturally as part of this regional process and eventually, by excluding the United States for the first time from an East Asian regional consultation—based on a Summit Conference including ASEAN, Japan, China, and Korea—Japan and China may achieve an 'Asian version of the reconciliation between France and Germany.'"[2] Since the views of China, Japan, and the ASEAN countries on regional progress are not entirely consistent, the expansion of this plan indicates not so much the spread of the idea of Asia as the growth of power dynamics among the region's various nation-states.

The course of Asian regional integration includes a number of complex and contradictory features. On the one hand, the name of the region, "Asia," appeals to supranational interests, but on the other hand, it incorporates nation-states into a larger, protective community. Thus, this regionalism includes an intention to challenge global hegemony through constructing regional autonomy, even as it is, at the same time, the product of global market relations under the domination of the "New Empire." From a historical perspective, the discussion of "Asia" is not an entirely new phenomenon, and over the course of the surge of nationalism in the modern period, we encounter two sharply opposed discourses on the region. The first is the colonialist conceptualization developed out of Japanese "continental policy," while the other is that of a vision of Asian social revolution with national liberation and socialist movements at its core. The former constructed the idea of Asia or *Tōya* (i.e., "Dongya," or "East Asia" as pronounced in Japanese) on the East/West binary, whereas the latter presented the issue of nationalism from an internationalist perspective. Any discussion of Asia, therefore, cannot avoid further inquiry into the modern colonialist and nationalist movements.

Asia and *Tōya:* A Derivate Proposition

Historically speaking, the idea of Asia is not Asian but, rather, European. In his 1948 essay "What Is Modernity?" Takeuchi Yoshimi wrote: "[In order to] understand East Asia, [we must appreciate that] what enables the concept to be realized are the same factors that brought about the realization of the concept of Europe. For East Asia to be East Asia requires reliance upon a European discursive context."[3] This view can also help us to explain Fukuzawa Yukichi's negative way of defining Asia, that is, with his call to "shed Asia" (*tuo Ya*, or *datsu A* in Japanese). Scholarly opinion differs on the role that "On Shedding Asia," an article published on March 16, 1885, in the Tokyo newspaper *Jiji shinpo*, played in the development of Fukuzawa's thought. As I see it, however, the important question is why the slogan developed from this article, "shed Asia and join Europe"—even though Fukuzawa never actually used the words "join Europe"—became a recurring theme in modern Japanese thought. The notion of "On Shedding Asia" included two ideas concerning Asia—first, Asia referred to a region with a high degree of cultural homogenization, that is, Confucian Asia. Second, the political import of "shedding Confucianism" was breaking away from China-centered imperial relations and turning in the direction of a European-style nation-state oriented toward "freedom," "human rights," "national sovereignty," "civilization," and "the spirit of independence." In the context of the continuous expansion of the new political form—with its new power relationships—of "the state," "Asia," seen as the cultural and political antagonist to the nationalist vision of modernization, was fundamentally negated.[4] According to the logic of Takeuchi's comment that "For East Asia to be East Asia requires reliance upon a European discursive context," "the Asian essence" implicit in Fukuzawa's proposal to "shed Asia," that is, Confucianism and its social system, is actually part of a European sequence of ideas. If "what enables the concept [of East Asia] to be realized are the same factors that bring about the realization of the concept of Europe," the birth of "East Asia" must result from East Asia's negation of itself. In this sense, Fukuzawa's proposal to "shed Asia" and Takeuchi's thesis both derive from the nineteenth-century European conception of "world history."

Just as European self-consciousness required knowledge of its "outside," "shedding Asia" was a way of forming self-consciousness through differentiating Japan from Asia. From this perspective, "shedding Asia," the embodiment of modern Japanese particularism, in fact derived from modern European historical consciousness. In other words, Japanese particularism derived from European universalism. In the words of Karl Jaspers, "Cutting away from Asia was part of a universal historical process, not a particularist European gesture towards Asia. It took place within Asia itself and was the path of humanity and the true path of history." He continued:

> Greek culture seems like a peripheral phenomenon peripheral of Asia. Europe broke prematurely away from its Asiatic mother. The question arose: Where and when and through what step did this break take place? Is it possible that Europe will once more lose itself in Asia? In Asia's depths and in its leveling-down that is destitute of consciousness?
>
> If the West emerged from the matrix of Asia, its emergence has the appearance of an act of daring in which human potentialities are set free. The act brings with it two dangers: first, that Europe might lose the foundation of its soul, and then, once it has attained consciousness, the continual danger that it might sink back again into Asia.
>
> If this danger of sinking back into Asia were to be realized today, however, it would be under new technological conditions which are transforming and destroying Asian itself; Western liberty, the ideas of personality, the amplitude of Western categories and its lucid consciousness would go by the board. In their place would remain the eternal characteristics of Asia: The despotic form of existence, the absence of history and of decision, the stabilization of the spirit of fatalism. Asia would be the universal, enduring world that outlives Europe and includes it. Whatever fashions itself out of Asia and must sink back into Asia is transitory.
>
> . . .
>
> Asia is turned into a mythical principle, that falls apart when it is analyzed objectively as an historical reality. The antithesis Europe-Asia must not be metaphysically hypostasized. Then it becomes a terrifying specter. As a mythical language at moments of decision it serves as a cryptogram that represents a truth only so long as it operates as an abbreviation for something historically concrete and intellectually lucid, and is not meant as an apperception of the whole. But Europe-Asia is a cryptogram that accompanies the whole of Western history.[5]

If "shedding Asia" was not the basis for Japanese particularism but rather a particular step in Europe's universal progress, what was the European context that gave rise to this "universal progress"?

In the eighteenth and nineteenth centuries, the European Enlightenment and colonial expansion provided the underpinning for the development of a new system of knowledge. Historical linguistics, race theory, modern geography, political economy, theories of the state, legal philosophy, the study of religion, and historiography all flourished at once, hand in hand with the natural sciences—in every respect they created a new worldview. The notions of both Europe and Asia were constituted as part of the process of this construction of new knowledge. In the works of European writers such as Montesquieu, Adam Smith, Hegel, and Marx,[6] the core of the European production of the idea of Asia was made up of the following features: multinational empires as opposed to modern European or monarchical states; political despotism as opposed to modern European legal and political systems; and nomadic and agrarian modes of production completely at odds with European urban and commercial life. Since the European nation-state and the expansion of the capitalist market system were considered at once the most advanced stage and the *telos* of world history, Asia and its characteristics were relegated to a lower historical stage. In this context, Asia was not only a geographic category, but also a civilization, representing both a political type defined as the antithesis to the European nation-state as well as a social type defined as the antithesis to European capitalism, or as occupying a transitional space between prehistory and history proper. Throughout most of the nineteenth and twentieth centuries, the discourse on Asia was embedded within a universalist narrative about European modernity that provided a common framework for the otherwise completely opposed historical blueprints of both colonists and revolutionaries. The three central themes and keywords of this narrative were empire, nation-state, and capitalism (or a market economy). From the nineteenth century on, the discourse on Asia has in one way or another been related to these three key concepts.

In many nineteenth-century European discussions on history, philosophy, law, the state, and religion, Asia was presented both as lying at the "center" of all the world's nationalities as well as being the "starting point" of world history; within the context of "shedding Asia," Chinese Confucianism was regarded as the source of history. These views about "source" or "starting point" arose from a need simultaneously to make connection and to break away. We may take the discovery by historical linguists of the connection between European languages and Sanskrit as an example, and thus see how a political economist like Hegel could connect this linguistic discovery with nineteenth-century European theories of race and the state so as to describe the implications of "Asia as the starting point of history":

> The great historical discovery some twenty odd years ago of the connections between Sanskrit and the European languages was like discovering a new world. In particular, the connection of the German and Indian peoples has been demonstrated, with as much certainty as such subjects allow of. Even at the present time we know of peoples that scarcely form a society, much less a State, but that have been long known as existing.... In the connection just referred to, between the languages of nations so widely separated, we have a result before us, which proves the diffusion of those nations from Asia as a center, and the so dissimilar development of what had been originally related, as an incontestable fact.[7]

Asia must, therefore, meet two conditions in order to constitute the "starting point" of world history. First, Asia and Europe must be two organically related parts of the same historical process. Second, Asia and Europe must occupy two drastically different stages on this historical continuum, with the main standard for evaluating these stages being "the state." The reason Asia occupied the "starting point" or prehistorical period was that it still lacked states and thus could not possess a historical subjective agency. In this sense, once the Asian region completed the transition from traditional empires to "states," from agrarian or pastoral to industrial or commercial modes of production, from village to urban or "civil" society, it would cease to be Asia.

Because his account of civil society, markets, and commerce derives from the Scottish school of political economy, Hegel's notion of a despotic Asia is linked to a particular economic system. If we contrast Hegel's historical philosophy of the four stages of human history—the Orient, Greece, Rome, and the Teutonic peoples—with Smith's four phases of economic history—hunting, pastoral, agricultural, and commercial—it is not difficult to discover the internal links between Hegel's historical description centering on political forms and Smith's historical stages based on forms of production. Smith treats the progression from agricultural society to commercial society as the transition from European feudal society to modern market society, thereby connecting the ideas of the modern era, the commercial era and European society in a single historical narrative. He sets out a model of the movement of markets as an abstract process: the discovery of the Americas, colonialism, and class differentiation are all presented as an economic process of endless market expansion, division of labor, technological advancement, and the rise of tax receipts and wealth. A model of the circulation of world markets is thus established through this formalist narrative, in which the market serves as both the result of historical development and the inner law of history; the concrete spatial relationships of colonialism and social differentiation become transformed into a temporal process of production, circulation, and consumption.

In *The Wealth of Nations*, Smith's division of four historical stages corresponds to a taxonomy of the conditions of different regions and peoples. When describing the "nations of hunters, the lowest and rudest state of society," for example, he mentions "today's native tribes of North America"; when discussing "nations of shepherds, a more advanced state of society," he names Tartars and Arabs as examples; when describing "[nations of husbandmen,] a yet more advanced state of society," he turns to ancient Greece and Rome (in a previous chapter he had also mentioned Chinese agriculture). As for commercial society, this is exemplified by what he refers to as the "civilized states" of Europe.[8] In Hegel's vision, all these issues were incorporated into a political framework concerned with the state, and the reason "nations of hunters" were "the lowest and rudest" form of society was that the scale of their communities was too small to produce the political division of labor necessary for state formation. In the words of Ernest Gellner, "for them, the question of the state, of a stable specialized order-enforcing institution, does not really arise."[9] Hegel's narrative of world history therefore explicitly excludes North America (characterized by lives of hunting and gathering) and situates the Orient at the starting point of history. If Smith divides history according to different economies or modes of production, then Hegel denominates historical stages according to region, civilization, and state structure, but both of them correlate modes of production or political forms with specific places (such as Asia, the Americas, Africa, and Europe), and both organize these places within a chronological structure.

The notions of Asia or China articulated by Montesquieu, Hegel, Marx, and Fukuzawa (as well as other modern Japanese thinkers) all developed through comparative descriptions of civilizations. In order to construct Asia as a particular type of civilization in contrast to Europe, it was necessary to elide its internal developments and transformations—even the historical conflicts between northern and southern Chinese ethnicities (i.e., what European writers called the conquest of China by the "Tartars" and vice versa) were not regarded as modifying the shape of history. In the words of Montesquieu: "[T]he laws of China are not destroyed by conquest. Their customs, manners, laws, and religion [were all] the same thing."[10] From this "culturalist" perspective, Asia has neither history nor the historical conditions or impetus for producing modernity. The heart of this modernity is the "state" and its legal system, its urban and commercial way of life, as well as its mechanisms for economic and military competition. In his critique of European delineations of the "Asiatic mode of production" and its "despotism," Perry Anderson wrote: "The concept of 'despotism' has from its origins been an outsider's appraisal of 'the Orient.' As far back as ancient Greece, Aristotle famously claimed that 'Barbarians are more servile by nature than Greeks, and Asians are more servile than Europeans; hence they endure despotic rule without protest.... But they obey established rules and pass them on from generation to generation, so they are secure.'"[11]

Modern European observations on the structure of the Asian state grow out of the long history of conflict between European states and the Ottoman Empire. Machiavelli's *The Prince* was the first to pit the Ottoman state against European monarchies, arguing that the Ottoman monarchical bureaucracy differed categorically from all European state systems. Similarly, Bodin, often regarded as the first European theorist of sovereignty, also drew a definitive line between European "royal sovereignty" and Ottoman "lordly power."[12] With the nineteenth-century expansion of European colonialism, this contrast eventually mutated into one between European nation-states and Asian empires, to such an extent that it is difficult today to recognize that the "despotism" or "absolutism" we associate with Asia in fact derives from European generalizations about the culture of the Ottoman Empire.[13] From this characteristically Western European perspective, modern capitalism is seen as the product of Western Europe's unique social structure, and there is thus a necessary or natural connection between capitalist development and the system of nation-states, with feudal states as their historical precondition. Under the influence of this conception of history, imperial systems (vast, multi-ethnic empires such as the Ottoman, Chinese, Mughal, and Russian) are viewed as the political form of Oriental despotism, incapable of producing the political structure necessary for the development of capitalism.[14] It was this notion of despotism derived from descriptions of empire that enabled later scholars to contrast European and Asian political categories (i.e., the distinction between democratic Europe and authoritarian Asia), and provided the theoretical premise for Fukuzawa and his successors to contrast Japan with Confucian China through the theory of "shedding Asia."

The idea of Asia in modern European thought was always closely connected with the vast territory and complex ethnicity of empire, with its antitheses the republican system of Greece and the European monarchical state—during the wave of nineteenth-century nationalism, republican systems or feudal monarchies were seen as both as predecessors of the nation-state and as political forms distinct from those of any other area in the world. In other words, despotism became closely associated with the idea of vast empire in the transition from feudal state to nation-state in the Western European context, with the result that the category of "state," as opposed to empire, acquired its superiority in terms of both value and history. In order to establish a unique self-understanding, European thinkers such as Montesquieu firmly negated a number of quite positive descriptions of the politics, law, customs, and culture of China that had been written by Catholic missionaries in that country—images that had been the basis for the European Enlightenment depictions of China, particularly the positive descriptions of Voltaire and Leibniz—and then proceeded to summarize the political culture of China with concepts like "despotism" and "empire." According to the classic explanation since Montesquieu, an empire is characterized by the following: the chief ruler monopolizes the distribution of property with his military power, thereby eliminating any aristocracy that could balance the sovereign's power and forestalling the creation of a nation-state.[15] If we analyze the self-understanding of modern Japan within the context of this European notion of a despotic empire of mixed ethnicity and vast territory, can we not discern the roots of the contrast between a mono-ethnic Japan turning from feudalism toward a modern state, and a multiethnic China, trapped in its Confucian empire, and the resulting notion of "Shedding Asia" and its concomitant proposition of "rejecting our flawed Asian friends"?

The modern Japanese idea of "East Asia" was also, in fact, founded upon this European culturalism. In the words of Maruyama Masao, this "reflected Japan's rapid process of *westernization* [English in original] following the Meiji period, for the cultural and political path formed through the confluence of the statism growing out of the 'national learning' *(kokugaku)* of the Edo period and post-Meiji *westernization* was so obviously different from those of all other Asian countries."[16] In explaining the formation of the modern Japanese "conception of the rationality of the state," Maruyama stresses that the sovereign states of modern Europe were born out of the disintegration of the Christian world-community symbolized by the Roman Empire, and their international society was an agglomeration of all independent states, whereas "Japan was the opposite; it began to develop as a nation-state only after it had been forced into it by international society."[17] This is why the modern Japanese notion of "equality among states" developed out of a struggle against the hierarchical Chinese Confucian notions of "differentiating between barbarian and civilized" *(yi xia zhi bian)* and "expelling the barbarians" *(rang yi lun)*. According to this antithesis between the principle of formal equality in European international law and the Confucian idea of "expelling the barbarians," modern Japanese expansionism can be explained as a result of lacking European-style "state rationality" or as a product of a Confucianist notion of "expelling the barbarians." Maruyama comments that for Fukuzawa: "Internal liberation and external independence were understood as a single issue. According to this logic, individualism and statism, statism and internationalism achieved a splendid balance—it was indeed a fortunate moment. Fukuzawa received his comeuppance, however, from the international context Japan found itself in and the harsh fact that this balance was soon shattered."[18] The notion of "expelling the barbarians" paved the way for the modern state's expansion and exclusionism, but if that is all there was to it, then the tragedy of modern Japan is merely one of "incomplete westernization" or "incomplete modernization" rather than a tragedy of Japanese modernity itself.

In a later article explaining the notion of "state rationality," Maruyama wrote:

> The concept of "state rationality" goes beyond the stage of absolute sovereignty, extending into the age of coexistence among all modern sovereign states. These modern sovereign states establish diplomatic relations according to the principles of international law and pursue their state interests through means such as treaties, alliances, and war. This *"International Community"* seems to have already taken shape in seventeenth-century Europe, where it was called the *"Western State System."* "State rationality" developed on the twin pillars of the principle of equality among sovereign states and the *balance of powers*.[19]

In both its 1874 invasion of Taiwan, however, and its 1894 invasion of Korea, Japan appealed to European "international law" and its notion of formal equality among sovereign states. Should we interpret these actions within a framework of "the decadence of state rationality," or, rather, analyze them as being part of a process of the coming into being or the pursuit of European "state rationality"? There is no real contradiction between such imperialist actions and the embrace of the notion of sovereign equality as part of an effort to cast off the imperial Chinese tribute system and the hierarchical barbarian/civilized duality. Rather than try to explain this issue through a binary opposition between tradition and modernity or barbarian/civilized and international equality, we would do better to consider the derivativeness of Japan's modern nationalism, colonialism, and discourse on Asia, or, in other words to examine modern Japanese expansionism within its "European context."

According to the classic model of nationalism forged in the French Revolution, the nation-state is the basic prerequisite for the individual as unit of power (i.e., the citizen). Without this political community and its concomitant precondition of national uniformity, the individual as a juridical subject cannot be established. As European writers have asked over and again, however, "will a free Europe take the place of monarchical Europe? The wars against other monarchs undertaken to defend the fruits of the [French] Revolution quickly became missions of liberation, then the annexation of territory and the crossing of natural borders. . . . The revolution and the Empire both tried to incite other nationalities to overthrow their monarchs in the name of liberty, but this expansionism eventually drove these peoples to unite with their traditional monarchs in opposition to France."[20] Here the key issue is that, on the one hand, the bourgeois nation-state and its individualist notion of citizenship were political passages toward casting off the aristocratic hierarchies of ancient empires while, on the other, they were the best political forms for the expansion of capitalism (especially the formation of national markets, the expansion of overseas markets, and the system of private property), and this expansion was never limited to the territory within the borders of a single nation-state. So even if they could have actualized the system of "rights" so anticipated by Fukuzawa, there was no way to guarantee that this "system" would not be aggressive or expansionist. In this sense, there is no real contradiction between the theory of "shedding Asia" and the reality of "invading Asia"—both are grounded in the "European context" from which they derive.[21] Pointing this out does not mean denying the historical connection between modern Japanese imperialist expansion and the political tradition of "respecting the emperor and expelling the barbarians," but is rather to highlight how the use of this political tradition was produced under new historical conditions as well as new sets of relationships, and that reflections on this political tradition should therefore become an organic part of reconsidering such new historical conditions and relationships.

Populism and the Dual Meaning of "Asia"

Twenty-six years after Fukuzawa published "On Shedding Asia," the Chinese Revolution of 1911 broke out. Shortly after the Provisional Government of the Republic of China was founded, Lenin, leader of the Russian Revolution, published "Democracy and Narodnism in China" (1912), "The Awakening of Asia" and "Backward Europe and Advanced Asia"

(1913), applauding China as "a land of seething political activity, the scene of a virile social movement and of a democratic upsurge,"[22] and condemning Europe, "with its highly developed machine industry, its rich multiform culture and its constitutions," which had under the command of the bourgeoisie remained "in support of everything backward, moribund, and medieval."[23] These observations constitute part of Lenin's theory of imperialism and proletarian revolution, where he argued that, as capitalism entered its imperialist phase, the various social struggles of oppressed peoples around the world would be integrated into the world proletarian revolution. This method of analytically connecting European and Asian revolutions can be traced back to Marx's "Revolution in China and in Europe," an article written for the *New York Daily Tribune* in 1853.

Lenin's and Fukuzawa's opposed conclusions are based on a common understanding that Asian modernity was the product of European modernity, and regardless of Asia's status and fate, the significance of its modernity manifested itself only in its relationship with the more advanced Europe. Lenin regarded Russia as an Asian country, but this orientation is defined not geographically but from its degree of capitalist development, or the progress of Russian historical advance. In "Democracy and Narodnism in China," he wrote that "Russia is undoubtedly an Asian country and, what is more, one of the most benighted, medieval, and shamefully backward of Asian countries."[24] Although he was warmly sympathetic to the Chinese Revolution, Lenin's position became "Western European" once the issue switched from Asian revolution to the transformation of Russian society. In the nineteenth and twentieth centuries, Russian intellectuals regarded the vitality of Russia as lying in the struggle and collision between two forces: the Eastern and the Western, the Asian and the European. In the quotation above, Asia is a domain compounded of such notions as barbarism, the medieval, and backwardness, and it was precisely because of this that the Russian Revolution had such a profoundly Asian character—that is, because it was directed against the "Asian," Russia's "barbarous," "medieval," and "shamefully backward" social conditions—even as it had at the same time a global significance.

The special position of Asia in the rhetoric of world history determined how socialists understood the task and direction of modern revolution there. After he read Sun Yat-sen's "The Significance of the Chinese

Revolution," Lenin criticized the Chinese revolutionary's democratic and socialist program for going beyond capitalism, noting it as being utopian and populist. Lenin observed that "The chief representative, or the chief social bulwark, of this Asian bourgeoisie that is still capable of supporting a historically progressive cause, is the peasant," since before the Asian bourgeoisie accomplished the revolutionary task that the European bourgeoisie had already accomplished, socialism was out of the question. He adroitly used historical dialectics to assert that Sun Yat-sen's land reform program was "reactionary" because it went against or beyond the present historical stage. He also pointed out that because of the "Asian" character of Chinese society, it was just this "reactionary program" that would complete the task of capitalism in China: "[populism], under the disguise of 'combating capitalism' in agriculture, champions an agrarian program that, if fully carried out, would mean the *most* rapid development of capitalism in agriculture."[25]

Lenin's understanding of the Chinese Revolution was based on his ongoing reflections on the Russian reforms of 1861, and, especially, on the failure of the 1905 Revolution. In 1861, after defeat in the Crimean War (fought with Great Britain and France over control of the Balkans and the Black Sea), Alexander II initiated reforms to abolish serfdom. Even if we sketch the contours of this reform in only the most abbreviated manner, we must not overlook the two following points: first, the reform did not arise out of anything internal to Russian society, but rather out of external pressures; second, the "Emancipation Decree" announced on 19 February 1861 was premised on the full protection of landlord interests, and the Russian peasants paid a heavy cost for this top-down process of industrialization. This is why Lenin argued that 1861 led to 1905.[26] From the reform of 1861 to the Revolution of 1905, the concentration of land did not give rise to capitalist agriculture, instead leading peasants from agrarian communes to demand vehemently the appropriation and redistribution of landlord lands.[27] It was against this background that Lenin closely linked his thoughts on the 1905 Revolution to solving Russia's land question. In 1907, Lenin wrote "The Agrarian Program of Social-Democracy in the First Russian Revolution, 1905–1907,"[28] focusing on the Russian land question, in which he described two models of agricultural capitalism as "the Prussian path" and "the American path." In the former case the state and feudal landlords allied to violently expropriate the peasants, destroy their villages and communal land ownership, and turn a feudal landlord system into a Junker-bourgeois economy. The American path, on the other hand, is a scheme that "may be carried out in the interests of the peasant masses and not of the landlord gang," those interests being "the nationalization of the land, the abolition of its private ownership, and the transfer of *all* land to the state, which will mark a complete break with feudal relations in the countryside. It is this economic necessity that has turned the *mass* of Russian peasants into supporters of land nationalization." In summing up the reasons for the failure of the Russian land reform and the 1905 Revolution, Lenin concluded that under Russia's social conditions, "Nationalization of the land is not only the sole means for completely eliminating medievalism in agriculture, but also the best form of agrarian relationships conceivable under capitalism."[29]

Lenin believed that the Russian Populist *(Narodnik)* agrarian program was bound to lead Russia to return to a small peasant economy in which village land was divided up into small plots, and that this kind of economic system could not provide the impetus for capitalist development. He endorsed the "American path," first because only the abolition of medieval agrarian relations through the nationalization of land would allow the possibility of developing agricultural capitalism, and second because Russia had large amounts of virgin land and was thus possessed of the conditions for the American path that other European countries lacked. The development of capitalist agriculture necessitated the coercive reshaping of prior social relations:

> In England this reshaping proceeded in a revolutionary, violent way; but the violence was practiced for the benefit of the landlords, it was practiced on the masses of the peasants, who were taxed to exhaustion, driven from the villages, evicted, and who died out, or emigrated. In America this reshaping went on in a violent way as regards the slave farms in the Southern States. There violence was applied against the slaveowning landlords. Their estates were broken up, and the large feudal estates were transformed into small bourgeois farms. As regards the mass of "unappropriated" American lands, this role of creating the new agrarian relationships to suit the new mode of

production (i.e., capitalism) was played by the "American General Redistribution," by the Anti-Rent movement [*Anti-Rent Bewegung*] of the forties, the Homestead Act, etc.[30]

Thus, "The Narodnik thinks that repudiation of private landownership is repudiation of capitalism. That is wrong. The repudiation of private landownership expresses the demands for the purest capitalist development."[31] It was from this perspective that Lenin saw the genuinely revolutionary potential of Sun Yat-sen's program. He marveled that this "advanced Chinese democrat" knew nothing of Russia but still argued like a Russian and could pose "purely Russian questions": "Land nationalization makes it possible to abolish absolute rent, leaving only differential rent. According to Marx's theory, land nationalization means a maximum elimination of medieval monopolies and medieval relations in agriculture, maximum freedom in buying and selling land, and maximum facilities for agriculture to adapt itself to the market."[32] In contrast, "Our vulgar Marxists, however, in criticizing 'equalized redistribution,' 'socialization of the land,' and 'equal right to the land,' confine themselves to repudiating the doctrine, and thus reveal their own obtuse doctrinairism, which prevents them from seeing the vital life of the peasant revolution beneath the lifeless doctrine of Narodnik theory." Through examining Sun Yat-sen's revolutionary program against the specifics of Russia's historical background, Lenin concluded that "The Russian revolution can succeed only as a peasants' agrarian revolution, and the agrarian revolution cannot complete its historical mission without carrying out nationalization."[33] If the main characteristic defining the "American path" in contrast to the Prussian and English paths was the nationalization of land, the "Chinese path" represented a bottom-up "peasant agrarian revolution."

The Russian reforms took place against the background of the Crimean War, the 1905 Russo-Japanese War, and the First World War, so Lenin's reflections on the path of Russia's reforms could not avoid addressing the international relations created by European imperialism. If Russia's land question could only be solved through "nationalization," then just what kind of "state" could shoulder the responsibility for this reform? Lenin wrote that the national state is the rule and the "norm" of capitalism; the multi-national state represents backwardness, or is an exception.... This does not mean, of course, that such a state, which is based on bourgeois relations, can eliminate the exploitation and oppression of nations. It only means that Marxists cannot lose sight of the powerful *economic* factors that give rise to the urge to create national states. It means that "self-determination of nations" in the Marxists' Program *cannot*, from a historico-economic point of view, have any other meaning than political self-determination, state independence, and the formation of a national state.[34]

Thus, when Lenin discussed "the awakening of Asia," his concern was not with socialism but with how to create the political conditions for the development of capitalism, in other words, the question of national self-determination. Two points are worth noting here: First, the "national state" and the "multi-national state" (i.e., "empire") are contrasted, with the former being the "norm" of capitalist development and the latter its antithesis. Second, national self-determination is "political self-determination," and under Russian and Chinese conditions, the necessary form of this self-determination was to use socialism to create the political conditions for capitalist development, that is, the political structure of the political nation or the nation-state: "[C]apitalism, having awakened Asia, has called forth national movements everywhere in that continent, too; ... the tendency of these movements is towards the creation of national states in Asia; ... it is such states that ensure the best conditions for the development of capitalism."[35] Given the specific conditions of "Asia," only a peasant-led agrarian revolution and socialist state-building could create the preconditions for capitalist development, so all reform programs opposed to peasant liberation and redistribution of land had to be rejected.

There is no need to exaggerate the influence of the 1911 Revolution in China on Lenin or on the Russian Revolution—in fact, we cannot ascertain any direct influence between the two. By contrast, we can easily determine that the October Revolution of 1917, which arose as a direct result of the European war, exercised a profound and definite influence on the Chinese Revolution. The importance Lenin attached to the 1911 Revolution resulted from his long-standing reflection on the problems of state, socialist movement, and people's democratic dictatorship.[36] Yet, two facts are seldom remembered: first, the October Revolution took place after China's Republican Revolution of 1911. The initial example of a revolution for socialism in one country can thus, to a great extent, be regarded as a response to the revolution in Asia—that is, the 1911 Revolution in China. Lenin's theory of national self-determination and his interpretation of the significance of revolution in backward countries in the era of imperialism were both introduced after the Chinese Revolution and were theoretically connected with his analysis of that revolution. Radek, later to become the principal of Moscow's Sun Yat-sen University, published a commemorative essay in *Pravda* after Sun's death in 1925, in which he stressed the following fact:

> One day in 1916, with the War at its most intense, a group of Bolsheviks gathered at Berne to discuss national self-determination. At the meeting Lenin suddenly proposed that in the future the Bolsheviks should unite with the Chinese revolution. At the time this proposal seemed like the dream of an idiot! He was, however, able to envision the Russian proletariat fighting shoulder-to-shoulder with millions of Chinese. Of the six or seven Bolsheviks present, however, one was able to imagine that, should they live long enough, they might just see such a fantasy come to pass.[37]

This piece demonstrates the persisting influence of the Chinese Revolution on Lenin's thinking about national self-determination and the future direction of the Russian Revolution. Soviet support for Sun Yat-sen and the Guomindang in the 1920s and its efforts for further cooperation between that party and the Chinese communists is closely related to Lenin's views on the first (i.e., 1911) revolution.[38] From the perspective of the history of the socialist movement, China's first modern revolution marks the point at which, owing to Asian social circumstances, the anticapitalist and national revolutions of European socialism began to turn toward movements of national self-determination. Lenin's 1914 ideas on national self-determination and his explanations of the significance of revolutions in backward countries in the age of imperialism all were developed after the 1911 Revolution, and had theoretical links with his analysis of it.

Second, the Russian Revolution greatly shocked and had an enduring influence on Europe—it can be regarded as the historical event that separated Russia from Europe. There is no fundamental difference between Lenin's revolutionary assessment and the notions of Asia in the writings of Smith or Hegel: all perceived the history of capitalism as an evolutionary process beginning in the ancient Orient and flowering in modern Europe, and moving through necessary stages from hunting and agriculture to modern industry and commerce. For Lenin, however, this world-historical framework began to have a double meaning. One the one hand, the global expansion of capitalism and the Russian uprising of 1905 that it stimulated were the main forces that had awakened Asia—a land that had been "standing still for centuries" and had no history.[39] On the other, since the Chinese Revolution represented the most progressive force in world history, it clearly indicated to socialists a point of rupture in the imperialist world system. In the protracted debate between Slavophiles and Westernizers among Russian intellectuals and revolutionaries,[40] Lenin, as a "Westernizer," via a dialectical comparison between "progressive Asia" and "backward Europe," developed a new sort of logic that could be called "shedding Europe—an imperialist Europe—and joining Asia—a progressive revolution in a backward region." It was within this logic that the Chinese Revolution provided a unique path combining national liberation with socialism—and it was this unique path that provided the premise for a new kind of revolutionary subject: the alliance between workers and peasants with the Chinese peasant as the principal component.

"Greater Asianism" from the Perspective of Social Revolution

Lenin's thesis provides a basic clue for understanding the relationship between modern Chinese nationalism and the question of Asia. It is worth noting that modern Japanese Asianism was first directed at "reviving" or "stimulating" Asia, but soon became intertwined with an expansionist "continental policy" and the imperialist scheme of "Greater East Asia." Under this shadow, the intellectuals and revolutionaries of China, Korea, and other Asian countries were never able to express any interest in any of the many varieties of "Asianism" that developed in modern Japan.

A limited number of writings on the question of Asia by Chinese revolutionaries such as Zhang Taiyan, Li Dazhao, and Sun Yat-sen were produced in Japanese contexts. The question of Asia for them was directly related to the Chinese Revolution, the social movement, and national self-determination. At the end of 1901, Sun Yat-sen published "On the Theories of Preserving and Partitioning China" *(Zhina baoquan fenge helun)* in the *Tōho Society Journal*. Addressing two theories then prevalent in Japan—that of preserving China or of partitioning it—Sun pointed out that "From the perspective of state power, there is no reason to preserve [China], [but] from the perspective of popular sentiment, there is no need for partition." There was no reason to "preserve" China because, from the perspective of revolutionary politics, the Qing state and the people had already been severed from one another, just as there was no need to "partition" China because from the same perspective one of the aims of the revolution was precisely to implement national self-determination.[41] In 1924, during his last visit to Kobe, Sun was invited to give a speech, in which he once again articulated his views on the Asia question—this was his famous address on "Greater Asianism,"[42] in which he rather ambiguously delineated two versions of Asia: one was the "birthplace of the most ancient culture," that lacked "any completely independent states," while the other was an Asia about to be rejuvenated. If the former seems to have an inherent connection with the complicated "multinational states" of Lenin's account, then what was the basis for this Asian rejuvenation or a rejuvenated Asia? Sun said the basis was Japan, since Japan had thirty years previously rescinded a number of unequal treaties and become the first independent state in Asia. In other words, it would be better to say that the basis was the nation-state rather than Japan. Sun also applauded the outbreak and the Japanese victory in the Russo-Japanese War of 1904–1905: "The Japanese triumph over Russia was the first triumph of an Asian over a European nation in the past several centuries.... All the Asian nations are astonished and overjoyed, and have become extremely hopeful." And what was this hope? The answer is: "They therefore hope to smash Europe and begin independence movements.... A great hope for national independence in Asia has been born."[43]

Sun brings up a delicate subject here, that is "all Asian nations"—this Asia is not only the origin of the most ancient civilization, but also an

Asia that contains a number of independent nation-states; it is not only East Asia of the Confucian cultural sphere, but also a multicultural Asia. The totality of the "Asian nations" is based on the independence of sovereign states. The notion of "all Asian nations" is the outcome of movements for national independence, not just an awkward imitation of the European nation-state. Sun insisted that Asia had its own culture and principles—what he called "the culture of the kingly way" *(wang dao)* as distinct from "the culture of the hegemonic way" *(ba dao)* of the European nation-state. He entitled his speech "Greater Asianism" partly because he connected the idea of Asia with the notion of "the kingly way." If we compare his speech with the imperialist idea of Asia, it becomes clear that although it preserves its association with such Confucian ideas as "the kingly way" and "virtue and morality," Sun's notion of Asia is not an Asia with a core of cultural homogeneity, but rather one made up of equal nation-states. According to this notion of Asia, the inherent unity of Asia is not Confucianism or any other unitary culture, but a political culture that accommodates different religions, beliefs, nationalities, and societies. Within the scope of this political culture, Sun discussed China, Japan, India, Persia, Afghanistan, Arabia, Turkey, Bhutan, and Nepal, and the tribute system of the Chinese empire. Cultural heterogeneity was one of the main characteristics of this idea of Asia, and the notion of nationality provides the vehicle for the heterogeneity inherent in it. In Sun's usage, cultural heterogeneity provided the historical basis for a nation-state's internal unity and its capacity for resistance against external interference.[44]

Although Sun mentioned the Chinese tribute system in his speech, he in no way meant to claim a hegemonic or central status for China in relation to surrounding areas, but instead to demonstrate the necessity of the kingly way. In the context of "Greater Asianism," Sun's normative idea of the "kingly way" stood as antithetical to the "hegemonic" logic of colonialism. He believed that the tribute model implied mutual recognition of a multiplicity of cultures, ethnicities and religions in which modern states would be able to find the cultural resources to overcome imperialism. When he referred to the tribute paid by Nepal to China, he did not do so with any intent to rekindle the dream of a greater China, but rather because he firmly believed that these tribute relations implied equality based on mutual recognition and respect. Sun supported the national liberation and independence movements in Southeast Asia, and his ideas about Asia and national independence profoundly influenced that region.[45] He hoped to be able to unite the pluralism of the culture of the empire with new types of relations among nation-states so as to resist the colonialist policies of imperialism and the tendency toward the high degree of cultural homogenization found in the nation-state. His vision of Asia consisted of Japan in the East, Turkey in the West, and nation-states founded on Hinduism, Buddhism, Islam, Confucianism, and other cultural subjectivities in the areas in between. He said, "We must insist on Greater Asianism and recover the status of Asian nations. As long as we use virtue and morality as the basis to unite all our nationalities, then all the nations of Asia will become powerful."[46] According to Sun, this "culture of the kingly way" will "come to the assistance of oppressed nationalities" and "a culture that rebels against the hegemonic way is a culture that seeks the equality and liberation of all peoples."[47] Sun clearly saw the relationship between nationalism and the concept of race, even as he saw that nationalism's logic of resistance also contained a logic leading in another direction, that is, the logic of oppression and power. Thus, when he appealed to the notion of race to legitimize national independence, he also raised the notion of "Greater Asianism." The proposition of "Greater Asianism," or "Pan-Asianism," is antithetical to the Japanese idea of "Greater East Asianism," presenting a multiculturalism that critiques the highly homogeneous Japanese concept of "East Asia."[48] "Greater Asianism" offers, therefore, not only a scheme transcending imperialism through self-determination, but also a multinationalism that transcends the homogeneity of ethnicity, culture, religion, and belief.

The close connection between "Greater Asianism" and socialist internationalism rests on this logic, with Sun defining Asia from an ethnic perspective even as he saw the Russian liberation movement as an ally of Greater Asianism in overcoming ethnic boundaries. He said:

> There is a new country in Europe that is discriminated against by all white Europeans, who regard it as inhuman, like a venomous snake or a wild beast and dare not approach it; many of us in Asia hold the same view. Which country is this? Russia. Russia is now parting ways

with white Europeans. Why is this so? It is because Russia insists upon the kingly way rather than the hegemonic way; it insists on virtue and morality rather than justice (universal principles) and might. It upholds fairness to the utmost, and objects to the oppression of the many by the few. Hence the new culture of Russia is entirely compatible with the old culture of the East, so it will therefore come to join hands with the East, and part ways with the West.[49]

Here the socialist "new culture" after the October Revolution is the true yardstick (rather than skin color)—"Greater Asianism" as a "mass liberation movement" of oppressed nationalities closely resonates with it. If we compare Sun's text with Li Dazhao's "Greater Asianism and New Asianism" and "New Asianism Revisited," both published in the journal *Guomin* in 1919, they all trace out the same line of an Asia based on national self-determination and internationalism, defined against the background of Japan's "Twenty-one Demands" made to China, and leveraged on Russia's October Revolution. Li Dazhao argues that Japanese "Greater Asianism" is really a "Greater Japanism" similar to the United States' Monroe Doctrine. Its substance is "not peace, but invasion; not national self-determination, but imperialist annexation of weaker nations; not Asian democracy, but Japanese militarism; not an organization suitable to the organization of the world, but an organization deleterious to that goal."[50] His "New Asianism" was made up of two key points: "the first is that, before Japan's Greater Asianism has [been] destroyed, we weaker Asian nations should unite to destroy it; the other is that, after Japan's Greater Asianism has been destroyed, the Asian masses as a whole should unite and join the organization of the world—only then will it be possible to join that organization."[51] What they valued was not alliance among states but rather an alliance among "the masses as a whole," since regional or world organization must be a "great alliance of the masses" premised on social revolution and social movements.[52]

The understandings of "Asia" by Lenin, Sun Yat-sen, and Li Dazhao were closely related to their understandings of the task and direction of the Chinese Revolution. As for Lenin's view of Asia, we can clearly see a synthesis between the logic of revolution and the definition of Asia in Hegel's conception of world history (i.e., a medieval, barbarous, ahistorical Asia).

This Hegelian plus revolutionary conception of Asia not only includes ancient (feudal), medieval (capitalist), and modern (proletarian revolutionary or socialist) modes of historical development; it also stresses the unique position defined for "Asia" (especially Russia and China) in the age of world capitalism and imperialism, emphasizing the unique path of capitalist development within a society with a peasant economy as its main component. The state question is argued in a double sense: on the one hand, national self-determination is sought within the imperialist international order, while on the other, the state and its violence must be directed toward peasant interests and capitalist development. These two together make up a revolutionary view on Asian social characteristics, and from this perspective, what makes Asia Asia is not any cultural essence abstracted from Confucianism or any other civilization, but rather the special position of Asian countries in the capitalist world-system. This special position was not produced out of a particular narrative of the structure of world capitalism, but out of a dynamic analysis of the class composition and historical traditions internal to Asian societies.

This is why there are extreme differences between the "Asia" seen from the social revolutionary perspective and that seen by the various culturalisms, statisms, and theories of civilization that emerge in modern history, with the former focusing on the study of various social forces and their interrelations. The question pursued by those promoting social revolution is this: With agrarian relations at the core, what kind of relationships exist between the peasantry, the gentry, the emerging bourgeoisie, warlords, and urban workers? Just as Mao Zedong set out in his "Report on an Investigation of the Peasant Movement in Hunan" and "Analysis of the Classes in Chinese Society," analyses of class composition are not structural, but rather political, and made from the perspective of the social revolution and social movements. These participants in revolutionary movements are not inquiring about the ordinary property ownership ratios of particular social groups, but instead seeking to explain the attitudes and potential of these groups regarding social revolution and social movements. So this sort of "class analysis" should really be thought of as dynamic political analysis within the general framework of class analysis—political analysis being characterized by attention to subjective agency. Ignoring this, it is impossible to understand why, in the class transformations of modern China, members from the middle and upper social strata could become the main force of the revolutionary movement, or why intellectuals from imperialist countries could become steadfast friends and comrades of oppressed nationalities—from the perspective of subjective agency it would be more accurate to say that internationalism is a political consciousness or awareness that stems from linking the liberation of one's own nationality with that of others, rather than from a refusal of or an amnesia about national identity. If we analyze "Asia" from this social revolutionary perspective, totalistic and static descriptions of "Asia" or "East Asian" lose their validity, because the perspective of "political analysis" requires a dynamic analysis of the international and internal relationships of different societies. From the perspective of the social revolution it asks, in other words, in this historical movement: Who are our enemies and who are our friends? And this question of friendship or enmity pertains to relations both among and internal to nations.

According to Machiavelli's venerable formulation, "politics" is related either to an active subjectivity or a subjective agency. A political perspective demands both that the cognitive subject be part of it and that various active subjects also be located—then it is a matter of distinguishing among friends and enemies and assessing the direction of the social movement. A "political perspective" is always "internal": it is one that places the individual person in a position of dynamic interaction between friend and enemy and puts the political actions of thinkers or revolutionaries into intimate relations with the cognition of Asia, China, Japan, and Russia. The most powerful aspect of this perspective is that it can overcome the nationalism and statism that inhere within international relations among nation-states by discerning different political forces in different societies. From this perspective, questions of opposition or alliance are founded not on fixed frameworks of relations among states or nations, but on forces internal to each society and their potential dynamics of interaction.

In order to illustrate the characteristics of this kind of political perspective or analysis, we may compare it with the notion of "state rationality" (perhaps including its opposite, "state irrationality") that Maruyama Masao used to discuss Fukuzawa Yukichi. According to Maruyama, one of Fukuzawa's contributions to the history of thought was his articulation of a "state rationality" appropriate to the needs of the times. From the viewpoint of this "state rationality," modern Japan's exclusionism and expansionism can be seen as resulting from either a lack of or a betrayal of this rationality. In other words, for Fukuzawa no politics is more important than the establishment of a true "state rationality." Carl Schmitt opened his now widely quoted *The Concept of the Political* with the words: "The concept of the state presupposes the concept of the political. . . . No matter what, the 'political' is usually juxtaposed to the 'state,' or at least brought into a relationship to it." The formula of "equating the state with the political," however, cannot represent the essential form of the political: "The equation state = political becomes erroneous and deceptive at exactly the moment when the state and society penetrate each other." His purpose in raising this was to illustrate that such a situation "must necessarily occur in a democratically organized unit."[53] My purpose here in differentiating the political and the state is not to delineate the characteristics of a "democratically organized unit," but to understand political practice during the era of the Russian and Chinese revolutions. In the context of social revolution, "the political" exists among various active subjects and in disputes among the self-conscious wills of classes, class fractions, and political parties—these forces attempt to influence, dominate, shape, or control state power, but the state does not have an absolute capacity to encapsulate "the political" within its "structural-functional" operations. From this perspective, the formula state = political (i.e., active subjects having already become "structural-functional" elements of state power) describes not the normal situation but rather the result of a process of depoliticization within the political domain.

In contrast to the analytical perspective of "state rationality," "political cognition" during a period of social revolution is not in a normative sense the mode of action of political subjects (e.g., states), but rather the actuality and momentum of implementing a historical movement from the perspective of "active political subjects and their interactions." This requires the cognizant to transform themselves into "active subjects," that is, to place themselves or the interests they represent on the chessboard of political analysis, out of which arises a political summons. Lenin perceived in Sun Yat-sen's program a link between the Chinese Revolution and "purely Russian questions," so he proposed a program of national self-determination, opening a train of thought concerned with what the revolutionary forces needed to rely upon, whom they must oppose, and which kind of state must be established in order for capitalism to develop in "Asia." The political decision to combine socialism with the state was the product of this political analysis. Similarly, Japanese intellectuals such as Miyazaki Tōten and Kita Ikki, based on their recognition that China's independence and liberation was a necessary step in the liberation of Asia, and even of humankind, in various ways either took a practical role in China's revolution or undertook direct investigation of the Chinese social movement, in this way producing both profound political analyses and the capacity for political action. After the 1911 Revolution, "What Kita Ikki saw was the wretched emulation of Great Britain in Japan's foreign policy." His analysis of the Japanese "theory of preserving China" was truly political: if Japan joined the group of six lending countries, "imitating European economic partitioning [of China]," would that not just be "to play the running dog, [helping to] partition [China] in the name of preserving it"? If one really wanted to "preserve" China, it was necessary to promote Chinese autonomy and national awakening, and that required a clear separation from traitorous warlords and allying with China's "emerging revolutionary classes." Lending money to warlords in the name of "preserving China" in fact demonstrated the relationship between state politics and the expansive aspirations of the Japanese *zaibatsu*.[54] Kita supported and participated in Sun Yat-sen's revolution, but he sharply criticized Sun's acceptance of loans from Japanese *zaibatsu* and his excessive reliance on foreign aid, saying that Sun failed to discriminate between "war and revolution."[55] Here the ideal of "liberating Asia" (i.e., Sun's "Greater Asianism") and the problems of the "Chinese revolution" and of "remaking Japan" showed how closely they were tied to one another, and from this political perspective, not only did the abstractness of the idea of "Asia" disappear, but even China and Japan ceased to be monolithic concepts impervious to further analysis.

Another example is Yoshino's "Do Not Vituperate against the Activities of Beijing Student Groups," an article published in *Chū kōron* in June 1919, where he revealed the superficiality of Cao Rulin's and Zhang Zongxiang's "pro-Japan faction" and the "anti-Japanese voices" of the student movement, reaching the conclusion that "if we want to extirpate the ominous fact of anti-Japanese [sentiment], the strategy should not be to assist Messrs. Cao and Zhang and their ilk and thus purchase popular unrest, but to [address] our own well-known policy toward China of supporting warlords and the *zaibatsu*"[56]—a perspective I see as being a "political" one. During the second year of the War of Resistance against Japan, after the Nanjing government had been forced to move to Chongqing, Ozaki Hotsumi perceived the deepening of the Communist Party's influence and the weakening influence of Zhejiang wealth, and concluded: "This has accelerated the demands for national liberation conferred on China by its modern history; the national liberation movement has already become a force that is difficult for the Republican Government to direct or control" and "China's 'reddening' is determined by China's particular complexities and their particular content; I think it is not necessarily to be considered as something of the same order as the Soviet Union"[57]—an interpretation I see as a "political" one. After the Marco Polo Bridge Incident, Tachibana Shiraki questioned his own understanding of China, saying: "In my efforts to grasp its various circumstances, my vision has been fixed on the objective aspects of China, and my consideration of the crucial subjective conditions has been too shallow. How will it be possible to posit a relationship between these two under current conditions? I must begin anew."[58] As I see it, this way of understanding China through returning to "subjective conditions" is also a "political mode of understanding."

In terms of intellectual history, these understandings of China or conceptions of Asia eventually and in different ways and different degrees all strayed from their initial courses, the primary reason being that, in the face of a powerful state politics, they could not carry their analyses through to the end. That is, in the face of "the state," the "active subject" at the heart of any political point of view simply disappeared—this tragedy of both thought and the activist reminds me of a powerful thesis proposed by a European historian: if we want to determine the most central theme of world history since the nineteenth century, that theme would have to be the nation-state. While reading Professor Nomura's research on the thought and actions of Miyazaki Tōten, I noticed that his analysis began with "Miyazaki's two major regrets": "First, why did he take part in this revolution as a Japanese and not as a Chinese?" And "Second, before devoting his life to the Chinese revolution, why did he not commit himself to 'bettering Japan?'" Nomura goes on to an extremely insightful analysis: "The issue between being 'a Japanese' or 'a Chinese' in 'devoting one's life to the Chinese revolution,' as well as the issue between 'bettering Japan' and the Chinese revolution are both encompassed within Miyazaki's two regrets, and we can say that his two questions were deeply influenced by the political situation from the Meiji through the Taishō periods. As far as the Miyazaki who devoted his life to the Chinese revolution is concerned, the basic source of this regret was the tragic sense of being 'torn in two' by the nature of the relations between the two countries."[59] After quoting Miyazaki's words from late in life in honor of the Japanese emperor and state *(kokutai)*, Nomura comments: "As a man of the Meiji era, Miyazaki never managed to break free from the shackles of this curse: the state's emperor system."[60]

Kita Ikki went much further than Miyazaki: he regarded Japan's internal revolutionary transformation as a precondition to the liberation of Asia even as he also claimed that "Our seven hundred million compatriots in China and India will never be independent without our support.... While the authorities on Euro-American revolutionary theory all stand on this superficial philosophy and cannot grasp the 'gospel of the sword,' the far-seeing Greece of Asian civilization has already constructed its own spirit.... People who eschew armed states have the wisdom of children."[61] Here, rather than carrying his political ideas about "remaking Japan" over into Sino-Japanese relations during the period of imperialism, Kita instead uncritically imagined Japan as the armed liberator of Asia. As in his 1903 description of the Russo-Japanese War as the "decisive battle between the Yellow and White races,"[62] notions such as "state" and "race" prevent him from making a political analysis of his own society, so that today it is easy to discover "a vast inconsistency between his ideal image of Japan as a 'proletarian,' 'revolutionary' state and its reality as 'one of the colonizers.'"[63] When Ozaki Hotsumi trumpeted an "East Asian Cooperative Community" *(Dongya xietong ti)* in the late 1930s against the background of Japanese aggression against Asia, or when, after the Japanese occupation of Manchuria in 1931, Tachibana Shiraki applied his analysis of the Chinese social organism to his imagination of Manchukuo as a "decentralized autonomous state," what we see is precisely the equation "state=political," and a deviation from the political mode of analysis that they had once insisted upon—in different ways political analysis halted at the gates of the "Japanese Empire." From the perspective of social revolution, this is "the statification (*guojiahua*) of politics," a moment at which the figures of the thinkers themselves overlap with the "Japanese Empire" they had earlier sought to transform.

In the visions of Lenin and Sun Yat-sen, national self-determination is a synthesis of nationalism and socialism, that is, they require both the establishment of a nation-state as the necessary condition for capitalist development even as they emphasize that this process of state-building must simultaneously transform traditional imperial relations through social revolution. Socialists believe that weaker nations' demands for self-determination always include demands for a certain degree of democracy, and, moreover, their support for national independence movements is always linked to support for democratic forces. In this synthesis of internationalism and national self-determination, not much space is left for a category like "Asia"—Asia is only a marginalized zone in the capitalist system, a geographical region that can only enter the world capitalist system and then the struggle against that system through national revolution. If we want to discuss the relationship of socialist thought and Greater Asianism, we must recognize that, in the modern context, they both have historical ties to certain forms of nationalism. The socialist idea of national self-determination is founded on the modern European binary between "empire" and "state" and efforts to found "colonialist autonomous governments" such as Manchukuo under the banner of "Greater Asianism" similarly employ the ideas of sovereignty, independence, and autonomy in order to incorporate Japan's imperialist policies in the guise of a narrative of progress. The Japanese intellectuals mentioned above expressed sincere sympathy for China's revolution and shared profound insights into China's social movement, so why did even someone as insightful as Kita Ikki eventually convert to the very state system he had once criticized, even to the point of supporting policies of imperialist invasion? I cannot discuss these issues in detail here, but two factors provide certain explanatory possibilities: first, modern Japan lacked the conditions for social revolution, so these keen intellectuals could not carry out the political insights they had developed through their observations of the Chinese Revolution within Japanese society. Second, lacking these social conditions, socialist thought could not develop the impetus necessary to overcome modern nationalism and statism.

With the ebb of the Chinese Revolution and the trend of Asian national liberation, the political vision of social movement and revolution combined with a political mode of analysis capable of linking the social movements of Russia, China, Japan, and other Asian countries eventually faded. Since the late 1970s, following the decline of the social movements of the 1960s and the end of national liberation campaigns, we entered an era of "depoliticization"—a process in which state mechanisms have gradually appropriated active subjectivity or subjective agency within "state rationality" in track with the global market. As the question of "Asia" again becomes a concern of many intellectuals, we seem incapable of finding the political mode of analysis linking different societies that last century's revolutionaries adeptly developed through blending themselves into revolutionary history. At the present time, discussions of the question of Asia center on a regionalism that is tied together by regional markets, regional alliances against terrorism and issues of financial security.

Asia in Narratives of Modern History: Land and Sea, State and Network

Today's academic discussion of "Asia" takes place in the context of neoliberal globalization. At the beginning of this essay, I mentioned two discourses of "empire": the first has the United States as its center and global organizations such as the World Bank, the World Trade Organization (WTO), and the International Monetary Fund (IMF) as its mechanisms. According to Sebastian Mallaby, the formation of this global empire "would not amount to an imperial revival. But it would fill the security void that empires left—much as the system of mandates did after World War I ended the Ottoman Empire."[64] The other is a discourse of regional empires, with the European Union (EU) as model, aimed at resisting the unipolar domination of the global empire. British prime minister Tony Blair's foreign policy advisor Robert Cooper calls this vision of empire a "cooperative empire." In his taxonomy, the two models of "postmodern states" are the EU as a "cooperative empire," and the "voluntary global economic imperialism" of the IMF and the World Bank, with both models operating according to a set of laws and regulations, as opposed to the reliance of traditional empires on centralized power. Cooper's ideas of "cooperative empire" and "the imperialism of neighbors" were both proposed in the shadow of the Balkan and Afghan wars. He associated "humanitarian intervention" with this new kind of imperialism, making "humanitarianism" the theoretical premise for "empire." The EU is the paragon of this new empire.[65]

Against the background of colonialism and imperialist wars, Asian intellectuals have generally explained history through an East/West binary, with the result that modern ideas of Asia often had strong culturalist overtones, inevitably tending toward essentialist perspectives in constructing and understanding "Asian" or "East Asian" identity. Not only, however, are ideas of Asia formed in this way unconvincing in practice, but even should they turn out to be tenable, do we really want to establish the kind of "cooperative empire" or "imperialism of neighbors" that can carry out interventions in the name of humanitarianism? How can such a group of politically, economically, and culturally complex Asian societies form a "linking mechanism" to provide a form of regional organization different from both the modern nationalist state model and the two "imperial" models described above? Having experienced both the cruel history of colonialism and powerful movements for national liberation, can we find our way toward a flexible enough mechanism that will be able to avoid the traps of both the "imperial" and the statist models?

Let us begin our consideration with different historical narratives of an "East Asian world." The construction of such a world as a relatively self-sufficient "cultural sphere" is the creation of modern Japanese thought, but there are different ways in which this world has been delineated. Nishijima Sadao described "the East Asian world" as a self-contained cultural sphere: geographically, China formed the center, surrounded by Korea, Japan, Vietnam, and the eastern portion of the Western rivers corridor between the Mongolian and the Tibetan plateaus. Culturally, it was characterized by four features: the Chinese writing system, Confucianism, Buddhism, and a legal system.[66] The effort to establish a connection between geographic region and culture aimed to construct East Asia as an organic whole, but how did this idea of an "organic Asia" come into being? According to Maeda Naonori, Japanese scholars did not ordinarily include Japan within the East Asian world:

> It is generally believed that before modern times, before the history of different regions in the world attained commonality, China was a world, and India was yet another world. From the perspective of cultural history, the world of China can be regarded as the world of East Asia, including Manchuria, Korea, and Annam [Vietnam], which is what people used to believe. Although we considered the possibility, we were hesitant to include Japan in this world, something only a matter of cultural history. We know almost nothing about whether the internal development of Korean or Manchurian societies, not to mention Japan, was connected or merely parallel to China. We know that in the European world, for instance, the development of British society was parallel to and interrelated to that of the European continent. But whether a similar phenomenon existed in East Asia, especially between Japan and China, was, except in the context of modern history, never clearly explained, to the point that one can say it has not even been phrased as a question. The received idea has been that the development of Japan's social structure, from ancient times to the medieval and modern periods, has been completely isolated from those on the continent.[67]

The view that set Japan apart from Asia was closely related to circumstances unique to Japanese history before it opened its ports and with the notion of Japan's particularity that subsequently arose. Connection and separation, shedding Asia and joining Asia are the antitheses that made up the paradoxical, at once contradictory and coordinated, narrative of Asia in the modern Japanese nationalist system of knowledge.

The impetus for constructing an organically whole or self-contained East Asian world has invariably come from the nationalistic, industrialized, and capitalistic "West." The notion of a "sphere of East Asian civilization" was an organic constituent of modern Asian nationalist knowledge, and people yearned to see behind this narrative not just cultural particularity but also the momentum for an "inherent" and "universal" nationalism, industrialism, and capitalism matching this particularity. Hence the effort to search for modernity in Asia broke up the Hegelian sequence of "world history," even as it reestablished the inherent principles of the Hegelian "world order": nationalism, capitalism (industry and commerce), and theories of the state that served to organize a metahistorical narrative of East Asian history. Miyazaki Ichisada, the most prominent representative of the Kyoto school, proposed a new definition of "East Asia": on the one hand, he no longer followed traditional scholars in regarding the "East Asian world" as part of the "Chinese world," instead relocating China and its history within the category of "East Asian history." On the other hand, through analyzing changes in trade and transportation during the Sui, Tang, and Five Dynasties period (581–960 C.E.), Miyazaki asserted that "one can make out in Song society obvious capitalistic tendencies and phenomena that clearly differ from what can be found in medieval society," then proceeded to develop a set of narratives about an East Asian modernity parallel to that of the West.[68] Via his notion of "communication," Miyazaki wove together the history of disparate regions and interpreted "Song Dynasty capitalism," "East Asian modernity," and "nationalism" *(kokuminshugi)* from this perspective.

In a chapter entitled "Nationalism in Modern East Asia," he analyzed ethnic relations from the Qin-Han period all the way to the Qing dynasty. He argued that during the Song dynasty, not only did "nationalist upsurges" appear in central China, in the north and in the south that went beyond tribute relations (as with the war between the Song and the Liao and the Song-Jin war, with its "peaceful relations between two countries"), but there appeared the Dayue (i.e., Vietnam) and Dali kingdoms, which, although nominally tributaries to the Song court, actually were "independent and unconstrained nation-states." Although the Mongolian Yuan dynasty terminated this process, it stimulated "Han-centric nationalism" in the Ming dynasty that followed. In this sense, the development of nationalism in Asia is treated as parallel to that in the West.[69] Miyazaki boldly employs various European categories—his observations of the Tang-Song transition and especially of the Song dynasty are organized around the notions of capitalism and the nation-state. Any such effort to find its own history in East Asia is unavoidably teleological, and we can locate the binary of "state" versus "empire" contained in the European discourse on Asia in the assumption of an internal link between "East Asian modernity" and the nation-state.[70]

In this regard, Hamashita Takeshi's discussion of the Asian tribute system is both a critique of "shedding Asia" and a refutation of particularism. In the field of economic history, he reconstructs an East Asian world order centered on China and woven together through the tribute system *(chaogong tixi)*, and in this way he affirms a set of historical "connections" within Asia—including those between Japan and China. Although he similarly emphasizes an impetus for modernity that comes from within Asia, contrary to Miyazaki's outline of "East Asian modernity" characterized by European-style nationalism, Hamashita and the school he represents builds his notion of the internal integration of Asia on this tribute network.[71] His theory is centered on three major premises: first, Asia forms a totality, not only culturally but also economically and politically. Second, this totality has Chinese civilization as its core and is tied together by a trans-state tribute network. Third, coupled with this tribute network is a set of "core/periphery" ties and corresponding practices of tribute and imperial bestowal *(ce feng)* quite distinct from European-style relations among "states." If Miyazaki's "East Asia modernity" is grounded in "nationalism," Hamashita's narrative challenges the idea of a necessary link between the nation-state and modernity, using tribute networks to construct an alternative version of regional and world history. In his view, moreover, the Asian tribute network was not completely destroyed by the expansion of Western capitalism, with "Asia as world-system" continuing to exist in the modern age. Hamashita's account is inspiring, as he not only discovers internal connections within the Asian world but also employs it as a starting point for envisioning the contemporary world. He also uses a peripheral perspective to expose the continentalism and dynastic orthodoxy in official Chinese historiography. His is a forceful criticism of the advocates of Japanese particularism who refuse to recognize the historical relations between Japan and the rest of Asia even as it provides a perspective for viewing China from its periphery for Chinese scholars who are accustomed to considering China only from within. This effort to search for East Asian modernity based on the tribute network—the imperial system—also upsets Eurocentrism and its empire/state and tribute/trade binaries.

The "fact" of an East Asian totality is a preconception or construct premised on the category of "East Asia," with Hamashita's discourse stressing the commercial aspects of the tribute system, especially maritime trading links that overlapped with internal Asian relations. Here I will attempt to build on Hamashita's work and open it up by supplementing, balancing, and developing it. To begin with, the tribute system was not a self-sufficient or integral structure, but rather the product of historical interaction among the agents participating in the system. In this sense, the tribute system was a constantly shifting process of multiple centers of power producing one another, and whenever a new force entered the picture, the internal power relations would change. Hamashita defined six types of imperial tribute relations: (1) tribute from local minority chiefs (*tusi*) and local officials (*tuguan*); (2) tribute relations to win over border peoples (*jimi*); (3) tribute states with the closest ties; (4) tribute states with two-way relations; (5) tribute states on the outer edge of the periphery; (6) states nominally in a tribute relationship, but actually with primarily "mutual market" (*hushi*, i.e., commercial) links.[72] This ostensibly exhaustive narrative, however, relies excessively on a static "core/periphery" classificatory framework, so it cannot account completely for the constant changes in the historical connotations of tribute practices. Miyazaki had already divided Chinese history into different periods from the perspective of economic history: from ancient to medieval times was the inland-centered period; from Song to Qing was the Grand Canal–centered period; and with the late Qing began the coast-centered period—a new situation that clearly came into being under European influence.[73] If core/periphery relations within China were constantly shifting, so was the tribute system. For example, the tribute relations that the Song court established under conditions of war with its northern neighbors could not at all be encompassed within Hamashita's framework of "core/periphery" relations, nor could the Qing court's tribute relations with Russia that began in the seventeenth century.

The instability of core/periphery relations is one of the most important characteristics of the modern capitalist world, but premising the changes in power relations within Asia since the nineteenth century on core/periphery relations with China is less than convincing. As Hamashita pointed out in an earlier essay: "Asia and the Formation of the Capitalist Colonial System:

The Penetration of British Banking Capital in the 1850s," the intensification of the Western capitalist powers' financial penetration into Asia—and especially China—was closely related to the expansion of international financial markets following the discovery of gold in the United States and Australia. Financially speaking, modern Chinese economic history can be regarded as the process by which the Chinese economy was woven into the fabric of a unified international settlement system centered in London. In this sense, the "modern age" of Asia is the process of Asia being gradually incorporated economically into modern world history, an incorporation characterized by financial relations of domination-subordination.[74] If we extend the core/periphery structure to nineteenth- and twentieth-century power relations within Asia, it will inevitably conceal the actual central status in the new world-system of what were traditionally peripheral categories. For example, if Japan's "shedding Asia" and modernization (including the first invasion of Taiwan and the first Sino-Japanese War of 1894–95) is explained within the framework of "shaking off tribute-state status" (i.e., the core/periphery framework), it will be impossible to account for the great changes in "core/periphery" relations that had been taking place since the Opium Wars. The binaries of "core/periphery" and Chinese empire/tribute state (i.e., Japan) actually reproduce the binary of empire/state in modern European thought. As Maruyama says, European "state rationality came into being on the one hand though resistance against such trans-state authorities as the Holy Roman Empire and the Roman Catholic pope, and, on the other, in the struggle against demands for autonomy by Medieval social powers such as feudal lords, autonomous cities and local churches."[75] Thus the "core/periphery" structure cannot explain the historical role of Japan in modern Asia, being unable to account for why it was precisely the "peripheral" countries—Japan, Korea, Hong Kong, Taiwan, and Singapore—that one after the other became the centers or subcenters of nineteenth- and twentieth-century Asian capitalism, while such traditional continental "core areas" as mainland China, India, and Inner Asia declined into "peripheral" or colonial status.

Hamashita's innovative research also makes it possible for studies of regions that are not centered on states but on networks, but it is exactly in the widened network perspective that the overly static structure of tribute/trade or core/periphery relations encounters a new challenge. As

Hamashita himself noticed, at the beginning of the nineteenth century the private overseas Chinese trade network successfully transformed the official tribute system into a system of private trade, the result of a long-term process of historical interaction. As Xu Baoqiang argues in his doctoral dissertation:

> When the Europeans arrived in East Asia at the beginning of the sixteenth century, they tried to connect with the official tribute system so as to promote the development of trade. But they realized that they were increasingly reliant on the extensive trade networks of the overseas Chinese, and they thereupon consciously encouraged the expansion of these networks. Especially after the beginning of the nineteenth century, the official tribute system centered upon China was merely a fantasy of government control that was never actualized because China was confronted with the growing hegemony and aggression of the imperialist powers. To a large extent, then, it was not the official tribute system but private overseas Chinese trade networks that integrated the East Asian regions into a single historical system.[76]

According to Xu, it was not tribute but rather private overseas trade—including smuggling—that established the most important links between the East and Southeast Asian trade networks. Under European imperialism in the nineteenth century, the development of the Southeast Asian market resulted less from tribute trade than from the breakup of that system—the salient characteristics of trade in Southeast Asia in the eighteenth to the nineteenth centuries were smuggling, arms trafficking, and European trading monopolies.[77] Here, the historical transformation of networks resulted from shifts in core/periphery power relationships.

Second, in the picture of "maritime East Asia" envisioned in the tribute network, historical routes of communication in inner Asia and their changes over time were reduced to subordinate and marginal status. If we compare Nishijima's "East Asian world" with that of Hamashita, structured as it is by tribute networks and concentrated mainly on the east coast of the Eurasian continent, its peninsulas and its islands, including Northeast Asia and Southeast Asia, the latter closely approximates the "maritime Asia" that so interests contemporary Japanese academia. Hamashita developed his idea of Asia in opposition to Eurocentrism, and his description focused on such things as trade and the circulation of silver. He stressed the historical relations between China and East and Southeast Asia—that is, trade links enabled mainly through marine transportation—an account, therefore, that echoes the economistic logic and the maritime theory frame of the European narrative of capitalism. In his following work, this notion of the maritime became a theory of modernity that grew increasingly central to his observations regarding the question of Asia, and it was a theory that corresponds precisely with the political economy of the modern treaty system. Although he used the tribute system as his structural framework, Hamashita clearly pointed out that the basic rules of this world-system needed to be modified, with the changes moving in the direction of establishing a new East Asia system centered on the sea but different from the Western system of trade.

Japan, as the first maritime state to challenge the tribute trade order via a system of treaties guaranteeing equality in commercial relations, thus stood in an exceptional position in its time. For this reason, this "historical world with its integral unity" centered on East and Southeast Asia stressed the importance of culture, political structure, and the sea in the formation of regional relations, especially regional trade relations. This totalistic view of Asia, however, lacks a penetrating account of the continental relations—between China and Inner, West, and South Asia, as well as Russia—that dominated the tribute system for many centuries, and it seldom touches upon the relationship between the formation of the maritime trading sphere and continental dynamics, nor does it provide a clear enough delineation of a "West" that had long been involved in Inner Asia. In fact, the so-called maritime age came into being in a context of European industrialization, the development of maritime military technology, and the formation of the nation-state system in Europe. Via colonialism and unequal terms of trade, this "maritime age" managed to play down continental historical and social relations, subordinating them to maritime hegemonies and economic interaction.

From the Chinese historical perspective, relations among the Northwest, the Northeast, and the Central Plain have been the fundamental force driving changes in China's social system, population, and modes of production, and even in the so-called maritime age, inland relations have played a vital role in China. In his *Sketch of the Origins of Sui and Tang Institutions*, Chen Yinke traced these to three major sources: first, the Northern Wei Dynasty; second, the Northern Qi, Liang, and Chen dynasties; and third, the Western Wei and Northern Zhou dynasties. He pointed out that Sui and Tang "artifacts and institutions spread widely—to the Northern desert, south to Jiaozhi [Vietnam], to Japan in the East, and to Inner Asia in the West, but monographs on these origins and later changes to them are rare, a regrettable lacuna in Chinese historiography."[78] His studies such as *Draft Account of Tang Dynasty Political History* (Tangdai zhengzhi shi shulun gao) and *On Tang Dynasty Border Generals and the Permanent Garrison Troops* (Lun Tangdai zhi fan jiang yu fubing) argue that, beginning in the Sui and Tang dynasties, Chinese institutions, its population, and its culture have been the product of multiple Eurasian sources. In his *Inner Asian Frontiers of China*, Owen Lattimore describes an "Asian continent" with the Great Wall as its center, which transcended political and ethnic borders, an account that provides us with a completely different view of the relationship between core and periphery. This idea of a "center" meant that on either side of the Great Wall were two interacting and mutually influencing social formations, one agricultural and one pastoral; these influences in turn reflected back or diffused into the modes of each society's social life.[79] This "Great Wall–centered" thesis of a "mutual frontier" serves to correct the one-sided Chinese historical account of an agricultural core and provides a contrast with the Yellow River–centered and post–Song Grand Canal–Yangzi Delta–centered narratives. This shift of the locus of historical narrative is linked both to the shift of core zones in different periods as well as to changing perspectives on how one evaluates historical change, especially the momentum driving historical change. According to Lattimore, it was only under the pressure of European colonialism and industrialization that the internal momentum of Chinese history changed from North to South to South to North, causing him to use the concepts of "pre-" and "post-West" to describe the transformation of internal relations on the Asian continent.

In discussing movement in the interior of the Asian continent, however, the differentiation between "pre-" and "post-Western" periods also becomes too simplistic. After the Manchus took control of the central plain, large-scale migration of population, economy, trade, and cultural features from the central plain to the north became an important phenomenon. In the seventeenth and eighteenth centuries, this South-to-North movement originated mainly out of factors internal to the Qing empire, and had little to do with the West. In an 1857 discussion of China's attitudes toward the maritime hegemonic powers, Marx made an important discovery, namely, that while the Western states were using military force to expand their trade with China, Russia was spending little but gaining more than any of the belligerent states, because while Russia had no maritime dealings with China, it enjoyed a unique overland commerce centered at Kiakhta. In 1852 alone, the value of merchandise bought and sold amounted to US$150 million, and, since the goods traded were relatively inexpensive in themselves, the quantity involved is striking. Because of this increase of continental trade, Kiakhta grew from an ordinary fortress and marketplace into a fairly important city and border capital, with direct and regular postal communication to Beijing, some 900 miles away.[80] Marx, in such essays as "The British and Chinese Treaty" and "The New Chinese War" and Engels in "Russia's Successes in the Far East," both pointed out how the Sino-British and Sino-French coastal conflicts made it possible for Russia to obtain vast territories in the Amur Basin and much commercial profit, with Engels predicting that Russia was "fast coming to be the first Asiatic Power, and putting England into the shade very rapidly on that continent."[81] He criticized the British media and the British cabinet for publicizing the content of the Anglo-Chinese treaty but simultaneously suppressing information on how Russia had gained greater advantage in China, Afghanistan, and other Inner Asian regions. If we understand the 1905 Russo-Japanese War's impact on the course of Japanese modernization and China's later alliance and subsequent split with the Soviet Union within a dialectic of continental and maritime relations, it becomes clear that interactions on the Eurasian continent have indeed been highly influential on East Asian modernity.

Theories of Asia based on the tribute system tend to emphasize economic relations (especially networks of maritime trade) at the expense of events such as wars and revolutions. Sun Yat-sen's description of overseas Chinese as "mothers of the Chinese revolution" serves as backhanded testimony to the influence of overseas networks (especially in Japan and Southeast Asia) on the modern Chinese Revolution, networks that overlapped with tribute routes. After the failure of the Hundred Days' Reform in 1898, Japan became not only a refuge for exiled reformers and the first generation of Chinese revolutionaries, but also the cradle of the Chinese Enlightenment; it was also in this period that a number of Japanese intellectuals became direct participants in China's revolutionary and reform movements. Overseas Chinese and their communities in such Southeast Asian countries as Vietnam, Malaya, the Philippines, and Burma—along with such places as Honolulu—not only provided material resources for China's reform and revolution, but also injected a special vitality into the wave of nationalism that eventually swept the entire region, forming a transnational network of social movements. Following the outbreak of the 1911 Revolution, this revolutionary movement based in peripheral overseas areas took root on the Chinese mainland and provided the initial impetus for the political revolution, the agrarian revolution, and the military struggles that soon developed. Thus did the interaction between coastal networks and inland areas manifest itself during the course of the revolution.

Similarly, the ties and differences between land and sea to a very real extent influenced the characteristics of Asian wars. In an appendix to *The Concept of the Political* entitled "Theory of the Partisan," Carl Schmitt centers his political thinking on the guerrilla or "partisan" or "irregular warfare," regarding this figure as an "irregular force" in contrast to the "regularity of the state and the military":

> There is no place in the classical martial law of the existing European international law for the partisan, in the modern sense of the word. He is either . . . a sort of light, especially mobile, but regular troop; or he represents an especially abhorrent criminal, who stands outside the law. . . . The partisan is . . . different not only from the pirate, but also from the corsair in the way that land and sea are distinguished as (two different) elemental spaces of human activity and martial engagement between peoples. Land and sea have developed not only different vehicles of warfare, and not only distinctive theaters of war, but they have also developed separate concepts of war,

peace, and spoils. The partisan will present a specifically terrestrial type of active fighter for at least as long as anticolonial wars are possible on our planet.[82]

Beginning with the Opium Wars, the external pressures facing China switched from inland to coastal areas, and traditional forms of warfare were likewise transformed. During the First Sino-Japanese War (1894), the Japanese navy thoroughly destroyed the Qing's Beiyang fleet and thereby took control of East Asian waters. But from the invasion of Northeastern China (i.e., Manchuria) in 1931 on to the full-scale outbreak of the War of Resistance in 1937, the mighty Japanese army nevertheless was unable to subjugate a poor and militarily backward China. Of course the war's outcome was determined by many complex political, economic, and military factors, so it is hard to analyze from a single perspective, but the failure of Japan's military victories on the regular battlefield to secure final victory is clearly related to the special form of this war, that is, to the interweaving of regular and partisan warfare, and of interstate and "people's war." Acting in concert with the regular army were flexible, irregular partisan forces dependent upon the nature of the land, with the latter closely linked to the general mobilization of the population, high political consciousness, and a clear demarcation between friend and enemy.

In this ethnically complex, geographically vast inland region populated mainly by peasants, China's revolutionaries synthesized mobilization for war and for revolution, bringing to bear unique military means to break with concepts of regular warfare—war among states—as defined by European international law, and laying a foundation for a postwar political and military topography completely different from that which had pertained prior to the conflict. China's revolution unfolded over China's inland mountain ranges, waterways, forests, and prairies, and through the intensification of agrarian revolution, modern China's political forces—especially the revolutionary party—imbued several generations of peasants and their descendants with a revolutionary and military subjective agency, thereby creating a new pattern of "peoples' war." Via the baptism of military experience and revolutionary mobilization, an agrarian society that, from a European perspective, is the eternal symbol of the backward and conservative, was finally able to become an active political force, and the revolutionary state-building, industrial planning, urban development, and new urban-rural relations that followed were all closely tied to the emergence of this new political subject. From this perspective a reappraisal of Mao Zedong's discussions of guerrilla strategy during the War of Resistance, his theories on protracted war, on the question of the role of peasants and villages in warfare, and his concept of New Democracy may yield a new understanding of China's wars and revolutions.

From each of the perspectives outlined above, the questions of how to understand the links between Asia's continental and maritime eras, how to understand Asia's internal totality as well as its diversity, and how to understand the assortment of its cultural and historical relationships are all topics that await further research. Simple maritime theory cannot explain the profound polarization between China's coastal and interior (especially northwestern) areas, and the coastal economy's domination of the inland economy. Nor can it explain the momentum behind China's (and Russia's) modern, agrarian-led revolution, nor the peculiarities of the twentieth century's Sino-Japanese War. More importantly, the tribute system is not simply a set of economic ties, as it encompassed ritual and political connections among a variety of social groups with differing cultures and beliefs. In the course of a long historical transformation, networks formed through tribute, trade, and migration were able to provide crucial elements for revolutions, wars, and other social interactions. In this sense, taking the next step to explain the multiple implications of tribute relations, and from this multiplicity discover their points of overlap or conflict with modern capitalism, constitutes a topic well worth further exploration.

Third, the discourse of the tribute system is defined in opposition to European nation-states and their treaty system, having prevailed over the earlier view that only the nation-state is capable of propelling modernization. The dichotomy between the tribute and the treaty systems, however, is also derived from that between empire and state. As early as the seventeenth century, the Qing state was already using treaties to define clear-cut borders in certain frontier regions (such as the Sino-Russian border), to create regular frontier patrol forces, to determine custom-duty rates and trade mechanisms, to exert sovereign rights over residents within its administrative sphere, and to establish tribute/treaty relations with European countries—all things regarded by modern social theory as peculiar to the nation-state. Hence the Qing was not only an empire composed of a complex of nationalities, but also a political entity with an advanced state system, with its well-developed tribute network also including treaty relations. If we understand Qing society merely through the opposition between state and empire, treaty and tribute, we ignore the historical overlap of the processes of the construction of the empire and that of the state, and we will thus be unable to understand the basic characteristics of modern Chinese nationalism. It is because of the composite relations between the tribute and state systems that we cannot describe the tribute system simply as a hierarchical relationship between center and periphery.[83] Here the real key issue is not whether East Asia or China is state-centered or part of a tribute system, but rather to clarify various notions and types of political structure, and various notions of state, so as to prevent the notion of state being completely enveloped within the history of modern European capitalism and its associated nation-states. Research on the tribute system and its networks is centered on economics and trade and is devoted to finding alternative forms of capitalism. We should not, however, overlook the fact that the tribute system encompasses ritual, politics, culture, internal and external relations as well as economics, thus representing a unique political culture.

If the tribute system is the product of a different type of state than the modern European sovereign state, we need to reinterpret the relationship between tribute system and state by comparing different types of both categories. In Chinese history, tribute and treaty relations are not completely opposed categories. For example, when the Qing government began to develop cross-border commercial, political, and military interactions with European countries, tribute links were a type of interstate relation. The Qing court's association with countries such as Russia, Portugal, Spain, Holland, and Great Britain were called tribute relations, but they were also in fact diplomatic and treaty relationships. Hamashita, when classifying different types of tribute, draws attention to one that he calls the "mutual market" relationship, which is very similar to the later "diplomatic" or "foreign trade" relationships. Within the tribute sphere, there was also a link involving tribute and returning gifts *(hu ci)*. Sometimes the tribute and the gift-in-return were of equal value, and sometime the return gift was worth more than the tribute, resulting in a double-sided tribute relationship that involved both economic and ritual interaction. Under such circumstances, there were overlaps between ritual inequality and substantial reciprocity, and between the ritual character of the tribute relationship and the actualities of tribute trade. If the defining feature of tribute practice is the overlap between state and tribute relationships, should we not consider the domestic and international relations of European states from another perspective, that is, to regard the treaty system not as a structural form but as the product of historical interactions among various forces and circumstances? For example, we may ask: Were Great Britain's nineteenth-century trade relations with India and North America defined by a treaty or a tribute relationship? Were the United States' (or the USSR's) twentieth-century relationships with its "allied nations" or "strategic partners" scattered throughout Asia, Europe, and Africa—particularly in the Cold War and post–Cold War periods—relationships among sovereign states or characteristic of a tribute system?

During the Opium War period (ca. 1840–1860), Wei Yuan (1794–1856) already recognized that the main difference between China and Britain in matters having to do with trade was not between a system based on tribute and one based on treaties, but rather the following: tribute goods were not the mainstay of China's economy, so there was no internal momentum for linking the imperial government and military directly to foreign trade. Britain's domestic economy, on the other hand, relied extensively on trade relations with its North American, Indian, and other colonies and on tribute goods, resulting in a drive from within the British domestic economy to link state institutions with foreign trade directly. If, as Wang Gungwu argues, China's overseas trade was a "commerce without empire," then what British merchants engaged in was an organized trade carried out under state auspices within a business-military alliance.[84] It was only in order to force China to sign unequal treaties that the Western powers recognized the Qing state as a formally equal legal subject, thus applying to a non-European entity the notion of sovereignty previously reserved for international law among Christian or "civilized" states. If one explains the Qing conflicts with Japan over the Korean peninsula and the First Sino-Japanese War according to a normative framework of either "tribute" or "treaty" relations (i.e., sovereignty based on formal equality), then the major changes in Asian power relations during the nineteenth century will inevitably be glossed over, thereby rationalizing European international expansionism under cover of a universal "rationality." If one proceeds on the premise of a binary of tribute versus treaty, or empire versus state, to attack such Eurocentric ideas by merely inverting the relations between the terms, the complexity of historical relations within Asia will in all likelihood be oversimplified. From this perspective, it is worth seriously considering how to define the simultaneously overlapping and opposed relationship between Asia's "center/periphery" mechanisms and those of the European "state."

The question of Asian "modernity" must eventually deal with the relationships both between Asia and European colonialism and between Asia and modern capitalism. As early as the 1940s, Miyazaki began to explore the "birth of Song dynasty capitalism" through the study of wide-ranging historical transportation links, believing firmly that the study of "the development of modernity after the Song has brought us to the point of needing to reflect on modern Western history in terms of the development of modern East Asian history."[85] That his theory of "East Asian modernity" overlapped with the Japanese idea of a "Greater East Asia" does not obscure the insight inhering in Miyazaki's observations. He saw that from the perspective of world history, the digging of the Grand Canal, urban migration, the ability of the circulation of commodities such as spices and tea to connect European and Asian trade networks, and the promotion of artistic and cultural exchange between Europe and Asia enabled by the expansion of the Mongolian Empire, not only changed the internal relations in Chinese and Asian societies, but also connected Europe and Asia by land and sea.[86] If the political, economic, and cultural features of "Asian modernity" appeared as early as the tenth or eleventh centuries, was the historical development of these two worlds merely parallel or more closely linked? Andre Gunder Frank responded to this question by noting that Asia and Europe were already profoundly tied together by the thirteenth or fourteenth centuries, and that as a result any discussion of the birth of modernity must proceed on the assumption of a world-system characterized by such relations.[87] The significance of communication is not the mere bundling together of two worlds; it is more like two gears connected by a belt: when one turns, the other must turn as well. So a logical conclusion is:

> If history were only European, the Industrial Revolution would never have eventuated, because it was not merely a matter of mechanization but a matter of the whole social structure. The rise of the petit-bourgeoisie was a necessary precondition for the Industrial Revolution, and it also required the capital accumulated through trade with East Asia. Making the machines work required not just motive power but also cotton as raw material and markets into which to sell the finished products, both of which were in fact supplied by East Asia. Lacking interaction with East Asia, in other words, the Industrial Revolution probably would not have taken place.[88]

Miyazaki's research centers mainly on Chinese history proper, and his writings on the intercourse between Asia and Europe are thin. Frank's research, on the other hand, is economistic and trade-centered, lacking convincing explanations of the internal dynamics of European history and the capitalism these dynamics produced. In their structured narratives based on a maritime world, wars, contingent events, and other historical factors are necessarily pushed into the background. Both accounts, however, from their different perspectives do provide us with the possibility to create new narratives of "world history."

In such an interactive historical narrative, then, the efficacy of the idea of Asia diminishes, since it is neither a self-contained entity nor a set of self-contained relations; it is neither the beginning nor the end of a linear world history. It would be better to say that this "Asia"—neither starting point nor end, neither self-sufficient subject nor subordinate object—provides the moment to reconstruct "world history." If we need to rectify mistakes in theories of "Asia," we must also reexamine the notion of Europe. As we correct the errors in the idea of Asia, we must also reexamine the idea of Europe. To borrow Lenin's phrasing, we should ask: Where does this advanced Europe come from, after all? What sort of historical relations have resulted in Asia's backwardness? Historical relations internal to societies are important, but in the historical long run, how should we appraise the effects of ever-extending interregional relations on a society's internal transformation? If the discourse on Asia continues to be based on notions of Europe that are taken as self-evident, and the motive forces that gave rise to the concept of Europe are not re-understood via a penetrating review of European historical development, this discourse will not be able to overcome its lack of clarity.

Conclusion: A Problem of "World History": Asia, Empire, Nation-State

These accounts of Asia demonstrate not so much Asia's autonomy as the ambiguities and contradictions in the idea of Asia itself: the idea is at once colonialist and anticolonialist, conservative and revolutionary, nationalist and internationalist, originating in Europe and, alternatively, shaping Europe's image of itself. It is closely linked to issues relating to both nation-state and empire, a notion of a civilization seen as the opposite of the European, and a geographic category established via geopolitics. I believe that as we examine the political, economic, and cultural autonomy of Asia we must take seriously the derivativeness, ambiguity, and inconsistency that were intertwined with the history of its advent—these are products of specific historical relationships and it is only from these relationships that they can be transcended or overcome.

First, the idea of Asia was always closely related to the issues of "modernity" and capitalism, and at the core of the question of "modernity" lay the development of the relationship between nation-state and market. The tension in the notion of Asia between nationalism and supranationalism is closely related to the reliance of capitalist markets on both the state and on interstate relations. Since any discussion of Asia is rooted in such issues as the nation-state and capitalism, the full diversity of historical relations among Asian societies, institutional forms, customs, and cultural patterns comes to be understood only through the narrative of "modernity," and analysis of values, institutions, and rituals independent of that narrative has either been suppressed or marginalized. It is in this sense that, even as we challenge the Eurocentric historical narrative, how we go about unearthing these suppressed historical legacies—values, institutions, rituals, and economic relations—and rethinking European "world history" become key tasks.

Second, at this point the nation-state is still emphatically the main force behind advancing regional relations within Asia, with the following manifestations: (1) Regional relations are the extension of state relations:

whether we are talking about the Asian Forum promoted by Malaysia, or the East Asian Network advocated by South Korea, or regional organizations such as ASEAN or the Shanghai Six, all of these are interstate relationships formed along the axis of developing economic association or state security collaboration. (2) Asian sovereignty has yet to be fully established: the stand-offs on the Korean peninsula and the Taiwan Straits and the incomplete sovereignty of postwar Japan all illustrate that the nationalism set in motion in the nineteenth century to a large extent still determines power relations in East Asia. (3) Since the new discourse on Asia tends to be directed at forming protective and constructive regional networks against the unilateral dominance and turbulence brought about by globalization, the national question still lies at the center of the Asian question. Imagining Asia often appeals to an ambiguous Asian identity, but if we examine the premises underlying the institutions and principles of the idea, the nation-state emerges as the political structure needing to be overcome. So, how to deal in the present with the legacy of national liberation movements (respect for sovereignty, equality, mutual trust and the like) and traditional regional relations is still a question demanding the most serious consideration.

Third, and closely related to the two questions discussed above, the dominance of the nation-state in Asian imaginaries arose from the empire/nation-state binary created in modern Europe. The historical import of this binary is that the nation-state is the only modern political form and the most important premise for the development of capitalism. The binary, however, not only oversimplifies the diversity of political and economic relations subsumed under the category of empire, but also underestimates the internal diversity within individual nation-states. Modern Asian imaginaries are based mainly on interstate relations and seldom deal with Asia's complex ethnicities, regional communication and forms of interaction that are conventionally grouped under the category of empire—for example, trans-state tribute networks, migration patterns, and the like. The question is: In an era in which the nation-state has become the dominant political structure, will the traditional Asian experiences of various types of communication, coexistence, and institutions provide possibilities with which to overcome the internal and external dilemmas brought about by the nation-state system?

Fourth, the category of an Asian totality was established in contradistinction to Europe and encompasses heterogeneous cultures, religions, and other social elements. Whether from the perspective of historical traditions or contemporary institutions, Asia lacks the conditions for creating a European Union–style superstate. Buddhism, Judaism, Christianity, Hinduism, Islam, Sikhism, Zoroastrianism, Daoism, and Confucianism all originated on this continent we call Asia, which comprises three-fifths of the world's landmass and contains over half of the world's population; thus, any attempt to characterize Asia as a unitary culture is not plausible. The idea of Confucian Asia cannot account even for China itself, and even if we reduce the idea of Asia only to East Asia, we cannot escape the issue of the region's cultural heterogeneity. Any new imagining of Asia must combine a vision of cultural and political diversity with regional political and economic structures. A high degree of cultural heterogeneity does not mean that Asia cannot form definite regional structures—it merely reminds us that any such structure must have a high degree of flexibility and pluralism. Two possible directions for imagining Asia are, therefore: (1) draw upon the institutional experiences of Asian cultural coexistence to develop new models that will allow different cultures, religions, and peoples to get along on equal terms within the context of the nation-state and the Asian region; and (2) form multilayered, open social organizations and networks linked through regional connections to coordinate economic development, mitigate conflicts of interest, and diminish the dangers inherent in the nation-state system.

Fifth, Asia has historically long-standing and unbreakable religious, trade, cultural, military, and political ties to Europe, Africa, and the Americas, so to describe Asia either on the model of, or to assume it to be something like, an enlarged nation-state are equally inappropriate. The idea of Asia has never been purely self-delimited, but rather the product of interaction with other regions; the critique of Eurocentrism is not an affirmation of Asiacentrism, but rather an attempt to eradicate a logic dominated by egocentrism, exclusivity, and expansionism. In this sense, discerning the disorder and pluralism within the "new empire" and breaking down the self-evident notion of Europe, are not only important preconditions for reconstructing the ideas of Asia and Europe, but also the path required to break out of the "new imperial logic."

Sixth, if the excavation of Asia's cultural potential is also a critique of Eurocentrism, then the reconstruction of the idea of Asia also constitutes defiance of the colonial, interventionist, and dominating forces that have divided it. The commonality of Asian imaginaries partly derives from subordinate status under European colonialism, during the Cold War, as well as in the current global order, and also arises out of Asian movements for national self-determination, socialism, and colonial liberation. If we fail to acknowledge these historical conditions and movements we will not be able to understand the implications of modernity for Asia nor the sources of its division and perils of war. People regard the fall of the Berlin Wall and the dissolution of the Soviet Union and the Eastern European socialist bloc as the end of the "Cold War," but in Asia, the structure of the "Cold War" has to a large extent been preserved and has even developed new derivative forms under new historical conditions. Contemporary discussions of the question of Asia, however, are carried out either by state actors or intellectual elites, and the numerous Asian social movements—whether of workers, students, peasants, or women—are indifferent to it. This stands in sharp contrast to the tempestuous surge of Asian national liberation in the twentieth century. If it can be said that the socialist and national liberation movements of the twentieth century have drawn to a close, their fragmentary remains can still be a vital source for stimulating new ways of imagining Asia.

By way of conclusion, let me emphasize once again what I have been attempting to convey: the issue of Asia is not simply an Asian issue, but rather a matter of "world history." Reconsidering "Asian history" at once represents an effort to rethink nineteenth-century European "world history," as well as an effort to break free of the twenty-first-century "new imperial" order and its associated logic.

2

How to Explain "China" and Its "Modernity": Rethinking *The Rise of Modern Chinese Thought*

The four-volume *The Rise of Modern Chinese Thought* was published in 2004 and sold out very quickly.[1] In the last three years I have read a number of reviews published by colleagues in China, Japan, the United States, and Europe, and I have also participated in four conferences called specifically to discuss the work in Shanghai, Beijing, and Tokyo. On the occasion of the work's reprinting I would like to try to summarize and reflect upon the train of thought running through the study, as well as to discuss certain issues that are raised and offer some preliminary responses.

Three Sets of Antithetical Concepts: Empire and Nation-State; *Fengjian* and *Junxian*; Rites/Music and Institutions

Scholars of Chinese history often have misgivings about the concepts and categories used to describe historical phenomena and the research paradigms

---

Translated by Wang Yang

related to them. These misgivings concentrate on two points: First, can one use existing theoretical categories and social scientific paradigms effectively to describe and interpret historical phenomena? For instance, the 1990s witnessed a debate within Chinese studies in the United States over the question of whether the concept of "civil society" can explain a similar historical phenomenon in China. Second, can Western concepts and paradigms be usefully applied to Chinese historical phenomena? As an example of this point, in the first section of my book *The Rise of Modern Chinese Thought*, I questioned the binary of "empire versus nation-state" in Western thought and challenged its derivative use in Chinese studies. Because these issues are conventionally examined in a binary context of Western theory versus Chinese practice, they lose their theoretical significance through being transformed into antagonisms between "the Western versus the local" or "universal versus particular." Arising out of these two levels of misgivings, many historians have attempted to activate traditional Chinese categories to explain historical phenomena. In my opinion, however, simple reliance on traditional conceptions and paradigms does not guarantee effective interpretation, since these things generally take on meaning only in light of modern thinking and theorizing. Therefore, although we need to maintain a careful and historicized attitude when applying theoretical concepts and social scientific paradigms, application per se is unavoidable. In order to allow such reasonable doubts to achieve their theoretical significance, we must break through the binaries of "Western versus local" and "universal versus particular" and rethink the complicated relationship between history and theory.

In *The Rise of Modern Chinese Thought* I consider three sets of antithetical concepts dealing with political institutions. The first set consists of the notions of empire and nation-state, both products of Western thought. In this regard, the study of Chinese history is dominated by two interpretive frameworks that are different from but closely related to each other. One of these views China as an empire (or civilization, or continent) as opposed to, or in contrast to, the modern Western nation-state, whereas the second holds that China long ago developed an early nation-state structure built upon a centralized administrative structure *(junxian zhi)*. Although these two approaches stand in opposition to one other, both are outgrowths of the empire/state binary generated by modern European thought. To be sure, my critique of this binary does not simply put aside the concepts of empire or state as such, but tries to integrate at another level the particular features of Chinese history revealed by these two narratives. The second set consists of the traditional Chinese categories of centralized administration and enfeoffment *(fengjian zhi)*. In discussing Confucianism from the Song to the Qing dynasties, I rarely use the concepts of empire or state in sorting out specific political interpretations, but instead approach these issues from the perspective of the notions of a centralized administration and enfeoffment, the terms generally invoked by Confucian scholars and the gentry. For example, in my explanation of how "Heavenly Principle" *(tianli)* came to be established during the Song dynasty, I pay particular attention to the Confucian debate that developed over the issue of a centralized administration versus enfeoffment, and try to analyze historical change from the perspective of questions inhering within this debate. Finally, the concepts of rites/music and institutions (the Chinese for "institutions," *zhi* in pre-Qin documents, later becomes *zhidu*) constitute the third set. In treating the Song dynasty, I talk about the differentiation of rites/music from institutions, yet do not take them as two descriptive categories completely at odds with one another. Instead, I discuss their differentiation from the perspective of Neo-Confucianism and Song dynasty historiography, and in so doing allow this differentiation, which appears to be an objective historical narrative, simultaneously to become the terrain of value judgment or of historical verdicts.

Let me begin with the last set of concepts. Whereas the Confucians of the pre-Qin period viewed rites/music and institutions as overlapping, Song Confucians divided them from each other, eventually advancing the proposition of "the differentiation of rites/music from institutions" to describe history. That is to say, during the Three Dynasties of antiquity (the Xia, Shang, and Zhou) *(sandai zhizhi)*, rites/music and institutions were completely integrated, while the dynasties that followed saw a separation grow between them. Thus, the differentiation of rites/music from institutions became a political topic. Because Song Confucians used the idea of rites/music to describe the ancient system of enfeoffment, and that of institutions to explain the centrally administered state with imperial authority at its core, the differentiation was closely related to the Song Confucians' political thinking about centralized administration and enfeoffment, and to their judgments on contemporary politics based on such thinking in particular. Song Confucians strove to integrate substantive elements from the regime of the Three Dynasties back into daily life, such as the patriarchal clan system (*zongfa*), the well-field system, and the system of enfeoffment. These efforts to return to ancient ways, however, cannot be viewed as mere archaism, but instead can only be comprehended in light of Song scholars' critical understanding of the standardization of the civil service examination system and a centralized bureaucracy. Although they opposed the examination system, they did not call for any simple revival of the ancient election system (*xuanju*), but were trying instead to improve and set limitations on the former within a new context. Their goal in advocating the ancient well-field system was to resist the implementation and the consequences of the dual tax system enacted late in the Tang dynasty—they did not really insist that Song society readopt the ancient system. They took part in practices to rejuvenate clan patriarchy in order to confront the historical realities of the scattering of genealogies and the steady formalization of political institutions after the Tang dynasty; they did not really think that all political institutions should return to the ancient system of enfeoffment. In fact, they acknowledged the legitimacy of centralized administration based on imperial authority.

The call for returning to ancient institutions was thus a critique of new institutions; it was not, however, a total negation, but instead a call for reform of the contemporary political order by absorbing crucial elements of the enfeoffment system into the framework of a central administration; it was a critique based on a judgment of current circumstances. Thus, although the Song Neo-Confucians gave priority to relatively abstract philosophical and ethical categories such as the Way of Heaven (*tiandao*), Heavenly Principle, and heart/mind versus nature, the historical narrative of the differentiation of rites/music from institutions clearly indicates the political thinking embedded in Neo-Confucianism. Absent consideration of the concepts of centralized administration and enfeoffment and the historical views they entail, one cannot explicate the political implications of either the *daoxue* or *lixue* strains of Neo-Confucianism; absent these political-historical relationships, neither can one understand why Song Confucians were so dedicated to developing the category of Heavenly Principle. The inherent historical dynamics for the establishment and deployment of the

Heavenly Principle worldview were clearly set forth in the exploration of the differentiation of rites/music from institutions, the comparison between the Three Dynasties and the eras that followed, and the discussion of the dialectic binaries of centralized administration versus enfeoffment, the well-field system versus the equal-field system, and the school system versus the civil service examination system.

From the Northern to the Southern Song, the thinking of adherents of *daoxue* (the learning of the way) centered around the notion of Heavenly Principle, which eventually coalesced into what came to be called Song Neo-Confucianism *(lixue)*. The idea of Heavenly Principle may seem very abstract, and also quite different from such closely related concepts as pattern *(li)*, material force *(qi)*, heart/mind *(xin)*, nature *(xing)*, and such issues as "investigating things and extending knowledge" *(gewu zhizhi)*; it is also much different from the issue upon which Confucians of the pre-Qin and Han-Tang periods focused. Consequently, many modern scholars, heavily influenced by modern European philosophy, proceed directly to make philosophical analyses of Song dynasty thought from within the framework of ontology, realism, and epistemology. In my opinion, however, such an analytical method is in itself extrinsic to Song thought, being an interpretive system based on the concepts, categories, and theoretical frameworks of European philosophy. At the same time, dissatisfied with this history of ideas method, other scholars have attempted a social-historical interpretation of intellectual history, an important venture. As I said above, the fundamental categories used to analyze social history are derived from modern social science, with politics, economics, society, culture, and their taxonomies having grown out of the knowledge and social divisions of modernity. Thus, when placing certain historical phenomena within these categories we lose the internal historical perspective of the period and the opportunity to rethink our own knowledge, beliefs, and worldviews from this perspective. In my studies, the "Heavenly Principle" worldview is not a simple abstraction, and by asking why, in the specific circumstances of the Song dynasty, it became the central idea of a new worldview, who advocated it, and under what conditions it was embodied or abstracted, I strive to reveal the internal connections between this seeming abstraction and social change. To do so, it is necessary to take an intermediate step, that is, to reexamine historical change and the value judgments of Song Confucians by analyzing the relationship between their metaphysical categories (like Heavenly principle) and the immediate social propositions set forth by Song thinkers.

The question of how to establish this relationship is, however, worth serious consideration. If we simply enter ideas or propositions like Heavenly Principle, material force, nature, and "investigating things and extending knowledge" into an economic, social, or political historical narrative, we will not only reduce these complex conceptual problems to mere components of these latter narratives, but once encapsulated as such, we will also have neglected their significance in the intellectual world of antiquity. Therefore, we need to examine these concepts within the framework of the particular worldview of the period, and then explain the phenomena that modern scholars have categorized as economic, political, military, or social in the context of their relationships with Confucian categories such as Heavenly Principle. I found my entry point in the historical narratives of Ouyang Xiu (1007–1073) and certain other historians, and their demarcation between the pre– and post–Three Dynasties periods in particular. As I see it, this demarcation is not merely part of an objective historical narrative, but also a historical process that unfolded from within a perspective internal to Confucianism, a process that reveals how the political ideals of Song Confucians developed via a historical narrative. The political, economic, and even military debates among Song Confucians more often than not involved issues like centralized administration versus enfeoffment, the well-field system versus the dual tax system, and the election system versus the civil service examination system, all of which were discussed in the context of the narrative of the demarcation between the pre– and post–Three Dynasties periods (or in relation to the laws of the Han and Tang dynasties). To be sure, working within the parameters of modern knowledge, we can explain these issues via the interpretive methods of political and economic history, but in light of the considerations of "the internal perspective," referred to above, we have to ask what the implications embedded in these issues are for the Confucian narratives of the demarcation between the pre– and post–Three Dynasties periods. These issues are political, economic, or institutional, yet, from the Confucian perspective, the relationship within each antithetical category is closely connected to the historical demarcation between the pre– and post–Three Dynasties periods as well as to "the historical differentiation of rites/music from institutions."

In this sense, politics cannot be expressed by employing only a simple political analysis; the same is true for economics. Because the issues of the dual tax system, the well-field system, patriarchy, imperial authority, and the civil service examination system were all deployed within the concept of enfeoffment, the ideal of the Three Dynasties, and the internal framework of the theory of the differentiation between rites/music and institutions, their implications cannot be encompassed by what the modern social sciences take as institutional problems. If we put the birth of the Song notion of Heavenly Principle together with the Confucian view of history, we find that the increasing importance of the former in the Confucian world bears a close relationship with Song Confucian observations on historical change: the Three Dynasties embodied a world of rites/music, a world where morality and ethics were completely integrated with rites/music, and their narratives were identical; there was thus no need for an ontology that transcended rites/music in order to provide its moral legitimacy. On the other hand, the period after the Three Dynasties constituted a world of a "differentiation of rites/music from institutions," such that institutions could no longer provide the moral legitimacy offered by rites/music and an account of institutions could be the simple equivalent of an account of morality. Morality, therefore, had to resort to an ontology beyond the real world or its institutions. This differentiation also exhibited itself in the transformation of the category of things *(wu)*: in the world of rites/music, things not only embody "everything" *(wanwu)*, but also represent the norms of rites/music with the result that things and pattern or principle *(li)* are completely united. In the world in which the Song Confucians had come to be situated, however, rites/music had degenerated into institutions without moral implication—they were simply material or functional. Consequently, the moral implications of things in a world ruled by rites/music had been sloughed off and Principle could be revealed only by the practice of investigating things *(gewu)*.

Therefore, the understanding of the birth of the concept of Heavenly Principle cannot be separated from an understanding of the Confucian understanding of historical change. In the book, I place particular emphasis on analyzing the concept of "the propensity of the times" *(shishi)*, since Chinese—or Confucian—historical consciousness bears a special relationship with this notion.² Time is a core domain of modern Western thought; it evolves in a linear fashion, is teleological, homogeneous, and empty. Nineteenth-century Europe experienced a change in its view of history whereby historical entities achieved identity with the temporal; a fusion resulting in history becoming imbued with teleology. My criticism of Hegelianism in the introduction to *The Rise of Modern Chinese Thought* expands upon this point. The narratives of modern nationalism and national subjectivity also center on this epistemology of time. Thus, my use of the concept of "the propensity of the times" is meant to reconstruct the epistemological framework of historical narrative. From the Confucian perspective, consciousness of "the propensity of the times," like the concept of time itself, is related to the conceptualization of history as well as to historical consciousness, but it does not proceed in a linear fashion, nor is it empty. It is, rather, an account of the natural unfolding of history and its internal dynamics, something not dependent upon any teleology. Purpose inheres in the searches conducted by people caught up in historical change for values (such as Heavenly Principle, rites/music, and those of the Three Dynasties) incorporated into our daily lives and practices. In Song thought, "the propensity of the times" became an inner matter, and the concept of "the historical manifestation of Heavenly Principle" *(lishi)* is representative of this move toward interiority. "The propensity of the times," however, was not exclusive to Song learning, as variations on it can be found in both Gu Yanwu's (1613–1682) and Zhang Xuecheng's (1738–1801) studies of the Confucian classics, as well as in their historical research.

Like other intellectual categories, "propensity" *(shi)* is a very old idea, but both "the propensity of the times" and its "historical manifestation" took on a special significance in Song thought. In considering the totality of social or historical change, Neo-Confucians paid particular attention to the differentiation of rites/music from institutions without passing any simple value judgments on either term, regarding this differentiation as the result of historical change. On the one hand, they yearned for the rites/music of the Three Dynasties, even as they held high the banner of Heavenly Principle on the other. Why, then, was their appeal for a return to antiquity translated into a call for the abstract category of Heavenly Principle that was also embodied as individual moral practice? Lacking a historical perspective, there is no way to connect these two. In fact, the differentiation of rites/music from institutions is not the Song Confucians' own expression, but my summary of their various historical narratives. But is not the demarcation between the Three Dynasties and the eras that followed how they basically understood history? Qian Mu's and Chen Yinke's (1890–1969) interpretations of the difference between rites/music and institutions in their accounts of Sui and Tang dynasty history have influenced my conclusions. The context of my explanation of "the differentiation of rites/music from institutions," however, is different from the one within which they were working. Qian Mu faults Chen Yinke for creating a problem by not distinguishing rites/music from institutions in his analysis, criticizing Chen for assigning to the category of institutions that which should rightfully belong to rites/music.

Yet, since there was no such clear separation between rites/music and institutions in the pre-Qin period, we may ask: Whence came Qian Mu's binary? From the opposite perspective, since in the post-Song context rites/music and institutions were taken as two distinct categories, we can ask why Chen Yinke fails to distinguish them in his study of medieval history. As we know, Chen Yinke deeply identified with the beliefs of Song Confucianism, but he was a historian who, in the same way that traditional Chinese historical narratives contain their own theories of history, never failed to incorporate his own historical ideas into his narratives. Thus, conflating rites/music with institutions or dividing the two from one another is not simply a factual matter. Many historical writings proceed on the basis of taking this split of rites/music from institutions as a historical reality, and in studies of the Northern and Southern dynasties and the Sui-Tang period this differentiation is probably necessary. Regardless of whether it is Chen Yinke failing to mark the difference or Qian Mu making a distinct separation between them, they both reflect a historical view derived from a post-Song perception of historical change. Why, then, are rites/music and institutions sometimes seen as not being different from one another while at certain other times it seems imperative to divide them? From the perspective of the Confucian tradition, this dialectic of integration and separation bears an internal relationship with Confucianism, and with Confucius's representations of the collapse of rites/music in particular. In this sense, the differentiation of rites/music from institutions is a question of historical viewpoint rather than one of historical fact; it is a question of from what perspective and from what value system one narrates history. Although we can describe the differentiation as a historical process, we must simultaneously understand that this historical process unfolded as a historical judgment from a particular perspective. It is also in this sense that both Song Confucian narratives concerning the practices of restoring patriarchy and the well-field system, as well as their criticism of the civil service examination system and harsh laws and punishments, constitute an evaluation via the rites/music of the Three Dynasties of the new institutional practices under a central administration. The demarcation between the Three Dynasties and later periods, and the antithesis between rites/music and institutions, have direct political implications, implications that are not simple and straightforward but are rather deeply imbued with the Heavenly Principle worldview.

In my opinion, we are interpreting Chinese history from within when we discuss the establishment of Heavenly Principle and we take up the issues summed up by modern historians in the categories of economic, political institutional, cultural, and philosophical history from a historical perspective internal to Confucianism. In this view, things now taken as purely economic or political issues cannot be explained simply in those terms when transferred to other historical contexts. For example, the ideas of centralized administration and enfeoffment constitute organic parts of the intellectually integrated world of Confucianism, and it is only within this conceptual arena that the real world and the changes in it take on significance and can be grasped. This internal perspective is produced through a process of ceaseless dialogue with modern times. Methodologically, the dialogue does not merely allow us to interpret modern times through antiquity, or antiquity via antiquity, nor does it simply enable a view of antiquity with a modern eye; it rather provides the opportunity for a dialogue to translate this perspective into a vehicle for our own introspection. By observing the demarcation between the Three Dynasties and the later period, and the differentiation between rites/music and institutions, we can also see the limitations of our own knowledge.

Empire and Nation-State in Historical Narratives

Since *The Rise of Modern Chinese Thought* developed its discussion of enfeoffment and centralized administration from a Chinese historical perspective, why, then, discuss the matter of empire and nation-state? Obviously, this is closely related to the main narrative of the entire book—that is, its inquiry into "early modernity." The focus of my inquiry is whether the formation of Song Neo-Confucianism (*lixue*) shows that there was an important transition in the Song dynasty, to what might be thought of as "early modern," in society, the state, and the world of thought. The force of this question has driven me back to some assumptions about Chinese history made by Japanese scholars more than half a century ago. For example, there is the hypothesis of a "Tang-Song transition" raised by Naito Konan in the 1920s and the later hypotheses of an "East Asian modern age" and "Song capitalism" raised by Kyoto School scholars such as Miyazaki Ichisada. They discuss "early modernity" by examining the decline of the aristocracy, the development and maturity of a central administration, the growth of long-distance trade, and the standardization of the civil service examination system, with Miyazaki, in particular, identifying Song philosophical Confucianism with the ideology of "nationalism" (*kokumin shugi*). I cannot go into the relationship between the Kyoto School and the politics of empire in detail here, but their scholarship raised a number of questions still worth discussing, with the matters of the Tang-Song transition and taking the Song as the beginning of East Asian modernity principal among them. My discussion begins with the relationship between "the establishment of Heavenly Principle and the development of a state with a central administration" and goes on to analyze the transformation of Confucianism, including a dialogue with and a response to Kyoto School assumptions. The questions that merit our concern here are: Why is the exploration of "early modernity" related to the problem of empire and nation-state? What is the relationship between the Kyoto School's hypotheses and this problem?

Eric Hobsbawm once said that if there is a main theme in historical studies since the nineteenth century, it is the nation-state, and we may add that capitalism constitutes an even more fundamental narrative. In post-nineteenth-century studies of political economy and in historical writings, narratives of the nation-state have been constructed through their contrast with other narratives, an opposition directly embodied by the distinction between the narratives of "empire" and "nation-state." In the nineteenth century the conception of history underwent a crucial transition, becoming the history of the subject, that subject being the nation-state. In this sense, there is no history without the nation-state. If, therefore, China was not a nation-state, or, rather, to say that China was an empire, is in fact to say China does not have history and cannot constitute a true historical subject. It was precisely in opposition to Western narratives of modernity that the Kyoto School posited the hypotheses of an "East Asian modern age" and "Song capitalism," and then reconstructed Chinese history with an internal, modern dynamic within the framework of "East Asian history." I would like to put aside for the moment the political relationship between this school and Japanese imperialism or colonialism, as I am primarily concerned with the Kyoto School's narrative approach: while it builds an account of an East Asian modern age as parallel to that of Western modernity, the point of departure of the former similarly relies on the core issue of the nation-state. Thus, there can be no narrative of an East Asian "modern age" *(jinshi)* that is not centered on the nation-state. The Kyoto School does talk of the schools of Neo-Confucianism *(lixue, daoxue)*, but simply views them as the ideology of a new nationalism, and behind this lies a historical interpretation that identifies a state with a centralized administration with the early modern nation-state, or *proto-nation-state*. In sum, when the Kyoto School opposes the notion of an "East Asian modern age" to Western narratives, it does so by constructing a narrative centered on the nation-state and capitalism that inverts the Western mainstream account: whereas the Eurocentric version portrays China as an empire, a continent, or a civilization, with the implication that China is not a nation-state, the Kyoto school posits the opposite. It sets up its hypothesis of an "East Asian modern age" by appealing to the categories of "a mature state with a central administration," or "nationalism."

In this way, my dialogue and dispute with the Kyoto School also implies a critique of the nineteenth-century European notion of "world history." In a nutshell, my differences with the Kyoto School—and with its representative scholars in particular—are over how to characterize the Song dynasty, and can be summarized as follows: first, in contrast to Miyazaki Ichisada, who identifies Song Neo-Confucianism as "a modern philosophy" or an ideology of "nationalism" in keeping with his description of the social transition in the Song dynasty, I contend that Neo-Confucianism and its concept of Heavenly Principle embody an antagonistic tension between its ideas and the Song transition; their historical relationship in fact develops by way of this antagonism. Methodologically, the Kyoto School exhibits a strong predisposition to social history, and their conceptual categories, which are mainly derived from the system of knowledge that has gradually developed in Europe since the nineteenth century, prevent them from being able to size up historical change from an internal perspective. Thus, the basic theoretical framework of the Kyoto School and its historical narratives actually derive from European modernity. For if the Song dynasty were, as they describe it, an "even more Chinese" China, how can one represent the Song transition from a Confucian perspective? And, if the substance of an "East Asian modern age" is early capitalism and a central administration similar to that of the nation-state, does not the Song Confucian view of history as characterized by the sharp distinction between "rites/music of the Three Dynasties and the institutions of the subsequent periods" embody not only their recognition of historical change, but also their resistance to a centralized administration and "early capitalism" (if this concept is really appropriate)?

The second point bears a close relationship to the first: whereas the Kyoto School depicts the "early modern" features of Song society and thought from within the intellectual framework of modern Western nationalism/capitalism, my description—for instance, my analysis of the binary of "empire versus nation-state"—strives to surmount such a linear, teleological narrative. The Kyoto School analysis of the Song dynasty as a mature state with a central administration enables their hypothesis of an "East Asian modern age," something premised on the historical relationship between European modernity and the nation-state, and which takes the nation-state as the internal measure of modernity—the specifics of their narrative of the "East Asian modern age" makes this clear. But how should one portray the social structure of the Yuan dynasty, or, even more to the point, the social system of the Qing? The reason I use a limited sense of the concept of "empire" is to inveigh against historical narratives that identify modernity with the nation-state—after all, compared with the long history of the category of "empire," that of the nation-state is still very short. If it is inappropriate to place the Ming-Qing transition in the same category as the "Tang-Song transition," then to define the change from the Qing to Republican China as a move from empire to nation-state is also problematic—otherwise, how can we explain the obvious connection between the Qing and the Republic in regard to such things as the makeup of the population, ethnic composition, the extent of the country's territory, and a number of key institutions?

Therefore, when we argue that there were some "early modern" components in the Song dynasty, to describe them we need a new theoretical framework that is different from that of the Kyoto School, one that breaks away from the temporal teleology of modernity even as it moves beyond nationalism. Some friends of mine once asked about the book's title, *The Rise of Modern Chinese Thought:* What is "modern"? What is "China"? What is "thought"? And what is "rise"? The phrase "the rise of modern Chinese thought" appears to be simply descriptive, but from beginning to end my book actually challenges our commonsense notions of each of the terms within it. When I wrote about the origins of modern Chinese thought, I was not writing a work on the origins of modern Chinese intellectual history; so what, then, is "rise"? One can explain it as the "production and reproduction" *(shengsheng)* portion of "production and reproduction are what constitute change" *(shengsheng zhi wei yi)*, which, according to the *Book of Changes,* is a process full of change and growth. If, then, the Song is supposed to mark the beginning of the "modern age," does the Mongolian Yuan dynasty that followed represent continuity or rupture? And if the late Ming is meant to have witnessed the early stages of enlightenment, does Qing thought represent a reaction or a resurgence, and how should we interpret the relationship of this period and its intellectual activity with modern China? What I am emphasizing, then, are elements that appear repeatedly in history, rather than absolute origins. Throughout the ceaseless changes of history, each dynasty constructed its legitimacy as a Chinese dynasty in its own particular way, a process that cannot be represented by a linear historical narrative. Based on this understanding of history, I do not see "the rise of modern Chinese thought" as linear, in contrast to the Kyoto scholars and their linear narrative stretching from the Song to the modern period. What I seek to provide through my interpretation of such concepts as "the propensity of the times" and *lishi* is a historical epistemology different from temporal teleology and embedded in the Confucian worldview and the epistemology of its times. If we take into account Benedict Anderson's argument about the relationship between the concept of time and nationalism, we will gain a deeper understanding of the significance of "the propensity of the times" in dynastic history and in the process of dynastic change.

It is from this perspective that I critique various discourses on "China." For example, I take issue on the one hand with such self-evident genealogies as the progression of Yao, Shun, Yu, Tang, Wen, Wu, the Duke of Zhou, Confucius, followed by the Qin dynasty, the Han, the Sui, the Tang, the Song, the Yuan, the Ming, and the Qing. On the other, I do not approve of reductively challenging—or negating—Chinese identity from the standpoint of national minority history. If Confucianism, and the rise of Neo-Confucianism in particular, embodies a determination to rethink historical discontinuities and continue the tradition, continuity must be premised on considerations of historical rupture, and thought of from the perspective of seizing historical initiative; from the standpoint of politics continuity must be understood as part of the endless process of refashioning legitimacy. Affirming that thinking about continuity is premised on the idea of rupture cancels out the notion of continuity as a natural process, understanding it rather as the product of a will to take historical initiative. What are the implications of this? The point is that "China" has no existence that is external to us, nor is it something other than the object of a particular historical subjectivity. "China" is closely tied to the thought and action of the people of particular eras.

Linking "the establishment of Heavenly Principle" with such matters as a state with a central bureaucracy, patriarchal enfeoffment, a land tenure system, taxation law, and the debates in both the Northern and Southern Song about Chinese versus barbarians *(Yi-xia zhi bian)* expresses the close relationship between this new weltanschauung and the reconstruction of social values and identity. And linking Confucian classical learning with such questions as the legitimacy of the Qing dynastic state, the dynasty's multiple legal systems, the relationship between the Manchu and Han peoples, and the internal and external issues revolving around the imperial tribute system and international relations also expresses the close relationship between the appearance of this new type of Confucianism—quite different from Song Neo-Confucianism—and the reconstruction of social values and identity. Linking the weltanschauung of Universal Principle *(gongli)* with such matters as the nation-state, the social system, rights, and cultural movements allows me to discuss new types of identity and their internal contradictions and difficulties. I examine the entity of "China" and its implications from various angles in order to liberate the concept from a simplistic notion of European nationalism. "China" is a richer, more flexible and more diverse category than the concept of the national would imply, and in constructing the legitimacy of a dynasty ruled by a national minority, in constructing equal relations among the different ethnicities under that dynasty, and in such enterprises as molding differing forms of foreign relations and tribute relationships with differing political entities, "China" demonstrated its particular flexibility and adaptability.

Accompanying the rethinking of the nation-state system and research on globalization, such issues as the historical experience of early empires and the dynamics of the transition from empire to modern nation-state have once again been brought within the scope of research. This has provided an opportunity to reexamine issues that had been constricted within the discourse of teleological modernity, such as the state structures and economic systems of early empires and interregional communication. Today two approaches dominate the discussion of empire, one focusing on the globalization of the "post-nation-state," with Michael Hardt and Antonio Negri's *Empire* being among the most influential examples.[3] The other approach consists of a renewed "empire studies," driven by dissatisfaction with or a rethinking of the nation-state system, embodied most directly in the efforts of a number of historians to reopen study of the history of early empires and to transcend the predominant existing narrative centered on the nation-state and its metrics. I see both approaches as responses to the contemporary crisis and to the study of history—they are, of course, connected, but they should not be conflated; *Empire and State*, the second volume of my book, hews more closely to the second approach. My intent in once again raising the issue of empire is thus to transcend rather than strengthen the narrative of the nation-state. In summing up the legacy of empire, beyond the interregional communication mentioned above, scholars have examined multiethnic political structures and cultural identity, internal colonization, the tendency to centralize political power, and the complex interrelationship of empire with the formation of the nation-state.

If, however, we should approach the relationship between empire and early modernity from the conventional binary of "empire versus nation-state," it is too easy to fall into or simply provide evidence for a nineteenth-century European historical view, which holds that China has no real political subjectivity. The key point here is not to affirm or deny the existence of a "nation-state" in Chinese history, but to clarify different types of political entity and their differing makeups, and in so doing free the concept of "state" from being completely encompassed within the history of modern European capitalism and the nation-state. Modern states have different political cultures, with socialist and capitalist states each having their own. Thus, since any discussion of modern states involves coming to grips with distinctive political cultures and traditions, addressing pre-twentieth-century states and their subjectivities only as abstractions is inadequate. The Kyoto School emphasizes the Song dynasty as a mature state with a centralized administration, in fact, a quasi-nation-state. Therefore, when Kyoto School scholars connect such a centrally administered state with early modernity, they once again affirm the "empire versus nation-state" binary. This binary can be portrayed in widely divergent ways, but none of them ever departs from positing an inherent connection between the state and capitalism, Miyazaki Ichisada's argument being a prime example. Within this conceptual framework, we cannot really imagine what a non-capitalist nation-state might be.

Because of these factors, I emphasize the overlapping relationship between establishing empires and nation-states rather than becoming entangled within the binary of one versus the other. Since the nineteenth century, virtually all studies of premodern history have been conducted within the category of the history of empire. S. N. Eisenstadt's *The Political System of Empires*, that representative work of the 1960s, is a good example.[4] This highly influential work synthesized historical studies of great world civilizations within a Weberian framework, placing "premodern" history under the rubric of the "political system of empires," a rubric that grew out of the binary of "empire versus nation-state" in nineteenth-century European political economy. Within this binary, "empire" constitutes all the features that are the opposite of modernity, and even when a relationship between empire and modernity is acknowledged, the relationship is only allowed retrospectively; for instance, it might be asked: What are the origins of despotism and authoritarianism in the modern nation-state? Or, why is the modern nation-state unable to break away from its inherently violent nature? In other words, all the manifestations of the crises of modernity will be traced back to the historical relationship between empires and the modern world. *The Political System of Empires* is an excellent example of how nearly all twentieth-century "premodern histories" were encompassed within the category of "empire."

In my volume *Empire and State*, I mainly discuss the following problems: First, how did Confucianism legitimize the Qing as a Chinese dynasty? How were pluralistic identities and pluralistic political/juridical institutions within the imperial system constructed? On the one hand, an important part of the exploitation of Confucianism by the Qing rulers to consolidate their rule was to identify themselves as a "Chinese dynasty." On the other hand, the Qing literati also used a thoroughly legitimate Confucianism to criticize the dynasty's ethnic hierarchy, with the result that certain principles and propositions of Confucianism were fused with the issue of equality within a specific historical context. Second, since a number of important post-nineteenth-century scholarly works take empires as the antithesis of the state, what are the historical relations between the construction of empire and the construction of the nation-state? As a response to this question, in my discussion of Qing classical scholarship, and *Gongyang* learning in particular, I emphasize that construction of the empire, including the expansion of the tribute system, and the construction of the Qing state are two sides of the same coin. In fact, phenomena defined as typical symbols of the nation-state, such as boundaries and administrative jurisdictions within those boundaries, already existed by or began to develop as early as the seventeenth century.

The phenomena that arose in the seventeenth and eighteenth centuries are not, however, simply embryonic elements of a nation-state, but rather an outgrowth of another political culture and other historical relationships. Thus, such things as the tribute system, pacifying "barbarians" *(hefan)* and forms of interaction should all be explained within the framework of the dynastic political culture. Failing to do this, it will be difficult to understand why the territorial boundaries, the population, and the administrative divisions of post-1911 Republican China and even the post-1949 PRC (People's Republic of China) so clearly overlap those of the Qing dynasty. In the book, I analyze the overlaps and differences between the tribute and the treaty systems as well as the specific process by which the Confucian classics came to be appropriated within the context of modern international relations. My question is: In the wake of colonialism, how was such "imperial knowledge" integrated into a new type of "Confucian universalism"? From the perspective of Confucian studies, my research is a corrective to research methodology that examines Confucianism merely within the framework of philosophy, history of ideas, ethics, or institutional learning. In respect to political history, Confucianism can be understood as legitimized knowledge: its various manifestations existed in a complicated relationship with the construction of the dynastic system and the construction of political legitimacy. Without recognizing this point, we cannot fully grasp its historical import.

A friend once asked me why I continue to apply "empire" in my studies, rather than "all-under-Heaven" *(tianxia)*, a more "native" or "Confucian" concept. The "All-under-Heaven" *(Tianxia)* chapter of *Zhuangzi* provides a universally appreciated interpretation of the concept of "all-under-Heaven," one also widely used by later scholars. "All-under-Heaven" is, in fact, a fascinating notion that bears within itself any number of theoretical and historical implications worthy of further study. In fact, there have already been scholars intent upon stressing the uniqueness of China who, in response to doubts about China's status as a nation-state, have declared China to be "all-under-Heaven" rather than a nation-state. While there are differences between the concepts of "all-under-Heaven" and "empire," they have in common, however, an explanation of Chinese history from within the empire/nation-state binary, and by invoking "all-under-Heaven," scholars are doing nothing other than distinguishing China from being a state, that is, a modern nation-state. This discourse ignores the fact that ever since the "states" of the Warring States period, Chinese history has been characterized by state forms unified under a central authority. Does not this failure to explore alternative implications of the "state" in effect signal a return to the core conception of nineteenth-century European of "world history," namely, that there is no history in China or East Asia? Even as I deal with the idea of "all-under-Heaven," I intend to hang on to the concept of "empire," but to impose a number of stipulations to it.

First, the term "empire" *(diguo)* is not a recent invention. It appears in ancient Chinese records, but the concept of empire recorded in these documents does not directly correspond to the modern category of empire introduced into China from Japan and the West. In the late Qing, the term *diguo* was rediscovered and thereafter incorporated into the modern Chinese language, and by now has become part of the Chinese historical tradition—an example of "translated modernity." During the wave of nationalism in the late nineteenth century the term gradually attained a Chinese intellectual pedigree and became an integral part of Chinese thought via translation. We thus cannot treat it simply as a foreign term extrinsic to Chinese history. Of course, were there to appear a more suitable idea, I would be delighted to use it, but at least up until now I have not been able to think of another core idea to undergird the discussion of these issues.

Second, the concept of "all-under-Heaven" is closely related to Chinese thinking about the universe, nature, and the world of rites/music, and can be traced back to far antiquity. If, however, we do not make simple comparisons with the European nation-state, but instead compare it with other historical civilizations, we can find similar expressions in other civilizations and religious worldviews. In this sense, to believe that only this concept is capable of rendering the uniqueness of China is merely a particularistic narrative of China from the epistemic perspective of the nation-state, rather than a result of any deep consideration. As Gu Yanwu's attempts to distinguish between "the collapse of all-under-Heaven" *(wang tianxia)* and the "collapse of the dynasty" *(wang guo)* would indicate, from the perspective of political analysis the concept of "all-under-Heaven" should not be equated with China as a particular political entity. "All-under-Heaven" embodies a special set of ideals and values, and should thus be kept distinct from the concept of "state." If the concept is to directly describe a given dynasty or political entity, it will lose the special implications conferred upon it by Confucians like Gu Yanwu.

Third, there is of course no problem in numerous scholars having described Chinese political history with the notions of "heavenly dynastic state" *(tianchao guojia)*, or "dynastic state" *(wangchao guojia)*. These two ideas are not, however, adequate to explain the differences among the Chinese dynasties, in particular those between the Yuan/Qing and the Song/Ming. Although all four were "heavenly dynastic states" or "dynastic states" with regard to the size of the territory controlled, their relationships with peripheral areas, and their internal political structure, the Yuan/Qing clearly differed significantly from the Song/Ming in spite of the fact that, according to Miyazaki, the latter pair have been defined as mature states with a centralized administration, or quasi-nation-states. Since the Kyoto scholars are determined to define the centrally administered Song dynasty as the beginning of the modern age, how can they evaluate the historical place of the Yuan and Qing? And since they identify Song/Ming Neo-Confucianism with the beginning of "nationalism" or modern thought, how do they interpret the relationship between Qing classical and historical studies and the political legitimacy of the Qing state? The Kyoto School's explanations of these two issues are inadequate. In discussions of late Ming capitalism or early modernity, Chinese scholars also often view the Qing as a historical rupture, with the Manchu invasion marking the demise of these two earlier developments; the Qing is thus eliminated from "narratives of modernity."

In my discussion of Qing *Gongyang* learning, I use the concept of "ritual China" *(liyi Zhongguo)* to explain Chinese territorial changes, the transformation of China's political structure, and new modes of interaction between the inside (China) and the outside (its neighbors). In my view, what is crucial is not to prove once again whether China was a nation-state or an empire, but to explicate fully the particularities of Chinese political culture and how it changed over time. The Mongol and Manchu dynasties share some similarities with what we call empires, but I do not explain this narrative of empire within the context of the empire/nation-state binary. Instead I strive to adduce the evidence for why the Qing should be legitimately included in the genealogy of Chinese dynasties. For example, by changing the dynastic name to "Qing"—a name congruent with "Ming"—making sacrifices to Yuan and Ming sacred implements, paying tribute to the descendants of the royal families of those two dynasties, restoring the civil service examination in Chinese, revering Cheng-Zhu Neo-Confucianism, and adopting the Ming judicial system, the Qing rulers affirmed themselves as the legitimate heirs of the Chinese dynastic system; in this sense, the Qing emperors were Chinese emperors.

At the same time, however, the Qing emperors ruled Mongolia, areas inhabited by Muslims *(Huibu)*, Tibet, and the southwestern areas through distinctive institutions (for example, the Mongol eight banners system, the *Kashag* political system in Tibet, the local chieftain *(tusi)* system in Southwest China, and a number of tribute relationships). Thus, in Central and West Asia, the Qing emperors were the legally constituted successors of the Mongol khans. Beyond this, the Qing emperor was at the same time the lineage head of the Manchus, responsible for Manchu identity and charged with maintaining their ruling position. As a result, he embodied a synthesis of three identities—emperor, great khan, and lineage head. The complications of Qing politics—such as the entanglements between imperial authority and Manchu and Mongolian aristocrats and the rise and decline of Han Chinese at court—grew out of this synthetic imperial authority and its vicissitudes. Therefore, to argue the case for the self-sufficiency of Manchuria and the eventual inevitability of the establishment of Manchukuo purely from the perspective of the imperial household's effort to preserve Manchu national identity will not hold up, even by considering the diversity of imperial authority. And even if we discuss the legitimacy of the Qing dynasty only from the angle of the Manchu-Han relationship, how should we interpret the repeated conflicts between the emperor and Manchu aristocrats in the early Qing? As I see it, these conflicts were ineluctable products of the antagonisms and vicissitudes inhering in the process of establishing dynastic legitimacy for a highly diverse imperial authority. The notion of "ritual China" arises repeatedly from these complicated relationships.

We can thus see that traditional Chinese concepts such as "all-under-Heaven" or "dynasty" cannot clarify the particularities of the political institutions and political culture of different dynasties, just as the binary of empire/nation-state cannot reveal the features of Chinese political culture. As it happens, within the scope of modern historiography, these traditional concepts constitute the basic components of the modern historical narrative. The China/West binary is closely related to this interpretive framework of history; it emphasizes that China is characterized by all-under-Heaven, and the dynastic and tribute systems, whereas the West is characterized by the nation-state and its system of formally equal sovereignty. In fact, in modern times colonialists often exploited the empire/nation-state binary for their own ends, using the culture of the "sovereign nation-state" to belittle traditional social relationships and political models. For example, Japan used conflicts between the aboriginal inhabitants of Taiwan and Okinawans as a pretext for its first invasion of Taiwan in 1874. Making use of the official Qing declaration that Taiwan aboriginals (as so-called savages [*shengfan*]) were "people beyond the pale of civilization" (*huawai zhi min*)—that is to say, outside the control of the central administration or Qing law—the Japanese authorities brought to bear the sophistical argument that its encroachment on the Taiwanese "savages" and their areas of habitation was not an invasion of Qing territory. At that time, European international law had already been introduced into East Asia, and the Japanese sought an excuse for their invasion by placing the pluralism embodied in the Qing notion of "adjusting to local customs and conditions" (*congsu congyi*) and the difference between "inner" and "outer" as recognized by the empire under the rubric of international relationships among sovereign nation-states. In evaluating this event, therefore, we should pay attention not only to the conflict between Japan and the Qing, but also to the conflict between the principles exploited by Japan in its invasion and the principles upon which Qing pluralistic social institutions were based, and, in particular, to the differing metrics and practical scope prescribed by these two sets of principles for dividing inside from outside.

Political Legitimacy and the "Continuity and Rupture" of History

An old platitude has it that Chinese history is continuous while that of the West is discontinuous. Through understanding the transformation I discussed above—that is, how a conquest dynasty changed itself into a Chinese dynasty—it can be seen that the so-called continuity of Chinese history is an illusion. China experienced ceaseless invasions and penetration of the center by the periphery, and ruptures both of politics and of ethnic relations took place repeatedly throughout Chinese history. In other words, this so-called continuity results from a process of continual intentional or unintentional historical fabrication. For example, the rulers of the dynasties established by ethnic minorities exploited Confucianism (including its various manifestations such as Neo-Confucianism, classical studies, and historiography) to make themselves Chinese. Thus, the matter of "ritual China" is not so much a ritual or moral issue but one of politics, or rather, a question of political legitimacy. The reason I use the notion of "self-transformation" here is to illustrate the substantial degree of agency in this process: the rulers of new dynasties (whether they were minorities or rebels) incorporated themselves within dynastic genealogy or orthodoxy (*daotong*)[5] by justifying their own legitimacy through orthodox Confucianism. Such "self-transformation" was, however, only a precondition, as this legitimacy was ultimately established through a whole series of relationships of mutual recognition, which is to say that "self-transformation" could only be confirmed via a particular "politics of recognition." To take the Qing dynasty as an example: many Han Chinese literati (as well as some of the kingdoms surrounding China) only came to accept the political legitimacy of the Qing by the Qianlong period (1736–1796). This is not to say that there was no progress toward a regime that integrated Manchus with Han Chinese during the Kangxi (1662–1722) and Yongzheng (1722–1736) eras, nor does it imply that conflicts between Manchus and Han completely disappeared after the Qianlong period. It does indicate, however, that in the broader sense, the position of the Qing as one link in the genealogy of Chinese dynasties was not affirmed until that time, a key historical transformation that has been uniformly ignored in past studies of the Qing. The reason I insist on a recurring redefinition of the category of "China" is that the understanding of China by its dynastic rulers, the literati, and the common people alike changed along with these redefinitions.

It is precisely at this point that it becomes necessary for us to reopen a historical perspective and to explore historical relationships outside the narrative of nationalism. Beyond a historical understanding of ethnic and geographical relationships, when seeking to explain the realm of pre-twentieth-century history, I suggest we need to pay attention to two questions: first, the "politics of recognition," that is, the historical formation of political legitimacy; and second, political culture, on which "self-transformation" relied. For example, what was the nature of the political culture upon which the Qing validated its legitimacy as a Chinese dynasty? How was such a political culture able to incorporate different ethnic groups, populations from different regions, and different religions into a flexible and pluralistic political structure? Clearly, understanding this requires a conceptual framework completely at odds with "nationalist knowledge," which depends upon such categories as ethnicity, language, and religion. This other type of knowledge has its own special concepts and forms, something that can be illustrated by the example of Classical Studies.

The Changzhou School of the late Qianlong period marks the beginning of the study of the New Text School by adherents of Classical Studies. After the Eastern Han (ca. 220 C.E.) New Text Confucianism declined, and aside from a few scholars like Zhao Fang of the late Yuan and early Ming period, it seemed to have disappeared completely until the rise of the Changzhou School. In their discussions of Qing Classical Studies, however, scholars of intellectual and academic history invariably fail to consider the efforts made by the Jurchen (*Jin*), the Mongols, and the Manchus upon entering China to use *Gongyang* learning—in particular the themes of "grand unification (*da yitong*)," *Tong santong* (linking with the Three Dynasties), and "distinguishing the inside (i.e., what is Chinese) from the outside" (*bie neiwai*)—to construct orthodoxy for new dynasties.[6] These works or proposals were written by Jurchen, Mongols, Manchus, and Han Chinese serving the regimes of the three non-Han ruling houses and were not research pieces devoted specifically to New Text Classicism, but rather political essays or memorials submitted to the throne. This shows, however, that many of the New Text themes had already been embedded in dynastic politics and the process of political legitimization. For example, when the Jin dynasty fought against the Song, Jin literati and officials used the study of the *Spring and Autumn Annals* and *Gongyang* learning in their attempts to legitimize their conquest of China. During the course of the Mongol conquest of the Song, the Mongol/Yuan empire not only considered establishing itself as a Chinese dynasty (with officials at court debating whether they should be the successor of the Liao, the Jin, or the Song), but around the period when the Taihe laws lost their force, Confucians discussed how to use the *Spring and Autumn Annals* to establish a legal foundation for the Yuan. After the Manchu conquest, the Qing government restored the civil service examinations, administered them in Chinese, made a commitment to Confucianism (especially Zhu Xi's teachings), and found inspiration in the *Gongyang* learning in constructing its own political legitimacy. If there were no political culture or theory of legitimacy centered on Confucianism, it would be impossible to discuss continuity among the dynasties. Historical continuity, then, was a product of self-conscious construction.

This discussion not only illuminates the necessity of understanding Confucianism from the angle of legitimizing knowledge, but also the need to investigate the political practices and the self-examination of pre-twentieth-century Chinese dynasties in dealing with ethnic relations. "Empire" is, of course, a mode of rule, an embodiment of power relations. When, however, a new, nationalist knowledge devalues traditional knowledge as being outdated, it is clearly important to reexamine this once legitimate knowledge and its implementation, and to look again at the experience of multiethnic coexistence of that period. This is of great value in understanding nationalist knowledge, its limitations, and, in particular, its tendency toward homogeneity.

The Construction and Questioning of Nationalist Knowledge

The advent of dominant East/West and China/West binaries is a historical creation, so viewing these binaries as methodologically absolute will bring along a number of impediments in its wake. For instance, in legal studies, there are many who posit a dichotomy between the Chinese ritual system and the Western legal system, something not entirely unreasonable. Nonetheless, it oversimplifies both China (Does not China have a legal tradition?), and the West (Does not the West have rites and moral education?). There are also many scholars who discuss the methodological problem of particularism and universalism, and, as far as I am concerned, we should of course take into account the particularity of a given historical period or society as the object of our research; and we especially need to critique Western universalism. Philosophically speaking, however, neither concept is viable, because, as we know, all narratives of "particularism" are universal particularism, while all the narratives of "universalism" are particular universalism. These two narratives appear to be diametrically opposed, but are actually interdependent. To a certain extent, what we must work for is a "singular," or singularistic, universalism. Within this framework of singular universalism, the pursuit of singularity is not merely a return to particularism, but, rather, is to reveal the universal implications of the singularity, and to ask how and under what conditions such singularity can be translated into universality.

At this point, allow me to refer to the third and fourth volumes of *The Rise of Modern Chinese Thought* to discuss the inherent relationship between modern knowledge and the problem of political legitimacy in the twentieth century. In the first two volumes I discussed the relationship between the Heavenly Principle worldview and a centralized administration as that between Classical Studies and dynastic legitimacy. So why follow that up with a discussion on the problem of knowledge? It is just as numerous intellectual historians have noted: no matter how much they might otherwise disagree on questions concerning the origins and beginning dates of modernity, historians of Europe all define the question of "modernity" in terms of science and new methodological concepts. As Isaiah Berlin wrote:

> The direct application of the results of this investigation of the varieties and scope of human knowledge to such traditional disciplines as politics, ethics, metaphysics, theology, and so on, with a view to ending their perplexities once and for all, is the program which philosophers of the eighteenth century attempted to carry through. The principles which they attempted to apply were the new scientific canons of the seventeenth century; there was to be no *a priori* deduction from "natural" principles.

It was precisely within this transformed epistemology that "[s]pace, time, mass, force, momentum, rest . . . are to take the place of final causes, substantial forms, divine purposes and other metaphysical notions. Indeed the apparatus of medieval ontology and theology were to be altogether abandoned."[7] This new idea had a decisive impact on all fields of knowledge: it not only permeated the work of philosophers who held the natural sciences in the highest esteem such as Locke and Hume, but it was just as clear to those deeply skeptical of the metaphysical assumptions of that science like Berkeley. It was also highly influential on the principal manifestos of the American and French revolutions, and, in fact, left its mark on virtually every aspect of the modern world. As a result, the social-historical significance of science and its methodology cannot be restricted to the scientific method per se, but rather seen as a scientific mentality that extended itself to the transformation of weltanschauung. Through analysis of scientific concepts and the worldview of "general truth" *(gongli)*, I sought to disclose the genealogy of the formation of modern knowledge.

A common thread running through *The Rise of Modern Chinese Thought* is the reciprocal relationship between knowledge and institutions exemplified by such things as the relationship between centralized administration and the notion of Heavenly Principle as well as that between general truth and modern nationalism and its institutions. In discussing Kang Youwei, for example, I stressed his re-creation of a Confucian universalism premised on a historical consciousness of the loosening of the hitherto self-evident relationship between that universalism and the notion of China. Under this premise, before attempting to demonstrate the universality of Confucianism, it had first to be acknowledged that China was but one part of the world, and that there was a substantial region outside of China, an expanse not just in terms of geographical space but also of culture, politics, and education. What, then, can we tell from this interaction between Confucian universalism and the image of China as existing among numerous other nation-states? I believe it explains the dependence of nationalism on a certain universal worldview and a genealogy of knowledge. In other words, the birth of this new type of Confucian universalism took place at the same time as the birth of China as a sovereign state in a new world system. This "Confucian universalism" is, in fact, nothing other than a circuitous modern manifestation of the idea of "general truth."

The relationship between universalism and the modern nation-state, or nationalism, involves the same logic. Since the late Qing, the epistemic structure of this universalism has been preserved, while the Confucian garb in which Kang Youwei invested it has been completely stripped away. The legitimacy of the modern nation-state is based on knowledge of this universalism and its taxonomic logic, while the institutions of the modern nation-state rely on the structures of this universalism and the division of labor among them. Regardless of whether it is the concept of sovereignty, or the justifications made by various political power-sources for their own legitimacy, or the historical idea of evolution and progress, or the rationality of institutions and theories supported by this historical concept, none of these can be independent of this universal knowledge. The establishment of modern nation-states is correlated with an antihistorical epistemological framework, and although nationalist knowledge often appeals to "history," "tradition," and "origins"—that is, to cultural particularism—its basis is this new epistemology and intellectual genealogy. Therefore, to discuss intellectual system and discourse today is in effect to talk about a new type of political legitimacy. A distinctive feature of nationalism is its ability to trace its own beginnings, whether that be ancestor veneration or cultural origins, but these more "ontological," "original," or "particular" forms of knowledge are generated by the new epistemology and its intellectual framework. So this new epistemology was not a product of "ontology" or "origins" per se, but rather the "ontology" or "origins" required by the epistemological structure of the nation-state.

It is not enough, however, simply to point out the constructed nature of nationalist knowledge or to engage in its deconstruction to be able once and for all to effect a permanent solution to the problems it poses—that would be wishful thinking. Even as nationalism is producing its own "ontology" or "origins," it is also appealing to mass mobilization: it is here that those who "take the initiative" (*zijue zhe*) strive to unite their thinking about the nation's fate under a given "propensity of the times" (*shishi*) with the values to which they have dedicated themselves. For example, the Chinese Revolution, as a sweeping social movement, a national liberation movement of rare scale and depth, took in a number of historical elements that cannot be encompassed within the category of nationalism—nationalism cannot encompass everything within twentieth-century China. Thus, a critique and negation of nationalist knowledge cannot be equated with a simple refusal to acknowledge an extremely rich and complicated historical process. If we acknowledge that modern China is built on the foundation of Qing dynasty history, can the modern China produced by the revolution be adequately described via nationalist knowledge? And by the same logic, in what sense can the Chinese Revolution be depicted as a "national revolution"? *The Rise of Modern Chinese Thought* does not study the twentieth-century Chinese Revolution in any depth, but the inquiry outlined above should provide a few avenues for reconsidering modern China.

In other parts of the book I bring up the matter of "anti-modern modernity." The third volume, *General Truth and Anti-General Truth (Gongli yu fan gongli)*, analyzes the thought of Yan Fu (1854–1921), Liang Qichao (1873–1929), and Zhang Taiyan (1868–1936), particularly the different ways they go about questioning modernity: these doubts were not totalist, but rather inhered within their very pursuit of modernity. To be sure, there are great differences among these men in the depth and ways of their thinking. For example, Yan Fu approached Western positivism through the teachings of Zhu Xi, translated and justified evolutionism through study of the *Book of Changes* and historiography, and touched upon the problem of freedom in Western thought through the theories of Laozi. His translations and interpretations of Western thought, however, in themselves constitute dialogue with, adjustment to, and tension with Western thought. Liang Qichao became familiar with Western political and religious knowledge through New Text Confucianism and the teachings of Wang Yangming (1472–1529); he translated and introduced modern European theory of science, German theories of the state, the philosophy of Kant, and James's pragmatism and his theory of religion. But his thinking also is imbued with critical reflection on capitalism, a utilitarian system of education, and the sense of a crisis of values. Zhang Taiyan was the most radical of the three, providing a systemic and intense critique of modernity from the standpoint of the consciousness-only school *(weishi xue)* of Buddhism and Zhuangzi's theory of seeing all things as equal *(qiwu lun)*. Beyond that, in the final volume's discussion of the community of scientific discourse, I analyze the internal complexity of the scientific community, and those individuals and groups who self-consciously resisted the hegemony of scientism. All these discussions show that Chinese thinking included an interrogation within its pursuit of modernity, a phenomenon that can be interpreted as the self-doubting or self-negation of Chinese modernity.

Within the framework of "anti-modern modernity," however, it was not just the scientific community, Hu Shi (1891–1962), and the "May Fourth" new culture movement that represented scientism, but humanists like Liang Qichao, Liang Shuming (1893–1988), and Zhang Junmai (1886–1969), who opposed scientism, must also be incorporated into its genealogy. Is there any way out of this quandary? I see the modern humanities as being a supplement to scientism that emerged out of resistance to it, and in this sense this humanism cannot provide a path out of the "crisis of modernity." At this point I need to explain my approach to this problem: I do not in any simple way take the thinking of these men as a solution, but I lay out how their thinking developed, that is, I try to show how possible solutions to modernity were incorporated into the process of pursuing modernity as a whole. I treat Yan Fu, Liang Qichao, and Zhang Taiyan the same way. I set out different possibilities and different avenues for thinking through this problem as found in their complicated intellectual entanglements, as well as in their individual responses to "the propensities of the times." In fact, intellectual diversity in itself constituted critical reflection on modernity and thinking toward a "solution," which is why I often describe Chinese modernity as "anti-modern modernity." We must take into account, however, that a basic trend of modern history has been to dispel this diversity by incorporating it into modernity itself, something that renders a "solution to modernity" a very simple problem that requires no self-struggle. My point here is that the way out of modernity is not simple, but that it requires a multitude of critical reflections, so as to create one, or a series of, possible directions—this is what I wish to do.

I began writing *The Rise of Modern Chinese Thought* in the bleak and depressing atmosphere of the aftermath of 1989, a time very different from the China of today. The book divides into four major subdivisions: "Principle and Things" *(Li yu wu)*, "Empire and State" *(Diguo yu guojia)*, "General Truth and Anti-General Truth" *(Gongli yu fan gongli)*, and "The Discursive Community of Science" *(Kexue huayu gongtongti)*, and seeks to pursue the following questions: How did the Song-Ming Heavenly Principle worldview take shape, and what was its historical dynamic? What, ultimately, is the relationship between the establishment of the Qing empire and the founding of the modern Chinese state? What intellectual resources can late Qing thought provide for understanding our complicated attitude toward modernity? How did the regime of modern Chinese knowledge come into being? What is the relationship between the modern "general truth" worldview and that of Heavenly Principle? Study of these questions provides us with a historical understanding of what is "China," what is "Chinese modernity," and the modern significance of Chinese thought. The above questions are closely related to the following double-edged inquiry: What is Chinese identity? This question is at once a meditation on the tendency toward social division inherent in modernity and an exploration of the historical dialectic between diversity and identity; it seeks to understand modernity's social relations and their tendency to expand. It is also a meditation on both the tendency toward the concentration of power under modernity and on the elements of traditional Chinese thought that seek to overcome this trend. As most scholars have discovered, once one has begun the process of study, the plentitude of history and its internal logic lead one forward, with the consequence that the best method becomes simply to develop the widest possible perspective. Therefore, respecting that perspective's internal logic and sorting out history's tangled tracks will provide us with a set of related and enlightening insights. At the conclusion of this introduction, however, I would like to add this: the motivation for my inquiries is rooted in a particular "propensity of the times," and both inquiry and study are attempts at cutting across the ruptures of history.

3

Local Forms, Vernacular Dialects, and the War of Resistance against Japan: The "National Forms" Debate

Many scholars have noted the clear historical links between the formation of modern nation-states and the process of the creation of a written language on the basis of a spoken vernacular.[1] In *The Civilization of the Renaissance in Italy*, Jacob Burkhardt described how, by writing in the vernacular as opposed to Latin, Dante made the Tuscan dialect the basis for a new national language.[2] Later, similar developments took place in many other European countries. In East Asia, first Japan and then Korea deployed their own spoken vernacular languages to resist the influence of Chinese and create their own national written languages. It is for reasons of this sort that in discussing Derrida's *Of Grammatology*, the Japanese scholar Karatani Kojin repeatedly emphasizes that phonocentrism is not just a "Western" issue, and that in the process of the creation of nation-states, "similar issues have arisen in all parts of the world, without exception."[3]

Translated by Chris Berry

The Chinese situation, however, seems different. For one thing, although there are evident links between the vernacular and the nationalist movements, the former cannot be seen as simply having been based on a particular dialect, and since it was a written language, neither can the replacement of classical by the *baihua* written vernacular be described as phonocentrism. Nor is this a question of a national language being adopted to replace an imperial language, as with Italian, French, or English replacing Latin, or with Japanese or Korean replacing Chinese. It was, rather, a case of one Chinese written language replacing another. Second, the movement to shift to a phonocentric scheme was not solely a product of the modern nationalist movement, but rather a legacy of the imperial period. For instance, in 1730, because Mandarin *(Guanhua)* was not spoken in Guangdong and Fujian provinces, the Court ordered the establishment of four Institutes for Proper Pronunciation *(Zhengyin guan)* in four cities in the south, even as it ordered that examination candidates *(jugong, tongsheng)* would not be permitted to sit for the examinations if they could not speak Mandarin, a stipulation that was to last for three years. In 1733 this restriction was extended for another three years. From the perspective of the cultural strategies of the imperial period, this royal policy of "Ordering Popular Customs" was, in fact, centered on the written language, because the standard for proper pronunciation was Mandarin, and Mandarin here refers not to the dialect of the capital region but rather to a tongue regulated by a written language that did not permit colloquialisms and slang within the scope of proper pronunciation. There were frequent discussions, research, and actual campaigns for the implementation of dialects during China's New Literature Movement, with one important instance being the discussion on "national forms" during the 1937–1945 War of Resistance against Japan. In the course of these discussions, local forms and dialects were linked directly to the nationalist movement, raising a challenge to the movement for the modern written vernacular. This challenge, however, ultimately failed and the modern vernacular was not toppled from its position as the common national language.

This essay will attempt to provide an explanation of the issues raised above via consideration of the debate over "national forms" and related matters. Following upon the movement for literary *(wenyi)* "massification" *(dazhonghua)*[4] of the 1930s, the "national forms" discussion caused a considerable stir in Chinese cultural circles between 1939 and 1942. Although the discussion gradually became less impassioned after 1943, it has continued to echo, and the problem of "national forms" has endured as a vital theme in the development of Chinese thought and literature. The discussion was opened up in Yan'an, where Ke Zhongping, Chen Boda, Zhou Yang, and Ai Siqi all took part, after which several dozen publications in Chongqing, Chengdu, Kunming, Guilin, the Shanxi-Shaanxi-Henan border region, and Hong Kong got drawn into the conversation; this eventually resulted in the publication of almost two hundred essays and treatises. Among those that attracted the most attention was the debate between Xiang Linbing and Ge Yihong as to whether or not "folk forms" were the core source of national forms. The discussion touched upon such literary issues as national forms, folk forms, and massification, but lurking in the background of each dispute were questions concerning how to appraise the May Fourth Literary Movement; how to reevaluate in the context of a national war the binary oppositions between old/new, modern/traditional, and urban/rural established during the "May Fourth" Movement; how to handle the class-based views on literature set forth during the 1928 debate on "revolutionary literature" and during the leftist literature movement of the 1930s; as well as how specifically to understand the relationships between the local, the national, and the global in regard to language and form. I would summarize these as contests between local forms and national forms, old forms and national forms, folk forms and national forms, mass culture and folk forms, national forms and internationalism, and national forms and cultural authority. All these problems circulated around "wartime state building" *(Kangzhan jianguo)* and the national aims of that state building. In this discussion, literature and its forms became an important means of forming "national" identity and mobilizing the "nation *(minzu)*."[5]

This essay intends neither to repeat what has already been said nor to touch upon all of the aforementioned matters,[6] but to begin instead with something rarely brought up by others, namely, the problem of local forms in the "national forms" discussion, and the problem of dialects and local patois in particular.

"Chinese Style" and "Chinese Flavor" as "National Forms"—Nationalist Politics and Literature in the Communist Movement

It is generally accepted that the formal source of the "national forms" discussion lies in a talk by Mao Zedong in October 1938, when he gave a report entitled "The Role of the Chinese Communist Party in the National War" to the Sixth Plenary Session of the Sixth Central Committee of the Communist Party of China, published on November 25 in the fifty-seventh issue of the Yan'an weekly magazine *Liberation* under the title "On the New Stage." The "Study" section of the essay dealt primarily with the problem of the "practical application of Marxism in China," not touching on literature at all. Mao stressed uniting revolutionary theory, historical knowledge, and practical campaigning, writing:

> If the Chinese Communists, who form a part of the great Chinese nation and are linked with it by flesh and blood, talk about Marxism apart from China's characteristics, that will be only Marxism in the abstract, Marxism in the void. Hence, how to turn Marxism into something specifically Chinese, to imbue every manifestation of it with Chinese characteristics, i.e., to apply it in accordance with China's characteristics, becomes a problem which the whole Party must understand and solve immediately. The foreign "eight-legged essay" must be banned, empty and abstract talk must be stopped and doctrinairism must be laid to rest to make room for the fresh and lively things of Chinese style and Chinese flavor which the common folk of China love to see and hear.[7]

The mid- to late 1930s and early 1940s was an important period in the formation of Mao's thought, one in which he attempted in numerous essays to rethink from a historical perspective the distinctiveness of China's problems and its revolution. The national war *(minzu zhanzheng)* China was fighting motivated Mao to redefine the major contradictions in Chinese society and to link the tasks of the Chinese Revolution even more closely with the issue of national revolution. At the beginning of the essay quoted above, Mao first discusses the relationship between internationalism and patriotism, pointing out that "only by achieving national liberation will it be possible for the proletariat and the toiling masses to achieve their own liberation.... Thus patriotism is simply an application of internationalism in the war of national liberation."[8] It is noteworthy that the "Chinese style and Chinese flavor" Mao speaks of is raised against the background of the China/international binary, that is to say, in the context of the national war, in which the international communist movement should be united with the national struggles of oppressed nations. The problem of the nation superseded the problem of class as the leading problem for the Chinese Communist movement during the War of Resistance. Within the framework of the international communist movement and Marxist theory the problem of the "national" is opposed to the problem of the "international," as a "local" problem in the general liberation of the proletariat.[9] And we cannot forget, of course, that the raising of the "national" problem within the scope of the communist movement had specific political implications and historical context: by appealing to the problem of the "national" one could win national autonomy within the communist movement. Or to put it more plainly, slipping free from Comintern control resulted in an independent and self-reliant Chinese Communist Party.

Against the backdrop of the popularization discussions and the national war, the most direct repercussion (in the literary world) to Mao's speech was over the issue of "national forms" in literature. The discussion gradually came to center on the two questions: What was "Chinese style and Chinese flavor?," and how should this "Chinese style and Chinese flavor" be created? The idea of "Chinese style and Chinese flavor" not only represented a direct link between the idea of the "nation" and "China" but also suggested a relationship between the discussion of "national forms" and Chinese-style Marxism. The first person to link Mao's speech to the "national forms" question was Ke Zhongping. In an article entitled "On 'Chinese Flavor,'" published in the February 7, 1939, edition of the Yan'an newspaper *New China News*, Ke elaborated upon Mao's formulation, pointing out that "each nation has its own flavor, formed out of its own economic, geographic, racial and cultural traditions.... The extremely rich Chinese flavor is currently being preserved and developed among the majority of the ordinary Chinese people."[10] Here, "each nation" is employed as a concept of the national in terms of the nation-state, namely, a modern nation in which each of the minority nationalities and the predominant nationalities in each region (locality) together constitute a united nationality within the scope of that nation-state. "Chinese style and Chinese flavor" thus refers to the problem of a united Chinese culture within a modern nation-state system.

The formation of Third-World nation-states is one of the historical achievements of modernity. In the process of struggling against imperialist colonialism, the gradual formation of new national and cultural identities that transcended the local created the conditions for independent and sovereign modern countries. The model of the "nation-state" largely based itself on the prototype of the modern European sovereign state, appealing to race, language, and religion as the fundamental underpinnings of national sovereignty. In other words, in the colonial era, Third-World movements for national self-determination plainly resorted to the model of the European sovereign nation-state. In the global context, however, states made up of only one nationality are extremely rare, and scholars of European history have demonstrated that a number of nations traditionally considered as being made up of one nationality in fact are not. So, as far as China is concerned, the process of establishing a modern nation was not simply one of self-determination for one nationality but also one of creating cultural identity, an identity that had at once to transcend and include localisms and cultural identities other than that of the Han. The creation of this identity not only made claims relating to race, language, and tradition but also to the times, hence the understanding of this identity as "new." The 1940s discussion of "national forms" was one of the primary forces behind the creation of a modern national cultural identity and subjectivity.

It should be stressed that because the discussion took place in areas as diverse as Yan'an, Chongqing, Chengdu, Kunming, Hong Kong, Guilin, and the Shanxi-Shaanxi-Henan border region, it clearly went beyond any particular class or political party, but whether in terms of derivation or the focus of the conversation, the "national forms" debate was primarily undertaken within the "left-wing" cultural sphere. At the same time, while in its efforts to define and explain "national forms," the discussion could not avoid appealing to the economics, geography, race, and cultural traditions mentioned by Ke Zhongping; almost all those who took part felt that these forms did not as yet exist but were something new and as yet to be created.

This clearly indicates that within the overall goal of "fighting a war of resistance and constructing the nation," all the various political and cultural forces felt that "national forms" were modern. These forms were neither "local" nor "old," neither the property of a majority or minority nationality, nor of a particular social class or stratum; all preexisting forms were only source materials for new "national forms" and not the forms themselves. The reason for this was clearly that within the imperialist colonial system, as a "nation" China was neither just a region nor a race but rather a modern national community. Therefore, "forms" could not be merely regional or ethnic but were instead modern, transcending locality; they were new creations, and "creativeness" was an important characteristic of "national forms," expressing the link between them and modernity.

The Context of Proposing the Idea of "Local Forms"— The Role of the War in Reconstructing the Urban-Rural Relationship

What, then, were the sources for the creation of new national forms? One of the important but often overlooked issues in the "national forms" discussion is the fact that the question of "local forms" was raised within the context of the national, and exploration of this issue eventually provoked a major debate on whether or not "folk forms" were the "core source of national forms."

Against the backdrop of mobilizing a modern nation for war, raising the question of the "local" may seem a bit odd at first, but upon further analysis it makes more sense. The first to raise this question was Chen Boda, who in an article entitled "Notes on the Question of National Form in Literature," published in the third issue of *The Literary Frontline* on April 16, 1939, echoed Mao Zedong's views on "Chinese style and flavor." In the thirteenth section of the article, he brought up the notion of "local forms":

> In matters of national form, we should pay attention to local form: we should thoroughly research the specific properties of the local songs, stage performances, dances and all literary works in each locality. In particular, literary workers in each locality should emphasize

fully developing their own local forms. This does not mean, however, that there is nothing other than the local. It should be noted that in China there are a lot of very different local languages and quite different local customs and habits, a situation even more pronounced among our country's different nationalities. It has been said, however, that the majority Han nationality has Chinese characters in common, which is correct. Whether written in the classical or the vernacular, it is basically the case that the same things can be read and understood by Han people everywhere. And it is a fact that great national works like *The Romance of the Three Kingdoms*, *The Dream of the Red Chamber* and *The Water Margin* can be read by Han people everywhere, provided they have even a little education. This then is a pan-Chinese national form, something also the case with something like "Beijing Opera." Pan-Chinese things like these should not only not be abolished but given even more attention and elaboration.[11]

This concept of "local forms," then, shows that the concept of "national forms" is a general idea, and subject to subdivision, since both "Pan-Chinese national forms" and local "national forms" exist, with the latter including the "local forms" of the "different nationalities within the country," such as spoken languages and local customs. In his use of the phrase "different nationalities within the country," Chen Boda lets it be known that his concept of "national forms" deploys the "national" as a political concept, and not in the ordinary ethnic or racial sense but rather in terms of the modern nation-state. The interchangeable use of the concepts of "minority nationality" and "local" also demonstrates that the notion of "national" in the "national forms" discussion cannot be separated from the idea of the modern nation-state. The concept of "local forms" invokes both the issue of massification and the question of the characteristics of "national forms." In discussing the question of "local forms," Chen Boda raised the matter of local spoken and written languages, especially the uniformity of Chinese characters. So, in the context of China's national war, why raise the question of the "local"? What is the relationship between "local forms" and the tradition of China's New Literature?

In order to analyze this issue, we must first briefly discuss the historical context in which the "national forms" question was raised.

One of the main triggers of the "national forms" discussion was the social mobility of writers, that is, the first large-scale cultural migration in modern times from the cities to the periphery. The formation of China's New Literature was accompanied by the gathering of large numbers of the educated from the towns and villages of the periphery and from overseas to such major cities as Beijing, Shanghai, and Nanjing. Because universities, the press, and state organizations were rapidly expanding in China's big cities, from the late Qing dynasty on, Chinese writers and intellectuals took these organizations as their base and gradually set up literary and intellectual groups. As a result, early native-place *(xiangtu)* literature was written in the large cities by writers who had left their homes behind. In the metropolitan context, neither provincial nor Western culture could be accepted by different audiences until it had been filtered through and subjected to the baptism of urban culture. The diverse rural backgrounds of urban men of letters also made it difficult for literature from any one particular locality to win wide acceptance. Within modern urban culture, and especially as a result of the modern urban educational system and print culture, a modern "common language" based on the traditional written language and that transcended local vernaculars gradually took form. In actual creative practice, however, this "common language" could also be marked by a certain degree of "local color" by, for example, adopting a few dialect words and idioms, and even using some dialect pronunciations.

After the outbreak of the War of Resistance, however, Beiping, Tianjin, Shanghai, Nanjing, Wuhan, and many other major cities fell one after the other and the better part of the writers who had congregated in them began to migrate to the Southwest and Northwest. This process was accompanied by such cultural events as the migration of universities, the transfer of cultural production, and the burgeoning of both new and old publications in the periphery, with Chongqing, Chengdu, Yan'an, Kunming, Guilin, and Hong Kong becoming new centers of culture. Of course, this movement of cultural centers was not restricted to cultural workers and organizations, but included changes in readership and the cultural environment, and, in particular, to the relationship between city and country. The conscious adjustments and forced movements that Chinese literature faced during the War of Resistance were directly connected to these historical vicissitudes. One of these adjustments was the establishment of the

All China Literary Association to Resist the Enemy ("Literary Association" hereafter) in Wuhan on March 27, 1938, in which writers of various political persuasions united under the banner of resisting Japan, promoting anti-Japanese cultural activities such as "going down to the countryside" and "joining the forces," encouraging writers to gain a deeper understanding of the realities of the War of Resistance, and organizing teams of writers to do battlefield interviews. In April of 1938, the Third Department of the Political Bureau of the Military Commission of the National Government of China was founded in Wuhan with Guo Moruo in charge. In August of the same year, the "Third Department" organized all the national salvation drama troupes and literary workers who had come to Wuhan—with the national salvation propaganda teams from Shanghai as the mainstay—into nine resist-the-enemy performance teams, four propaganda teams, one children's theater troupe, and a film projection unit. These groups were sent out to perform all over the country and carry out literary propaganda work to support the war.[12] The question of the "local" arose at the same time as writers and artists were leaving the cities and going to the various dialect areas. When confronted with the cultural environment in the periphery, the creative work of the writers had to be readjusted to suit the needs of the readership and the local culture—this was the "forced transformation."

In fact, it was not only the debate about "national forms" but, even more importantly, the cultural migration itself that profoundly reshaped the cultural relationship between city and country. This was the historical turning point represented by the emergence of the "folk" issue, and as Xiang Linbing said in his debate with Guo Moruo: "We must distinguish between urbanized, refined folk culture and standard rural folk culture. In the case of the latter, neighborhood gossip replaces the classical, oral verse replaces poetic rhyme and the thirteen meters of classical Chinese poetry, and local patois replaces classical composition."[13] Because of the profound and ineluctable links between urban and colonial cultures, the raising of the "local forms" issue in the context of the discussion of "national forms" also posed a challenge to urban-centered "modern culture," a challenge with "folk language" at its core. For example, Gao Changhong even insisted that "folk language is the real source of national forms"[14] and the "folk language" he was talking about was by and large rural folk language.

The popularization *(pingminhua)* and massification of literature had been an enduring theme in discussions about the new Chinese literature after May Fourth. The "Plain and Simple Social Literature"[15] and "Literature of the Common People"[16] of the "May Fourth" literary revolution, however, were mainly aimed against classical and aristocratic literature, whereas the explorations of literary popularization in the 1930s were directly linked to issues of class.[17] Between the "literary revolution" of "May Fourth" and the "revolutionary literature" of the 1930s there had been significant changes in content, but as far as form and the target readership was concerned, they were both basically urban.[18] The modern written language characterized by the *baihua* vernacular had been circulated mainly via middle and primary school textbooks, newspapers, and magazines, and had become the "common language" of a modern, unified country. This "common language," however, was primarily the written language of urban life and its circulation had not supplanted local dialect. The latter mainly took the form of spoken idioms, vocabulary, and variations in pronunciation. In broad areas of the countryside, the written language did not become a widely used "common language" because of very low literacy levels. The discussion of "literary massification" during the War of Resistance clearly linked massification to the idea of the nation, and its first turning point was the change in target readerships. Such slogans as "Literature of the Trenches" and "Literature of the Villages"[19] and the calls for "Writing to the Countryside" and "Writing to Join the Forces"[20] demonstrate that the aim of the discussions about literary massification was to turn the arts into "a weapon to arouse and mobilize the masses,"[21] and using "old forms" or "putting new wine into old bottles" arose out of "starting out with a definite political propaganda result [in mind]."[22] The various small-scale literary works that appeared widely during this period, such as battlefield reports, reportage, street theater and poetry, poetry recitations, and popular literature, were all intended for an ordinary mass readership. It is worthy of particular note that as part of the widespread mobilization for the War of Resistance, literary forms were already not merely written but included all sorts of performative forms such as theater, traditional operas, vaudeville *(shuochang)*, and recitations; in most of the countryside, print had ceased to be the dominant cultural form. The reason that dialect and local tunes became important issues was clearly connected to changes in literary genres and their forms of expression.

The Problem of the "Local" and the "Pan-Chinese"

That the urban literary movement, and especially the movement for the adoption of the written vernacular, were cultural initiatives directly connected to the creation of the modern state presented a problem. The formation of a modern common language that would transcend dialect was a cultural prerequisite for China to become a modern "nation-state." To put it another way, the modern vernacular is a stereotypical "national form," but under the special circumstances of the War of Resistance, whether or not this "national form" transcended the local was put into question.

On the one hand, the discussion about "national forms" was a continuation of the discussion of literary massification, but on the other it was about raising the "national" as an integral part (in both content and form) of the new art. During nationwide national mobilization, the primary issue facing the new art was the connection between the creation of "national forms" and "local forms," and not the problem of art and class that dominated urban literary debate in the 1930s. This was primarily because the war against Japan was national rather than a matter of class, but also because Japan had occupied the major metropolises and most Chinese writers had moved from them to the countryside and to peripheral cities. Under these new historical conditions, national form and massification were not abstract theoretical topics, but practical creative problems: What forms should writers use, especially what language, and who were the readers?

Ke Zhongping, a popular theatrical troupe leader in Northern Shaanxi and the Jin-Cha-Ji (i.e., Shanxi-Inner Mongolia-Hebei) border region, discussed this topic more concretely than did Chen Boda. In his essay "Introducing *Checking the Travel Permits* and Creating New National Operas," he says that his troupe's anti-Japanese operas "take democracy as the foundation but at the same time hold onto the good points of the old dramatic forms, and move from absorbing old artistic techniques to developing a new Shaanxi opera." *Checking the Travel Permits* adapted melodies from Shaanxi opera and that province's Mei and Fu counties, being a success not only when performed in the countryside but also applauded by intellectuals in Yan'an. As a result, Ke Zhongping believed that "this opera has local characteristics, but at the same time it has also gone beyond the boundaries of local opera." Toward the end of the second part of his essay, he concludes:

> When we performed among the ordinary people of Northern Shaanxi, we were received warmly by the local people because all the actors were locals speaking the local language and singing local tunes. Today, with our major cities and lines of communication occupied by the enemy, maintaining links between places is very difficult, so it is absolutely essential that our mobilization work occur in every part of the countryside. In our rural activities, making art local has become a top priority, but most local things can also become pan-Chinese—especially today when there is so much population movement. Because Chinese localities have always been part of China, with the exception of a few rather special cases, they all have real life experiences that the whole country can understand and common language usages that are reasonably close to one other. While such productions emphasize the local, they can also fully bring out the pan-Chinese common elements that exist in the local, thus being both local and pan-Chinese. *Checking the Travel Permits* already exhibits these strong points.
>
> If this opera is performed in another locality, some of the local language from this area can be replaced with localisms from other regions, so as to make it more effective when performed.²³

Like Chen Boda, Ke Zhongping believes that "local forms" can either be advantageous to or transformed into "pan-Chinese" resources. In other words, local forms are not and should not be resources for the formation of local identity, but aid in the formation of national identity instead. Similarly, the use of local dialect in operatic performance is to help construct a "national" rather than a local identity.

Raising the question of "local form" is based on this premise. In "On National Forms in Chinese Music," Xian Xinghai stresses that "because the Chinese nation is so great, its written and spoken languages and its styles and customs are highly complex and varied. If we really want to use national forms effectively, we must first unify the spoken and written languages.

Second, we must improve our own classical music, submitting it to modern scientific change and improving it so that it can be used in compositions to express more national color."[24] Du Ai added that "If we find the common elements, the pan-Chinese, in these various different local forms, they will constitute an integral national form."[25] Zong Jue even states categorically, "Those things that are most local are also the most national in the most profound sense of national life, because the forms of a large nation are usually assembled from a blend of many local characteristics." According to this logic, if "'the global is in the local,' it is also in the national." From his perspective, the issue of local forms also encompasses the national minority literature of the Southwest and Northwest:

> During today's united War of Resistance, this issue has a particularly deep political significance.... It is the major premise under which we develop their national forms so that they become a powerful national troop in resistance war literature.... Regardless of whether one is considering pan-Chinese national forms, local literary forms or national minority literature, they all necessarily take the War of Resistance as their subject matter. This is unquestionably a direct result of the political requirements of the united national War.[26]

Among "local forms," "national minorities forms," and "national forms," the problem was that the connection between the "local," "national minorities," and the Chinese "national" was not completely consistent, as under certain conditions the "local" could become an obstacle to the "pan-Chinese." In the discussion of "national forms," there is no evidence of a direct connection between the "local" issue, local politics, and local cultural identity, and the intellectuals who had come to the countryside and the periphery from the cities did not represent local culture. However, we can neither ignore the reality of long-term political and military separatism in modern Chinese history nor the particular features and cultures of the areas where the national minorities live. As regional militarism developed in the Qing dynasty[27] and central authority weakened, local political and military power became increasingly important in the makeup of the country as a whole. After the 1911 Revolution, a political pattern of local separatism took shape with provincial military governors and warlords as the main political and military powers, and the connection between local culture and local politics was obviously an important feature of the political and cultural terrain. Even if during the War of Resistance all the political and military forces of each faction accepted the leadership of the nationalist government under the banner of resisting the Japanese, this did not change the situation of local military and political separatism. Add to that the difficulties in communication, and a common language could not prevail in these localities, so the use of dialect was unavoidable.

Examined in terms of the historical development of the new literature, attention to the connection between the national and the local leads toward two conclusions: One, taking the "May Fourth" New Literature standpoint of "Literature in the National Language, and the National Language in Literature," critiques and reforms dialects and local forms so as to create common national forms. The other, taking the standpoint of local forms or rural literature, critiques the urbanization and Europeanization of May Fourth New Literature. The most sensitive and important issue here is the relationship between dialects and a common spoken language *(putonghua)*. Prior to the emergence of the "national forms" discussion, however, the main critique of the "May Fourth" cultural movement was generated from the standpoint of class theory, with the "local" and "dialects and local patois" almost never used as the springboard for the critique. The writers who had left the cities and entered the special zones—that is, the localities—could not completely avoid the political, military, and cultural realities of those localities. If local forms, dialects, and patois were directly connected with local political identity, then this would be a serious threat to the formation of a united nation-state. It was, therefore, quite natural that under circumstances that necessitated the use of dialects, there was continual emphasis on the dialectical unity between the local and the national.

The Modern Language Movement and the Dialect Issue

In his analysis of this issue, Huang Yaomian said:

> The first problem is the contradiction between the common language and dialects. Mr Li Dazhao has pointed out that if we want to

achieve true massification and Sinification we must make greater use of local patois, and he was quite correct. Some people, however, have responded that if writers all use their own dialect, then only those from the same locality will be able to completely understand their work and those from other areas would find it very difficult to comprehend; would this not, in fact, run counter to massification? I believe there really is a contradiction here, and that the way to resolve it is to take the common speech in circulation today as the foundation and keep adding dialect from other regions so that it becomes richer day by day. Although the result may seem a bit awkward at first and it may even be necessary to add annotation, habit and usage will eventually make these additions component parts of the language. Furthermore, we will not block the writing of literature in pure local patois specifically for people in that area to read, and by promoting regional literature of this sort, we will assuredly discover much local talent. I believe that such work is sure to have a decisive impact on the literary movements of the future.[28]

Although Huang realized there was a contradiction between dialects and the common language, he basically believed that dialects could enrich that language and thus become an organic part of it.

The issue is, however, clearly more complicated than Huang Yaomian's analysis here, since Xiang Linbing and others had already made those "folk forms" which included dialect the sources of "national forms" and used this idea to launch a stern critique of cultural achievements since "May Fourth." In the context of national war, specifically regional "folk forms," with dialect and patois as their medium and local literature as their vehicle, became the negation of the critique of the modern culture movement. In his "On the Primary Source of 'National Forms,'" Xiang Linbing pointed out that "two literary forms pre-exist national forms: One is the new literary forms that have developed since May Fourth and the other is the folk literary forms to which the masses have long been accustomed. Which of these, then, is to be the source for the creation of national forms?"[29] He concluded:

On one hand, folk forms are the antithesis of national forms, while on the other they are the same; therefore, so-called folk forms themselves constitute an essentially contradictory unity, because it is a developing domain of naturally self-negating elements and also because by its very nature it is full of embryonic national forms.... The application of the critique of folk forms lies in initiating the creation of national forms and the completion of that process is the ultimate purpose of the use of folk forms. In other words, those who subscribe to realism should find the primary source of national forms in folk forms.[30]

Xiang Linbing had already explicitly used "folk forms" as a point of departure for his critique of the May Fourth cultural movement. He felt that if, as had been the case with "May Fourth," newly emerging forms were the source of national forms and that if folk forms were dissolved and dispersed into the new literary forms—as the folk vocabulary had been woven into the modem vernacular—"because its oral expressive quality have been emasculated, the possibility of direct enjoyment by the masses is also lost."[31] The "oral expressive quality" of folk literature that Xiang Linbing mentions here demonstrates that his concept of "folk literature" is intrinsically linked with the spoken language, dialects and other performative forms. This orientation toward folk literature is clearly in conflict with the fundamental approach of the modern language movement taking place within urban culture, even though both were driven by nationalism.

Both the formation and the promotion of the modern vernacular were the historical products of the Chinese educated classes' quest for modernity, and we can understand the connection between the modern language movement and modernity on at least two basic levels. First, the modern language movement was an antitraditional, scientific, and cosmopolitan activity, and, second, it was a movement to form the common language of a modern nation-state. In modern times, literary change has always been accompanied by linguistic change, and scholars generally believe that the foundation of the modern vernacular movement was a unity of the spoken and written languages *(yan wen yizhi)*, that is, fusing everyday speech and the written language. From Huang Zunxian's remark, "My hand should write as I speak; how can we allow ancient ways to hold us up?" to the "May Fourth" vernacular movement, the modern literature movement and its promoters clearly saw it as moving ever closer to the spoken language, and that included its grammatical structures, vocabulary, and pronunciation.

As for the orientation toward unifying the spoken and written languages and the connection between this and nationalism, modern linguistic change in China was similar to the situations in Japan and Korea.[32] Questioning the modern language movement from the perspective of local patois or vernacular dialects, however, raises the question of what the practical historical significance of "the unity of the spoken and written languages" actually was, and in what sense the modern language movement was directed toward the oral language. From the standpoint of linguistic change, what was the significance of the cultural movement following "May Fourth"?

We will examine the situation in Japan and Korea first. Around the fifth century C.E., Chinese books were transmitted to Japan and became the basis for a widely used system of writing. The Japanese, however, used their own pronunciation to read Chinese characters. In about the sixth century, the *Manyogana* system appeared, which used Chinese characters to represent Japanese words phonetically, but with variations in both pronunciation and meaning.[33] In this way two reading systems were created in Japan, one of which was the *Manyogana* set of signs for the Japanese indigenous spoken language, although these signs themselves were Chinese characters. In the ninth century, the *hiragana* and the *katakana* writing systems also came into being, which partially replaced Chinese characters as linguistic signs.[34] The grammatical structure of *manyogana*, however, bore absolutely no relation to Chinese. The other reading system was derived from the Chinese character documents that came to Japan from Korea, and it retained the character of the original Chinese, with its characters, vocabulary, and syntax.

Prior to the Meiji Reformation of 1868, the use of dialects in Japan remained very common, with different dialects used in the different territories or *han* of the various feudal lords *(zhuhou)*, making interaction difficult. Following the development of communications after the Meiji Reformation and in the context of the movement for unifying the spoken and written languages, in 1885, Miyake Yonekichi proposed a national inquiry into dialects, with the aim of using dialects as the source material for a common language, and with the Tokyo dialect as the standard. Also in 1885, Shimano Seiichiro advocated using the Tokyo language as the basis for uniting writing and speech,[35] and Katayama Junkichi linked the unity issue with that of primary school texts. Starting with these texts, mass reading material aimed at ordinary people was to pull together writing and speech. We can see from this that the lack of linguistic unity manifested itself not just in grammar and vocabulary but also in differences between pronunciation and written texts. The language unification movements that appeared at the end of the Edo Period and the beginning of Meiji not only called for the use of everyday vernacular forms in writing, grammar, and vocabulary, but also sought for the use of the *kana* phonetic syllabary to partially substitute for Chinese characters. In 1900, the Ministry of Education proclaimed the Regulations for Implementation in Primary Schools, with the third regulation, on the national language, calling for attention to the common language. The next year the Essential Regulations for Higher Normal Schools on the Implementation of Japanese Language Courses in Ordinary Primary Schools was also proclaimed, which formally proposed that the Japanese used in language instruction should take the current correct pronunciation and grammar of the Tokyo middle classes and above as its basis.[36] In short, modern Japanese was formed on a base of dialect, using a phonetic method to produce a writing system different from the Chinese.

The situation in Korea was very similar to that in Japan. As early as the fifteenth century, Korea had already formulated the *Hunmin Chong-um* script, but Chinese writing remained dominant. The broad dissemination of the national written signs occurred during the modernization process of opening up and two forms derived from the *onmunchae* writing system appeared—*kukmunchae*, or "national writing," and *kukhan-munchae*, or "Korean-Chinese writing." Much like China's vernacular, *onmunchae* had been used in classical novels and to an extent in everyday life, and it was the written form closest to a unified writing and speech. At the time of the opening up to the outside world, this written form developed into the unified language of *kukmunchae*. This "national writing," however, did not become the written language in general use. Instead, the newly established mixed *kukhanmunchae* became the general written language, even though it added auxiliary words to Chinese characters to perform grammatical functions and was thus quite far from uniting writing and speech.

Eventually a new hybrid form of written language derived from the *kukhanmunchae* and unifying speech and writing became fixed in place.

At the same time as this process was underway, another important theme appeared in the national language movement, the standardization of the phonetic *onmun* system of writing. In the five centuries following the formulation of the *Hunmin Chong-um* system, because there had not been a process to establish a national language or a common writing system, its orthography had gradually become irregular, and by the end of the nineteenth century people had a strong desire to sort through the various spellings and unify them. Research on this began in 1907, and the "Agreement on Research into the National Language" of 1909 summed up the findings on national language of the "Opening of the Ports" period. It clarified the origins of the national language and the evolution of its writing system and pronunciation, advocating the deletion of eight symbols that had been formulated in the *Hunmin Chong-um* but were by then no longer in use. The program thus sorted out the chaotic system of linguistic signification that prevailed at the time. The "Agreement" was integrated with research on the national language undertaken during the colonial period that followed, and in 1933 the Unified System of Korean Orthography was enacted. We can deduce several characteristics of the changes in Korean language: it threw off the shackles of Chinese characters, standardized the *onmun* phonetic writing system, and unified pronunciation.[37] The Japanese and Korean language movements were directly connected to the formation of national identity, using national writing systems and standard pronunciation in order to break the ties to the Chinese language and create modern written languages that were either new or a mixture of the new and the old. Because of the links between the language movements and nationalism, and because nationalism here took the form of directly re-creating language with the spoken tongue as the core, the creation of a common national language was closely connected to the issue of national "pronunciation," or, in other words, dialect.

The movement for the unification of speech and writing in China took a similar approach as those in Japan and Korea, namely, the creation of a new national language. In the Chinese case, however, and with the movement for the vernacular in particular, the abandonment of characters was not an issue, nor was the formulation of a phonetically based written language. Attempts to abandon characters, such as the Romanization and Latinization movements discussed in more detail below, all failed. Because there was no question of using the "national" or "folk language" to replace a language of empire, the vernacular movement did not arise out of a confrontation between a native language and an imperial one, but was rather oriented toward its own confrontation in values between the poor and the "aristocrats" and between the vulgar and the refined. The aim of the so-called shift to oral language of the vernacular movement was not toward real "oral language" at all, but rather opposition to the rules for versification of classical poetry and the ornate stuffiness of the classical writing in general. Thus, the modern language movement was first constituted as an opposition between old and new, vulgar and the refined, and not as an opposition between written language and dialect. *Baihua* was thus spoken of as the "modern language" and classical Chinese as "ancient," with the modern setting store by the "vulgar" and the ancient valuing the "refined." As a result, the antithesis between modern and ancient also clearly bespeaks the different cultural values of the ordinary people and the upper classes.

After the *Minbao* (People's voice) ceased publication in 1908, for example, Zhang Taiyan and Qian Xuantong co-published a *baihua* magazine called *Jiaoyu jinyu zazhi* (Modern language education), demonstrating that the vernacular language movement from the late Qing to "May Fourth" was oriented toward the values of "the present" *(jin)*, "the new," and what was later called "the modern," even though the vernacular was not itself something purely modern. The primary source of the modern vernacular was the traditional written vernacular, with the addition of some colloquial vocabulary and syntax as well as some elements of Western languages and their grammar and punctuation. The opposition between the classical language and *baihua* already existed in the Chinese written language, and cannot be understood as a simple opposition between classical and the oral vernacular. In taking the written vernacular as its primary source, the modern vernacular not only stood in opposition to classical Chinese, but also transcended dialect to create a common spoken language. The eventual result was that the plan for a "common speech" *(putonghua)* based itself on Northern Chinese, with Beijing pronunciation as the standard, thus establishing a common language that transcended dialect by taking a dialect as its foundation.[38]

The "shift to the oral language" implies challenging the classical and demanding popularization *(tongsuhua)*, which is formally expressed as opposition between the classical and the vernacular, and in content the division between refined and vulgar. This antagonism did not begin in the modem period; it is just that modern-day people construe it as being "modern."[39] In other words, this antithesis is not something that arose only after nationalism became an issue. Opposition to the dead written language of classical Chinese necessarily touches upon the idea of living language, which also leads to the matter of dialect. In the 1920s, beginning with the research on folk songs following the founding of the "Beijing University Dialect Investigation Society" (January 1924), there was a period in which Chinese research on language focused on descriptive linguistics. This period was characterized by taking living language as the object of research, phonological description, and comparing these with traditional phonetic notation *(qieyun)* in an effort to discover patterns in phonetic change over the years.[40] From the 1950s on, however, the emphasis in dialect research shifted from actual dialects and their historical transformations to comparisons between local pronunciations and the common language. Of course, the motivation for the effort to find patterns of correspondence between dialects and this *putonghua* was to work for the latter's popularization.[41] It can be said that before this, dialects and common *baihua* were contrasted primarily in regard to the written language, for example, the use of dialect vocabulary. The "oralization" of vernacular Chinese mostly emphasized grammatical structure and vocabulary, with less attention to phonology, indicating that the vernacular, like classical Chinese, was primarily a written language, without a fixed system of standard pronunciation.[42]

To put it another way, so-called oralization only occurred in the process of forming the modern standard written language, because when it comes to speech there were only dialects and no common spoken language. Clearly both Beijing and Northern Chinese are also dialects, and they became a "common national shared language" through systematic stipulation and implementation by a modern nation. As de Saussure said, "The privileged dialect, after it has been promoted to the rank of official and standard language, seldom remains the same as it was before. It acquires dialectal elements and becomes more and more composite, though without losing completely its original character."⁴³ What Saussure calls "literary language" in this context designates not only the language of literary work, but also and in a more general sense all types of cultivated or uncultivated language that either formally or informally serve the whole community.⁴⁴ In regard to its relationship with modern nationalism, *putonghua* has been an important resource for social mobilization and the construction of national identity. During the "May Fourth" New Culture Movement, the vernacular was proposed primarily as a written language and the issue of dialect pronunciation went basically untouched.⁴⁵ This was because the basic orientation of social mobilization during the wave of modern nationalism was to bring different areas and social levels toward nationalist goals and complete the task of establishing a modern unified nation; it was not toward local separatism, and the language movement was an organic part of this nationalist movement. Under conditions where there was no common spoken tongue, it was only possible to attain the objective of a National Language *(Guoyu)* through the unification of writing.⁴⁶ The proposal and implementation of the concept of "National Language" made it clear that the fundamental import of the "May Fourth" vernacular movement was not to call for the use of a true spoken language (or dialect) in the production of literature, but rather to use the vernacular written language, while drawing on oral elements, as the basis for creating a modern, unified written language. This is why the concept of National Language was plainly aimed against the traditional written language, even as it implicitly took dialects as its antithesis. The debate on using the Roman alphabet for phonetic spelling that took place about the time of "May Fourth" was focused on the issue of phonological unity and not on dialect. The "National Language" movement supplied linguistic resources for the foundation and identity of the modern unified nation-state, but dialect and its intrinsic link to local identity was a potential obstacle to national mobilization. In short, although dialect was understood as a crucial component of a common spoken language, especially as a resource for vocabulary, it was completely impossible for the modern language movement to adopt dialect as the guiding principle for change.

With this background in mind, we can understand why some of the basic norms of the modern written language are not derived from either the oral language or from dialect. For example, the first publication to use new punctuation and print horizontally rather than vertically was the monthly *Science*, established in 1915, adopting this completely Western style to publish scientific essays and formulae. The modern Chinese nationalist movement ran parallel to the westernization movement in culture, with the modern Chinese language reform movement exhibiting a trend toward westernization that manifested itself in a linguistic cosmopolitanism favoring the adoption of a Western phonetic script. Even before the 1911 Revolution, Wu Zhihui and others advocated the abolition of Chinese characters, suggesting that even if it were impossible immediately to adopt Esperanto, English or French could be used in the interim.[47] Many members of the May Fourth generation saw Chinese characters as a tool for keeping the masses ignorant and as the most obdurate enemy representing an evil tradition. For example, Qian Xuantong wrote, "If we want to get rid of Confucianism, we must first get rid of Chinese characters"[48] and "Unless we overthrow *(geming)* Chinese characters, we will not be able to have popular education, National Language literature will certainly not be able to develop fully, and writing in the National Language will not be able to give expression freely and easily to the new truths, scholarship and knowledge that is the public property of the world's people."[49] Following the movement to adopt the vernacular, language remained thereafter a central and constant issue in debates about literature. For example, there was the massification movement that began in 1930, the debate about "Chinese common speech" (*putonghua*, as a literary language) of 1932, and in 1934 the controversy about mass language and the Latinization movement. All these movements for language change were connected to the creation of a new national language and were all deeply influenced in their orientation by Western phonetic spelling. In fact, Chinese grammar had been constructed according to the basic standards of Western languages since *Ma's Language Reference (Ma shi wentong)*.[50]

Among the lasting influences of the modern Chinese literature movement was the creation of the conditions, standards, and conventions for the formation of a modern written language, and through this the formation of a sort of "general language." This provided a linguistic basis for unifying the nation even as it gradually drew closer to Western language through what was called at the time becoming "scientific," "logical," and "phonetic." In other words, the new language had both a double orienta-

Local Forms, Vernacular Dialects, and the War of Resistance

tion and double function, being both cosmopolitan and nationalist in its deployment of "scientific" methods to construct a general common modern national language, that is to say, *putonghua*. This is not to say, of course, that there were no experiments with "dialect" in the modern Chinese language and literature movements, but, generally speaking, such experiments as Liu Dabai and Liu Bannong's use of dialect to write poetry clearly never entered the mainstream. The mass language movement also touched upon the dialect issue, but it was clearly linked to questions of class, and raising the idea of the language of the lower classes as a sort of "language" basically does not fall within the scope of regional "dialects." It should be noted, however, that class transcends nation, with the framework of class theory obviously including a cosmopolitan tendency, and the cosmopolitan can generally accommodate the local even as it excludes the national. Of course, there is no logical inevitability to the connections between these various elements, and they were mostly determined by historical circumstances. For example, the Latinization movement, closely connected to the mass language movement as it was, produced a dozen or so plans concerning dialects, and under the historical conditions of the War of Resistance, these dialect plans in themselves created the conditions for mass mobilization and became organic components of the nationalist movement.

If we focus our attention more closely on the relationship between the movement to reform Chinese characters from the late Qing dynasty on and the moves toward the adoption of phonetic spelling, that is, the relationship between written language and pronunciation, then the historical link between the formation of a modern Chinese national language and westernization—the cosmopolitan orientation—becomes even clearer. Linguists have already noted the close connection between the phonetic spelling movement of the late Qing dynasty and the activities of Western missionaries, origins that can be traced back to 1605, when Matteo Ricci published a volume in Beijing entitled *The Wonder of Western Characters (Xi zi qiji)*, the first work to systematically use the Latin alphabet to spell out the sounds of Chinese characters. In 1625, the French Jesuit missionary Nicolas Trigault (1577–1628) revised Ricci's alphabetization work and completed the lexicon for the spelling of Chinese characters using the Roman alphabet entitled *The Ear and Eye Assistant to Foreign Scholars (Xi ru ermu zi)*.⁵¹ Their straightforward method of phonetic writing immediately inspired a desire for this type of phonetic writing among Chinese phonologists.⁵² As Chen Wangdao noted, "Everything they did was for the convenience of their colleagues, so they often used the roman alphabet to record the sounds of Chinese characters, which led to reflections that letters could be used to record or spell Chinese characters, something that gradually evolved until two centuries later it produced the trend towards the use of the national phonetic or *pinyin* alphabet."⁵³

Chen calls this "period in which they planned to make it convenient for themselves to study Chinese characters" the first stage in the "phonetic notation and *pinyin* phonetic spelling wave."⁵⁴ It is worth noting that toward the end of the Qing dynasty, missionary activity connected local dialects and phonetic spelling—this was what Chen Wangdao called "the period when church people prepared to spread phonetic spelling everywhere for the sake of the illiterate," something he labeled the "Church Romanization movement." For the sake of their proselytizing, the missionaries successively translated the Bible into the spoken form of local languages, sometimes using Chinese characters, at other times using Roman letters. According to statistical summaries, by the end of the nineteenth and the beginning of the twentieth centuries, the Bible had been circulated in at least seventeen translations using local dialects spelt out in Roman letters.⁵⁵ A clear conflict emerged between the "Church Romanization movement" and the Chinese writing system, with some missionaries proceeding to advocate replacing Chinese characters with the Roman alphabet and promoting phonetic writing. This shows how the move toward oral expression within the early language movement was not just toward regional speech, but also represented an attempt to erode Chinese culture and language by Western religious culture and language—it was aimed at linguistic colonialism rather than at some sort of nationalistic linguistic movement.

It is also clear, however, that this movement had a very important effect on later Chinese language reform, moving gradually from the phonetic spelling of dialects to the creation of a unified spoken language and pronunciation, that is, promoting a unified pronunciation under the impetus of the nationalist movement, using phonetic spelling as the main tool. The period between the publication of *First Steps in Complete Understand-*

ing at a Glance (A new phonetic script for the Amoy dialect) in 1892 by Lu Ganzhang (1854–1928) of Tongan in Fujian Province and the Xinghai Revolution in 1911 marked the first stage in the creation of Chinese phonetic spelling. During this time, twenty-eight schemes for phonetic notation came out, of which those by Wang Zhao (1895–1933) and Lao Naixuan (1843–1941) were the most prominent. Influenced by Japanese *kana*, Wang Zhao created the "Mandarin alphabet" and published *The Mandarin Phonetic Alphabet* in 1900. He took Beijing pronunciation as standard and used a dual system to spell out vernacular Chinese.[56] Lao Naixuan's "simplified phonetic characters" was a scheme for the spelling of southern dialects based on Wang Zhao's "Mandarin alphabet," but with the addition of some elements peculiar to southern local speech; his aim was to "take local patois (i.e., southern dialects) a simple step towards the unification of spoken Mandarin (i.e., Beijing accent)," in order to promote popular education and unify the National Language.[57] In 1910, after examining six petitions entitled "Explaining Our Request to Promote Simplified Mandarin Characters," Yan Fu drafted a report in which he wrote, "It is widely held that there are two reasons why our country is difficult to govern: education is not widespread, and the National Language is not unified, both of which result from the failure to use Mandarin phonetic spelling."[58] This demonstrates that the movement for the construction of a modern nation-state and the process of creating a common language on the basis of dialect went hand in hand, with the unification of the National Language plainly speeding up after the establishment of the Republic in 1912.

In regard to pronunciation, the Church Romanization movement was very different from the movement for the promotion of language reform on the part of Chinese intellectuals and the modern nation-state: the former manifested itself in the phonetic notation of dialects using the Roman alphabet, whereas the latter used a unified phonetic notation to overcome differences among dialects. The plan for a "phonetic alphabet" after the establishment of the Republic grew out of the late Qing dynasty movement for phonetic notation. "The Central Provisional Conference on Education" convened in Beijing in 1912 set out a "plan for the adoption of a phonetic alphabet," and in 1913 the Ministry of Education convened a "Conference on the Unification of Pronunciation" that approved the official national pronunciation for all characters, certified the total number of sounds in the language, and selected letters to express each sound.[59] The proposal for a "phonetic alphabet" with standard pronunciation formed part of the backdrop to the rise of the "May Fourth" *baihua* movement: although this vernacular movement did not set out to create the written language anew by basing it on pronunciation, it did include a process of authorizing a new standard pronunciation.

Not long after Hu Shi published "My Humble Suggestions on Literary Reform" *(Wenxue gailiang chuyi)*, in which he discussed the improvement of both the form and the content of literature,[60] Qian Xuantong, Fu Sinian, and others began to propose plans for more radical language reform that included the elimination of Chinese characters and their replacement with phonetic spelling. *New Youth (Xin qingnian)*, *New Tide (Xin chao)*, *National Language Monthly (Guoyu yuekan)*, and other journals published one article after another discussing the reform of Chinese characters, including Fu Sinian's "Preliminary Discussion on Changing over to a Phonetic Script for Chinese," in which he explicitly advocated the substitution of Chinese characters with phonetic spelling,[61] and Qian Xuantong's "Revolutionizing Chinese Characters," in which he opined that the fundamental reform of Chinese characters would be "the use of a Roman-style alphabet."[62] In 1923, Qian proposed a "Request to Organize a Committee on National Language Romanization" to the "National Language Unification Commission," the aim of which was to establish a "National Language Romanization Committee" that would carry out specific research, gather opinions from all quarters, and "fix a practical and standard 'National Romanization.'" In September 1926, the National Language Romanization Committee formally convened and adopted the "Rules on National Language Romanization," which it formally requested the Education Ministry to promulgate.[63] Experts on Chinese linguistic history consider that:

> National Language Romanization was the first nearly mature plan for phonetic writing following the Chinese character reform movement of the late Qing dynasty. It not only took into account the entirety of the writing system and various special characteristics of the Chinese language itself, but also had an internationalist perspective in its choice of symbols. It was theoretically and methodologically

more creative and better developed than all previous plans for a phonetic writing system, so the National Language Romanization movement holds an important position in the history of the efforts to reform Chinese characters.[64]

There was always a close connection between the modem Chinese national language and an "internationalist perspective." In 1933 and 1934, just when the discussion on "classical Chinese, the vernacular and massification" was going on in China, news of the movement for a new Latinized writing that was taking place in the Soviet Far East was introduced inside China, drawing a quick response.[65] The Latinization movement was closely linked to the issue of mass language, so it was not solely a question about national language, as the cultural impetus behind it already encompassed class theory and an internationalist perspective. The Latinization movement heralded the end of the National Language Romanization movement. The orientation of the Latinization movement did not particularly emphasize the National Language, but was marked, instead, by many schemes for the Latinization of dialects, including those of Shanghai, Guangzhou, Xiamen, Ningbo, Sichuan, Suzhou, Hubei, Wuxi, Guangxi, Fuzhou, and Wenzhou. Directly linked to the "national forms" issue discussed here is the fact that, after the rise of the anti-Japanese movement to save the nation and the full outbreak of the War of Resistance, Latinization was well suited to mobilization of the masses, popularizing education, and anti-Japanese propaganda, so it swept rapidly across the whole country. Not only were there more publications than ever before, but also such things as the thousands of New Writing classes for refugees and "New Writing night schools for farmers," numerous "training classes in Latinization for cadres," and the establishment of all sorts of related organizations and associations; it was the high point in the modern phonetic writing movement.[66] In fact, the conflicting orientations between the Latinization movement and the National Language Romanization movement was already quite apparent at the time, and a number of scholars who had advocated Romanization of the National Language firmly resisted Latinization, publishing a number of highly pointed critiques.[67] The reasons for the eventual failure of the Latinization movement are no doubt quite complex, but its failure to establish a real "literary language"—in the Saussurian sense—was no doubt one of them.

It can be said with certainty that the modern language movements of China, Japan, and Korea were processes of constructing "national languages" motivated by nationalism. Apart from the early "Church Romanization" and Latinization movements, the basic direction of the Chinese language reform movement was to work for a unified written language and a unified system of national pronunciation, in order to produce the conditions for the creation of a unified national language. As a result, the vernacular movement that was the hallmark of modern language reform did not create new symbols for the written language or take the pronunciation of any of the dialects as the basis for its reinvention. The effort to unify pronunciation was not in order to reinvent Chinese characters, but to overcome the pronunciation differences among dialects. At no point in the history of the Chinese modern language movement was the dialect issue central; it was, on the contrary, overcoming the differences among dialects that constituted the mainstream of the modern language movement.[68]

It is precisely because of this that the "local forms" issue and in particular the "dialect" issue came up as part of the "national forms" debate, and were in basic conflict with the orientation of the modern language movement. The war created separate de facto regimes within China, forcing men of letters to move far from the metropolitan cities and to settle in unfamiliar dialect environments. The creators of the New Literature were for the first time faced directly with the opposition between the "general language" of the large cities and the "dialects" of the rural areas. The challenge to the history of the New Literature posed by dialects or local forms was connected to the actual political situation. This specific political situation, however, in no way altered or caused a divergence from the nationalistic path of establishing a sovereign nation-state. As a consequence, all the debate sparked by the local forms issue could only be carried out within the basic logic of modern nationalism. For example, Pan Zinian understood the issue of "national forms" as one of "Sinification," and when discussing the language issue, he pointed out that vocabulary and grammar were the most pressing issues facing the Chinese language at the time. He cited the contributions of Goethe to German and Pushkin to Russian as examples, noting that the Chinese modern language lacked that sort of creativity:

For example, so far there is no grammar of the Chinese language. *Ma's Language Reference* is a reasonably comprehensive Chinese grammar, but, first, it uses foreign grammar to annotate the rules of Chinese language and is not a work that sorts out its grammar rules on the basis of the Chinese language itself; it cannot, therefore, either avoid being far-fetched and strained at times, or prove up to the task of investigating the particular grammatical characteristics of the Chinese language. It thus cannot be spoken of as a real Chinese grammar. Second, it confines its research to classical Chinese—the ancient language—and not colloquial or modern spoken Chinese. As a result, it can only be considered a grammar of written Chinese at best, and not the grammar of the spoken language that we need.[69]

In distinguishing between the grammar of "written" *(wen)* and "spoken" *(yu)* Chinese, Pan Zinian noted the fatal weakness in Chinese language reform. For in his view, although vernacular Chinese had more or less triumphed over the classical after "May Fourth," in fact it had only created a "vernacular classical" at best, and "it had not produced a real *baihua* corresponding to the language the ordinary people use every day," or: "[It has not] created a Chinese national language out of the daily lives of the ordinary people—in part it is merely classical Chinese and in part merely foreign. As a result, although classical Chinese has been pushed aside for the time being, nothing new has been found to replace it. One either has to resort to using 'vernacular prose,' which is neither classical nor plain and sooner or later leads back to the classical, or one uses 'Europeanized sentences,' which are neither Chinese nor western."[70] Pan summed up the two requirements for the formation of a modern national language as a rich vocabulary and a comprehensive grammar, with the latter in some respects more important. A national language that met the requirement of having a "comprehensive grammar" could not be a dialect but had to be a new standard or generally used language. Therefore, he commented that "only after a common language or dialects and local patois that can be made a common language have contributed sufficient raw material for study can there be a real Chinese grammar."[71] The problem was how to decide which language was the "common language" or constituted "dialects and local patois that can be made into a common language."

What is missing here was the political relationship among localities, for what determined which dialect was the common language was not language itself but relationships dominated by politics, culture, and economics. Marx felt that natural languages were elevated into national languages, "partly as a result of the historical development of the language from preexisting material, as in the Romance and Germanic languages, partly owing to the crossing and mixing of nations, as in the English language, and partly as a result of the concentration of the dialects within a single nation brought about by economic and political concentration."[72] De Saussure said, "The reasons for the choice differ widely. Sometimes preference goes to the dialect of the region where civilization is most advanced or to the province that has political supremacy and wields the central power. Sometimes the court imposes its dialect on the nation."[73] As far as China is concerned, "the historical development of the language from pre-existing material" was among the reasons for Northern Chinese becoming the common language, because over 70 percent of the Chinese population used the northern dialects, but political authority was obviously an even more important factor. There are internal differences among the northern dialects, but the common speech clearly excluded such differences. Pan Zinian believed that the sources for a "grammatically complete language" included classical literature, folk and foreign languages, but never made clear the implications of the term "grammatically complete." If there was as yet no "grammar," how could which sort of language was "grammatically complete" be determined? We can see clearly that a "grammatically complete language" could not be a dialect or a local patois, nor could it be pure spoken language, but instead could only be "a brand new form."[74]

On December 15, 1939, Huang Sheng published an essay entitled "National Forms and the Language Issue" in the literary supplement of the Hong Kong newspaper *Da gong bao*, in which the logic of the exposition was very similar to Pan's. He pointed out that "The creation of national forms marks a new stage in the development of literature and signifies a movement for literary reform. At the beginning of this stage and as the reform is put into practice, we will immediately run into a crisis of language. The national forms movement must be accompanied by a reform movement in literary language."[75] Huang Sheng thought through the "national forms" issue from the linguistic angle, particularly oral language, regarding the "creation of national forms" as a reform movement in post–"May Fourth" literature, and raised clear doubts about the limits of the movement for vernacular writing: "In relation to the demands for the creation of national forms, how should we deal with literary language after May Fourth?"[76]

The importance of Huang Sheng's essay lies not only in the fact that he so clearly approached the issue of "national forms" from the linguistic perspective, but even more in his clear awareness of conflict between the westernizing tendencies of the "May Fourth" *baihua* movement and "national forms," dialects and local patois in particular. It was from this that he developed his critique of the limitations of the "May Fourth" language reform movement, even as he ultimately critiqued the Chinese national language by reaffirming that "May Fourth" was characterized by its basis in Western language. This is evidently because, first, if dialect and local patois are made to be characteristic of "national forms," this eliminates the possibility of a unified set of "national forms" taking shape, even eliminating the possibility of "localizing" the "national" linguistic issue. Second, it is because dialect and local patois are in conflict with the post–"May Fourth" language movement in two respects: one conflict was with the cosmopolitan tendency toward phonetic spelling, the scientific and the logical, while the other was with the class-theory-based framework of "mass language." On one hand, Huang critiqued the limitations of the vernacular movement and its tendency to compromise, saying "the real living spoken language is relegated to an auxiliary position, along with classical Chinese." On the other hand, he also criticized "the adoption of foreign languages, as the casual importation of European and Japanese grammar divorces literary language from the masses," even going so far as to reaffirm Qu Qiubai's sharp critique of *baihua* during the mass language movement, saying that the vernacular is "the exclusive property of the high bourgeoisie and the intellectuals. Furthermore, it has come to a sudden halt and it could even be said that it long ago set out on the road of compromise and surrender, producing a kind of comprador writing system completely incomprehensible to the masses and full of the taint of both Europeanization and the eight-legged essay style."[77]

On the basis of these two ideas, Huang Sheng concluded: "National forms are the negation of the literary forms that have developed since May Fourth, and they are unavoidably the sublation *(yangqi)* of literary language since that time."[78] Criticizing "May Fourth" language from within the framework of class theory was expressed mainly as a demand for greater "massification," but was not a negation of the basic trend toward developing a "common language." If, however, the criticisms of the "May Fourth" vernacular movement were linked to the issues of dialect and localism, then the possibility of conflict with massification could have arisen. This would have been unacceptable as part of the historical process of nationalism, so, after making the judgment cited above, Huang immediately added "dialectically":

> It is important to note that so-called sublation is not entirely a matter of discarding but rather a combination of elimination on the one hand and preservation and development on the other. As far as the literary language since May Fourth, we cannot but preserve and develop its actively progressive elements. To be consumed by fear that "the masses will not understand" and therefore completely avoid new literary vocabulary and idioms would be foolish.[79]

In order to explain the historical rationality of "Europeanized *baihua*," he develops his argument in two ways. First, he uses the concepts of the times and of progress to link the language issue to the question of the "consciousness of the times," thus completely substituting the relationship between the old and the new times for that between the "intellectuals" and the "masses" as a way to resolve the absolute opposition between the two.

> Language changes with change in social consciousness. The language of the feudal era expressed feudal consciousness, whereas the language of the democratic revolutionary era expresses the consciousness of the democratic revolution. Therefore, literary language since "May Fourth" is without question more progressive than that which went before and some of that must be taken up in national forms. To try to avoid it deliberately would not only belittle linguistic art but also obstruct the expression of advanced ideas.

Second, he uses the scientific tendency in modern culture to criticize the traits of the Chinese language and to reiterate his Western perspective on language:

Linguistic poverty and an absence of tight organization are the innate failings of our nation, and drawing on language from outside is a way to remedy this. Vocabulary and grammar from outside have, in fact, enriched our literary language, and thus have an actively progressive significance. We must, therefore, organically fuse European and Japanese vocabulary and grammar into national forms. In fact, the complexity of thought entails greater richness and tighter organization of language no matter what. The form of artistic works should draw closer to the masses, but neither can we scant them depth and range of thought. Cultural workers must draw closer to the masses even as they must absorb the complex language of advanced countries to educate them.[80]

Whether resorting to the concept of the times or to the logical nature of the Western languages, Huang Sheng's deliberations on the national form of language always reaffirm modernity as well as the cosmopolitan and nationalist trends in linguistic transformation. He can only take dialect and local patois seriously under the premise of modernity. Hence, the original query that required answering—"In relation to the demands for the creation of national forms, how should we deal with literary language since May Fourth?"—now turns in another direction and becomes an almost completely opposite question: "In relation to the demands for the creation of national forms, how should we deal with old forms, i.e., the language of folk literature?"[81] Reflection upon linguistic modernity is thus transformed into a proposition on linguistic modernity, and the challenge to the modern vernacular posed by "national forms" is turned into critique of "old forms." As a result, Huang's conclusions change completely: the transformation of social consciousness has led to the language of work popular with the masses becoming "the dead vernacular of old novels"; the writing of men of letters in the "old forms" mixed in many classical Chinese elements, and has become "the stale prose of the old literati"; "much of the language of folk literature is ordinary, 'ready made,' 'uncreative,' derivative. . . . It is monotonous;" the work of literati hacks is chock full of "fatalistic and reactionary feudal consciousness, something unavoidable even in the writings of the masses. It is a poisonous language that depends on this consciousness for its existence." Thus, although "national forms" in theory represent a new stage in linguistic transformation since "May Fourth," Huang in fact reaffirms "May Fourth" values, condemning the folk, feudal, and literati linguistic heritage, adding only that "adopting the language of the masses" should be taken seriously and invoking the quite ordinary slogan of "reinvention:"

> Therefore, we advocate learning language from the masses and using vernacular dialect and local patois critically so that our work may gain local color and so that national character can be expressed through this local color. Naturally, we do not advocate the indiscriminate use of dialect and local patois, nor do we recognize the possibility of so-called "local patois literature." For the most part, local patois is backward, disorderly, and pays no attention to grammar. Only after selection, refinement and reinvention can it be of any literary significance.[82]

We can now see that the mainstream of the modern language movement—that is, the vernacular movement—not only took the extinction of the multiplicity of oral language as a price it was willing to pay, but that it was also accompanied by a kind of cultural filtering. In this sense, the formation of the dominant position held by the modern nation-state over culture was closely connected to the modern language movement.

The Negation of the Negation of the "May Fourth" Vernacular Movement

In fact, treating "national forms" according to this logic, one can only affirm that the new forms created by "May Fourth" are also "national forms." Ba Ren, for example, held:

> It can be said that the new literary forms since May Fourth are mostly reflections of urban life, and in this they have taken on the key characteristics of western European literary forms. These forms have also, however, become national forms in our own literary history and, while they have not been widely accepted by the masses of our people, are evidently progressive. Although they depart from the unsophisticated formal structure of the actual language of the

masses, they are clearly already partially able to communicate relatively subtle thoughts and emotions. This strength is not something that must be abandoned, but, quite the contrary, must be taken up and developed further.[83]

Starting out by advocating linguistic transformation and "national forms" eventually leads back to modern history. And speaking of literature, this initially leads back to a reconsideration of "May Fourth," which is the basis for all the different positions of advocacy around these issues. What can be confirmed is that the main direction of the "national forms" discussion and the positing of the main criteria used in arguments about "local" and "folk" forms proceeded from reaffirming the historical significance of May Fourth and the value of modernity. For example, Zhou Yang maintained that:

> Seeking out vernacular novels from old folk forms and placing them in a position of literary orthodoxy has been one part of the work of the "May Fourth" literary revolution; another part has been the import into *baihua* of substantial quantities of foreign vocabulary and grammar suitable to the requirements of Chinese life. This has been done in order to make a more complete and rich modern Chinese language, to change the traditional Chinese novel into a freer and more concise modern form, and to have the old vernacular verse forms metamorphose into free verse. The distinct traces of the styles and tones of the old novel and verse forms could still be found in the vernacular novels and poetry of the early "May Fourth" period, although these were no longer old forms, but new ones. It cannot be denied that because of the short history of the new literature and the long separation between the Chinese written and spoken languages, the new national literary forms have yet to be perfected and there are still serious shortcomings in linguistic form. But it is beyond question that when compared with old forms, the new forms are progressive from any perspective. Their vocabulary is richer, their grammar more precise and their genres are freer and more lively, which bespeaks their power to give accurate expression to contemporary reality, that is, a heightened ability to do so.[84]

The examples of Pan Zinian, Huang Sheng, and Zhou Yang all show the steadfast and unshakable universal connotation of "national forms," and the use of dialect and the spoken language had to follow its logic. In fact, the linguistic logic of this universalism was not just nationalistic but also "internationalist," or cosmopolitan. This is why "local forms," which were characterized by dialect and spoken language, were accommodated under the rubric of a general language, even though this general language and its norms had yet to actually take shape. If, however, we read Hu Feng's "On the Putting Forward and Debate of the National Forms Issue," we can see that urban and Western languages still determined the proposed norms.

In this essay, Hu Feng lays out the historical process produced by literary massification. When he comes to the 1930s debate on "mass literature," he recalls that the starting point for that debate was "the negation of the 'vernacular' of the new literature of 'May Fourth,' which was said to be a 'new Europeanized classical Chinese . . . divorced from the masses of the ordinary people' and that revolutionary mass literature should use 'the common speech of the rising classes, . . . an already extant Chinese common speech being produced by people who have come from all across the land to the big cities and modern factories."[85] Hu Feng saw the debate about the language used in "mass literature" as

> striving to develop all the self-criticism attempted by the massification movement . . . because as soon as that movement moved on to creative practice—which could represent the lives of the masses and be understood by them—it was inevitable that it would bump into the differences between the language of literature and the spoken language of the masses, which produced a problem concerning the basic component of literature, the written language. . . . The raising of this issue did not yield any great theoretical results aside from the fact that the two points of contention—the criticism of the new May Fourth *baihua*, and the counter-criticism of that criticism (which proved analytically that the "common speech of the rising classes" did not actually exist and that "the new westernized classical Chinese" required re-evaluation) contained some truth—even if only partial. But the discussion also raised the issue of demands for dialect

literature and of a phonetic spelling of dialects and local patois, followed hard on its heels by advance notice of a great new movement for linguistic reform.[86]

Hu Feng concludes that the great contribution of the "massification movement," the "demands for dialect literature and of a phonetic spelling of dialects and local patois" was deeply significant over the long term. This demonstrates that modern language reform was not a movement to use the spoken language or dialects to refashion the written language, but rather to create a new pronunciation via the movement for phonetic spelling to accompany the formation of a modern written language, which would lead to a "general language," namely, common speech (*putonghua*). Thus, the modern language movement, with written and spoken forms consistent with one another as its defining feature, did not take existing spoken language as the basis for the reform of written language, but produced a new, phonetically driven language that included spoken and written components. In evaluating the 1934 movement for linguistic reform, Hu Feng made a point of adding the attributive "national citizenry" before the concept of the "masses," something plainly done to accommodate the nationalism of the War of Resistance, but that also resonates with the "May Fourth" idea of "National Language." He wrote:

> By the time the movement for mass language had developed into the New Latinization Writing Movement, the nature of the problem had already moved far beyond what literary language was being used to become a link in the cultural portion of the national citizens' mass movement for liberation. This movement, headed by Lu Xun, explained in theory that the writing system had to be able to record, refine and improve their spoken language, and to reflect the content, color and rhythm of the their lives, so that it could be used by the citizens themselves as a weapon for the reflection and critique of life. This is a case of moving from a high degree of diversity (dialect culture, the dialect literary movement) toward achieving a singular unity as rich as the life of the citizens itself (the national unified language and citizens' literature of the future).... Furthermore, young scholars of linguistics have undertaken substantial practical activities: the

creation of a program for a living alphabet for Northern Chinese and some publications, plans for alphabets for the Shanghai, Ningbo, Cantonese, and Amoy dialects, the publishing of dialect serials and textbooks, establishing research associations and classes for local dialects. . . . This has laid a foundation that, although far from meeting our actual needs, can nonetheless serve as a starting point. Thus, the mass language movement has not only spread the substance of massification to the entire creative sphere via the issue of literary language, but also, through the matter of the linguistic refashioning of the national citizenry, it has also made the substance of massification into one wing of the political movement of the citizenry and the masses against old consciousness and of the struggle for the new. Thus, the cultural struggle of the national citizenry and the masses has become conjoined by this particular process, a union that clearly expresses the much remarked upon "advanced consciousness."[87]

Hu Feng mentions the recording of spoken language, and stresses refinement and improvement even more, not to mention moving from a high degree of formal diversity toward achieving a singular unity. He describes the Latinization movement as a "struggle against the fetishism of Chinese characters,"[88] but it is just these characters that have kept modern Chinese together, that have given it its "singular unity." Even as he affirms the necessity of research into dialect and dialect literature, Hu Feng also affirms "the new 'May Fourth' literature and its 'vernacular'" and opposes seeing *baihua* as "a new westernized classical Chinese."[89] He quotes commentators to the effect that, formally, the basic vernacular vocabulary and grammar is also a fundamental part of the spoken language of the laboring masses, and that, in content, the vernacular had created a good deal of advanced literary work and that it was the only tool for the translation of theory.[90] It is precisely on this basis that Hu Feng insists that "massification cannot be divorced from the 'May Fourth' tradition, because it must constantly conform to the demand for realistic reflection of and critique of life; the 'May Fourth' tradition cannot separate itself from massification, for its natural orientation is toward union with the masses."[91]

It is not coincidental that in the end the issues of "local forms" and "dialects and local patois" could only be subsidiary in the debate over "national forms." In the quest for setting up a modern nation-state, a general national language and artistic forms that transcended the local were always among the most important means for building cultural unity. Between the old and the new, the urban and the rural, the modern and the folk, the nation and class, local culture could not garner an autonomous theoretical basis. At some later stage, I will take a look at the relationships between new and old and the modern and the folk so as to further interrogate the modernist logic that dominated the "national forms" debate.

4

The "Tibetan Question" East and West: Orientalism, Regional Ethnic Autonomy, and the Politics of Dignity

Prologue

On March 14, 2008 (and for a short period thereafter), in Tibet, in the Aba region of Sichuan, and in the Tibetan areas of Qinghai and Gansu, there occurred riots that took the form of successive attacks on local shops—mostly those belonging to Han people and Muslims—and antigovernment demonstrations. The attention of the Western public immediately focused on Lhasa, the Dalai Lama, and the Tibetan exile community, with the official Chinese media launching a counterattack on Western public opinion. Both sides focused on the violence and on the overseas Tibetan independence movement, devoting little attention to discussing the causes of the "3/14" incident from the perspective of the social crisis it represented. At almost the same time, the passing of the Olympic torch through the entire world had just begun and in such West-

Translated by Theodore Huters

ern cities as Paris, London, and San Francisco encountered serious obstruction from Tibetan exile groups as well as from Western supporters of Tibetan independence, with Western politicians and the mainstream media offering one-sided criticisms of China. Spurred on by this situation, Chinese students and citizens studying and working abroad launched efforts to support the Olympic torch as well as massive demonstrations of protest against the prejudice expressed in the Western media and the movements to boycott the Olympic Games. Within China, aside from official reports relating to these events, the younger generation began an Internet campaign—an unprecedented phenomenon—to oppose these Western expressions of public opinion. All of these events created a highly dramatic situation, one that contained within it the potential for any number of transformations: how to understand the attitudes of Western society toward the question of Tibet; how to understand the Tibet crisis in the context of Chinese market reform; how to regard the intervention into this matter by a new generation of people, both at home and abroad. Even more important, however, is the question: Why did these two quite opposed responses concentrate on nationalism and not on the social conditions that occasioned the Tibetan crisis? All these are highly significant questions posed both to contemporary China and to the world at large. I am not an expert on Tibet, but given the gravity and urgency of this issue, I will put myself at some risk to venture forth a few embryonic opinions of my own, in the hope of eliciting further discussion and criticism. The two extremes of opinion on Tibet represented by the response to the events of March 14 make it difficult to find any middle ground on which to carry out a discussion in which both sides can participate. It is my hope, however, that by analyzing the situation in the light of a series of factors peculiar to Tibetan history and the international relations of the region, at least some of the confusion might be cleared away.

The Phantasms of Two Orientalisms

Following the outbreak of the Tibetan riots, the intensity of the attitudes of the Western media and society as well as the political response of Chinese all over the globe attracted a good deal of notice. Let us first take up the question of the reaction of Western society to this question. In fact, a variety of people are supporting "Tibetan independence," and aside from those critiquing Chinese politics from the viewpoint of democracy and human rights, there are three matters worthy of particular note from a historical perspective. First is that Western knowledge of Tibet is deeply rooted in an orientalist mind-set, and while this has been analyzed by scholars, such analysis has yet to exert any fundamental influence on the attitudes of Western society toward Tibet.[1] Relatively speaking, this factor has been particularly influential on Europeans. Second is the manipulation of public opinion by a specific political force and the organization of a political operation, something particularly relevant to the United States. Third, sympathy for Tibet contains an admixture of concern, fear, aversion, and rejection of China, as well as toward its rapid economic rise and, specifically, toward its radically different political system. On this last point, aside from a substantial number of Third-World countries, the entire world has been affected. These three points are related not only to nationalism, but even more to colonialism, imperialism, the history of the Cold War and global inequality. The three questions are not isolated from one another, but they do need to be kept analytically distinct. I will first take up the question of orientalism and its influence on Cold War cultural politics. When I was in Switzerland in 2001, I visited a museum exhibit entitled "Dreamworld Tibet—Western and Chinese Phantoms." The curator of the exhibit, the anthropologist Dr. Martin Brauen, had a passionate devotion to Tibetan Buddhism culture from an early age, as well as having adored the Dalai Lama, but as he grew a bit older, he began to wonder just why it was that he had developed his passion for Tibetan Buddhism and culture in the first place. It was just this process of self-reflection that brought him to the decision to use the form of a museum exhibition to portray the images of Tibet, Tibetan Buddhism, and the Dalai Lama in the Western world. This exhibit curated by Dr. Brauen, as well as the recent release of the American CIA files on the Tibet of the 1950s, provided me with important leads for thinking about the "Tibet question." In the space below I will sum up the materials I saw at the museum as well as analyze the reading I did later on the subject.

    Edward Said took the study of Islam as the centerpiece of his analysis of European orientalism. He regarded this field of study as the means by which the Orient was dealt with and positioned in the Western European experience, with the Orient becoming a constituent part of the composition of European culture and material civilization, the "other" against which Europe established itself. As far as Europe was concerned, the Orient was neither a pure fabrication nor a phantasm, but was also not a natural entity—it was, rather, a structure of praxis and theory created by humans, which contained a long historical accumulation on the material level. The study of Tibet has all along occupied an important place in orientalism, something that has never been seriously sorted out. Tibet has also never been studied from within the framework of Chinese studies, something that has been the case from the very beginning of orientalism and continues up to the present, and from this taxonomy of knowledge, one can get a sense of the relationship between China and Tibet in the Western imagination. The form of the relationship is precisely as Said described it—it is more accurate to think of it as a system fabricated by the human mind rather than as a natural occurrence.

The Swiss scholar Michael Taylor's *Mythos Tibet: Entdeckungsreisen von Marco Polo bis Alexandra David-Neel* describes the exploration of and incursions into Tibet by Europeans from the 1245 visit by the disciple of Saint Francis himself, Jean-du PlanCarpin, right up until the beginning of the twentieth century, thereby providing us a rich set of original materials about the early period of Tibetan studies.[2] The object of the visits of early missionaries to Tibet was to locate lost Christians, as they believed that Tibetans were the descendants of Prester John, the twelfth-century Christian king of legend who defeated the heterodox, the Persians, and Medeans in battle. According to legend, Prester John had lived somewhere in Central Asia. In other words, in the early European imagination the Tibetans were the disciples or adherents of the Christians who had propagated the gospel throughout Asia Minor, Central Asia, and China during the early medieval period. Of course, not all missionaries shared this view of the Tibetans—the Capuchins and Jesuits differed, holding that Buddhism was the creation of Satan, because only the cunning of Satan could have produced a religion so clearly similar to Christianity. These two diametrically opposed views of Tibet and Tibetan Buddhism have never really disappeared, and they surface and vanish in various incarnations throughout the Enlightenment and secular eras. Regardless of whether Tibet is seen as another home of Christianity or a world "clearly similar to Christianity" created by "the cunning of Satan," both views are part of the way in which "the Orient was dealt with and accommodated on the basis of the position of the Orient in the Western European experience," and I accordingly label them as two phantasms of orientalism.

One of the founders of Tibetan studies in Europe was the Roman Ippolito Desideri (1684–1733), another Catholic missionary who followed in the steps of the Portuguese missionary Fr. Antonio de Andrade, who had visited Tibet in 1623. Desideri left Rome on September 27, 1712, for Lisbon, where he embarked, eventually arriving in Goa on September 23 the next year. After traveling through India with some companions, he departed from Delhi for Srinagar in Ladakh, finally reaching Lhasa on March 17, 1716. He lived in Tibet for five years, experiencing the invasion of the Dzungar Mongols, thoroughly studying Tibetan culture, and translating five works into Tibetan so as to propagate the gospel. His views of Tibet clashed with those of the Capuchin monks, and he also criticized a number of the misleading views and prejudices of Western missionaries. For instance, he reported on such things as the Tibetans' wars and their combative character, but in the end settled upon the fixed perspective that Tibet was a peaceful land, a perspective that was to prove exceedingly influential for the view of that land in the West.[3]

Herder, Kant, and Hegel on Tibet

Eighteenth- and nineteenth-century European philosophers like Rousseau, Kant, and Hegel were all critical of Tibetan Buddhism, but Herder and a number of others, basing their views on the similarity between Tibetan Buddhism and Christianity, had a relatively favorable view of the Tibetan religion. No matter what their outlook on Tibetan Buddhism, however, the perceptions of these modern European thinkers can not only be traced back to missionary narratives, but they were also rooted in different attitudes toward Catholicism. Let us look first at Herder's positive view of Tibetan Buddhism:

> Between the mountains and wastes of the vast Asian mass there has been established a religious kingdom that must be regarded as unique; it is the realm of the Lamas. In spite of the fact that small-

scale revolutions have separated the religion from secular authority, they eventually and invariably were reunited. In respect of the constitution of imperial power in the hands a group of high-ranking monks, there is no place like it. In accord with the notion that the soul of the Sakyamuni or the Buddha can be transmitted to the next generation, the soul of the great lama can be transmitted to become a new lama after his death, and be regarded as a manifestation of the sacred. This definitive sacred order establishes a chain linking the great lama to the various other levels of lamas. There have been almost no other examples of such a firmly established theocratic rule such as this one arising out of the tenets of this religion from the roof of the world.[4]

This description reveals a faint debt to the legend of the lost Christians in Tibet. Buddhism's origins in the warm south in such places as India and Siam show up in its characteristic mercy, pacifism, forbearance, gentleness, and stagnation, but because of the harsh natural conditions in which it was situated, Tibetan Buddhism developed characteristics similar to those of Catholicism. As Herder wrote:

If we ask which religion regards the mortal world in the most horrible and terrifying light, that would be Lamaism. It is as if—and this is something that cannot be entirely ruled out—the most severe tenets and rules of Christianity have been transplanted here and have on the Tibetan plateau taken on a more fearsome visage than anywhere else. It is a matter for rejoicing, however, that this stern Lamaism has not been able to transform the national spirit, just as it has been unable to transform their needs or the climate.[5]

In another passage, Herder directly compares the Dalai-Panchen system to the papal institution of the Catholic Church, believing that Tibetan Buddhism is a "papal religion":

Tibetan Buddhism is a papal religion, like that of Europe in the dark middle ages; the latter, however, lacks the commendable order and morality of the Tibetans and Mongolians. Among the people of the high plateau, and even among the Mongolians, Lamaism propagates a kind of broad learning and textual language that is a real contribution to humanity, and is perhaps a supplementary cultural means of preparing these people for maturity.[6]

Herder's concern for Tibet was concentrated strictly in the realm of religion, something that is still quite prevalent today. Differing from Herder's Catholic theological view of Tibetan Buddhism, Kant's perspective was ethnological and linguistic. His discourse provided the thread for Hegel's reconstruction of "world history." In his 1795 "Third Definitive Article of Perpetual Peace, *'Cosmopolitan Right Shall Be Limited to the Conditions of Universal Hospitality*,'" Kant initially takes "hospitality" as a "question of right," and defines this right as a "right of temporary sojourn," different from the "right to be a permanent visitor." This is a right "to which all human beings have a claim, to present oneself to society by virtue of the right of common possession of the surface of the earth. Since it is the surface of a sphere, they cannot scatter themselves on it without limit, but they must rather ultimately tolerate one another as neighbors, and originally no one has more of a right to be at a given place on earth than anyone else." When people exercise this "right of hospitality," "In this way, remote parts of the world can establish relations peacefully with one another, relations which ultimately become regulated by public laws and can thus finally bring the human species ever closer to a cosmopolitan constitution."[7] Western "sojourners," however, in the name of "establishing economic undertakings," conquered other lands and peoples, thus overstepping "the privilege of foreign arrivals." "America, the negro countries, the Spice Islands, the Cape, etc., were at the time of their discovery lands that they regarded as belonging to no one, for the native inhabitants counted as nothing to them. In East India (Hindustan) they brought in foreign troops under the pretext of merely intending to establish trading posts. But with these they introduced the oppression of the native inhabitants, the incitement of the different states involved to expansive wars, famine, unrest, faithlessness, and the whole litany of evils that weigh upon the human species."[8]

Following close upon this passage, Kant brought up the intercourse among Europe, China, and Japan. He wrote: "China and Japan *(Nipon)*, which have attempted dealing with such guests, have therefore, wisely, limited such interaction. Whereas the former has allowed contact with, but not entrance to its territories, the latter has allowed this contact to only one European people, the Dutch, yet while doing so it excludes them, as if they were prisoners, from associating with the native inhabitants."⁹ In discussing China, Kant brought up China and Tibet by way of a footnote, demonstrating a disposition to define China from the perspective of Tibet. He wrote:

> In order to call this great empire by the name it gives itself (namely, *China*, not Sina, or any other sound similar to this), one need only refer to Georgius's *Alphabetum Tibetanum*, pp. 651–654, note b in particular (Antonio Agostino Giorgi [1711–1797], *Alphabetum Tibetanum missionum apostolicarum commodo editum* [Tibetan Dictionary Published for the Convenience of Apostolic Missions] [Rome, 1762], a Latin-Tibetan dictionary, based in part on works of Francesco Orazio). Actually it uses no particular name to refer to itself, according to Professor *Fischer* from Petersburg (Johann Eberhard Fischer [1697–1771], Quaestiones Petropolitanae (Questions from St. Petersburg) [Göttingen, 1770]); the most common is the word *Kin*, which means gold (the Tibetans express this with *Ser*), which explains why the emperor is called the King of *Gold* (of the most magnificent land in the world). In the empire itself, however, this word probably sounds like *Chin*, which is pronounced by the Italian missionaries as *Kin* (due to their inability to pronounce the guttural consonant *ch*).—This leads one to conclude that the Land of the People of *Ser*, as it was referred to by the Romans, was China, but silk was transported via *Greater Tibet* to Europe (presumably through *Lesser Tibet*, Bukhara, Persia, and so on), which has led to many speculations about the age of this astonishing state in comparison to that of Hindustan by means of its association with *Tibet* and, through the latter, with Japan. The name *Sina* or *Tschina*, on the other hand, which neighboring territories give this land, leads to no such connection.¹⁰

Kant's interest in China arose out of an interest in world history in which east and west were connected via the Silk Road, but he was never clear about the true thread underlying this thoroughfare. There are three notable points in Kant's discussion: first, that he understood China through European missionary knowledge of Tibet; second, his stress on the notion that "there is no definite word used in that country as its name," resulting in its seeming natural to delimit China via Tibetan phonetics; third, his separation of Greater and Lesser Tibet so as to explain that the Silk Road linking China and Europe had Tibet as its intermediary.

The article of faith that there was an ancient and mystical link between Europe and Tibet constituted the core of Kant's view of Tibet. In the paragraph that followed, Kant discussed Tibet by pursuing the connection between ancient Greece and Tibetan religion rather than addressing it from the perspective of the relationship between Tibet and European religion, with his discourse being framed in philological terms. He wrote:

> Perhaps the ancient, although never widely known connection between Europe and Tibet also can be explained by what has been passed on to us by *Hesychius* (Hesychius of Alexandria, fifth- or sixth-century grammarian who compiled a Greek dictionary) regarding this, namely, the Hierophant's (Hierophant: in ancient Greece, leader of the Eleusinian cult) call *(Konx Ompax)* in the *Eleusinian Mysteries* (cf. *Journey of the Young Anacharsis* [Jean-Jacques Barthelemy, *Voyage du jeune Anacharsis en Grèce, dans le milieu du quatrième siècle avant l'ere vulgaire*, 5 vols. [Travels of the Young Anacharsis through Greece, in the Middle of the Fourth Century before the Beginning of the Common Era] (Paris, 1788)], part 5, p. 447 et seq.). For according to Georgius's *Alphabetum Tibetanum*, the word *concioa* means *God*, which bears a striking similarity to *Konx*, whereas *Pah-cio* (ibid., p. 520), which the Greeks may well have pronounced like *pax*, means *promulgator legis*, the divinity that suffuses all of nature (also called *Cencresi*, p. 177).—But *Om*, which La Croze (Mathurin Veyssiere de La Croze [1661–1739], Benedictine monk and historian) translates as *benedictus (blessed)*, applied to divinity can hardly mean anything other than the *beatific* (p. 507). Yet given that Father Francisco Orazio (Francisco Orazio [1680–1747], the Capuchin monk who provided descriptions of life in Tibet, where he lived from 1716 to 1732), having often asked the Tibetan *Lamas* what they understood God *(Concioa)* to be, always received the following

answer: *"It is the gathering of all blessed ones"* (i.e., of all the blessed souls that have returned to the deity through rebirth as the lama after many migrations through all manner of bodies, and thus as *Burchans*, souls transformed into beings worthy of adoration [p. 223]), the mysterious word *Konx Ompax* is likely to mean the *holy* (Konx), *blessed* (Om), and *wise* (Pax) highest beings existent throughout the entirety of the world (personified nature) and, as used in the Greek *Mysteries*, likely referred to the *monotheism* of the epopts in contrast to the *polytheism* of the people, even though Father *Orazio* (loc. cit.) detected a variety of atheism here.—But how that mysterious word came to the Greeks via Tibet can be explained in the aforementioned manner and, conversely, make a case for Europe's early contact with China through Tibet (a connection perhaps even more likely than that with Hindustan).[11]

Prior to the discovery of the Indo-European system of languages by European historical linguists in the nineteenth century, many Europeans believed that Tibetan and the European languages belonged to the same family, and Kant's view represents the expression of this common belief. By consulting Kant's writings on questions of race from his "pre-critical period," we find the key racial components of his understanding of Tibet. In his "On the Various Races of Mankind," published in 1775, Kant used the methodology of Botany and Zoology to divide humankind into four races, that is, the white race, the black race, the Huns (*Xiongnu*, that is, the Mongols or Kalmyks) and the Indians or Hindustanis. The Tibetans were part of the ancient Scythians (also translated as "Skutai"), with Indians, Japanese, and Chinese being the product of mixing between the Scythians, the ancient Indians, and the Huns.[12] In the ethos of eighteenth-century European thought, discussion of racial origins and national characteristics was closely intertwined with discussion of the spirit of the times. Kant used "sublime" to praise the spirit of antiquity while using "strange" to denigrate contemporary transformations. For instance, he described the Crusaders and medieval chivalry as "adventurous," while calling the duels that resulting from the remnants of the latter spirit as "strange." The passion evoked in principled self-restraint he regarded as "sublime," while venerating sacred bones and wood and the holiness of the lamasery were seen as "strange."[13]

It is difficult to judge whether or not Kant's views of Tibet influenced those of Hegel. The latter was inspired by the discovery of the Indo-European family of languages, but he never addressed the matter of the Tibetan language. His attitude toward Eastern religions was in the same vein as Kant's Enlightenment views, resulting in a particular definition of Tibet resting between the ancient "sublime" and the modern "strange." Hegel basically did not acknowledge that China had any religion, and when he happened to mention the Dalai Lama, he put the latter in the category of primitive worship of the supernatural. In thus contrasting philosophy and religion, Hegel manifests a distinctively Enlightenment attitude. In the *Philosophy of Mind* he wrote:

> To substitute polytheism for atheism in castigating philosophy is largely the product of contemporary education, that is the New Piety and the New Theology; in their view philosophy has too many gods, they being assured these gods being so numerous as to make God be everything and everything be God. Because this sort of theology reduces religion to a more subjective feeling, not to mention denying any capacity to know God in His essence, only an ordinary god lacking any objective qualities remains. It has no interest in any concept of a real and substantive god, and takes any such concept as something that people once were interested in. Moreover, it treats anything belonging to a theory of substantive divinity as a kind of historical artifact. An unspecified god can be found in any religion; any form of piety—that of Indians towards monkeys and cows or the piety toward the Dalai Lama; the piety of the ancient Egyptians towards bulls, etc.—are all examples of worship of something, and no matter how absurd the stipulations of the worship of that object, they all manifest the type, the abstraction of the universal divinity.[14]

In terms of knowledge of Tibet, "treating anything belonging to a theory of substantive divinity as a kind of historical artifact" is a common practice, and, in fact, is the virtual equivalent of knowledge about Tibet. This form of knowledge is produced not just by understanding Tibet as a religious society, but also derives from a disposition that combines a resolve to enlightenment with determination both to discard religion and not really discard it. As Hegel wrote: "direct knowledge should be the standard for truth, and from this we can derive a second condition, namely that all superstitions and veneration of idols have been declared to be truthful, and even the content of the most unfair and immoral wills has been taken as proper. Indians did not go through a so-called indirect process of cognition, consideration and reasoning to conclude that cows, monkeys, Brahmins and Lamas are sacred, but this is rather a matter of belief."[15] The contrasts between truth and superstition, knowledge and faith is one of the most important tenets of the Enlightenment, and Hegel bases himself on this in placing Tibetan Buddhism and other things he regards as vulgar myths and idol worship in the same category. Even in Hegel's lifetime, however, the power of religion had not completely faded away, and in his narrative of world history the mystical East availed itself of this universal historical narrative to embed itself firmly in history's depths.

Theosophy and the Image of Tibet

Following in the wake of industrialization, urbanization, and secularization, a new kind of mysticism targeting Enlightenment idealism began to permeate social life and culture. Since it resulted from doubts concerning modernity, it was unlike early religious faith, but this new mysticism took on a new life, similar to Herder's misgivings about the modern—the links between European views about Tibet and modern mysticism took hold in this context.

In the nineteenth and twentieth centuries, knowledge about Tibet became connected to Theosophy, a body of theory that posits wordless intuition as the means of communicating with the spirits. Helena Petrovna Blavatsky (1831–1891), who was born in the Ukrainian area of what was then Russia and died in England, became known for having founded Theosophy. From the time she was a child she had been afflicted by hysteria and epilepsy, often becoming possessed by strange and terrifying visions. She had several marriages after her first at age 17, but she claimed to have remained a virgin throughout. She also claimed to her biographer that between 1848 and 1858 she had traveled the world, visiting Egypt, France, England, Canada, South America, Germany, Mexico, Greece and, most important, having spent two years in Tibet before arriving in Ceylon and formally converting to Buddhism.

In 1873 she immigrated to the United States, where she proceeded to demonstrate her capacity for transcendence through the quasi-religious practice of spirit mediation and calling back the spirits of the dead, using such techniques as levitation, clairvoyance, out-of-body projection, telepathy, and clairaudience. In 1875 she joined with Henry Steel Olcott and a number of others to found the Theosophical Society.[16] Blavatsky claimed to have interacted spiritually with Tibetan masters, and published a series of mystical letters from Tibet. In fact, she had never been to Tibet, and the letters that were supposed to have been written by Tibetan lamas came from the Aryan Mahatmas instead. These letters, however, not only had a powerful influence on the study of Tibet, but also had a decisive influence on the formation of Theosophy. Blavatsky and her Theosophist followers disseminated a racialist perspective, holding that by far the greater part of the human race belonged to one of four root races, one of which was Tibetan. It was said that after the submergence of Lemuria and Atlantis, some survivors took up residence in a place near the Gobi Desert called Shambhala, and these people were the prototype of the fifth root race. Blavatsky thought that Shambhala was the motherland of the natural aristocracy of the earth, made up of Indo-Arians and Caucasians. According to Jackson Spielvogel and David Redles, Blavatsky's doctrines on root races, once combined with the interpretations of her German followers, were a "decisive" influence on Hitler's mental development.[17]

Theosophy created an ideal and surreal image of Tibet—a place unpolluted by civilization, marked by spirituality and mysticism, without hunger, crime, or drunkenness, a land separate from the world, inhabited by a race still possessed of an ancient wisdom. This image is greatly removed from the reality of the period of agricultural serfdom in Tibet, but has in various ways fashioned the Western understanding of the Orient, particularly of Tibet. At the core of this image lies a transcendent spirituality. Aside from Hitler, there are a substantial number of prominent and extremely influential people who were influenced by Blavatsky and Theosophy. I list just a few of them here: Sir Edwin Arnold (1832–1904), the English poet and journalist who wrote *The Light of Asia;* Swami Sivananda

Saraswati, the famous spiritual leader of Yoga and Vedanta; Mohandas K. Gandhi (1869–1949); Guido Karl Anton List, or Guido von List (1848–1919), Austro-German poet, mountain climber and important leader of the movement for a Teutonic revival, of Teutonic mysticism, and of the movement to revive the ancient Runic script; Alexander Scriabin (1872–1915), the Russian composer, pianist, and most important representative of the music of Russian symbolism; James Joyce (1882–1941), the Irish author of *Ulysses*; Wassily Kandinsky (1866–1944), the founder of Russian modernist painting and aesthetic theoretician; Alfred Kinsey (1894–1956), American biologist, entomologist, and famous sexologist; and William Butler Yeats (1865–1939), Irish poet and playwright. The links between Theosophy and this group of influential twentieth-century romantics, modernists, and nationalists are without exception based on misgivings about modernity—they were all engaged in an exhaustive and urgent search for an "alternative" world. I list these names not because of any particular opinions they have on Tibet, but rather to explain how in the modern Western cultural imagination, social psychology and political movements are all thoroughly suffused with mysticism, and the position of Tibet in the contemporary Western mental world is rooted within this.

1960s Gloom and the Image of the Lamas in Western Popular Culture

The study of Tibet in the postwar period has made great advances, and has attracted a number of outstanding scholars and important contributions. In James Hilton's *Lost Horizon*, Arnaud Desjardins's films about the secret lives of Tibetan spiritual masters, *Le Message des Tibétains: Le Bouddhisme (première partie)*, 1966 (I); *Le Message des Tibétains: Le Tantrisme (deuxième partie)*, 1966 (II); *Himalaya, Terre de Sérénité: Le Lac des Yogis (première partie)*, 1968; *Himalaya, Terre de Sérénité: Les Enfants de la Sagesse (deuxième partie)*, 1968, and other popular works like it, however, the influence of academic scholarship has been negligible, even if in academic work the shadow of orientalism has yet to completely disappear. Hilton's fabricated name of "Shangri-la" has already been adopted by the Zhongdian region of Yunnan Province as its new name. The Shangri-la story actually is an offshoot of Blavatsky's myth: a tale of Caucasian Buddhists living in a remote fastness. In this story, Tibet is but the background, with the author and actors being the Westerners who fantasize about Shambhala and Shangri-la. Hollywood films and all sorts of other forms of popular culture ceaselessly perpetuate these stories of Shambhala or Shangri-la, but they are doing nothing more than giving expression to fantasies from the Western world. Following upon catastrophic wars and the trauma of industrialization, Tibet—although it would be more accurate to label it Shambhala or Shangri-la—has become the fantasy world of numerous Westerners: a world at once mysterious, spiritual, inspiring, without modern technology, dedicated to peace, moral, and with access to a supernatural intelligence.

Matthieu Ricard, one of the two authors of *Le Moine et le Philosophe* (The monk and the philosopher), has said:

> It's a fact probably unprecedented in human history that of Tibet's population up to twenty percent were ordained—monks, nuns, hermits in retreat in caves, learned lamas teaching in the monasteries. Spiritual practice was beyond any doubt the principal goal in life, and lay people too saw their daily activities, however necessary, as being of secondary importance compared to their spiritual life. The whole country was centered around its religion.
>
> . . .
>
> I had the impression of seeing living beings who were the very image of what they taught. They had such a striking and remarkable feeling about them. I couldn't quite hit on the explicit reason why, but what struck me most was that they matched the ideal of sainthood, the perfect being, the sage—a kind of person hardly to be found nowadays in the West. It was the image I had of St. Francis of Assisi, or the great wise men of ancient times, but which for me had become figures of the distant past. You can't go and meet with Socrates, listen to Plato debating, or sit at St. Francis's feet. Yet suddenly, here were these beings who seemed to be living examples of wisdom. I said to myself: "If it's possible to reach perfection as a human being, that must be it."[18]

With the passing of time, the role of the Aryan lamas and the Caucasians in this myth has gradually faded away, replaced by the Tibetan lamas—

and it is better said that they are the creation of Westerners rather than the descendants of Tsong-kha-pa (1357–1419).[19] What I am addressing here is not the direct manipulation of Tibetan exile politics by the United States from 1959 on, but rather the role that a few lamas have come to play in Western elite and popular cultures. This role represents the accumulation of a complex self-understanding of modern Western society. Jean-François Revel describes how Tibetans represent a particular methodology resembling that of the original ancient philosophy of the West, where theory and practice "went together." "So we're talking about an attitude that certainly used to exist in the West—not just to be content with teaching, but to be the reflection of what you teach, in your very way of life. . . . In the age of classical philosophy, therefore, there was no fundamental difference between West and East."[20]

The image of Tibet circulating in the West deals directly with various sorts of alienation in modern society, like the slippage between the notion of a moral life and the creation and perfection of knowledge, such that it manifests itself as a model of spiritual life. "A lot of Westerners turn to a religion other than their own, like Islam and Buddhism, because they're disappointed by the religion they were born into. But in your case, you moved to Buddhism from a state of indifference to any religion, a kind of religious weightlessness."[21] It is in this sense that the crisis of modern society has created the outcome for the great Tibetan teachers in the West. Prior to May of 1968, just when the depression of Western youth had reached a peak and was about to erupt, numerous people turned their eyes in two different directions: one was a China brimming with cultural revolution and the other was a quiet and peaceful India, where lived the great Tibetan masters. What the two had in common was taking seriously spiritual practice and the transformation of the interior life.

> It was the year before 1968. All these people were looking for something different. Some were there to smoke marijuana, some were on a spiritual quest, visiting Hindu ashrams; others were exploring the Himalayas. Everyone was looking for something, here, there, and everywhere. Ideas and information were being exchanged all the time: "I met such-and-such an extraordinary person there . . . I saw this amazing landscape in Sikkim . . . I met this or that master of music in Benares . . . this or that Yoga teacher in south India," and so

on. It was a time when everything was being questioned, everything being explored—not only in books but in reality.²²

In 1971 the first group of Tibetan masters traveled to such Western countries as France and the United States and their followers gradually increased from the hundreds to the thousands to the tens of thousands and more. Many of these followers lived with these Tibetan masters in the Himalayas: "It's called 'mixing your mind with the teacher's mind,' the teacher's mind being wisdom and your mind being confusion. What happens then is that by means of 'spiritual union' you progress from confusion to wisdom. This purely contemplative process is one of the key points of Tibetan Buddhist practice."²³

From these two similar but quite opposite directions taken by Western youth in the 1960s, we can see that this move back to ancient philosophy via the mediation of the spirit of Tibet is, in fact, closely related to the political ideology of the Cold War period. We can say that those young people who looked toward China in seeking out the socialist ideal were following the Enlightenment tradition in moving toward Marxism, and those who believed that "the alliance of happiness and justice would no longer come about through the individual quest for wisdom but through the rebuilding of society as a whole. And before building a new society, the old one first had to be completely destroyed," found in the concept of "revolution" the possibility of combining theory and practice. On the other hand, the "liberal revolution" rejects the idea that the individual can find salvation by belonging to a collectivity, and believes that this idea will bring about political totalitarianism.²⁴ Tibet thus provides a way of conceiving of modern society outside the Enlightenment tradition—particularly in providing a path for thinking about high-technology society and its forms of political control. Revel sums up his political views as "rejecting both political and religious totalitarianism." "And that brings us back to what's called 'first philosophy,' focused on the personal attainment of perspicacity and wisdom."²⁵ From this perspective, the pursuit of spirituality and its attendant critique of modern society are allied with notion of an "open society," and at absolute odds with the socialist system—which in the liberal tradition is thought of as totalist—and its ideology.

With the end of the 1960s, the spirit of that period gradually infiltrated its way into popular culture; the oppositional spirit lost its internal tension and was gradually turned into a popular spiritual/commercial product, incorporating, intentionally or not, the ideologies of the Cold War and even of racism. All manner of related films, commercial products, works of art, and jewelry can be found in major stores, cinemas, and art galleries. "Dreamworld Tibet—Western and Chinese Phantoms" had many examples of this sort of thing as part of its exhibit, about which the curator inquired: "Why does it never occur to people that printing these sacred images on t-shirts is a sort of blasphemy?" Tibetan Buddhism encourages selfless dedication, but these commercial products exist in the service merely of a selfish desire for possession. Some Christians who have lost their faith have turned to Tibetan spirituality, but the Tibet they are turning to seems to be the abode of fashion rather than of spirit. Many Hollywood celebrities—who perhaps know nothing of Tibetan actualities—have become adepts of Tibetan Buddhism and antagonists of China. That such things have taken place in the central place of Western fashion should perhaps not be so surprising—we should at least gain an understanding of the cultural ethos at work here.

Tibet has a great civilization, and Tibetan Buddhism constitutes a venerable tradition, but their significance does not reside in the hallucinations of orientalism. Tibet must liberate itself from the images held by Westerners and the myths of Shangri-la before it can make genuine progress. The common image of Tibet presented by orientalism is nothing more than the self-projection of the West. In his discussion of orientalism, Said invoked Gramsci's notion of "hegemony," of which he said: "[it is] an indispensable concept for any understanding of cultural life in the industrial West. It is hegemony, or rather the result of cultural hegemony at work, that gives Orientalism the durability and strength I have been speaking about.... [T]he major component in European culture is precisely what made that culture hegemonic both inside and outside Europe: the idea of European identity as a superior one in comparison with all the non-European peoples and cultures." And "In a quite constant way, Orientalism depends for its strategy on this flexible *positional* superiority, which puts the Westerner in a whole series of possible relationships with the Orient without ever losing him the relative upper hand."[26] To this day,

Western society has not shaken off this sort of orientalist knowledge. Thus, those who are disappointed in their own society and the modern world can readily turn to the image of Tibet for spiritual solace, without a thought for the fact that their "Theosophy" or spiritualism not only runs counter to Tibetan history and current actuality, but also wounds those Chinese who have turned to them with open arms. Most Chinese have no idea that what they are facing are Westerners saturated in several centuries of orientalist knowledge, for whom Tibet is something purely internal or, rather, a wholly fabricated internal other. And when Westerners become aware of the huge gap between the actual Tibet and the factitious entity, there is an up rush of resentment—the existence of the Orient/Tibet is a necessary premise upon which their selfhood is constructed, so if this "other" suddenly takes its leave of this Western self, where is it going to lodge? In fact, Shambhala has long since ceased to exist in our globalized world, and if people have lost faith within their own world, there is no place else they can find it.

Orientalism is no longer exclusive to the West, but is also something we have created in China. The Zhongdian region of Yunnan Province's Tibetan areas has been formally renamed Shangri-la by its own local officials—the reason for the coronation of a territory inhabited by a number of ethnicities, including Tibetans, with this name from a Western fantasy is strictly to attract more tourists. When I visited the area in 2004, I went to a "model village" of Tibetan culture. In this tiny village was gathered virtually all varieties of Tibetan architecture and furnishings, but there never has been such a village thus characteristic of Tibetan culture. With symbols of Tibetan spiritualism having been transformed into emblems of commodity fetishism, just what sort of new Orientalist Theosophy and spiritualism are the masses of visitors trooping there from all over the world and all over China creating, with these cultural exhibits of "local" and "ethnic" products crafted to suit the Western imagination? And what are we doing in changing a living ethnic culture into an "other" suitable for tourists? When we criticize the Western orientalist imagination, do we not also need to take the analysis a bit deeper? In respect to these sorts of questions, we are in need of a good deal of self-criticism.

Variations on Colonialism and Nationalism

The Concept of Suzerainty and the "Politics of Recognition" in International Relations

The question of "Tibetan Independence" arose simultaneously with the extension to Asia by the West of its own imperialist politics of recognition, that is to say, a system of recognition based on the nation-state as the unit of sovereignty. When Western views of civilization, nationality, and sovereignty transformed the preexisting historical relationships of the Asian region and became norms for the entire world, older modes of political linkage that had been in effect for centuries in this region ceased to work. The distinguishing characteristic of the "Tibet question" is this: all Western countries, including the United States and Great Britain, recognize Tibet as part of China, as one of the autonomous regions of China—there is not a single country that publicly denies Chinese sovereignty over Tibet. This was true even in the late Qing and early Republican periods at the beginning of the last century, when Chinese sovereignty over Tibet was recognized, with a few exceptions, by Western countries in the various unequal treaties they imposed on China. From the perspective of international law the status of Tibet is completely clear. This issue, however, requires some explanation, to avoid having our sightlines blurred by this "politics of recognition."

First, historically there were throughout the world a number of complex types of relationships, such as that between the Ming dynasty and Tibet, and the pattern of fealty or the tribute system that characterized the relationship between Tibet and the Qing government. This fealty or tribute system, however, did not cohere to the pattern of the European nation-state, and as soon as these traditional relationships were incorporated into the system of European sovereignty, trouble followed. In the course of the nineteenth- and twentieth-century colonial history of Asia, Great Britain and the other powers concluded a number of different sorts of treaties, using the notion of "suzerainty" [English in original] to translate and define the complicated tribute/suzerain relationships in the Asian region, forcing the Qing dynasty to abandon its relationships of suzerainty over the kingdoms surrounding it, then moving these kingdoms into the sphere of control of the Western powers. This was the shift of suzerainty in the colonial era. In the discourse of European nationalism, the concept of "suzerainty" was originally used to describe the Ottoman Empire and its relationship with the territories that surrounded it, but during the nineteenth-century colonization of Asia, it came to be applied to the Qing and its relations with territories around it. The key point here is that relationships of suzerainty include different historical forms, or that there are different types of suzerain relationships. In the nineteenth and twentieth centuries suzerain relationships among imperialist countries and colonies mostly took place between suzerain industrial countries and agricultural or less-developed areas, with close relations of economic dependence between them. Once imperialist suzerain relationships were established, the colonial economic structure not only became part of the suzerain nation's industrial system, but social relations and the political structures of the dependencies were also substantially transformed. In contrast, the Asian tribute network did not generally demand such a compulsory division of labor, the economy of the suzerain nation not requiring economic contributions from the dependencies.

Suzerain relations under imperialism and those of the Asian tribute network and its dependencies diverged sharply from one another, differing in essence. Once the suzerain imperialist nations used the concept of suzerainty to describe European imperialist history and to equate it with enfeoffment, tribute, and dependency relations in the Asian region; and to create in the Chinese context an intertranslatability between "suzerainty" on the one hand and "tribute-enfeoffment-dependency" on the other, not only did the important historical differences among the two sets of ideas disappear, but the complex evolution of the relations between Tibet and the central Chinese empire was also ignored. "Tribute" is an ambiguous concept, taking different forms in different historical periods. The relationship between Tibet and the Yuan, Ming, and Qing dynasties is often described in terms of the concept of tribute, but there were important differences in each case. For example, the Yuan established a central office—the *Xuanzheng yuan*—specifically dedicated to managing Tibet as well as matters having to do with Buddhism. It also divided the Tibetan region into three districts under Offices of Pacification *(xuanwei si)*. The Ming carried on the Yuan system of rule, but changed the three

Pacification Offices into three offices of Commandatory Emissaries *(zhihui shi si)*. Under the influence of the notion of "discriminating between the Chinese and outsiders" *(Hua-yi zhi bian)*, however, the relationship between the Ming court and Tibet gradually changed from one between center and locality to a classic tribute relationship.

The Qing imperial authority combined in itself the multiple roles of the rule of Mongol Khans, the central emperor, Manchu clan elder, and the Manjusri Buddha sacred to Tibetans. The Resident in Tibet and the stationing of troops there indicate the relationship of subordination between Tibet and the central government, but this relationship of subordination was not like that with the provinces of inland China, something that can be seen clearly from the establishment of the Court for Managing the External *(Lifan yuan)*. The Court had been set up in 1636 as the Mongol Office *(Menggu yamen)*, but in 1639 the name was changed to the *Lifan yuan*, and placed under the Ministry of Rites. As part of the central government the *Lifan yuan*, aside from managing affairs having to do with Mongolia, Tibet, Xinjiang, and other border regions, prior to the creation of the *Zongli yamen* (Ministry of Foreign Affairs) in January of 1861, also took care of matters concerning Russia. The six offices within the *Lifan yuan* managed such things as rank and emoluments *(juelu)*, tribute, setting borders, officialdom, military punishment, household registration, farming and herding, taxation, post-houses, trade, and religion. The Court also set up separate organizations like the Internal Office *(neiguan)* and the External Office *(waiguan)*; institutes for Mongolian, Tangut, Todo, and Russian studies; for management of the imperial hunting ground *(mulan weichang)*; the lama registration bureau *(lama yinwu chu)*; and a statute office *(zeli guan)*. Since there was no strict demarcation in tribute relationships between internal and external; the concept can be used to describe both relations between the dynasty and its dependencies *(shudi)* (such as Tibet and Mongolia) and between the dynasty and its vassal states *(fanshu)* (such as Myanmar, Nepal, and the Ryukyus). It can even be used for the relations between the Chinese dynasty and Russia or the nations of Europe. Thus, within the frame of reference of the norms of modern international relations, linking the notion of tribute to such concepts as "suzerainty" and "sovereignty" risks distorting historical understanding.

Following upon the development of liberation movements in the colonies, their rejection of these suzerain relationships and their economic dependence, the search for national self-determination and liberation became the emblematic appeal of the times. With this came the easy application of the concept of suzerainty within the context of nationalist knowledge to describe traditional relationships within the Asian region. In reference to China, the notion of suzerainty generally has had a dual meaning: on the one hand, it contrasts with the traditional division between the imperial power and the fiefdoms, separating Mongolia, Xinjiang, Tibet, Manchuria, and other such portions of "Outer China" from so-called China Proper or "Inner China." On the other hand, the notion of suzerainty came to be contrasted to sovereignty, with the former used to describe empires (like the Ottoman or Chinese) and their relationships with the territories surrounding them, taking the surrounding territories as belonging to the suzerain country in the diplomatic sense, while being autonomous political entities internally. The latter term described relations among equal countries. Combining both of these senses, however, the concept of suzerainty established a distinction between an internal and an external China, a distinction that was defined through the optic of relations among European sovereign states—it is an autonomous region situated in an amorphous ground between sovereignty and subordination. In fact, this ambiguous concept of autonomy is derived from the translatability between "suzerainty" and "tribute-vassal-dependency," and permeates the policies of Britain, the United States, and other Western states toward Tibet. Within this relationship of translation, the concept of sovereignty has clearly become formalized and has lost the important historical distinction between the suzerain relations of European history on the one hand and tribute-vassal relations on the other.

For example, at the Simla Conference convened by the United Kingdom between October 1913 and July 1914, Britain's position was that Tibet should become a British protectorate and stay on only nominally as a highly autonomous region under China—this so-called high degree of autonomy did not mean that Tibet should actually be autonomous, but was an indication of the authority of the British protectorate. In 1943, in light of the antagonism developing between the Chinese central government and Tibet, Britain planned to drop its recognition of Chinese suzerainty and publicly support Tibetan independence. A document in the British Foreign Office archive entitled "Tibet and the Question of Chinese Suzerainty" states quite clearly: "Chinese plans and propaganda for a post-war settlement in the Far East aim at securing independence from British rule for such territories as India, Burma and Malaya. The real motive, so far as the two latter are concerned, is undoubtedly to clear the ground for Chinese political and economic domination" and that "In order to give effective support to Tibet's claim to complete independence, we should, I submit, abandon our previous willingness to acknowledge China's suzerain rights."[27] On November 15, 1950, Hector David Castro, the head of Salvador's delegation, acting under the instructions of the United States, requested that the United Nations General Assembly discuss China's "invasion of Tibet," with the U.K. Foreign Office once again clarifying the matter of suzerainty in order to prove that Tibet was not part of China but was, rather, an independent country. There was also the following statement in a telegram from the British Foreign Office to the British high commissioner in India:

> The actual control which China in virtue of her suzerainty exercised over Tibet varies at different times. In 1911 Tibet threw off Chinese control and expelled all Chinese troops from her territory. By 1913 she had established independence of China and she participated in a tripartite Conference in Simla in 1914 in her own right. As a result of this Conference representatives of Britain, China and Tibet drew up a Convention recognizing Tibetan autonomy under Chinese suzerainty but expressly precluded China from incorporating Tibet as a Chinese province.... Though China did not sign the Convention, it was only on the faith of the conditions in it that Tibet agreed to accept Chinese suzerainty again.... Our recognition of Chinese suzerainty over Tibet after 1914 was conditional on the recognition by China of Tibetan autonomy; in other words the suzerainty which we recognized was the nominal kind envisaged in the Simla Convention, and we have since 1914 accepted the right of Tibet to enter into direct relations with other states.[28]

This position was also taken by India. In September 1950, Nehru said the following to a Tibetan delegation: "The Government of India will continue the policy of the British period in considering Tibet outwardly a part of China but internally independent. We will request the Chinese not to send their troops into Tibet, but if the Tibetan representatives say that Tibet is completely independent, it will be very difficult to reach an agreement."[29] As a result, the fact that Western nations recognize Chinese sovereignty over Tibet does not prevent them supporting Tibetan separatism from another perspective, the guise of autonomy. The origins of this apparently contradictory phenomenon lie in the politics of translation of the term "suzerainty" in the European colonial era, with its distinction between things internal and external to China.

Second, the politics of recognizing sovereignty has never been as stable and immutable as it is held out to be. The break-up of Yugoslavia provides a good example: in the beginning Western countries recognized Yugoslav sovereignty in accordance with international law, but as the situation developed, they quickly came to break the rules of that law, exemplified by Germany's unilateral recognition of Croatian and Slovenian independence; in this Germany not only violated international law, but its own postwar constitution. The recent case of Kosovan independence is another case in point, as it not only violated international law but also the commitments of the Western powers. This was a point that Boris Yeltsin was probably able to anticipate, but his death preventing him from acting on it. After the Tibetan riots of March 14, Fred Halliday, writing on the Website *Open Democracy*, equated the Tibetan question with that of Palestine, labeling them both part of "the syndrome of post-colonial sequestration." Halliday argued that looking at all struggles for sovereignty from the perspective of their historical positioning is incorrect, since the independence is not decided by historical factors, but rather by international recognition. He raised the example of Kuwait, a strictly "man-made" state, but because it had received international recognition, it was provided with aid by the entirety of international society when Iraq invaded in 1990.

Both Tibet and Palestine, on the other hand, because they were not taken seriously and did not receive international recognition at certain key periods, forfeited their chances for independence. Because of this, "even if Tibet *had* been an integral part of China for centuries, this would not gainsay its *contemporary right*—as a territory with a clearly distinct language and culture, and with several decades of *de facto* and modern sovereignty before 1950—from claiming independence. After all, Ireland was long ruled by England, Norway by Sweden, and Finland, Ukraine and the Baltic countries by Russia, without this contradicting their right to independence in the 20th century."[30] In likening Tibet to the other countries and colonies that he lists, and by equating the relationship between the Qing dynasty and Tibet with relations between European countries and the colonies or nations they occupied, Halliday commits what is from the perspective of historical research an unacceptable error. But Halliday's point about the formation of sovereign nations not being wholly decided by history but rather by the status of international recognition is not completely wrong. Lacking the instigation of Western imperialism, there would have been no Tibetan independence movement in the early part of the twentieth century,[31] and without the support of Western public opinion there would have been no independence movement in present-day Tibet.

The Chinese and Tibetan Views from the Perspective of the Nation-State

In any discussion of Tibet, we must pursue the following questions: At the same time that Western countries generally recognize China's sovereignty over Tibet, why do so many Westerners sympathize with or support "Tibetan independence"? This question contains a number of highly complicated components, and I would like first to analyze two of these that are not encompassed by the debates over religion and sovereignty already discussed:

First, Western nationalist knowledge has played an important role in creating views on China and Tibet. The 1911 Revolution in China destroyed the national dynasty of the Manchus and established a republic in the form of a state of five nations, which immediately faced a crisis similar to that confronting the multinational European empires at the very same time: movements for independence or autonomy took place in Tibet, Mongolia, and in a number of provinces in "China proper." This new volatility corresponded to the influence "Wilsonism" was exerting during the initial decade of the Republic. From the standpoint of the European "principle of nationality," both the movement to expel the Han that took place in Tibet in the years after 1911 and the current movement for "Tibetan independence" based outside of China adhere to the logic of ethnic nationalism (based on a particular ethnicity, language, religion, and culture) in pursuing a nationalism in which national borders overlap with ethnicity and language, or what is known as "Linguistic nationalism."[32]

Beginning in the nineteenth century, the entire world came to be organized within the system of nation-state sovereignty. In spite of the fact that in many countries there existed highly complicated patterns of ethnic nationality, in general, nationalism manifested itself as an extremely simple political principle, namely, in the words of Ernest Gellner, that the "political and national unit should be congruent." "In brief, nationalism is a theory of political legitimacy, which requires that ethnic boundaries should not cut across political ones, and, in particular, that ethnic boundaries within a given state—a contingency already formally excluded by the principle in its general formulation—should not separate the powerholders from the rest."[33] According to this idea, feelings of nationalism are inspired either because of anger at the violation of this principle, or because of the feeling of contentment brought about when this principle is observed. Following the end of World War I, the nineteenth-century "principle of nationality" prevailed under the aegis of Wilsonian "national self-determination," but it was not an inevitable part of national progress. It was, rather, "the result of two unintended developments: the collapse of the great multinational empires of central and eastern Europe and the Russian revolution which made it desirable for the Allies to play the Wilsonian card against the Bolshevik card. For, as we have seen, what looked like mobilizing the masses in 1917–18 was social revolution rather than national self-determination."[34]

In fact, however, in postwar Europe, multinational states were the norm and we can see from this that the new nation-state did not actually supplant the traditional "prisons of nations" form of traditional empire. In the post–Cold War period, the reconsolidation of the system of international relations was based on appeals to "democracy," "human rights," religion, or nationalism, and a number of resistance movements—including resistance movements directed at the nation-state—have been multi- or transnational. In Eastern Europe and the areas formerly part of the Soviet Union, however, it would be better to say that the probability of success for new nation-states lies in whether or not they are pro-American or adhere to the needs of the American global strategy rather than to slogans like "democracy" or "human rights." But, on the question of nationalism, historical "practice did not conform to theory,"[35] and the historical fact of the widespread existence of multiethnic societies cannot change the prevalence of "the principle of nationality" in Europe. In regard to certain powers (like the power of nationalism or that of hegemony), the congruence of the national and political unit represents the most convenient means of expression, and if this principle coincides with differences in religious faith, it is even easier to spark ethnic antagonisms. There were a number of complicated factors involved in the breakup of both the Soviet Union and Yugoslavia, but the form of each breakup corresponded to this basic precept of nationalism. The earlier breakup of India and Pakistan also adhered to this formula—the tragic violence that accompanied the breakup being something with which we are very familiar.

In the contemporary world, China is perhaps the only society in the world still to preserve the territory and social makeup of a pre-twentieth-century dynasty or empire, but it has long since ceased to be the Qing empire and become a sovereign nation. For many Westerners, precisely how to describe this China, a "trans-systemic society," which is not only multinational but holds within itself a number of religions and cultures, poses a problem. From the perspective of comparative cultural history, the roles of Christianity and Confucianism in determining the respective natures of cultural Europe and cultural China are generally similar, but there is a crucial difference, which is, as R. Bin Wong puts it: "Christianity transcends the political boundaries of European states while Confucianism fuses the cultural and political into a single, though complex, compound. . . . Were we to grant the premise that the fusion of politics and culture is a unique feature of modern nationalism, we would face the awkward dilemma of treating imperial Chinese state-making strategies as 'modern.'"[36] For European thinking, just how to understand this fusion in Chinese history of cultural and political boundaries into one collectivity constitutes an epistemological challenge. In order to avoid this "awkward dilemma," it became necessary to offer additional explanations about China.

A ready example can be found in a recent textbook on Chinese history published by Penguin, which is marked by this characteristic difficulty in describing Chinese history. The first sentence on the first page begins thus: "The state, people and culture known in English as China are in profound general crisis." Just what is this "general crisis"? Only at the end of the book does the author provide his answer: "It is the crisis of an inherited cultural and political order and of the spirit in which they are encoded, of the present consequences of past glories, or an empire in the guise of a modernizing unitary state whose long-term continuation seems to be just as seriously threatened by the switch to capitalism of a kind as it would have been by prolonging attempts to keep Maoist socialism alive."[37] The phrase "an empire in the guise of a modernizing unitary state" provides the key to the book—China has failed to adhere to the principle of the congruence of the boundaries of ethnicity and politics, its language is better described as an imperial rather than a national language and its historical narrative is better described as the religion of empire rather than a national history. In sum, China resembles neither Jenner's concept of a nation nor that of a state, and it not only mixes numerous ethnicities, but incorporates many civilizations. In his view, China is thus an empire lacking internal cohesion, relying strictly on the power of an authoritarian politics to hold its disparate regions together.

Prior to Jenner, the noted American sinologist Lucian Pye offered an even more elegant explanation: "The special importance of political culture for understanding China also lies in the ways in which China is unique in both the collective and individual levels. As a collectivity, China is not just a normal nation-state; it is a civilization trying to squeeze itself into the format of a modern state. At the individual level, no society makes more of the importance of molding children into people who will honor correctness in both thinking and conduct."[38] In other words, according to these views, China can be a civilization, a continent, an empire, but can under no circumstances be "an ordinary nation-state" or a "modern state." Here, "ordinary" and "modern" are based on a standard produced by the Western self-imagination, a Western exceptionalism brought about by forcing themselves into a frame of universalism—or so-called universal value. This narrative of China created within the context of nationalist knowledge is predicated on a standard model of the European nation-state, and according to this standard model, the political community must be centered on a national community. From this perspective a complex multinational or even multi-civilizational society formed through a long historical process can only be seen as artificial and coerced.

Contesting the Rules: The Expansion of Colonialism, the Chinese Revolution, and the Genesis of the "Tibetan Question"

Second, nationalist knowledge is not merely the way the West treats China, but is also a historical force that has relentlessly developed along with an expanding capitalism and nationalist movements—political relations in all areas of China, including Tibet, have been remolded by it. Owing to the incapacity of the Qing dynasty to resist the incursions and encroachments of British colonialism, the traditional relations between Tibet and the Qing were altered, resulting in antagonisms and estrangement, a direct consequence of this colonialism. After the Opium Wars, in order to cope with its coastal challenges, the Qing government, on its own initiative, abandoned the right of its commissioner in Tibet to inspect the commercial income and expenditures of both the Dalai and Panchen Lamas, as well as certain military rights.[39] Between 1841 and 1855, when Britain was instigating the Kashmiri army to invade Tibet and the Nepalese to attack the Tibetan border, the Qing government was embroiled in the Opium War and the Taiping Rebellion, and was thus utterly unable to come to Tibet's rescue. During the time of its various incursions into Tibet, Britain sought to separate it from the Chinese government in order to secure special rights there.

The Qing dynasty was in no position to offer Tibet military assistance, so it obliged the latter to adopt a policy of compromise as the only means of protecting itself. For example, in 1856, under the auspices of the Qing commissioner there, Tibet was forced to sign the Tibet-Nepal Treaty; the articles in the Cheefoo Convention signed by the Qing and Great Britain in 1876 pertaining to Tibet were the product of the same policy of compromise; between 1886 and 1888, the questions surrounding the Tibet-Sikkim border and the defensive positions at Lungthu brought Tibet and Britain into sharp conflict, but the Qing government instructed its Tibet Commissioner to withdraw from forward positions, which met with strong opposition from all quarters of Tibetan society; in March of 1888,

Britain launched its first invasion of Tibet, occupying strategic points like Lungthu Mountain, the Jelepla Pass, Yatung, and arrested the Chogyal ["religious king"] Thutob Namgyal (1860–1914) of Sikkim, who had been resident in the Chumbi Valley, and held him prisoner at Kalimpang. At the conclusion of the war, between late 1888 and 1890, the Qing government was obliged to dispatch the Assistant Amban (minister) Sheng Tai, with the assistance of the Briton James H. Hart, to conduct negotiations with the British at the latter's military posts and in Darjeeling.[40]

Finally, on March 17, 1890, the Convention between Great Britain and China Relating to Sikkim and Tibet was signed at Calcutta. Containing eight articles, aside from demarcating the border between Tibet and Sikkim, the Convention made a special point of affirming that "it is admitted that the British Government, whose Protectorate over the Sikkim State is hereby recognized, has direct and exclusive control over the internal administration and foreign relations of that State, and except through and with the permission of the British Government neither the Ruler of the State nor any of its officers shall have official relations of any kind, formal or informal, with any other country."[41] This brought about the complete collapse of Qing suzerainty over Sikkim.[42] On December 5, 1893, the Qing court was forced to sign articles appended to the convention (the "Tibet-India Treaty"), which dealt with all matters pertaining to "trade, communications and pasturage." According to this treaty, in 1894, China would open Yatung as a trade mart, to which the Government of India was permitted to "send officers to reside . . . to watch the conditions of British trade." For a period of five years after 1894, all goods traded, expect the banned "arms, ammunition, military stores, salt, liquors, and intoxicating or narcotic drugs," were to be tariff exempt, and the matter of the Indian tea that the Qing had long forbidden entry to Tibet was to be resolved within that period of time. As even the British aggressors confessed, "as a matter of fact, this treaty has proved itself to be completely useless—the Tibetans have never recognized it, and the Chinese authorities are completely unable to compel the Tibetans to comply."[43] In 1903–1904, the British once again launched a large-scale war against Tibet, and the Qing government, acting via the agency of its Commissioner for Tibet, prevented the Tibetans from resisting, with the result that over a thousand Tibetan soldiers were slaughtered by the British army. On the day the British occupied Lhasa, Youtai, the Qing Commissioner even paid a call on Colonel Younghusband, the leader of the invading force, and presented awards to the British army.[44]

The British invasion brought a centrifugal tendency to Tibet, which only gave rise to Qing efforts to control it more directly. The Qing rulers had finally come to understand that Tibet could very possibly be reduced to a British protectorate like Sikkim and Bhutan. Accompanying the transformation of the struggle between Britain and Tibet into antagonism between Tibet and the Qing government, the Qing altered its previous mode of action toward Tibet and began to intervene directly into its affairs, resulting in intensified antagonism between the two. Because of this steady increase in antagonism and misunderstanding, the Thirteenth Dalai Lama fled to Mongolia in 1904 and to India in 1910, both times declared as having been deposed by the Qing government. In 1905 the Qing announced a decree to reduce the number of monks and monasteries in Batang in the Kham region of eastern Tibet, to prevent the ordination of new monks for a period of twenty years, and to give land to Catholic priests in the area, something that evoked resistance from the monks and monasteries.[45] The Sino-British treaty signed at Beijing on April 27, 1906, in fact negated one of the key results of the British war against Tibet of 1903–1904. Against the background of the post-1901 "new policies" implemented by the Qing, the government dispatched Zhang Yintang—recently returned from the United States—as "deputy general" to serve as Deputy Amban, charged with "overseeing Tibetan affairs."

In October of the same year, in order to slow the return of the Dalai Lama to Tibet and thus help consolidate Qing control of the region, the Qing emperor ordered him to stop over at the Kumbum monastery in Qinghai on his way back from Mongolia. In 1907 the Qing government sent Lianyu as Amban to Tibet, where he entered into discussions with Zhang Yintang about governmental reform. They agreed on a plan to train a strong military force, to set up secular governmental agencies, and generally to secularize the Tibetan government. They also devised proposals for highways and a telegraph system as well as plans to develop Tibet's natural resources; they even planned to use Confucian ethics and modern ideas to transform Tibetan customs. In 1907 they opened a Chinese language school in Lhasa, and in 1908 a military school.[46] In 1908, after pacifying an uprising in Kham, the commissioner in charge of the Sichuan-Yunnan frontier, Zhao Erfeng, instituted a large-scale program of bringing regional chieftains under central control. These "new policies" had a profound effect on the Tibetan social system of religious government and also "bore the deep imprint of Manchu and Han nationalism."[47] It must be noted, however, that these "new policies" were produced in response to British invasion and attempts at domination. In order to pacify and cope with the resistance and disturbances of the Tibetans toward the "new policies," in 1910 the Qing government sent Zhong Ying and a force of 2,000 troops from Sichuan to Lhasa, leading directly to the second flight of the Dalai Lama. In 1911, when news of the revolution that year reached Lhasa, it immediately incited internal strife and mutiny among the Qing resident army—they went on a rampage, looting monasteries and shops, even killing locals; the demise of the Qing also foreshadowed the separatism of this period—together, these events stirred up the enmity and spirit of resistance of the Tibetans toward the Han.[48] In 1912, after the Qing was overthrown, the Nepalese mediated the complete expulsion of Qing officials and military from Tibet, thereby signifying the complete collapse of the Qing system of rule there.

This dual transformation of relations between Tibet and the Qing and the centrifugal tendencies among the Tibetan upper classes complemented one another. In 1912, the Thirteenth Dalai Lama, still not returned from India, issued an "Edict Expelling the Han," in which he said:

> The people of the interior provinces [i.e., "China proper"] have expressed a determination to overthrow the emperor and establish a new country. Prior to this time no official documents or governmental orders sent by the Han to Tibet have been obeyed. . . . Han officials and armies sent to Tibet have long since lost their credibility by indulging themselves in pillage, trampling on our sovereignty, causing my officers and people to go into restless exile, and to flee to the four quarters—the dragging out of this viciousness has reached an extreme. . . . From this point on, . . . should there be any remaining Han in our territory, they should be expelled completely, and those areas without Han people should be strongly defended against them;

it is to be hoped that the Han will vanish from the entire precincts of Tibet; this is something of the highest import.[49]

The locution "the people of the interior provinces have expressed a determination to overthrow the emperor and establish a new country" established the legitimacy of the "expulsion" on the basis of a new model, which is the "politics of recognition" of nationalism. This "politics of recognition" differs completely from the traditional model linked to religion and the tribute system. It echoed the movements for independence and autonomy taking place in every Chinese province after the 1911 Revolution even as it embodied an ethnic component of dividing Han from Tibetan and a nationalistic "establish a new country" factor even clearer than the movement for autonomy it shared with each Chinese province. Twenty days after he returned to Tibet, the Dalai Lama announced a unilateral declaration of sovereign powers to his officials and people, defining the traditional system of relations between Tibet and the Ming and Qing dynasties with religious and the tribute relations at its core as "sacrificial and donor relations" *(gong-shi guanxi)*. This definition is, in fact, based upon the dual factors of nation and state. If we look at these components in light of the 1912 Mongolian declaration of independence and the agreement between Tibet and Mongolia signed in January 1913, we can see clearly movements of nationalist separatism in pursuit of the goal that the "political and national unit should be congruent." The agreement states that "Whereas Mongolia and Tibet, having freed themselves from the Manchu dynasty government and separated themselves from China, have become independent States, and whereas the two States have always professed one and the same religion, and to that end that their ancient and mutual friendship may by strengthened."[50]

This pursuit of an "independent" "politics of recognition" was not, however, produced "independently." First, aside from Britain's two wars on Tibet, and the two unequal treaties signed at their conclusion, throughout the course of the twentieth century powers from other regions and from all over the globe began to intervene in matters having to do with Tibet. Prior to the British invasion of Lhasa in 1904, the Czar used his special connection with the Russian subject and Buryat Mongol Agvan Dorzhiev, who was also a tutor to the Thirteenth Dalai Lama, to try to persuade the

Dalai to seek the patronage of Russia. The Dalai intended to ally with Russia in order to resist the British invasion, but his original motivation was not independent. When he was fleeing to Mongolia, he stated openly that "I will first go to Mongolia, and then go on to Beijing to have an audience with the Empress Dowager and the Guangxu Emperor."[51] In February of 1910, just when the Qing was implementing its "new policies" in Tibet, the Dalai, who had only recently returned there, fled once again to India. When in January 1913 he sent Dorzhiev to the outer Mongolian capital of Urga (now Ulaan Baatar) to sign the treaty in which each signatory declared themselves to be "independent states," the hand of Russia was clearly visible. In October 1913 at the Simla conference attended by China, Britain, and Tibet, the Tibetan representative, Shatra Pal-jor Dorje, raised a plea for "Tibetan independence" at the instigation of the British and at the end of 1915, a conference between Britain and China over Tibet was convened in London, its agenda being primarily concerned with the original 1906 treaty and its appended stipulations.[52]

From that point on, Tibetan elites have continually tended toward seeking "independence," such as with the 1942 resurrection of the Tibetan "Foreign Affairs Bureau," which resulted in antagonism with the Chinese Republican government. At the end of the same year, Captain Ilya Tolstoy (grandson of the Russian author) and Lieutenant Brooke Dolan of the American OSS entered Tibet carrying a letter and gifts from President Roosevelt, with Tolstoy stating that "he was recommending to his government that Tibet be represented at the Peace Conference to end the war."[53] At the end of 1946 a Tibetan delegation was invited to India to attend an "Asia Relations Conference."[54] In late 1947, the Tibetan Kashag (governing council) sent a "Trade Mission" led by its "Minister of Finance," Tsepon Shakabpa, on a visit to the United States, the United Kingdom, France, and Italy with the intent of seeking support from Western nations for "Tibetan independence." In Washington, the delegation was received by George Marshall, the Secretary of State, and by W. Walton Butterworth, the Director for Far Eastern Affairs. Marshall disregarded the American rule that gold could only be sold to sovereign states and agreed to sell 50,000 ounces to Tibet.[55]

In March of 1950, a delegation led by Shakabpa reached Calcutta and had secret discussions at the American consulate there, and the decision was reached to cache weapons along the Tibetan border in Sikkim, Nepal, and Bhutan so that the Tibetans might use them; in May, the United States and India reached an agreement to the effect that the United States would unload large quantities of rifles, machine guns, hand grenades, and ammunition in Calcutta so as to aid the Tibetans. The shipments would proceed uninspected and would be escorted by armed Americans via Darjeeling to Tibet.[56] On November 1, Secretary of State Dean Acheson castigated the People's Liberation Army for its "aggression" against Tibet, and two weeks later the head of the Salvadoran delegation to the UN, Hector David Castro, with American backing, "telegraphed the U.N. secretary-general requesting that the 'invasion of Tibet by foreign forces'" be discussed by the General Assembly.[57] After the Seventeen-Point Agreement between a Tibetan delegation and the Chinese government was signed in Beijing in May of 1951, the United States not only urged the Dalai Lama and his group to raise the "Tibet issue" at the UN, but also tried to persuade him to flee to Bhutan, Sikkim, or Nepal and assented to allow the Dalai and a hundred of his followers to take refuge in the United States. Following this, the United States and the Kashag entered into a long series of talks concerning such questions as Tibetan independence.[58] In the spring of 1955, the American CIA recruited a group of Tibetan troops in the outskirts of Kalimpong, and carried out secret training in such places as Taiwan, Okinawa, Saipan, and Guam—this was the prelude to the instigation and support of the Dalai Lama's armed rebellion and subsequent exile.[59] The "internationalization" of the "Tibet question" is the product of this process.

Second, the Tibet crisis is not an isolated matter, but rather the result of a systematic transformation. Beginning in the late eighteenth century, the diverse collection of areas in traditional tribute relationships with the Qing on the southern flank of the Himalayas fell one by one within the British sphere of influence. Although what I am calling tributary relationships here refers to the system that had the Qing at the center, it also was marked by a complex system of overlapping relations, including differences between vassal and dependent states and distinctions among both vassal and dependent states themselves. For instance, Nepal paid tribute to the Qing court, but was in military conflict with Tibet; Assam was a vassal of Myanmar, but the latter paid tribute to the Qing; Ladakh was a dependency of Tibet, but Tibet was a Qing vassal state; Sikkim was vassal to Tibet, but was also controlled by the Qing; Bhutan was vassal to both the Qing and to Tibet even as it was in conflict with the Chinese vassal state of Nepal. Accompanying British invasion and encroachment, however, Nepal in 1816, Assam in 1826, Ladakh in 1846, Sikkim in 1861, Bhutan in 1865, and Myanmar in 1886, all, one after the other, fell under British control.

British colonial activity in this area had two unique features: one, although it used military force to open the gates of these countries, it did not rely upon direct military occupation. It obliged the countries to sign unequal treaties and used "treaties among countries" to affirm their status as protectorates, after which it broke up traditional regional relationships, particularly the tributary ties between these places and both the Qing and Tibet. British colonialists of course worked in the name of the East India Company to commence wars and to sign treaties, but the form of the treaties still accorded with the basic structure of treaties among European states. British control of Nepal began with two invasions launched by the East India Company in 1767 and 1769, but since it encountered the fierce resistance of the Gorkhas, they were obliged to redirect their efforts to Bhutan. Regardless of which country was the proximate target, however, the real goal was to enter Tibet. When the East India Company occupied three Bhutanese fortresses in 1772,[60] the Sixth Panchen Lama addressed a letter to the British Governor-General in India, stating that Bhutan belonged to the Dalai Lama. This provided the pretext for the British to sign a treaty with Bhutan and to send George Bogle to Tibet. The Panchen Lama refused Bogle entry, citing the fact that Tibet "is subject to the Emperor of China" as his reason,[61] but with the assistance of the monk Purangir Gosain, Bogle was able to enter Tibet and stay for a number of months. In 1775 the British government in Bengal twice dispatched the physician Alexander Hamilton, who had accompanied Bogle on his mission of the year before to Tibet via Bhutan, only to once again encounter the opposition of the Panchen Lama.[62]

In 1814, the British East India Company invaded Nepal and Sikkim and in 1816 signed the Treaty of Sagauli with Nepal, in which the latter ceded 10,000 square kilometers of its southern territories to British India, further stipulating that in the event of any dispute involving Nepal or Sikkim the British government was to adjudicate. In February 1817, the Company signed the Treaty of Titalia with Sikkim, which stipulated the return to that country of Terrai and western Morang, territories that had been occupied by Nepal; the treaty also requested that Sikkim agree to the Company taking control of Sikkim's external relations and to provide protection and exemption from taxation to British Indian merchants. Through this treaty Britain secured the right to pass through Sikkim to Tibet for trading purposes. In 1853 the British carved off for themselves Darjeeling and all territory south of the Ranjit River, and in 1890 forced Sikkim to accept the status of British protectorate. In 1864 the British launched an armed invasion of Bhutan, forcing that country to sign the Treaty of Sinchula in November of the following year. The treaty not only obliged Bhutan to cede Kalimpong and other substantial pieces of territory, but also put Bhutan in the position of being a British dependency.[63] In 1887 Britain forcibly occupied a Sikkim that still recognized Qing suzerainty and dispatched a resident commissioner, while in March of 1888 Britain launched its first invasion of Tibet, eventually forcing the Qing to sign the Anglo-Chinese Conventions of 1890 and the further "Regulations Regarding Trade, Communication and Pasturage" in 1893. The former recognized the British protectorate over Sikkim, while the latter opened up Yatung to commerce, with the English gaining special trading privileges and rights of consular adjudication. From this point on Sikkim was reduced to the status of British protectorate and the door to Tibet was opened.[64]

Second, the British invasions of Nepal, Bhutan, and Sikkim were all undertaken with the goal of entering Tibet, and entering Tibet was part of opening up China. Thus, Britain and its activities in the Himalayan region were completely coordinated with the British opium trade on the southeast coast as ways of opening the door to China. For example, in 1788 and 1791, Nepal invaded Tibet twice, and the second time occupied Shigatse and sacked the Tashilhunpo monastery, which initiated a war of the Qing against Nepal. During the second war, Lord Cornwallis, the Governor-General of British India, disregarded the opposition of the Dalai Lama and supplied weapons to the Nepalese, on the condition that Nepal sign a treaty with Britain. On March 1, 1792, Nepal was obliged to sign a commercial treaty with the East India Company's representative in Benares Jonathan Duncan; on September 15 of the same year, Cornwallis sent a letter to the king of Nepal stating that Britain could not provide further aid to Nepal because of British commercial relations with China.⁶⁵ According to the findings of Gao Hongzhi, Britain refused to send military assistance to Nepal for three reasons: (1) the war between China and Nepal coincided with the Macartney mission to China, so Britain did not wish events in Nepal to influence the negotiations Macartney was undertaking with the Qing court on matters having to do with trade; (2) the years between 1790 and 1792 were the same years in which Britain was engaged in fierce fighting with the Kingdom of Mysore in south India, so it lacked the capacity to also become involved in Nepal; (3) on September 15, 1792, Cornwallis received an intelligence communication from a British agent to the effect that Nepalese defeat was a certainty. His attitude thus changed from leaning toward supporting Nepal militarily to one of trying to mediate the conflict. After the China-Nepal War, the Qing court strengthened its control over Tibet, and in 1793 promulgated the "Imperially Authorized Regulations for Remedying the Tibet Internal Situation," which stipulated administrative measures concerning such things as the Golden Urn lottery [for choosing the Dalai and Panchen Lamas], fiscal and currency administration, as well as military affairs; the Regulations also confirmed that the Qing Ambans were of equal status and had authority equal to the Dalai and Panchen Lamas.

It is particularly worthy of note that Sino-British conflict in the Himalayan region resulted from a contest between two types of political legitimacy and the laws based on each type. Unlike Britain, which deployed treaties in order to encroach upon the region, Qing control never overstepped the Dalai and Panchen Lamas, the Golden Urn lottery system and other religious, tribute and ceremonial forms. The subordinate political situation of Tibet in the Yuan, Ming, and Qing dynasties rested upon the political, military, and economic dependence of Tibet on the metropolitan dynasties. Not only that, but this long-standing relationship benefitted from a highly flexible tribute system that subsumed a number of complicated forms of religious and ritual association. This system was based on the dynamic relationships of its participants and thus was in constant flux, regardless of whether Tibet and China were close (as in the Yuan and Qing) or relatively distant (as in the Ming)—it cannot be explained in terms of the notions of unification and division characteristic of the era of nationalism. From this perspective, Qing Tibetan policy was not just the product of interaction between center and periphery, but was from the beginning closely related to geopolitical developments in the broadest sense. My basic point here is that the signing of the unequal treaties between the Qing and the powers took place against a background of the entirety of regional relations and the changes they underwent.

This change in the rules represented a transformation from the traditional and multifaceted relationships that characterized the tribute system to relations among nation-states in the context of colonialism, a transformation from recognition that notions of internal and external were relative to recognition of sovereignty in which the internal and external were clearly demarcated. The former revolved around the universal monarchy and its diverse relationships of recognition (such as those of religion, politics, and the multilayered interactions among Mongolia, Dzungaria, Manchuria, and China proper), while the latter are premised on recognizing sovereign nation-states. Once the system of state sovereignty was established as the standard of international relations, the relationship between center and periphery that held under the traditional tribute system could not but fundamentally shift, with territory, ethnicity and religion coming to serve as the essential markers that distinguished different political communities. Among these factors, administrative jurisdiction over a given territory became the predominant means of expressing modern national sovereignty. Chinese policy toward Tibet after the 1950s must be placed within this change in the rules before it can be fully comprehended. If we say that the move toward separatism that took place in late nineteenth-century Tibet was a product of the crisis and decline of China under threat of colonialism, then the same tendency after the 1911 Revolution was already rooted in a new concept—that of the sovereign nation-state.

Autonomy of Ethnic Regions and the Incompleteness of "Unity in Diversity"

Three Types of Chinese Nationalism

In the nationalist movements of the nineteenth and twentieth centuries, the key to the issue of political identity came to congeal around the relationship between "nation" and "state." From the time of the founding of the Republic in 1912 to the founding of the People's Republic in 1949, there were pushes for independence or separatism in all parts of China. Not only were there centrifugal movements at various times in ethnic regions of Tibet, Mongolia, Qinghai, and the Liangshan area of Sichuan, but even the Northeast (i.e., "Manchuria"), Guangxi, Hunan, Guangdong, Sichuan, Guizhou, and Yunnan at different times witnessed movements for independence, autonomy, and separation. Since the late Qing, aside from these inclinations to separate from the central government, Tibetan society has been riven by internal rifts, such as during the 1904–1906 flight of the Dalai Lama to Mongolia, when Britain encouraged a split between the Dalai and Panchen Lamas by inviting the latter to visit India. In 1912 and 1913, the Panchen Lama refused to participate in the Dalai's banishment of the Han (Chinese) and after the passing of the Thirteenth Dalai Lama in 1933 there was also serious strife between Tibet and the Kham region. These different sorts of fissures were the products of the same political crisis, but because those pertaining to Tibet had to do with ethnic identity and took place on the frontier, they were more serious.

In order to resist the incursions of imperialism and overcome internal divisions, modern Chinese nationalism attempted to reshape the understanding of China, with its main effort devoted to demarcating China as a sovereign nation-state and thereby confirm its independent position in international relations. The Chinese national salvation movement had no appeal other than to the world order created by colonialism and its principles of political legitimacy. The ethnic, religious, and national elements represented by the 1912 exile of the Han from Tibet ordered by the Thirteenth Dalai Lama and the Tibet-Mongolia Treaty of 1913 were perfectly consonant with the upsurge of Han ethnic consciousness and political nationalism of the late Qing and early Republican periods—while their demands differed, each was influenced by the nationalist tide. In the wake of the collapse of the universal monarchy and social dissolution, the idea of "one country, one nation" was imbedded in all national discourses, being the notion that "nationalism is a country established on the basis of unifying one race and excluding others."[66] The general norm of one nation and one state, however, created numerous complications surrounding the national question in the modern Chinese revolution: how to go about constructing a "nation-state" out of a Chinese society containing such a complicated assortment of ethnicities, religions, languages, cultures, and customs.

It can be concluded that three principal forms of Chinese nationalism have come into being since the late Qing: (1) In order to overthrow the Manchu Qing dynasty, prior to the 1911 Revolution, revolutionaries like Sun Yat-sen and Zhang Taiyan promoted the notion of a Han nation-state centered on opposition to Manchu rule, producing such things as the slogan "drive out the Tartars and restore China" and the veneration of the Yellow Emperor as the Chinese national ancestor. As many commentators have pointed out, however, this Han nationalism worked as a theory of revolution, but as soon as the goal of political power was achieved, it had to change in one of two ways. (2) Kang Youwei and Liang Qichao, basing themselves on the idea of international competition, advocated the concept of "saving the country by uniting the people," or "greater nationalism." This notion assumed that the Han, Manchu, Moslem, and Manchus had long since amalgamated and should thus form themselves into a nation- or citizen-state under a constitutional monarchy. In reality, the advocacy of Kang and Liang and those of like mind to preserve a constitutional monarchy with Confucianism as its national religion revealed an anxiety: although they thought that the Manchu, Mongols, Tibetans, Moslems, and Han all belonged to the "Chinese nation," in terms of religion, bloodline, language, and custom there were actually serious differences, so it was necessary to find a political form and an ideology that could accommodate them.[67] (3) The classic expression of the ideas of "taking the state boundaries of the Qing empire to demarcate the scope of nationalism" or "national unity in diversity"[68] after the founding of the Republic of China in 1912 was the proclamation of Sun Yat-sen on taking office as the Provisional President of the Republic: "The state is based on its people, and uniting the Han, the Manchus, the Mongols, the Moslems and the Tibetans in one country, and uniting the Han, Manchus, Mongols, Moslems and Tibetans into one people is what we call the unification of the nation."[69] After this, Sun's desire to fuse all of China's ethnicities into a "Chinese nation" came to occupy an important position in the nationalist thought of the Guomindang and the intellectuals surrounding it. For instance, in *China's Destiny*, Chiang Kai-shek wrote:

As far as the history of the development of the nation is concerned, *our Chinese nation is an amalgamation of many ethnicities.* These numerous ethnicities have fused into the Chinese nation through the ages, but the impetus behind the fusion is culture rather than force, and the means by which fusion is fashioned is assimilation rather than conquest. . . .

Based on what I have explained above, we know that the Chinese nation has a high degree of consciousness, that its strength is tenacious, and that its culture is vast and enduring. This prevents the Chinese nation from being encroached upon even as it keeps us from encroaching upon others. And since we cannot accept encroachment upon us, even should another people occupy our land, the Chinese people will determine themselves to rise up, expel them and recover our ancient lands and rivers. And because we do not encroach upon others, even as our nation relieves itself of the pain of humiliation and calamity, we are able to meld with our neighbors through the agency of our vast and enduring culture and *create a single national clan.*[70]

As Gu Jiegang said in a letter to Hong Weilian: "There is no such thing as the Han ethnicity in China, the Han ethnicity is nothing but the union of a number of smaller ethnicities via the agency of culture."[71] This view is not only in the same vein as Kang Youwei's refutation of the anti-Manchu nationalism of the late Qing revolutionaries through his discourse of the hybrid nature of Chinese history, but also shares a common tenor with Chiang Kai-shek. In 1934, when the Nationalist government sent Huang Musong on a diplomatic mission to Tibet, the streets of Lhasa were filled with bilingual slogans proclaiming that "The relationship among the five peoples of China is like that within a single family,"[72] demonstrating that this concept guided the Tibetan policies of the Nationalist government.

The Korean scholar Ryu Yong-Tae believes that all of these different discourses of Chinese nationalism are premised on the notion that the "Chinese nation" is predicated on the majority nationality (the Han) assimilating and absorbing other, minority, nationalities.[73] Therefore, an "internalized imperial nature" constitutes an important part of modern Chinese nationalism. Modern China was formed on the geographical and population base of the Qing dynasty, and as far as its national political form is concerned, modern China (the Republic and People's Republic alike) has certain features that overlap with the earlier empire. I need, however, to add three supplemental points here: (1) The formation of modern Chinese nationalism presupposes China having suffered foreign aggression—its emphasis on the principle of "one Chinese nation" represents a response to the crisis of disintegration brought about by imperialist aggression; national amalgamation and sovereign independence are the common objects of the entire twentieth-century national liberation movement. (2) In administrative terms, assimilation or absorption advocate extending the traditional system of "centralized bureaucracy" *(junxian zhi)*,[74] or provincial administration to what was the realm of the tribute system within the realm of the old empire. The system of each political entity being a single state differs completely from the "imperial nature" of the old tribute system, as the theoretical foundation of the former is "the entire Chinese nation is equal, without respect to ethnicity, class or religion."[75] (3) These propositions concerning the population being an "organic whole" differ from the nationality policies of the Chinese Communist Party—the autonomous regions of the People's Republic are premised on the recognition of ethnic difference and encouraging ethnic cooperation, contact, and common development. Even assuming that China's historical cultural amalgamation and political unity provided a firm basis for the creation of the modern Chinese nation, we cannot depart fundamentally from the way in which the Chinese revolution coped with the way in which modern China was established—the notion of the Chinese people was born at the same moment as the notion of popular sovereignty. If we talk of modern China and its similarity to the structure of the empire in the absence of this revolutionary process and its values, we will not be able to grasp the concept of China as a political nation.

Ethnic Autonomous Regions and Their Basic Principles

All revolutionaries, from Sun Yat-sen on through the Communist Party, pursued the Leninist theory of national self-determination under the principle of ethnic equality, but eventually each pursued different approaches in trying to find institutional arrangements suitable to China. The system of local ethnic autonomy put into practice in contemporary

China is the product of the modern Chinese Revolution, and while in its intentions it inherits a number of features from that revolution, it also contains numerous innovations. From the standpoint of institutional structure, the ethnic autonomous regions differ from a unified, centralized administrative structure in systemically distinguishing ethnic regions from other regions in respect to differences among them in ethnicity, culture, religion, language, customs, and social development. From a political perspective, the theory of the ethnic autonomous region differs from either the theory of national self-determination or that of a federal system within a nation-state (or the theory of a Soviet-style union of republics) in not denying the organic unity of the Chinese nation. In terms of its connotation, these regions differ from the political principle of ethnic nationalism, because the autonomous entity is not established completely via a hereditary *(zuyi)* demarcation, but rather on the demarcation of "ethnic region." Local ethnic autonomy draws upon the traditional Chinese experience of managing the borders through "following the appropriate local customs" shaping the relationship between center and periphery according to differing social conventions, cultures, institutions, and historical circumstances. The contemporary system, however, does not simply replicate history, but is an entirely new creation, the key difference being that the current social system made out of a unitary state sovereignty with mass politics at its core is at variance with a tribute system under monarchial sovereignty. I see it as a synthesis of the imperial legacy, the nation-state and socialist values. This synthesis is neither happenstance nor opportunistic, but rather the result of a continuing process of exploration, innovation, and praxis based on precepts of equality, development, and diversity.

What are the basic principles of local ethnic autonomy? The first principle stresses cooperation among ethnicities and is opposed to separate ethnic establishments *(fenli)*. The concept of "separate establishment" is distinct from "separatism" *(fenlie)*, with the former emphasizing that within a political community, ordinary relationships should be carried out via contact rather than via separate institutions. The notion of cooperation among ethnicities is premised on the recognition of multiple ethnicities and engages in a double critique of greater or lesser nationalisms intent upon "separate establishment." Cooperation is based on ethnic equality—not merely equality between the Han and minority ethnicities, but on equality among each minority ethnicity. In his discussion of this issue, Zhou Enlai said:

> Historical developments have given us the capacity for ethnic cooperation, and the revolutionary movement has given us a basis for cooperation. As a result, after Liberation we adopted a system of local ethnic autonomy suitable to our national circumstances and beneficial to ethnic cooperation. We do not advocate separate establishment for our ethnicities. Were we to do this, the forces of imperialism would immediately take advantage of it. Even were these forces to be unsuccessful, they would complicate cooperation among our ethnicities. Prior to Liberation, for instance, there were reactionary elements in Xinjiang engaged in separatist activities, such as the "East Turkistan" movement that the forces of imperialism took advantage of. Reflecting upon this, when we set up the Xinjiang Uygur Autonomous Region we did not approve using the term "Uygurstan." The Uygurs are not the only nationality in Xinjiang—there are twelve others, so we could not create thirteen "Stans." The Party and the government ultimately decided to establish the Xinjiang Uygur Autonomous Region, and comrades in Xinjiang agreed. In calling it the Xinjiang Uygur Autonomous Region, the "hat" is still worn by the Uygurs, as they are the principal nationality in Xinjiang, with seventy percent of the population, so the other nationalities also wear this hat. The meaning of the two characters "xin" and "jiang" is "new land," which carries no connotation of conquest, thereby differing from "Suiyuan" (pacifying the distant).[76] Both "Xizang" (Tibet) and "Nei Menggu" (Inner Mongolia) have double meanings, referring at once to places and ethnicities. The naming issue would seem to be of secondary importance, but in fact carries great significance in regard to the issue of China's ethnic autonomous regions, as it carries with it the matter of cooperation among ethnicities. It is important to be clear about this.[77]

The second principle of local ethnic autonomy is that, while recognizing ethnic diversity, it does not take into account only ethnicity as the unit of autonomy, but rather makes the region the unit of autonomy. Taking the region as the autonomous unit rather than using the form of a federation or union of republics so as to implement ethnic cooperation is also something that has roots in Chinese history. Also in 1957, Zhou Enlai, in his "Ethnic Regional Autonomy is Advantageous to National Unity and Common Progress," compared the different situations in China and the Soviet Union, his main points being that in China the Han are overwhelmingly dominant and that different ethnicities have long histories of having lived among one other; if a union of republics or a federal system based on ethnicity were put into effect, it would lead to ethnic isolation and conflict. He said:

> The situation in our country differs from that in the Soviet Union. In our country people of Han ethnicity are extremely numerous, but the area they occupy is relatively small; ethnic minorities are not very numerous, but the area they occupy is extremely large, which creates a huge disparity. In the Soviet Union, on the other hand, the Russian people are numerous, but the area they occupy is also quite large. Were China to adopt a federal system, creating new geographical borders among the various nationalities, the result would be to increase ethnic strife. Since in our country many ethnic minorities have for a long period of time resided in the same area as the Han, such that in certain regions, like Inner Mongolia, Guangxi and Yunnan, the Han constitute the majority population. Thus, if a federal system based on strict separation of individual ethnicities were to be put in place, many people would have to move, something that would be highly disadvantageous to both national unity and development. So we have not implemented a federal system, but have put in place instead a policy of ethnic regional autonomy.[78]

In the spring of 2004, I attended a conference on "Tibetan Culture and Biological Diversity" in the Zhongdian region of Yunnan. At the meeting the anthropologist Xiao Liangzhong reported on the tendency for increased separatism among ethnic minorities. Xiao is from that area himself, and is a member of the Bai ethnicity, although there are four ethnic groups represented in his ancestry. He pointed out that this tendency toward separatism is partly a function of the fact that foreign investment—in this case largely via projects sponsored by non-governmental organizations (NGOs)—is concentrated in Tibetan areas, and that the imagination of the Western world in regard to Tibetan culture has encouraged Tibetans to have a sense of self-pride. The flow of investment runs in accordance with the ways in which these NGOs are able to raise money in Western society—aside from an interest in the Tibetans and the Naxi, Western society neither knows nor cares about any other ethnic group in the region. We all respect and admire Tibetan culture, but as Xiao inquired: Do none of the other ethnic cultures really care at all about protecting biological diversity? The intervention of outsiders here has brought about ill feelings, antagonisms, and moves toward separation among different groups that had previously lived harmoniously in a multiethnic region. In a multicultural society, any politics based on the principle of equality has to suppose that all cultures are of equal value, and if there is a systemic raising up of one culture and ignorance or belittling of others, then there will be a separating out and great damage done. There is no harm in asking at this point, when so many people are raising the question of national autonomy: Just how many of them really understand the cultural situation and the relations among the ethnicities of these mixed regions?

According to Zhou Enlai's explanation, local ethnic autonomy should be distinguished from a federal scheme based on ethnic self-determination; the issue that most concerned him was the relationship between ethnic intermixing in one area and the institutional arrangements set up to deal with that. The scope of the autonomous region and the composition of its population must, therefore, respect historical tradition and take into consideration how best to facilitate ethnic cooperation. On that basis one must make the best possible institutional arrangements, creating different structures in accordance with different circumstances. For instance, in the 1950s the Tibet region was actually divided up into three large administrative regions, the region controlled by the Dalai Lama and the Kashag, the region controlled by the Panchen Lama and the Khenpo Assembly (of spiritual elders) and the region controlled by the Chamdo People's Revolutionary Committee.[79] The Panchen Lama at first suggested creating autonomous regions based on this division, but after having taken into consideration the relative homogeneity of the peoples in the Tibetan region as well as historical tradition, the central government suggested establishing a unified Tibetan autonomous region based on the characteristics of the homogeneity of the Tibetan population and the unity of the religion.[80]

Had the new People's Republic not been based on the foundation of the profound sympathy of the Chinese Revolution for oppressed nationalities, it would have, just like the old dynasties, implemented policies of divide and rule in minority areas, while the process of establishing a unified Tibetan autonomous region as well as the setting up Tibetan autonomous counties and prefectures within regions inhabited by other nationalities provides a clear contrast with the ways by which the traditional dynasties ruled their border regions. This is not to say, however, that the ethnicity of the population is the sole standard for establishing autonomous regions. The lines of demarcation among the places where Chinese ethnic minorities reside are not clear, composing a pattern of what the sociologist Fei Xiaotong called "intermixed through larger regions, together in small localities." As far as the Tibetans are concerned, in the early 1950s, aside from the million-plus Tibetans residing in the Tibetan Autonomous Region, there were another million-plus living among other ethnicities and scattered throughout the provinces of Qinghai, Sichuan, Gansu, and Yunnan. At present there are over 5 million Tibetans and the fact of living among other ethnicities has not changed—actually, owing to increased population mobility intermixing at present is even more pronounced. How to deal with popular sentiment in this time of multiethnic mixing is a complicated question and its solution cannot be a one-size-fits-all system of local ethnic autonomy, but must take into full account conditions in each area. At a working meeting held in Qingdao in 1957, Zhou Enlai addressed this question:

> In implementing regional ethnic autonomy, we will create not merely autonomous regions for a particular ethnicity, but also autonomous prefectures (*zhou*), counties, and townships. For instance, although the Inner Mongolian Autonomous Region occupies a vast area, the ethnic Mongolian population represents only about two-thirds of the Mongolian population of the whole country, or just over a million out of 1.4 million people. The remaining several hundred thou-

sand, representing slightly less than one third of the total population, are scattered about various other regions, such as the Northeast [Manchuria], Qinghai, and Xinjiang, all of which contain Mongolian Autonomous Prefectures or Counties. In the soon to be created Ningxia Hui [Moslem] Autonomous Region, the Moslem population is only 570,000 out of a total of 1,720,000, or about a third. This in turn represents only a small fraction of the total of over three and half million Moslems in the country as a whole. So what is the disposition of the other three million that are widely disbursed throughout the rest of the country? The solution, of course, is to set up autonomous prefectures, counties and ethnic townships in areas where the Moslem population is concentrated. In the areas controlled by the Preparatory Committee for the Tibetan Autonomous Region, there are only about a million Tibetans, with another million spread out among Tibetan Autonomous prefectures and counties in the provinces of Qinghai, Gansu, Sichuan and Yunnan; these autonomous regions have close economic relations with the provinces in which they are situated, making for ease in cooperation.[81]

By 2006, the population of the Tibetan Autonomous Region was 2.8 million, with those of Tibetan ethnicity representing 92 percent of that number, an increase of more than 1.6 million over the 1951 total of more than 1.1 million. The number of Tibetans residing outside the Autonomous Region increased at a similar rate, and represents half of the total Tibetan population.

The third principle of regional ethnic autonomy is that of joint progress. Those who designed the system of regional ethnic autonomy determined that considering the multiplicity of these ethnicities it would be "appropriate to unite, inappropriate to split," but this is not a call for simple ethnic assimilation, otherwise it would not have considered the particular circumstances of specific regions, like the question of ethnic unity in the Tibetan region. In setting up the ethnic autonomous regions, regardless of whether ones looks to Mao Zedong or Zhou Enlai, they both advocated that the Han people sacrifice and contribute more, in order to prevent Han chauvinism. At the same time, however, they also stressed that whether one was criticizing Han chauvinism or local nationalism, one needed to speak in concrete terms rather than in abstractions. Otherwise the facts would be distorted, creating internal divisions and antagonisms among ethnicities. The goal of regional ethnic autonomy was to allow different ethnicities to progress together, not to isolate them from one another; expanding the autonomous regions and encouraging interethnic cooperation became the means by which different ethnicities could share the fruits of progress. In taking the example of the Guangxi Zhuang Autonomous region, Zhou Enlai said:

> In dealing with the issue of creating a Zhuang autonomous region, we used the same logic to persuade the Han people to go along with us. The question came down to one of whether it was more beneficial to create a Zhuang Autonomous Region in Western Guangxi or to set up a Guangxi Zhuang Autonomous region of provincial scale? An autonomous region made up exclusively of Zhuang people was an impossibility, as even if one took all the areas of Guangxi inhabited by concentrations of Zhuang and added the adjacent portions of Yunnan and Guizhou that also have concentrations of Zhuang and made it into one autonomous region, there are still over a million Han people in the area, not to mention two Yao Autonomous Counties containing over 400,000 people. In other words, even an area with the maximum concentration of Zhuang would still be inhabited by between one and two million Han and Yao, so even such a unit would not be exclusively Zhuang. Moreover, dividing the territory up this way would leave the Autonomous Region isolated, and would not be advantageous for economic development—in the transportation sector, the railroads would be divided up between the Zhuang and the Guangxi Han, with the economy split between the agricultural regions of the east and the industrial and mining sectors of the west. All of these factors are not good for economic development, so being united is for the best. In sum, the Guangxi Zhuang Autonomous Region is also a region of ethnic cooperation.[82]

The idea of combining regional and ethnic autonomies thus contains two fundamental precepts: First, that different ethnicities can coexist, interact, and still maintain their ethnic characteristics. Second, building autonomous regions based in specified areas can aid ethnic minorities in economic development and thus avoid having these minorities become isolated from mainstream society, as happened to the Native American population in North America or, as is the case with so many small minorities, coming to play what Kautsky called the role of "antiques" as the mainstream population advances.

"Unity in Diversity" and the Hybrid Nature of Ethnic Regions

The system of regional ethnic autonomy is premised on "the structure of unity in diversity in a Chinese nation." In the same way that this system differs from a union of republics, the concept of "unity in diversity in a Chinese nation" is not the same as the nationalist the "Chinese nation is one" or the "Chinese nation is an amalgamation of many ethnicities" discourses of the Republican period. In contrast with those discourses of "the Chinese nation," the concept of "unity in diversity" accentuates the unification of diversity and hybridity. First, different from the notions of "one" and "amalgamation," with their sense of the Han absorbing the minority ethnicities, "unity in diversity" stresses the long duration of hybridity and amalgamation—it is not simple assimilation. As Fei Xiaotong put it: "For the most part, this unity in diversity was formed through a process by which innumerable separate and distinct ethnic units came into contact, mingled, united and amalgamated even as they sometimes split and vanished, eventually forming a body containing much individual character, a good deal of coming and going and in which parts of me were in you and parts of you were in me. This is perhaps the common process by which all nationalities in the world were formed."[83] Second, Fei's theory of "unity in diversity" not only refers to the co-existence of multiple nationalities, but also to the internal diversity of any social unit demarcated as a particular ethnicity. As a result, the notion of unity in diversity is equally applicable to the Chinese in general, the Han ethnicity and each of the ethnic minorities.

When I visited Tibetan and Qiang villages in the northwestern part of Sichuan, I found the two groups living adjacent to one another, and interacting closely, even as they maintained their cultural distinctiveness. When conducting research in Yunnan and Guizhou and attending Miao local festivals, I found that the young people of other ethnicities would attend the festivities. Village identity is not necessarily predicated on "ethnicity," but can also be based on geography (such as proximity to mountains or rivers) or other indicators. In southwestern China many villages are inhabited by multiple peoples, and even individual families contain a variety of ethnicities among their members. A "township" is in itself a hybrid category that is also quite fluid. For instance, in the Jinshajiang [upper Yangzi] River valley, there are many different ethnicities represented in any given village, with the Tibetans among them mostly having migrated in or having married into the region. The harmonious coexistence of many ethnicities in the Chinese southwest is a model of multiculturalism for today's world, with a multiplicity of cultures, systems, customs, and sorts of intelligence encompassed within its scope. It is very much worthy of attention. If, however, we were to rigidly segregate each ethnicity into its own closely defined area, using nothing but "ethnicity" as the means to divide up the territory, would not tragedy ensue?

In taking up the notion of "Unity in diversity," diversity is relatively easy to argue for, with unity being the more difficult concept to demonstrate. "The Chinese nation" refers not just to the national entity in itself that gradually took shape over the course of several thousand years, but also to what political resistance to the Western powers over the past century transformed into a self-conscious political body. As for the meaning of the former term, "unity" refers to the close relations among ethnicities that were developed via daily life, common experiences, and the historical tradition—including local customs and the political tradition. As for the definition of the latter, "diversity" refers to the political community that was produced on the basis of the relations described above. As a result, this is not a concept of nation based on a notion of essential ethnicity, but rather a political entity composed of a community of citizens, subjects making up "the people." And because "the Chinese nation" is a political entity rather than a settled fact, it is still something in a continuous process of formation that has always depended upon generation after generation of experimentation and social practice. A number of Western scholars of history and culture have spent a good deal of time and effort using the notion of "diversity" to deconstruct "unity," but there has seldom been any research into the political and historical implications of "unity."

They have even failed to realize that this "unity" contains "unitary" minority peoples and "unitary" ethnic regions, and thus cannot understand that this so-called unity ultimately is nothing more than an "interactive unity," what I call a "trans-systemic society."

Many of those who study culture fear the idea of "unity," believing that "unity" is something artificial and created by governments, while diversity or ethnicity are primordial (at least relative to state-created identity), natural, and more authentic, leading to conclusions as to how state identity suppresses ethnic identity. This view seems on the surface to be in opposition to nationalism, but is in fact predicated upon the politics of national identity. The process of making distinctions among ethnic identities in the 1950s demonstrated that many of the ethnic identities so distinguished were actually the creations of the state. To take the "White-horse People" (*baima zu*), who live in the northeast corner of the "Tibetan-Yi Corridor" (they are primarily concentrated in Wen County in Gansu Province and in Pingwu County and the Aba Tibetan-Qiang Autonomous Prefecture of Jiuzhaigou County in Sichuan). The "Biographies of Southwestern Barbarians" section of *The Records of the Grand Historian*[84] refer to a group known as the "White-horse Tribe" (*baima di*), and the historical record thereafter labels the group by the various names of "Di," "Yi," "Baima yi," "Baima di," "Longzhou man" and "Diqiang." When the "Committee on Ethnic Autonomy in Pingwu County" was established in 1950, they discovered the differences among the "baima fan," the "baicao fan," the "mugua fan," but the "baima fan" could not trace out their own ethnic line of descent.

After much discussion, it was decided that the "Longan sanfan" recorded in the history books were all to be considered Tibetans, and in July of 1951 the "Committee on Tibetan Autonomy of Pingwu County" (the name was later changed to the "Pingwu County Tibetan Autonomous Region") was set up. In practice, however, prior to the creation of these ethnic distinctions, the "Baima di" did not consider themselves to be Tibetan. In 1954, when the Dalai Lama made a tour of the region and the Tibetan students attending the Southwestern College of National Minorities paid their respects, the Baima among the students almost got into a fight because they failed to pay their respects to the living Buddha by presenting him with a ceremonial white scarf (*hada*). In 1978, Fei Xiaotong, in his "On the Question of Distinguishing Ethnicity in China,"[85] raised the possibility that the "Baima Tibetans" were not, in fact, Tibetans. Subsequently, a good deal of research was carried out in the ethnic studies community on this question, with an eventual decision being made on the basis of maintaining political stability to continue to claim the "white-horse" people as Tibetans.[86] This example not only serves to explain how the self-definition of ethnicity is no more authentic than that of larger social groups, but also illuminates the many problems inhering in theories of ethnicity themselves. These are all problems generated by the discourse and practice of modern nationalism. I raise the issue of transcending the episteme of nationalism because only when the limitations of this manner of knowing are transcended will a multiplicity of different types of intelligence both ancient and modern come to the surface. And only in this way will the possibility of the practice and theory of a politics of equality predicated on diversity become possible.

The concept of "region" as in "ethnic" or "autonomous" region is worth particular attention, as the concept transcends categories like nation, ethnicity, and religion even as it combines these in a mélange of nature, culture, and tradition. Fei Xiaotong distinguished six macro-regions and three corridors in the area inhabited by the Chinese people. The six macro-regions included the northern grasslands, the northeastern mountains and forests, the Tibet-Qinghai plateau in the Southwest, the Yungui plateau, the coastal zone, and the central plain. The three corridors include the Tibetan-Yi corridor, the passes to the southern regions, and the northwest corridor. The Tibetan-Yi corridor includes the Luo-Yu region from Gansu in the north to the southern slopes of the Himalayas—where areas of Han, Tibetan, and Yi ethnicity intersect, and which also contains a number of other ethnicities.[87] Compared with the notion of a simple ethnic nationalism, this particularly Chinese view based on different regions allows an understanding of the pattern of interregional ethnic diversity. If one were to compare regional ethnic autonomy with the discussions of regional autonomy that have developed since the late Qing, there would be both many points of similarity and of difference.

Kang Youwei's (1858–1927) essay "Citizen Self-rule" is a case in point,[88] in which Kang, basing his idea on a comprehensive discussion of the experience of autonomy in China as well as in Western countries, posited a complete system of local autonomy with the township as the fundamental unit. With local autonomy based on such a relatively low and small-scale foundation, Kang held that such a system would be able to foster activism on the part of the citizenry even as it avoided the tendency to despotism inhering in autonomous units that are too large—such a system would also actually help guarantee the unity and stability of the nation. Kang did not discuss the problem of ethnicity in his essay, but his thinking on local autonomy was consistent with his critique of the anti-Manchu nationalism of the revolutionaries of the time, as well as being consistent with his views on the multiethnic history of China ever since the Northern Wei (386–534 C.E.). Taking into consideration the local ethnic diversity of a multiplicity of areas in northwest and southwest China, positing the township as the basic unit of autonomy does justice to this diversity. In the southwest and northwest of China, grassroots autonomy would perhaps differ little from "regional ethnic autonomy." Accompanying advances in communications technology and other sorts of networks, spurring on network-type links between different regions and among cities will perhaps require China's administrative divisions to move toward a smaller scale. In such situations, the natural choice will almost certainly be to eliminate, reduce, or weaken province-level governmental units, establish a system of directly ruled cities and counties, and to grant more autonomy within the counties themselves.

By now everyone is familiar with the difference between China's Tibetan Autonomous Region and the Dalai Lama's idea of "Greater Tibet." This "Greater Tibet" not only includes the Tibetan Autonomous Region, but also the entire province of Qinghai, half of Sichuan, half of Gansu, a quarter of Yunnan, and the southern portion of Xinjiang; it incorporates numerous areas with no Tibetan population and occupies a quarter of China's landmass. There are two points that need to be kept clear when discussing the question of "Greater Tibet." First, the concept of "Greater Tibet" is completely new, and is not consistent with such traditional Tibetan geographical designators as mNga' ris skor gsum, dBus gtsang ru bzhi, and mDo khams sgang drug. According to Shen Weirong's research, Mar yul, one of the three enclosures of mNga' ris, includes the Ladakh and Baltistan regions of what are now India and Pakistan, which were called the great and little Balur (Bru zha) in the Tang dynasty. In the

Yuan, the Tibetans divided Tibetans into three administrative regions (*Tufan sanlu,* or *bod kyi choi kha gsum*) that accorded precisely with the territory demarcated by the Yuan Three Province Pacification Office *(San dao xuanwei si)*—that is, "mNga' ris skor gsum" and "dBus gstang ru bzhi" were combined into a geographic unit approximately coincident with the area administered by the present Tibet Autonomous Region ("dBus gstang"). Amdo (mDo smad) and the Kham (mDo stod) region were separated off into two independent Pacification Offices. If the notion of "Greater Tibet" is set in this context, two questions immediately come to mind. First, since Amdo and the Kham region have been administratively split off from Tibet for over seven hundred years, and the population of those regions has undergone a significant transformation in that time, what could justify reincluding them in "Greater Tibet"? Second, since regions like Ladakh, Bhutan, and Sikkim were separated from Tibetan territory only under the influence of modern colonialism, why are they not included within the scope of "Greater Tibet"? Does this distinction between what is included and what is not in the putative area not in effect recognize the results of modern British colonialism?[89]

Second, as Shi Shuo has pointed out, in order to comprehend how this region took shape, we must first discard the idea that regards Tibetan culture as from its origins a cultural dependency of China proper, followed by an understanding of how Tibetan culture has been expanding eastward for an extensive period of time, such that there has been a long history of it mutually interpenetrating with the culture of China proper. From a temporal perspective, it was only in the Yuan dynasty that Tibet was incorporated into the Chinese dynastic system of control. As Shi Shuo writes, "Prior to the thirteenth century, however, Tibetan civilization had for some time demonstrated a marked tendency toward moving east, whether spatially or as a matter of culture. The spatial manifestation of this tendency can be seen in the eastward progression of Tibetan civilization from the seventh century on, something made possible by the expansion of the military might of the Tufan (Tubo) kingdom."[90] The Tufan expansion went in all directions, but it ran into seriously difficulties in moving west and northwest, resulting in the momentum eastward. At the beginning of the seventh century, there lay between the Tang and the emergent Tufan kingdom an "extremely large and relatively weak territory," which is now the territory encompassed by Greater Tibet. Within this territory there was an assortment of nationalities and the tribes, running from north to south, included the Tuyuhu ('A zha), the Dangxiang, the Bailan Qiang and the Dongnüguo, all of which were eventually conquered by the Tufan. Each tribe, however, maintained its own language, while the Yellow River zone of what is now Gansu Province was always territory inhabited by the Han. In summing up all these factors, it is clear that "the time of the formation of the Tibetan ethnicity was neither the unification of the various tribes of the Tibetan plateau by Songtsän Gampo (Srong gstan sgam po, 617?–649), nor the period of the Tufan kingdom, but should be regarded as the historical period following the extinction of the Tufan kingdom and prior to the thirteenth century."[91] In other words, the creation of the Tibetan nationality was also a matter of "unity in diversity."

With the expansion of Mongol power in the thirteenth century, the hundred-year Mongol rule of Tibet caused the relationship between Tibet and China proper to develop to a new stage, such that even after the demise of the Yuan, the succeeding Ming dynasty was able to rapidly establish its rule over Tibet. Setting up this ruling relationship was not the result of a unilateral coercion on the part of the Ming, but included the Tibetan side speedily entering into the relationship. The Qing was able to gain ruling authority in Tibet on the basis of each Mongol nation acknowledging its allegiance to the dynasty, and after the defeat of the Galdan rebellion in 1696, the direct Mongol rule over Tibet steadily passed to the Qing, and the 1720 expulsion of the Zunghars from Tibet by Qing troops marked the establishment of direct rule. Tibetan efforts to move east did not stop even with the entry of Western—particularly British—colonialism into Chinese affairs, as on October 10, 1913, under British leadership the Tibetan side at the Simla Conference pushed for an eastern border that included a great expanse of fertile territory inhabited by Han people. In response to this, the Chinese side, in addition to reaffirming its claims to sovereignty, advocated a Tibetan border only 100 kilometers from Lhasa, in the Jomda region. In the peace agreement following the 1918 conflict in the Kham region, the Tibetans even advocated extending their borders to the Jinshajiang ('Bri chu, i.e., upper Yangzi River) region. In the present Tibetan Autonomous Region, aside from

Tibetans, there are also Han, Moslems, Monbas, Lhobas, Naxis, Nus, and Derungs as well as Deng people and Sherpas, who have lived there for generations. From the standpoint of its historical development, elements that have been incorporated into the Tibetan ethnicity include Han, Mongol, Manchu, Qiang, and the Naxi, and over the course of time segments of the Tibetan population have also been incorporated as Han, Mongol, Moslem, Qiang, and Naxi.

The notion that it was only under the compulsion of force from China proper that Tibet entered into the Chinese realm is simply the result of mechanical thinking. This historical region is the product of a series of processes resulting from the eastward development of Tibetan civilization and the western expansion of the civilization of China proper. Not only did the Dalai Lama never historically rule a Tibet of this scope, but even in the Tibet of the period prior to the democratic revolution, he and the Kashag government never controlled all of what is now the Tibetan Autonomous Region, as the area around Shigatse and Northern Tibet controlled by the Panchen Lama and (as well as the small area ruled by Sakya Trizin) were never under his rule. Were all areas inhabited by Tibetans placed under the aegis of the Tibetan Autonomous Region—with no attention paid to the fact that these regions are the product of a long historical process of mixed habitation—and to suddenly demarcate regions strictly on the basis of ethnicity, the inevitable result would be the oppression of, discrimination against, and eventual removal of the other ethnicities in the region. From this perspective, Zhou Enlai's proposal to take into account the diversity of the structure of autonomy by enlarging the autonomous regions so as to enable the different ethnicities in each region to interact cooperatively and to develop together was a scheme containing much historical insight.

"Post-Revolutionary" Development and Depoliticization

How to Read the Crisis of Ethnic Policy

In our present-day world, with its frequent clashes among ethnicities, the coexistence of multiple ethnicities in China's minority regions represents something to be valued. The system of local autonomy in the minority regions is the culmination of the Chinese historical tradition and the experience of the revolution, providing the organizational framework by which the multiple ethnicities in China's minority regions are able to live together. Like all systems, however, if the people of each ethnic group do not actively participate, if they do not have a sense of agency and of identification with it, the system itself will calcify, become conservative, and turn into a merely top-down order of social control and management. If the government fails to respect the culture and customs of minorities and from its superior position merely raises up or belittles the position of any given ethnicity in accordance with the thinking of mainstream society, then it could very possibly violently alter local ethnic relations and create antagonisms and conflict. Following the outbreak of strife on March 14, 2008, the institution of regional ethnic autonomy has been put into question from different perspectives, with the research of Professor Ma Rong being the most incisive and profound.

According to Ma's analysis, the crisis facing China's nationalities policy is most evident in the following: (1) as part of the expansion of markets in contemporary China income disparity has risen dramatically, something that has manifested itself in disparities among regions, occupations, educational levels, and different ethnicities, but because the system of regional ethnic autonomy places ethnicity at its core, complicated sources of inequality that are actually not related to ethnicity tend to congeal around ethnic antagonisms, becoming the catalysts for these antagonisms. (2) Following the foundation of the PRC, in order to implement complete ethnic equality, every level of the government has put into effect a system of policies that are preferential to minorities, consisting primarily of (a) a preferential policy on birth control for minorities in which they are either not subject to the rules or in which the rules are liberalized for them; (b) minority students generally receive preferential treatment in the university entrance examinations; (c) government policy extends varying degrees of preferential treatment in economic matters such as loans, welfare assistance, and financial aid to members of minority groups in the autonomous regions. Implementation of these preferential policies is, in effect, discrimination toward those who do not receive their benefits, something that has created two groups—those who receive preferential treatment and those who do not; this has created antagonisms and discriminatory relationships between the majority and minority populations.[92] Ma Rong's general summary is as follows: resolution of the question should consist of concentrating on reducing differences among regions, and classes or social strata; implementing administrative regulations that solidify the differences among ethnic groups will only create antagonisms and conflict among them.

Any given policy or administrative arrangement grows out of specific historical circumstances, and adjustments to them are inevitable. Ma Rong's criticism of China's nationalities policies is based on a large amount of factual data, and I would agree completely with his critique of the artificial distinctions among ethnic groups. Should we, however, thus deny the system of ethnic regional autonomy altogether, and replace it with the system of provincial administration that facilitates the total unification of institutions and citizenship status—citizenship status here includes ethnic difference—throughout the country? In principle, the equality of each citizen should be a basic goal, but formal equality and actual equality often differ from one another, a worldwide truism. The thinking behind ethnic autonomous regions was to try to effect a balance between formal equality and actual equality, to recognize the difference between the equality of all citizens at the statutory level and actual differences in social practice so as to advance real equality. Aside from this, globalization, marketization, and modernization have combined to produce cultural similarity all over the world, so one of basic concerns must be consideration of just what methods can be adopted to further equality even as cultural difference is maintained. If we regard local ethnic autonomy as the source of the Tibetan crisis, we may in fact be passing over the true crux of the matter.

In order to better enable us to make a choice between eliminating ethnic regional autonomy and reforming, perfecting and developing it, I believe that we must separate the policy question from the idea behind it. According to Zhou Enlai's authoritative interpretation, regional ethnic autonomy is not to be equated to ethnic autonomy—while it does focus upon on a particular region, by demarcating the region as an ethnic region, it is able to take into account the ethnic, cultural, customary, and productive capacities that distinguish areas where other ethnicities outnumber the Han. Compared with Han core regions, these areas generally lag behind economically and educationally. In principle, the idea behind regional ethnic autonomy is precisely to further ethnic cooperation, coexistence, and merger so as to create a new society based on universal equality—it is quite opposed to notions of autonomy with an essentialized vision of ethnicity at their core. In this sense, examining "unity in diversity" in Chinese society and looking back at nationalities policy during the socialist period does not mean assuming a universally applicable and inflexible institution, but rather to seek to understand under what circumstances the system provides the prerequisites for peaceful coexistence among a multiplicity of ethnic groups, and under what circumstances it creates the conditions for crisis and antagonism. If a crisis emerges in an ethnic autonomous region, why has it been produced under current conditions and not earlier, in the socialist period?

The crises facing the system of regional ethnic autonomy have been produced by social change. The Tibetan region is a snowy plateau and has a relatively unitary Tibetan population, but that does not mean it is an isolated world unto itself—its fate has been closely intertwined with the changes that China has undergone. In a letter he wrote to Hu Jintao, the first-generation Tibetan revolutionary, Phuntsok Wangyal, noted that Tibet depended upon aid from the central government and from other provinces and cities for 95 percent of its financial resources,[93] and that this assistance includes direct financial aid as well as assistance for Tibetan economic development. Even during the Cultural Revolution period [1966–1976], financial assistance from the central government to Tibet increased by 9.09 percent annually on average. In the reform period, Tibet has provided its population free medical care, education, technical assistance, and veterinary care, with other necessities of life and raw materials all receiving substantial subsidies. As a result, the GDP of the Tibetan region has grown by an average of 12 percent a year since 2000. The rise in the standards of housing and in personal income is generally acknowledged, with the *Far Eastern Economic Review* admitting in a commentary published after the riots in Tibet that the income of Tibetans has increased by several times.[94] In fact, in the face of accusations in the Western media, the Chinese government and media used the example of Tibetan economic growth as its defense. The question, then, is this: Why did the crisis in Tibet continue to worsen in the years between 1980 and 2008?

The Chinese government has charged that there is an organized unity of response between outside influence and the power of the exile community, something for which there is considerable evidence. In his "Tibet and the (Mis)Representation of Cultural Genocide," Barry Sautman described this situation some time ago. In 2001, when the International Olympic Committee announced in Moscow that Beijing had won the right to hold the 2008 Olympic Games, the Dalai Lama's special ambassador to Russia, Ngawang Gelek, said to journalists, "China has long conducted ethnic and cultural genocide in Tibet," and that the Olympic Committee should not have given Beijing the right to hold the games. He added, "Chechnya in the Russian federation has a hundred times more freedom than does Tibet in China." As early as the late 1980s and early 1990s, a leading official of the Tibetan Youth Congress (TYC) said, "There is not one innocent Chinese in Tibet and the war will target every [Chinese] civilian there." In 2003, the leader of the TYC spoke of an intention to train guerrilla fighters, and added: "I am going to ask the Dalai Lama: 'If killing a hundred Chinese a day will win Tibetan independence, will you do it?' If he says no, then he cannot lead the Tibetan people." Between 1995 and 2000, the TYC plotted nine bombings in Lhasa.[95] More recently, a German media organization revealed news concerning a plan involving a Tibetan exile group and a number of politicians from Western countries to oppose the Olympics that were held in China.

Even granting that "Tibetan independence" enthusiasts are only an elite minority inside and outside Tibet, it would be incorrect to assume that the Tibetan riots were based simply on a political plot without more fundamental causes. Chinese economic growth between the late 1980s and the present has been a stunning achievement, with the number of people lifted out of poverty unprecedented among the developing nations of the Third World. This economic growth, however, did not cause the social crisis to fade away, but, on the contrary, under the influence of developmentalism, the opposite occurred: the division between rich and poor, between different regions and between city and country, not to mention the environmental crisis, all reached major proportions, with massive population movement also constituting an important source of social turbulence. In the past few years all sorts of "group actions" have become extremely frequent, some them actually quite large. The difference between these spontaneous social movements for self-protection and the Tibetan riots is that the latter have been violent. Because of this, aside from the organized violence and the existence of a divisive external influence, the Tibetan question cannot be explained as being completely unique or exceptional—it must, rather, be analyzed in the context of the entirety of China's current social transformation. By my rough estimation, the transformation of the following three interrelated factors is vital to an understanding of the present situation in Tibet: (1) the complete disappearance of the class politics of the socialist period and the complete reorganization of social relations, with the administration of the original ethnic autonomous regions having undergone serious upheaval; (2) the complete permeation of market relations, with a consequent change in the makeup of the population and increases in economic and educational inequality; (3) the crisis in ethnic cultural identity, with the revival of religion and rapid growth in the number of Buddhist monasteries and monks. All of these matters took place against the background of China's rapid economic expansion and grave social divisions. I sum these factors up under the rubrics of "depoliticization," "the expansion of the market," with the cultural crisis and its attendant "expansion of religion" advancing in tandem with one another.

The Mass Standpoint, the Ethnic Standpoint, and the Politics of Two Different Identities

First, I take issue with Halliday's concept of "the syndrome of postcolonial sequestration," believing instead that the Tibetan crisis is rooted in the process of "depoliticization" that has developed in the context of "post-revolutionary" China. As I explained above, the Chinese nation is a political community with the people as subject; its established institutions, its social and ethnic policies must always keep this basis of the political community in mind. Any institutional arrangement or social or ethnic policy that betrays this principle can be seen as "depoliticized." As a result, the "politicization" element in "depoliticization" differs completely from the concept of "politicization" that creates hostility between us and others based on ethnic relations.[96] Most of the disputation over Tibet centers on questions concerning its historical situation, such as noting that in the thirteenth century the Yuan dynasty for the first time included Tibet within Chinese political borders; the legitimacy of the seventeenth century Qing dynasty rule of Tibet; the fact that Tibet historically was recognized as being under Chinese sovereignty throughout the nineteenth and twentieth centuries; the relationship between the Nationalist government and the Dalai Lama;[97] the signing of the "Agreement between the Central People's Government and the Tibetan Regional Government on Measures for the Peaceful Liberation of Tibet" (generally referred to as the "Seventeen-Point Agreement") signed on May 20, 1951; and the question of which side scrapped the "17-Point Agreement."

The question of Tibet's status, however, is neither simply dependent upon international recognition nor upon the agreement between the Chinese central government and the Dalai Lama–Kashag government. From the time of the establishment of the People's Republic of China in 1949 up until October 25, 1971, when China's seat in the United Nations was returned to it, China never received recognition by a United Nations that was under the effective control of the United States, but did that mean that China was not a sovereign state? And during the 1959 suppression of the Tibetan rebellion, which elicited such a clamorous response in Western public opinion, were there any Western governments that recognized Tibet as an independent state? This fact demonstrates that the political subjectivity of New China was established on the basis of the foundation of its own historical activity, and if one fails to grasp this premise, there is nothing further to discuss. From my perspective, failing to pay attention to this political process while discussing the Tibetan question is an example of the discourse of "depoliticization."[98]

Since the nineteenth century, colonialism and capitalism have created a particular set of global conditions in which revolution and change are neither absolutely internal nor absolutely external, but rather the result of interaction between the two. As part of this interaction, new political subjectivities have been formed. In dealing with the idea of the Chinese nation, if one fails to understand national identity from the perspective of the modern Chinese Revolution, it is impossible to fully grasp the national question in postrevolutionary China. In discussing the French and American revolutions and the concept of nation in this period, Eric Hobsbawm pointed out that "if 'the nation' had anything in common from the popular-revolutionary point of view, it was not, in any fundamental way, ethnicity, language and the like, though these could be indications of collective belonging also. As Pierre Vilar has pointed out, what characterized the nation-people as seen from below was precisely that it represented the common interest against particular interests, the common good against privilege."⁹⁹ As a result, although ethnic difference, common language, religion and territory, and a common historical memory are factors perennially appealed to by modern revolutions, these were not the only things that were decisive in the formation of the Chinese nation. The Chinese nation would have had a hard time becoming a self-conscious historical subject had there been no innovative political process and resistance to foreign powers, and without the practical experience of the people of every ethnicity joining the common struggle to construct a new China, the Chinese nation would never have become a self-conscious political fact. As far as Tibet is concerned, between the time of the peaceful liberation of Tibet in 1951 and the 1959 suppression of the rebellion and the gradual unfolding of the land reform there, the course of history in Tibet was not merely the result of a process of negotiation between the Chinese central government and the rulers of Tibet, but rather a process of social liberation. Without modern colonialism and the Chinese Revolution, this process would not have been possible, while it is equally true that the process could not have taken place without the resistance of the Tibetan people to foreign aggression and to internal oppression.

From 1772, when the British East India Company used the quarrel between Cooch Behar and Bhutan as a pretext to send emissaries into Tibet, to the battle of Mt. Longthu in 1886–1888, to the signing of the Sino-British Treaty on Tibet in 1890; from the conflict surrounding the demarcation of the border in 1894 to the British incursion into Lhasa in 1904, the Tibetan people and clergy having engaged in a long series of struggles with the forces of imperialism. During the later years of the Taiping Rebellion [i.e., the early 1860s], Tibetan and Qiang people in northwestern Sichuan launched an uprising against the Qing government, echoing the social struggles taking place in other parts of the country. Qinghai, Yunnan, Guizhou, and Sichuan were all places the Long March passed through in the 1930s,¹⁰⁰ and revolutionary politics was also influenced by contact with ethnic minorities. Advocacy of a united national front against the Japanese invasion was obviously quite different from the advocacy of simple self-determination for individual ethnicities that characterized the period prior to the Long March. Prior to that time, there were very few members from minorities among the revolutionary ranks, but after that their membership increased, to the point that during the Yan'an period the Central Party School established a minority cadre-training course. Those trained there later became the backbone cadre sent to minority areas, each with a double status of local resident and revolutionary. After the founding of the PRC, minority leaders made great contributions to the development, stability, and unification of China's minority regions. In fact, long before the establishment of the new China, there appeared the "Tibetan Revolutionary Party" led by Rab Dgav, who was close to the Nationalist Party and believed in the ideas of Sun Yat-sen. There was also a number of groups active in the region, such as the "Tibetan Communist Movement," which included the "United Tibetan Liberation League," the "League of Popular Autonomy of East Tibet," and the "Communist Working Group of the Tibet-Xikang Border Region"; the activists who took part in these groups went on to become leading cadres in various areas of Tibetan society.

Compared with other regions of China, however, there were unique features to the transformation of Tibet in the 1950s. There were two sorts of special circumstances: (1) Tibetan society was marked by a highly developed relationship between high politics and the religious apparatus, so any large-scale social change could not circumvent some change to this structure. (2) Tibetan society had witnessed reform efforts in the nineteenth and twentieth centuries, but such efforts were quickly suppressed by the combined pressure of Western imperialist invasions and conservative indigenous rulers, with Tibet thus forfeiting the chance to transform internally. The social changes that took place in the 1950s were thus not the product of internal social reform or of a class liberation movement, but rather a peaceful liberation resulting from negotiations between the Chinese central government and the Dalai Lama and Kashag government that took place against the background of the victory of the Chinese Revolution. In 1956 the central government gave assurances that for the time being ("six years of no change") it not would carry out a democratic revolution in the Tibetan regions, but would maintain the old system. These assurances, however, did not mean that the government gave up on the idea of a democratic revolution in Tibet. The Chinese government and the Tibetan elites were both clear about this. The events that took place in Tibet in 1959 were closely related to the influence on other Tibetan regions of the land reform in eastern Tibet in the 1950s—the Tibetan ruling class panicked even as there was a surge of liberation and change. The 1959 suppression of the rebellion was a major political crisis, which witnessed the complete breakdown of any cooperation between the central government and Tibet's ruling elites. Basing itself on changing land relationships and on class politics, the Chinese government used this moment to completely eradicate the system of serfdom, bringing about a momentous transformation to Tibetan society.

The system of land tenure in Tibet had been related not just to the institution of the nobility, but was also thoroughly intertwined with the landholdings of the monasteries, and serfdom was "the foundation on which thrived the manorial system and the interrelationship between politics and religion." As a result, in this social system in which "politics and religion" were merged, the implementation of land reform and the liberation of the serfs could not help but affect the religious sphere. As Melvyn Goldstein points out, "the two types of economically productive landholdings in Tibet were manorial estates held by aristocrats, monasteries, and incarnate lamas, and land directly held by the government. The majority of the country's land and people were organized into manorial estates: recent Chinese accounts state that they accounted for 62 percent of the total arable land, 37 percent in the form of religious estates and 25 percent in aristocratic estates."[101] Tom Grunfeld's research has demonstrated that prior to the democratic reform, the Drepung monastery, the largest monastery of the Gelugpa order, owned 185 estates with 20,000 serfs and 300 pastures with 16,000 herders.[102] These relations of domination of both land and labor permeated society down to the smallest village;[103] thus, the implications of land reform for the religious realm. And because in comparison with other places the Tibetan land reform was carried out more from the top down (from the standpoint of the Tibetan aristocracy, it was instituted from the outside), the violence involved in the process was particularly acute. The letter the Panchen Lama submitted to the central government in his later years has numerous descriptions of this, and regardless of the accuracy of his depictions, violence during land reform was an extremely serious problem. In the 1980s, the central government, as part of its efforts to ameliorate the consequences of the Cultural Revolution, carried out assessments, investigations, and rectifications of the tragic errors that took place in the Tibetan regions during that time, giving further confirmation of the many problems that were part of the Tibetan democratic reform.

Reassessment of and reflection on history should not, however, negate the important fact that as a result of land reform ordinary Tibetans gained new political and economic status, becoming members of society in a sense quite different from the tenants, hired laborers and serfs they had been during the period of "a merged politics and religion" and serfdom. Without this predicate, there is no way to explain why, in spite of the various crises visited upon Tibet between the 1950s and 1980s, the antagonisms and destruction (for example, the extremist policies of the "democratic reform" and the destruction of religious institutions and artifacts and factional struggles during the "Cultural Revolution") of all of these crises differed completely from the identity crisis of today's "Tibetan question." The report entitled "An Investigative Report into the Social and Economic Causes of the March 14 Incident in the Tibetan Areas" (*Zangqu 3.14 shijian shehui, jingji chengyin diaocha*) and written by a group of young scholars clearly demonstrates my point here. Their report states:

> In Amdo and Tibet proper, the central government beginning in the 1950s successively carried out land reform, the elimination of the monastic economy and the basic institutions of the tribal chieftain system, the abolition of relations of feudal dependency like serfdom, and distributed productive resources like land and livestock to the farmers. Via this fundamental transformation of the basic means of production, the farmers and herders who received these saw their overall standard of living rise significantly. At the time, the core productive activity in Tibet was still agriculture and stock raising. The reform of this economic base greatly transformed the living standard of the Tibetan people, and to a very real extent was successful in establishing a new legitimacy and sense of identity.

The worship of Mao Zedong maintained by some Tibetans even today is not simply a religious matter, but is rather a product of the sense of social subjectivity newly created in Chinese society in the 1950s and 1960s. "In the planned economy, the Tibetan region began to receive significant personnel, material and financial support. The transformation of the political and economic systems enabled the Tibetan regions in their totality to reach institutional identity with Han regions. At the same time, the social structure of Tibetan society also underwent change."[104] It was precisely the creation of this new social subjectivity that turned the matter of relationships with the Han that had been vastly exaggerated by the traditional rulers of Tibet into a question of social liberation. In other words, the system of local ethnic autonomy had under socialist conditions effectively established a regime of legitimacy and a sense of identity.

The Tibetan "democratic reform" established two principles, political equality and the separation of politics from religion. These principles not only caused the system of serfdom that was so closely related to religion to completely collapse, but also provided Tibetan politics and economics with a new subjectivity—a people's subjectivity produced through class liberation and ethnic equality. The term "emancipated serfs" was actually the basis for a new political legitimacy. Looked at historically, the creation of a subjective agency of the people was closely related to the class politics of that era, and any review of the antagonisms and tragic results produced by "class politics" should not occlude the tremendous effort that, through the land reform, effected enormous changes in the entirety of Tibetan social relations—the change in status of a "million serfs" provided the revolution with political legitimacy. The current "Tibetan question" has come to the fore against the background of China's market reforms and its gradual assimilation into the global economy, which has also produced shifts to the two principles set out above. From the perspective of the politics of equality, the "democratic revolution" rooted out a hierarchical system based on agricultural serfdom and went on to remake class relations. Market reform, however, has remade economic relations, dividing and rationalizing society around relations of property rights. The political foundation produced in China in the 1950s and 1960s was gradually reconfigured in the 1990s, and the ethnic regions were no exception: following in the wake of new social divisions, the political legitimacy of the early revolutionary period fell into crisis.

If the process by which a socialist country transformed the unity between religion and politics in a religious Tibetan society marks a radical secularization, then market reform is an even more radical process of secularization. The main difference between the two processes is this: in the course of pushing for a separation between politics and religion, the former not only reformed the politics of Tibetan society, the economic structure, and relations among classes; it also created for the Tibetan people a quasi-religious value system (i.e., a new unity between politics and religion),[105] while the latter has been the exact opposite effect of destroying the value structure of the socialist period via the force of the economy and the market; this process of secularization has, in turn, provided a new basis for religion. The increased separation between the state and its citizens produced by marketization has increased the possibility of religious penetration of all aspects of society, and Tibetan society now compared to the thirty years after 1949 once again approaches being a religious society—a religious society set between market conditions and globalization. Under current conditions, not only has the religious structure been penetrated by the force of globalization, marketization, and secularization, but the function of that structure has also undergone a major change: Buddhism has increasingly become the major source of personal identity in Tibetan society. Clearly, the processes described above accompanied the failure and retreat from the politics of universal identity created in the socialist period, the result being that the politics of universal identity have been displaced by an identity politics (political and religious) predicated on social division.

Many scholars have observed that "contradictions among the people" are produced primarily by regional difference, polarization between rich and poor and inequalities among the market competitiveness of workers rather than by any ethnic antagonisms that grew out of the idea of regional ethnic autonomy. What they have not dealt with, however, is the fact that these deep social divisions have brought crisis to the principles of equality and separation of politics and religion, thereby undermining the very rationale supporting the notion of regional ethnic autonomy. There are numerous statistics showing that during the reform period the central government, in order to promote Tibetan economic development and allow the Tibetan people to escape poverty and hardship, not only extended the system of contracting for land and self-management of stock farming from China proper to Tibetan regions, but also made substantial investment in basic infrastructure and provided considerable assistance in the form of social benefits like free education, public institutions, and aid for the poor. The central government also adjusted its former guiding principles toward Tibetan language education and religious life, adopting freer and more open policies. Unlike the advantages that accrued to the great majority of Tibetans under the reforms of the 1950s and 1960s, however, even as the developments of the post-1990 period furthered economic growth, they also heightened the differences between country and city in the Tibetan regions, the differences between China proper and the border regions, the differences between different social strata, and the differences between Tibet and China proper. According to social research undertaken by the group of young scholars cited above, "The majority of young Tibetans, even those born after 1980, have only a grade school education, a standard far lower than our young peers in Han regions. And even three to five years ago the drop-out rate from Tibetan primary schools was as high as 30 percent, and the average educational level was only primary school."[106] With such educational backgrounds and in the context of market competition, young Tibetans have a difficult time competing with people of the same generation from the Chinese core regions. And because outsiders play increasingly important roles in commercial and entrepreneurial activities in Tibetan areas, these outsiders generally have the advantage in competition within the labor force.

This research also shows that the farmers and herders with experience of the 1950s, 1960s, and 1970s have a fairly strong identification with the state, but in the late 1980s and 1990s a change took place, with those who were born and grew up in this later period having strong reactions to the differences between the Tibetan areas and external regions. If we step back a bit and take a look at the discrepancy between the support the state provides for Tibetan regions and the feelings of Tibetan society, we can clearly see a fissure: while the Chinese state provides substantial funding and assistance to Tibetan regions so as to raise their economic level, from the perspective of the Tibetans, these investments are merely expressions of the penetration and control of Tibetan lands by the advanced regions, that is the advanced Han regions. Economic integration has not spawned a sense of social integration, but rather given rise to a sense of social division. In Tibet, as in many other areas of China, mistrust of officials and the bureaucracy is not merely related to the spread of corruption, but is also rooted in a crisis of legitimacy that is part of a process of social transformation. Those who participated in the events of "March 14" were not older people who had experience of the period from "serfdom—land reform—reform and opening up," but were rather "Tibetan youth born after 1970, who grew up in Tibetan areas and who have suffered the effects of modernization and globalization."[107] For them, the old legitimacy lay far removed from current conditions. The events of "March 14" (and many things like it) were not political struggle, but rather eruptions of social retaliation, which explains why Tibetan society lacked the political space to solve such a social problem. In this context, crises in society, politics, economics, and culture all turned into ethnic conflicts.

This crisis is one of "depoliticization." I need to make it clear that my discussion of "depoliticization" is not rooted in some sort of nostalgia for the socialist period, but rather uses the concept to point out a basic problem that is more often than not ignored: the Tibetan crisis is one portion of the general crisis facing post-socialist China. Because the source of the crisis lies in the very course of contemporary history itself, ethnic issues cannot be explained purely by focusing on economic inequality alone; they also manifest themselves in cultural politics. Between 1950 and 1980, for instance, in the literary, musical, artistic, dramatic, and cinematic spheres that concerned themselves with national content, minority culture always played an extremely important role. It is worth pointing out that national policy having to do with minority culture not only expressed itself in the cataloguing and preservation of epic poetry, popular music, literature, and the general cultural heritage of Tibetans, Mongols, and other minorities, but even more through the creation of a new political and cultural identity. In the 1965 musical epic *The East Is Red*, the Mongolian and Tibetan folksongs sung by such characters as Hu Songhua and Cedain Zhoima (Tshe bstan sgrol ma) occupied an extremely important position in the work as a whole. Films centering on stories about national minorities like *Five Golden Flowers* (*Wuduo jinhua*, 1959), *Heroic Sisters of the Grasslands* (*Caoyuan yingxiong xiao jiemei*, 1965), *Ashma* (*Ashima*, 1964), *Serfs* (*Nongnu*, 1963), *Visitor on Ice Mountain* (*Bingshanshangde laike*, 1963), and *Third Sister Liu* (*Liu Sanjie*, 1960) are the classics of the Chinese cinema of that period. And during the entire period between 1950 and 1980, oil and brush paintings as well as murals depicting portraits and stories of

Xinjiang, the Mongols, the Tibetans, and minorities from the Southwest as well as the Northwest occupied an important place in artistic production. With hardly any effort we would be able to add a long series of other work to the above list.

Accompanying the "depoliticization" process of society as a whole in the 1990s, however, this array of representations ceased—the cessation I am referring to here is not just to the end of the large scale introduction of work on national minority themes, but also to the gradual linking of minority culture to the development of the tourism market, with the latter providing the social basis for the renewal of orientalism in China. Were we to compare works on minority themes from the two periods, the aim of the former would be a new and universal status achieved through socialist culture, while the latter seeks to accommodate the market via an accentuation of the "orientalism" of minority culture. While not getting into an evaluation of the political and artistic quality of minority cultural creations of the socialist period, I wish only to point out the following two facts: the former sought to create a new universal identity on a base of minority culture, while the latter takes minority nationality as essential difference; the former emphasizes the universal in the unique, while the latter creates a particularity out of the unique. And along with this change, cultural creation featuring minority themes has in general gone into decline in contemporary China. In my opinion, the rise of religion and its power is closely related to this decline.

Religious Society, the Expansion of the Market, and Population Mobility

The Expansion of Religion during Secularization

In response to the destruction of religion and the monasteries during the Cultural Revolution, in the 1980s the Chinese government in Tibet lifted all its restrictions on religion. Respect for freedom of religious faith is, of course, completely reasonable. In fact, even in the period of land reform, Mao Zedong and the Chinese government clearly expressed the idea that the land reform and religious questions should be kept separate, with the idea that land ownership needed to be reformed, while religious faith needed to be respected. Researchers have pointed out that as of the end of 1997, the Chinese government had allocated funds to restore 1,787 monasteries and centers of religious activity; the number of monks and nuns living in those monasteries and nunneries had reached 46,380 or 1.7 percent of the total population of Tibet. Such activities and ceremonies as studying and debating the sutras, abhiseka [devotional activities] and monastic discipline as well as Buddhist rites like sutra recitation, prayer, imprecations against catastrophe, blessing through touching the head, and expiating the sins of the dead all came to be practiced regularly. Aside from Tibetan Buddhism, there are 88 Bön monasteries, over 3,000 monks, 93 living Buddhas, and over 130,000 adherents; there are also four mosques and over 3,000 Moslems, and one Roman Catholic church with 700 believers. Among the religions listed above, Tibetan Buddhism occupies the key position and its institutes of Buddhist teachings, journals, and other publications have flourished. In Tibetan regions outside Tibet proper the force of Tibetan Buddhism also greatly increased. In the monasteries I have visited, those of medium scale had about 800 monks and acolytes in residence, while large-scale institutions had over 1,500. In these places I observed large numbers of young boys reading scripture by yellow lamplight, and the scale of the kitchens and their equipment—not to mention the mountains of firewood stacked up behind the buildings—was incredibly impressive.

The religious question has not, however, been resolved, with antagonisms cropping up in two areas. First, Tibet is a religious society, but the government's policies in regard to religion are formulated in accord with the logic of a secular society—there are thus conflicts between the religious and the secular in regard to the understanding and implementation of religious creed, knowledge, procedures, and protocols. As a Tibetan intellectual explained to me, according to the provisions of Tibetan Buddhism, the process by which lamas study religious knowledge must be in accordance with religious protocols—for example, certain texts may only be studied at certain monasteries, while other texts must be studied at monasteries in Qinghai or Gansu provinces. At present, however, religious knowledge is imparted by the Institute of Buddhist Studies *(Foxue yuan)*, so even if a student learns at another location the same thing as would be taught at the stipulated place, it would lack legitimacy. As the antagonisms within Tibetan society have intensified, however, and in light of the fact that monasteries themselves have become involved in the resulting conflicts, the government has grown extremely wary of mobilization and movement among monasteries. Another Tibetan intellectual said that another factor behind the March 14 riots was the divergent viewpoints between the government and monasteries over the age requirements for monks. Many Tibetan children are quite young when they go to a monastery to study and become lamas at the age of 15 or 16, and because of the economic growth of monasteries, becoming a lama has become another profession at which one may make a living. In accord with its rules about employment age, the government has changed the old age limit of 16 for becoming a monk to 18, thereby giving rise to antagonisms between the government and the monasteries. The religious question in Tibet is closely linked to the question of a religious society rather than to the issue of religious freedom in a secular society. Thus, as social antagonisms turned into ethnic and religious conflict and the religious question and political identity became ever more closely intertwined, the relationship between religion and politics emerged in a new form.

Second, this new expansion of religious activity has proceeded apace with the expansion of market society, one factor being that along with the market reforms, tourism and consumer society have both embedded themselves into the everyday life of Tibetan areas, another being that a substantial amount of wealth has flowed into the monasteries. Many visitors to Tibetan regions have been profoundly struck by the contrast between the magnificence of the monasteries and the general poverty characteristic of life in these areas. In relatively wealthy regions, the competition to keep up with the neighbors—while not necessarily the product of marketization—is quite evident in the building materials people have chosen for their houses; even if not a function of marketization, however, such display is an interesting reflection of contemporary consumer society. Some officials use the achievements of economic development to explain the importance with which the government regards minority regions, without understanding that development may, in fact, be the cause of the problems. Several years ago, in an editorial note in *Dushu* magazine, I introduced a discussion among several young Tibetans who were working in the field of rural reform. The three slogans they had put forward were (1) protecting the environment, (2) protecting Tibetan culture, and (3) protecting collective ownership.[108] The first two of these are easy to comprehend, but the third seems quite strange to enthusiasts of property right reform. The property rights characteristic of market society, individualism, and consumerism have all posed serious challenges not only to religious society but to local communities. In advocating the protection of collective ownership those who seek to construct local Tibetan communities do not wish to return to the commune system, but rather to protect the domestic Tibetan mode of life. This is the reason that I take the link between the simultaneous advance of religion and the process of marketization as the key to understanding the social problems of ethnic minority communities.

For the "Tibetan independence movement" to take the changes that contemporary Tibet is undergoing as "cultural genocide" represents a fundamental misunderstanding. In fact, as early as the 1930s, and even without any intervention by the central government, modern reform in Tibet (the Lungshar Reforms) had already come into conflict with the system of serfdom and its union between religion and politics—the antagonism between modernization and a religious society has been there since the inception. After 1959, Tibetan economic development took place under the auspices of the state, taking the form of investment from the more economically developed areas of China; in the 1990s, however, this was augmented by the new expansion of markets. We should not fail to be aware of the unprecedented crisis affecting the social system and cultural heritage of Tibet that has taken place in the course of this process of modernization. As is the case with the rest of Chinese society, which globalization and marketization are reorganizing in its entirety, Tibet is an organic component of this process. Taking this crisis as ethnic strife is a dangerous misunderstanding, but because the conflict between Tibetan religious culture and the logic of market society is so plainly evident, the pain and perplexity Tibetans are feeling is notably acute. On a visit to the Deqin (bDe chen) Tibetan region in 2004, I had the good fortune to travel with both a living Buddha from Qinghai and the Ganzi scholar and author of *A Comprehensive History of the Tibetans*, Mr. Zeren Dengzhu (Tshe ring don grub), and to be able to hear their discussions with the young people of the region. Based on questions raised in these discussions that confirmed my own observations and reading, I believe that the crisis facing Tibetan society manifests itself most clearly in the following areas.

The first crisis is that facing religion in a general process of secularization, which shows up mainly in two places, one of them being the antagonism between modernization and religious society. Late nineteenth-century Tibetan society witnessed a brief experiment in modernization, but it was nipped in the bud by British colonial incursions, resulting in the hostility of the religious authorities to modernization. Melvyn Goldstein and other Western scholars have already provided thorough accounts of this. But the real problem lies in the following: the issue of the relationship between Tibetan religious and secular society is not the same as the issue of freedom of religion or faith in the West, nor is it the same as the problem of the relationship between a religious and a secular society discussed in the rational context of social theorists in the West. The core of the religion question in Tibet is the antagonism and opposition between religious society and modernization, that is to say, how religious society copes with secularization. Since modernization has expressed itself most often as having spread from more economically developed areas to Tibet, the form this process takes is more often than not seen as "sinification."

The first steps toward secularization were taken with the separation of religion and politics in the late 1950s, and beginning in the late 1980s, and especially after 2000, this process was rendered even more acute by the radical expansion of markets. Although Tibet is regarded as a religious society, political and economic initiative no longer lies in the monasteries and with the monks. The stronger the sense of cultural crisis, the stronger the sense of identity based in Tibetan Buddhism and of living on the snowy high plains becomes. Ironically, however, the stronger this sense of identity, the greater becomes the perplexity at how to deal with the dual challenges posed by modernity and "sinification." And because of the split between religion and politics as well as between economics and religion the strengthening of religious identity naturally creates an ever greater tension between politics and religion and religion and economic society. As a Tibetan scholar attending the meeting reminded the young people who harbored a sense of cultural crisis, there is no getting around the challenge of modernity. This struck me as being similar to what then-President Kim Dae-jung of South Korea told a group of a dozen or so foreign scholars in 2000: globalization is a challenge, but South Korea has no alternative but to join in full-bore. The French sociologist Pierre Bourdieu was a participant, and I recall that at this point he pointed out skeptically the contradiction between globalization and cultural diversity. If in the Tibetan regions, however, modernization is regarded as the equivalent of "sinification," the conflict between religion and secularization will turn in the direction of conflict between Tibetan and Han.

The second crisis is that facing religious institutions in the process of secularization. In a religious society, the monastery lies at the heart of social life, but when politics and economics split off from religion, economic society becomes a challenge and a temptation to the religious order. I once heard an older Tibetan intellectual say that when those of his generation get together, what vexes them most is the corruption of religion and the monasteries. Aside from amassing wealth via taxation, many of the monks live double lives, generally failing to observe their vows and disciplines, going "to work" at the temple by day, and returning home at night to another sort of life altogether. The corruption of their religion readily stirs the moral consciousness and heartfelt religious faith of a Tibetan youth already imbued with a profound sense of anxiety, and when this faith and sense of morality is pulled toward matters of ethnicity, it was not difficult to predict radical social action. The people who suffered the most harm in the Tibetan riots were Han people and Moslems engaged in commercial activity, and most of those doing the attacking were monks and acolytes, a fact clearly related one way or the other with the crisis of religion in Tibetan society. The source of the hatred is rooted in the superficial overlap between secularization and "sinification." I say superficial not because there is not a real relationship between the two, but because the so-called sinification when set in another context would express itself as "Westernization," "globalization," "capitalism," or other such "-ations" and "-isms."

When people talk of Tibet now, they mostly repeat Hu Yaobang's comment of the 1980s that all Tibetans believe in Tibetan Buddhism, which is still pretty much the case. In different regions of Tibetan society and among different social strata (such as ordinary farmers and herdsmen versus the elites), however, views on the question of religion are not the same; within the society of believers there are different sects, and outside that society there exist nonbelievers or, perhaps better to say, secular Tibetan intellectuals, who mostly respect religious faith but also respect the freedom of religious belief. Within Tibetan society there are different tendencies, groupings, and voices, including voices critical of Buddhism, but it is precisely because of this profound crisis facing Tibet that many Tibetan elites tie their ethnic identity exclusively to their Buddhism, thereby consigning to oblivion the full diversity of voices that characterizes Tibetan society. In the realms of research on history and religion, there are a number of Tibetan scholars looking with renewed interest at the traditions of the Tufan period, inquiring about the aborted efforts toward modernity in the late nineteenth century and reflecting upon the origins and decline of the Bön religion, clearly in search of alternative traditions for Tibet. In the ever more insistent context of identity politics, however, these voices have come to be slender reeds. Thus, to understand Tibet and its religion it is necessary to break with the tendency to totalize that religion, the kind of totalizing so often used by Westerners when they analyze China. I need to add here that not only do we need to listen attentively to alternative voices from within Tibetan society, but we also need to attend to the voices of other minorities from China's Southwestern and Northwestern regions. Without hearing the diverse voices of the Moslems, the Uygurs, the Qiang, the Yi, the Han, the Mongols, the Derungs, the Naxi, the Bai, the Miao, the Dai, the Primi, the Lisu, and many others, it is impossible to understand either the Chinese Southwest or Northwest; neither should we rely strictly on different ethnic voices per se, but must rather attend to people from different social strata: the differing perspectives from the city and the country, from the rich and the poor, from those with different levels of cultural and educational attainment, from those who live in the mountains and those who live on the plains, from those in the river valleys and those from areas afflicted by drought—all these voices need to be allowed to emerge.

Marketization, Globalization, and the Linguistic Crisis

The second sense of crisis is of linguistic origin. In Tibetan regions, primary schools at the regional and municipal level conduct classes primarily in Chinese *(Hanyu)*, with Tibetan also offered; below these levels, and in agricultural and pastoral regions, classes are conducted primarily in

Tibetan, with Chinese also offered. After the Cultural Revolution, the government has made considerable investment in Tibetan education and culture, with a significant amount of that being in education in the Tibetan language. With the spread of urbanization and markets, however, more and more Tibetan youth—especially those who live in ethnically mixed areas—are showing less interest in learning Tibetan, a problem faced by all ethnic minorities.[109] There are certain similarities here with the situation facing Chinese under the impact of English, but the difference lies in the population base of Chinese speakers being so massive that it cannot be compared to the sense of linguistic crisis facing the Tibetans. If the status of the Tibetan language is compared to the languages of even smaller ethnic groups, however, Tibetan appears to be full of vitality. The crisis confronting the languages of even smaller and weaker minorities groups in the course of modernization merits our earnest attention. For instance, policies could be implemented to advocate for and strengthen bilingual or multilingual education, and legal arrangements could be made to protect minorities and their cultures through guaranteeing social and employment rights.

This issue, however, needs to be considered in the context of reflection on modes of development rather than simply discussed under the rubrics of "cultural genocide" or "ethnic conflict." In the seminars conducted by Deqin, some of the young people present brought up the fact that the proportion of young Tibetans able to speak Tibetan has gone down precipitously and they even wondered how, since with even a number of Tibetan scholars attending a conference on the study of Tibetan culture not being able to speak Tibetan, how could they seriously engage with Tibetan culture? In fact, all the scholars at the seminar could speak Chinese (*putong hua*). Later, a Tibetan scholar of the Bön religion with whom I became acquainted at the meeting told me that he did not like the formulations *Hanyu* (literally, "language of the Han people," generally translated as "Chinese") or *Guoyu* ("the national language"), because he had from the time he was in primary school learned both Tibetan and *putong hua*, and that *putong hua* was just as much their language as anybody else's, so the languages should not be distinguished by the ethnic labels of "Han" and "Tibetan." I wholeheartedly agree with his view; since the Han people are an amalgamation that has formed itself over time, the language carries within it components from every ethnicity within China; moreover, since Tibetan and the Chinese share a common origin, demarcating language from the perspective of modern views of ethnicity does little to facilitate interaction among peoples. This loose attitude toward the definition of language is easy to accept in areas with mixed populations, but in places where a single ethnicity dominates, linguistic change inevitably will elicit a much more powerful response than in mixed regions. This problem is not in any way diminished even when the government supports the minority language.

Radical Change to Modes of Ordinary Life

The third sense of crisis originates in changes in the modes of ordinary life. Even if monasteries and the religion have developed with extraordinary rapidity over the past thirty years, changes brought about by enhanced transportation, the media, popular culture and its associated life styles have transformed Tibetan society in even more startling ways. The late nineteenth- and early twentieth-century contention between traditional culture and Westernization in China is still freshly lodged in our memories, but from the late nineteenth century on there has been a strong tide of reform and enlightenment among Chinese intellectuals, which corresponded to the changes in the Chinese state apparatus taking place at the same time. This movement has had an enduring influence on the immense changes that have taken place since in Chinese society. For its part, Tibetan society has been immersed in a process of social change that is, if anything, even more extreme than that which confronted Han culture in the late nineteenth and early twentieth centuries, even as it has witnessed the expansion and development of religion in the postrevolutionary period. It has not, however, produced large-scale internal reform and cultural enlightenment movements like the 1911 Revolution or the "May Fourth" New Culture Movement. The modern traditions of enlightenment and of religion are entirely different and one's awareness of the very same event may be completely at odds, depending on in which tradition one is situated.

For example, for the vast majority of Chinese wearing Western clothes or jeans has become quite ordinary, with no one feeling the intense resentment that someone like Gu Hongming felt in the period around

1920.[110] When many contemporary Tibetans wear Western clothes, or jeans, or mountain-climbing gear, however, there are other groups of Tibetans who consider this symptomatic of the Tibetan cultural crisis. I have a number of Tibetan friends who rarely wear traditional Tibetan clothes, but when they attend cultural conferences they make a special point of dressing in traditional garb, demonstrating the conflicts and tensions they feel concerning matters relating to "culture." Accompanying the advent of urbanization, there has begun a transformation in the style of traditional housing in Tibetan villages, with many younger Tibetans now preferring to live in multistoried buildings, in which the living areas are arranged completely differently than in the traditional Tibetan house. At one conference an older scholar complained of how the way modern housing includes toilet facilities inside the house totally contravenes Tibetan tradition. This is, of course, the feeling of someone who is older, and those younger may not care much about it—many who heard this comment even thought it was quite funny, but to Tibetans who are greatly concerned with a sense of cultural crisis it is a very serious matter. These small matters having to do with ordinary life are the surest indicators of the profundity of cultural change, and our taking this concern as a matter for humor explains more than anything else just how much our own society has moved toward "Westernization" in the last hundred years.

Social Mobility, Rights of Immigration, and the Crisis of Ethnic Regions

The fourth area of cultural crisis arises out of population mobility, which may the most powerful catalyst of all. Such mobility certainly was present in traditional China, the mass migrations to the northwestern regions and into Manchuria starting in the eighteenth century being a good example. Population migration encompassing whole villages is, however, quite different from that growing out of the new division of labor that characterizes market society. The development of a market economy, the loosening of the *hukou* household registration system[111] and improvements to transportation have combined to enable massive population mobility. Following the vast expansion of the urban infrastructure, the construction of the Tibetan railway, and the development of the tourist and service industries, the Tibetan economy has opened up to an unprecedented extent. This opening has been accompanied by great numbers of outsiders—principally Hans and Moslems—entering Tibet, principally as laborers, technicians, service employees, and tourists. Nationally, the basic pattern of migration has been from the interior to the coastal regions and from the country to the city, and it has been on a large enough scale to put substantial amounts of pressure on such core cities as Beijing and Shanghai. Even with the great amount of state investment in Tibet, however, discrepancies among different regions are growing. The strategy behind "The Great Opening of the West" has been to reduce these discrepancies by accelerating economic development in China's West, and the result has inevitably entailed more population movement on the high plains, mostly in urban areas. If in comparison with the activity in the eastern regions of China the number of Tibetans engaged in this movement has been relatively small, it has mostly been concentrated in Lhasa and other core cities, with most of it consisting of seasonal employees and itinerant merchants (these movements have, by the way, in no way fundamentally transformed the basic composition of the population of these places, as the Western media has reported).

As the research of Ma Rong and Danzeng Lunzhu (bsTan 'dzin lhun grub) has pointed out, however, "The western areas of China are where the ethnic minorities reside, and portions of the Han floating population moving there will intensify and broaden the interaction among different ethic groups. The opening of the West will not only increase the scope for ethnic interaction and cooperation, but will also make more evident the cultural and religious contrasts among these different ethnicities, not to mention the fierce competition for employment and resources. The result will be a vastly more complicated set of relationships among ethnicities in the west."[112] Opening up to investment, population mobility and a labor market are the basic constituents of the formation of market society, and tourism is an even more fundamental tool of economic development in the west. Migration and mobility are the basic rights of every citizen, but within the logic of developmentalism, to ignore substantial differences in education, culture, language, and the distribution of social resources among different groups in different regions when looking at large-scale migration is to ensure the preferential treatment of some groups at the expense of others in terms of resources and incomes. As for Tibet, "those who profit most from economic prosperity are outsiders, not the Tibetans, who, because they lack any real capital or technical assistance, have become increasingly marginalized."[113] Within the crisis of religious society described above, the question of secularization gets crisscrossed with the relationship between indigenous peoples and those who have come in from the outside, with the result that a crisis brought about by secularization gets projected as an issue of "sinification." Against a background of market economics and large-scale population mobility, the questions of how to combine the protection of multiculturalism and social equity, how to effect a balance between protecting the interests of minorities and guaranteeing the right of population migration are the keys to perfecting local ethnic autonomy and furthering equal interaction among ethnicities.

The key question here is this: even though the division between rich and poor exists throughout Chinese society, in minority regions this split is invariably closely linked to the traditions, customs, language, and positions vis-à-vis the market economy of different ethnicities. As a result, it is not even necessary to posit widespread corruption in contemporary China as the cause of ethnic antagonism: even under conditions of perfect markets—the so-called equal start—market competition would result in new divisions in the absence of attention to cultural differences among ethnicities. For example, in certain minority areas, because members of different ethnicities have different positions in relation to the market, wages, working conditions and opportunities differ among members of these groups, giving rise to ethnic discrimination.[114] In sum, whether or not economic growth can foster ethnic harmony depends upon a variety of circumstances, but there is no necessary relationship between growth and harmony in themselves—the real question still concerns precisely how to develop and how to explain this development.

"The Politics of Recognition" and the Question of Equality in Ethnic Minority Society

The complicated situation in Tibet reflects the profound crisis that a religious society has been undergoing since the nineteenth century, a crisis of modernity that no region or social group has been able to really solve. Pointing out the factitiousness of the reproaches of China coming from the West is one thing, but actually coming up with ways of coping with the details of this complicated situation is quite another. Ten years ago, in an introduction I wrote for the book *Culture and the Public Sphere*, I raised two core questions: one, can modern society under certain circumstances place guarantees for collective rights over those of the individual? And, two, in a modern society based on a formal legal system, should we adopt perspectives that take matters of social substance into account?[115] In the process of editing and translating the selections for that book and in writing the introduction, I pondered the question of "the politics of recognition" in a culturally diverse society, but the problematic was quickly submerged in the hubbub surrounding globalization and Chinese nationalism.

A legally guaranteed market economy, individual rights and the right of private property comprise the core intellectual propositions of contemporary China. Even though theses notions are explained differently, it is clear they have in common a programmatic and depoliticized set of liberal rights. In fact, this discourse of liberalism merely replicates modernization theory. My critique of the theory of private property is not based on opposition to protecting rights to private property, but rather opposition to turning this concept into a limitless, universal truth. In our diverse society, with its complicated ethnic relations, the equal protection of individual rights often runs athwart the equal protection of collective rights. According to a rights-based liberalism, neither the constitution nor the law can protect any collective objective and any attempt to do so would be discriminatory. Based on a communalist *(shequn zhuyi)* perspective, however, this abstract concept of equal individuals and their rights is the product of a particular culture and society, and to apply it to other social circumstances would also be discriminatory. Thus, equal respect should not apply just to the individual person, but should take into consideration collective objectives, such as the particular demands of ethnic minorities, women, and immigrants.

Chinese policy toward its ethnic minorities does, in fact, recognize such collective objectives. During the early years of the ethnic autonomous regions, there were many who raised doubts, from a variety of perspectives. Some of the questions asked included: "The oppression of minorities has already been abolished and equality put into effect, so all that remains is the question of democracy among the various ethnic communities—so is there really still a need for local autonomy? Cadres from minority backgrounds are already in positions of real governmental authority—is this not already local autonomy? Some of the minorities in these areas resemble the Han in their social and economic lives, or they have no written language—is there still a need for local autonomy in these areas? Will not putting such stress on formal ethnicity foster a narrow nationalism?" Others asked whether democracy is absolutely necessary for local autonomy and whether it was not necessary to first work on ethnic relations outside the autonomous regions.[116] Local autonomy represents a method of incorporating both local initiative and interdependence, particularity and universality—it recognizes the character of the collective, but does not take these collective rights or characteristics as being in opposition to universality.

But do these special arrangements cause these distinctive policies toward minorities to be discriminatory toward other people who live in the autonomous regions? For instance, in regard to birth control, ethnic minorities are either subject to much less control or to no control at all, while the majority population is restricted to one child per family. Another example is that minorities have access to a number of staples of life that are in short supply, while the Han majority has either little or no access. In the past such preferential policies elicited a good deal of discontent among cadres and technicians assigned to aid Tibet or Xinjiang, believing they were not being treated equally. If one considers the population and special customs of the minorities, however, these policies and laws exemplified the principle of respect for equality. In fact, the institutions for treating ethnic minorities in China are closely related to certain characteristics of the Chinese political tradition, such as the various mechanisms developed on the principle of "following [local] custom and what is suitable" for rule in the Qing dynasty, the appointment of hereditary headmen in minority areas (the *Tusi* system), the system of "tribal" (*Buluo*) control, the "league-banner" system *(mengqi)* used in Mongolia and the unity between religion and political control. In each case, these mechanisms were adjusted and modified in line with the principle of adapting to local custom. In other words, these institutions all recognized difference, but from the perspective of formal equality, recognizing difference is simply recognizing a social hierarchy, and must thus be regarded as invalid.

How to respect simultaneously the two principles of equality and social difference presents an enormous challenge for a diverse society. Western societies are dominated by structures of rights, and because social inequality is produced under conditions of the formal equality of rights-based liberalism, the struggle for rights among minorities in those societies generally takes the form of a politics of identity. Communalists would hope to transform this politics of identity into a "politics of recognition," that is, to implement the values of equality via recognizing difference, and thereby mend social divisions. In this context, recognizing that different societies are of equal value is a logical postulate or starting point rather than a substantive judgment—it is premised on the idea that the politics of recognition is carried out through public association. This notion of so-called public association incorporates two ideas: one, as Charles Taylor has theorized, if this process of public association does not encompass the space for each culture to celebrate its own particular brilliance, the practical result is that the recognition of other cultures amounts to little other than condescension, and condescension is obviously directly at odds with the politics of equality or what might better be called the politics of respect.[117] Because of this, unity in diversity must be based on a principle of diversity, and if this principle does not stand, the "unity" becomes merely an imposition from the top.

Two, public association refers not just to the dialogue and interaction among different ethnic cultures, but also to the full rights of association within each ethnicity—should this premise be neglected, the politics of recognition can very easily become merely a process by which a small minority takes control of ethnic politics. Thus, if one seeks to prevent diversity from becoming the basis for a separatist nationalism but becoming instead the premise for coexistence, each "component" must be an interactive participant able to take political initiative, rather than being regarded only as something isolated and fixed in itself. In this sense, "the recognition of difference" is not to essentialize difference, but to be predisposed toward diversity and equality so as to further association, coexistence and mixing among divergent ethnicities. What we lack most acutely today is just this sort of interaction and equal dialogue among the intellectuals of each ethnicity or among those of different ethnicities. If we say that prejudice exists in contemporary China, the main form it takes is not open discrimination, but rather imperceptible ignorance and neglect.[118] For instance, at the time of the Tibetan riots, how did Tibetan intellectuals discuss this among themselves? What were the different points of view and explanations that they offered? If we don't hear their voices in the public media, we lose the opportunity for dialogue and contact among intellectuals of different backgrounds.

The Tibetan question involves the dual questions of the freedoms and protections guaranteed to minority culture as well as rights of migration in the context of widespread population mobility. Because of globalization and the spread of the market economy, the system of local ethnic autonomy needs to be adjusted, but this does not mean we should completely do away with it and bring into play a newly fabricated system to cover over existing differences. The recognition of cultural difference does not imply that these differences are essential and immutable such that we must return to forms of purely ethnic politics—in regard to this, I completely agree with the criticisms many scholars have made of the systematization of ethnic relations that has taken place during the course of identifying ethnicity. This does not mean, however, that we can overlook historical difference and forcibly cram different cultures and ethnicities into a single system of formal rights. Aside from promoting association and coexistence, the real challenge lies in ascertaining whether or not we will be able to transcend our already settled status politics and, as class politics fades away, recreate a universal politics capable of enabling different peoples to participate in and preserve social diversity. In sum, lacking a mass political basis—one accommodating initiative and dynamism—questions of ethnicity can only become a kind of game between minorities and the government, which could easily fall into the trap of becoming the Han/Tibetan dualism that Western mainstream opinion and various ethnic nationalists so fervently wish to create. If we want to break up this dualism between Han and Tibetan, we need to establish a new basis for a politics of equality by thoroughly reconsidering our developmental logic, creating a more tolerant public arena and allowing the voices of ordinary people fuller expression in that space.

The Protest Movement Is a Form of the Politics of Dignity

The Tibetan question has been created under complicated historical circumstances, reflecting the general crisis brought about by the twin processes of China's marketization and globalization. After the Tibetan incidents, however, we are faced with two sources of misinformation: for one, Western mainstream opinion not only has been unable to reflect upon the enduring damage done to other regions by its own colonialist history, but has, on the contrary, twisted a weighty question with which the Western world has had a centuries-long and very close involvement into an anti-China chorus. This has had a profoundly damaging effect on young Chinese living abroad who cannot help having been deeply affected by this discriminatory ideology. Second, even as the Chinese media attempted to confront Western opinion, it failed to focus on the deep crisis of Tibetan society—in fact, Chinese society as a whole failed to avail itself of this opportunity to think through the relationship between the logic of developmentalism in China and the Tibetan crisis. As a result, following the transformation of the Tibetan crisis into a controversy over seizing the Olympic torch, the Tibetan question was set to one side. As far as I am concerned, this is a "clash of ignorance" rather than some "clash of civilizations," but augmented by neo–Cold War politics.

Any large-scale social movement is made up of any number of separate intentions, making it impossible to explain the motivations of every participant. We heard any number of narrow-minded remarks from the Chinese student protest movement—the younger generation, like the Western media, knows little about the "Tibet question." But to simply say that the whole movement is characterized by a "parochial nationalism" is clearly to miss the substance of the question. To begin with, this movement was a defense of the Olympic torch, not a Chinese torch, and implicit in it was the search for world peace and protecting the right of the peoples of the world to interact under the Olympic flag. Second, in the face of systematic distortion of the violence in Tibet by the mainstream Western media and the prejudiced reports of the events surrounding the passing of the torch, Chinese students and residents overseas sought for a clear accounting of what actually happened even as they protested the violence that took place in Tibet. A good portion of the Western media they criticized had played a shameful role in reporting the Kosovo, Afghan, and Iraqi wars. The insulting words such mainstream outlets as CNN uttered against China and the Chinese people not only revealed their own ingrained racial prejudices, but also inflamed the "parochial nationalism" in their own societies. As a result, during the course of the protest movement, some of the students involved strove to link their protest with the antiwar movement, expressing their wish to join Chinese concerns with a world perspective and with internationalism.

Third, it is necessary at this point to distinguish clearly between the critique of hegemony and organized violence on the one hand and the complicated thinking involved in working through questions concerned with respect for ethnic minorities and general issues of ethnicity within a changing contemporary society on the other. The overseas student movement expressed with great clarity its rejection of the forces of international hegemony and separatism, thereby allowing the entire world to hear the voice of Chinese society. Absent this voice, the relationship between China and the West would have been perpetually stuck in the realm of diplomacy, without any popular participation. Today, when a mainstream Chinese media under the control of a small group nonetheless constantly declares itself to be the voice of the people, the power that the students demonstrated—whatever one thinks of it—provided a powerful instance of just what the voice of the people consisted of. This has been a turning point, a point where a new generation of people might gain a new understanding of China, and of China's antagonisms and predicaments—it is a moment where one can gain an understanding of China's true position in the world's contemporary order.

What I am stressing here is this: the logic of the politics of dignity and equality should be extended to all social relationships in Chinese society, including ethnic relations, and not limited merely to protest against the unfair words of the Western media. The Tibetan crisis was not a matter of happenstance, but was deeply rooted in the contemporary transformation of Chinese society. If the protest movement cannot extend the principles of the politics of dignity to defend the dignity of Tibetans, Uygurs, and other minorities, it will lose its implicit idea of equality. If the protest movement is suborned by feelings of ethnic hatred and enmity, it will also turn its back on the political principles of ethnic equality, cooperation, and mixing in its efforts to form a political community of citizens. In a period of depoliticization, the movement for the recognition of equality and dignity may present a moment for the birth of a new politics. In the course of this movement, a new situation stimulated the political enthusiasm of a new generation, enabling them to participate in the public life of contemporary life of China and the world. The spirit of self-sacrifice manifested by the younger generation of Chinese following the Wenchuan earthquake in Sichuan in May 2008 is closely linked to this moral enthusiasm and political concern. The epicenter of this earthquake was in the Aba Tibetan-Qiang Autonomous Prefecture, where reside people of a number of ethnicities, including Tibetans. The volunteers who came from all over the country never used racial or communal perspectives when they showed up to assist the victims—such a view never entered the consciousness or even subconscious of the volunteers; they came for no other reason than to struggle to save their compatriots. The bonds of "unity in diversity" are displayed in these powerful feelings and in the acts of mutual assistance that were characteristic of the time. I hope the public spirit displayed during this period of crisis can not only be turned into an enduring impetus for democracy, but can also be a moment that can produce a new recognition of Chinese society along with its different regions and cultures. We are facing a time marked by a steady stream of crises, and if we fail to employ substantial social force to change the logic of developmentalism, these crises cannot be resolved. In order to bring about the birth of this new politics, this new self-knowledge of Chinese society urgently needs to be in dialogue with intellectuals of different ethnicities.

5

Okinawa and Two Dramatic Changes to the Regional Order

In discussions on war and peace in Northeast Asia, Okinawa occupies a unique but often neglected position. As a creation of the Cold War, as well as the embodiment of the military structure of globalization, the American military occupation remains in place. On May 15, 1972, Okinawa was "restored" to Japan by the United States, but discord ensued: first, Japan was not in full administrative control over Okinawa "post-restoration," and the power relations of the Pacific War were still represented in Okinawan airspace. Second, historical relations between Okinawa and Japan cannot be properly encompassed by the term "restoration." If the concept of "restoration" recognizes the history of modern Japanese expansion, it also signifies the conflict that the Okinawan anti-occupation movement is bound to develop with the Japanese government. Even if we can get around the concept of "restoration," the sovereignty of Japan is even now limited by the political configurations of the Cold War era.

Translated by Zhang Yongle

Therefore, from the standpoint of nation-state logic, Okinawa will have to vacillate between the two options of identifying with Japan or seeking independence from it. (During the early postwar years, Okinawa was even obliged to consider the possibility of becoming a part of the United States.) As a result, while in the rest of Japan the discussion about Okinawa has been centered on the American occupation, in Okinawa itself the discussion has revolved around whether the area is a part of Japan or whether it should seek independence. Because the matter of military hegemony is involved with issues concerning labor and land rights, as well as Japan-U.S. relations, the U.S.-Japan Security Treaty, and the military alliance between Japan and the United States, any discussion of Okinawa is impossible without reference to the United States, Japan, Russia, China, and surrounding areas, as well as to the post–Cold War configuration of hegemony. The future Japanese role in this region also depends on changes to this structure of international relations. In this sense, the Okinawa problem is not just an East Asian issue, but essentially reveals the development of capitalism and imperialism in the region.

With American global hegemony in decline, how is peace to be maintained in Northeastern Asia? What changes are now taking place and will take place in the future to the order of this region that was given its shape by World War II and the Cold War? Is it possible to find a mechanism for keeping the peace from within the local traditions of this area? Aside from the antiwar and anti–military base movements, Okinawa has also raised the aforementioned epistemological and or historical questions. Based on the fate of Okinawa from the 1870s through the 1940s, this essay will analyze two dramatic changes in the East Asian international order. Through close reading and analysis of historical documents, I will attempt to show that the contest among China, Japan, and the United States over Okinawa is simultaneously a series of conflicts, compromises, and coordinations between two visions of order. It is, in fine, a conflict between nation-state relations on the Western model of international law, and the traditional regional order based on the "tribute system." In discussing peace and conflict in this area, we cannot avoid the key problem of how to determine a new order for the region.

The Okinawa Question, Regional Relations, and the Dramatic Transformation of International Rules in the Nineteenth and Twentieth Centuries

Since the mid-nineteenth century, imperialist expansion has brought Western nationalism to a position of great influence in Asia. Although some scholars contend that there has been a corresponding endogenous nationalism within Asian societies, a new type of sovereign state was born under the influence of Europe. Some of the new themes or new roles that have emerged in the Asian region derive from these new power relations and newly legitimized knowledge. Okinawa (called "the Ryukyus" at the time)[1] was an exceptional kingdom that had long maintained a tributary/suzerain-feudal relationship with China. In order to preserve its position, it actually established tributary relations with both China and Japan. Regardless of the specific geopolitical and cultural situation, however, the Ryukyus' status was upheld within a mode of order utterly different from that of the sovereign or nation-state. For the moment, let us use the not entirely appropriate term "tribute system" to refer to this mode of order, as, in general, it means that modern nationalism did not grow out of it. No matter what we call it, however, nationalism could only be formed following the demolition of this set of traditional relationships. As a consequence, Japanese domination of the Ryukyus did not take place under the old form of relationship, but under a new one, that is, an imperialist-nationalist relationship.

My basic argument is this: changes since the nineteenth century do not simply derive from changes in the hegemonic positions of China and Japan in the region, but also stem from drastic changes to general international rules. This dramatic change of rules cannot be described simply in terms of the relations between one state and another, as it refers to the transformation and rupture of the basic principles underlying the political entities and communities in the region. Without realizing the extent of this rupture and transformation, we cannot understand the modern history of Okinawa, the 1894 Sino-Japanese War and subsequent cession of Taiwan, the colonization of the Korean peninsula, the establishment and collapse of Manchukuo, or the political-military logic of the Greater East Asia Co-Prosperity Sphere. This new order takes European international law as its basic conceptual framework.

On December 23, 1871, the Meiji government sent out a diplomatic delegation, which, in a period of twenty-two months, visited twelve countries, including the United States, Britain, France, Germany, Russia, Italy, and the Austro-Hungarian Empire. It is said that this delegation spent one million Japanese yen, amounting to more than 2 percent of the fiscal revenue of the Meiji government in 1872.[2] In *An Explanation for the Dispatching of the Ministers Plenipotentiary (Haken tokumei zenkentaishi jiyū sho)*, the Meiji government set out one of the missions of the group as being to "explain to and consult with the governments of other nations on the aims and hopes of our government," so as to "revise past treaties and enact an independent and unrestrained system" "according to international public law *(Wanguo gongfa)*."[3] On March 15, 1873, this Iwakura diplomatic delegation paid a call on Otto von Bismarck, the German "Iron Chancellor," whose influence on modern Japanese thought cannot be underestimated; Okubo Toshimichi admired him immensely. Talking of the transformation of a poor Prussia into the great German empire, Bismarck told the delegation that "all the states in the world today communicate through friendly etiquette, but this is only on the surface—the reality is of the strong bullying the weak and the great humiliating the small. . . . So-called international law is said to be the standard by which the rights of all nations are protected, but when great powers contend for their interests, if observing international law is expedient, they observe it punctiliously; if it is not expedient, however, they quickly resort to force. It is thus never observed without exception."[4] Of this, Okubo wrote to Saigo Takamori: "After hearing these words of Bismarck's, I began to feel that Japan has a bright future."[5]

The extent of this event's influence was not limited to Japan's self-strengthening, as the Meiji government's efforts to use Western international law to gain space for itself in Asia eventually turned into a logic of imperialism and expansionism. The Pacific War was the result of the direct conflict between this logic and a similar American logic at work in the same region. In the early days of the Meiji period, Japan several times sent emissaries to China seeking the Qing government's signature to commercial treaties patterned after those signed with the Western powers. Behind these demands lay the desire to expand into Korea and the Ryukyus. The policy of those who controlled the government in the early Meiji period, such as Iwakura Tomomi and Kido Takayoshi, was to invade China and Korea, using the forces that had toppled the Shogunate, so as to consolidate the power of the center. At the time, Korea was nominally a dependency *(shubang)* of China, so when the Japanese government sent a delegation to Korea requesting that it open its ports to commerce, the Koreans asked Japan to sign a commercial treaty with China first, and only after that sign one with Korea. So the Japanese government's active pursuit of the conclusion of a Sino-Japanese commercial treaty was, on the one hand, to solve domestic conflicts, and on the other, to gain the qualifications for access to Korea.[6]

From the perspective of this logic, the narrative that has the Pacific War—"the struggle for living space"—as completely different from the "Great East Asian War"—imperialist expansion, invasion, and colonization—does not hold up.

Japan itself has undergone a fundamental transformation in the process of adapting to changes in international law. As Japan attempted to establish its own foundation after the Meiji restoration, its expansionism became ever more robust, and its using the regional relationships of the time to gradually annex the Ryukyus is a specific example of this tendency. Japanese expansionism, however, did not begin in the Meiji period. Toyotomi Hideyoshi's military action in invading Korea and his plans built on that invasion to sweep into Ming China and India, for example, are clear illustrations of an earlier expansionism. Prior to the Meiji, Tokugawa Ieyasu's fear of the Ming as well as considerations of commercial interest kept Japan from taking over the Ryukyus, and Zheng Jing's (1642–1681) dispatch of his lieutenant Xiao Qi to attack the Ryukyu tribute ship to the Qing court was another outgrowth of this situation.[7] This shows the long-standing historical motivation on the part of Japan to contest its sphere of influence with China. Such expansionist activities, however, differ little from traditional offensive and dynastic wars in Asia, and cannot explain events of the nineteenth and twentieth centuries. Thus, aside from this endogenous impetus to expand, we still must ask: What principles did Meiji Japan bring into play in gaining control of these areas? How did Japanese expansionism in this new period differ from what it had been in the past? I think that the self-conscious use of the new form of international law was one of the most important new things here.

The American missionary W. A. P. Martin's *International Public Law (Wanguo gongfa)*, a translation into Chinese of the American jurist Henry Wheaton's (1785–1848) *Elements of International Law* (1836), was initially published in 1864 and was quickly transmitted to Japan. This represented the introduction of Western nation-state logic into East Asia—both the Chinese and the Japanese were instructed that their conflicts and antagonisms with the West derived from their own ignorance and misunderstanding of international law, and that any change in behavior needed to take place in accordance with this law. In this way they could establish themselves as the embodiment of a new zeitgeist, that is, as nation-states under international law. It should be noted that although Japan in the early Meiji was also encumbered by unequal treaties with Western states, it still made every effort to employ such treaties in order to expand into China and Korea. In fact, even before the Iwakura delegation visited Europe and America, Japan had begun to imitate the model of the Western powers in its relations with surrounding areas. For example, during the negotiation of the 1871 Sino-Japanese treaty, Japan tried to "follow the Western example," but China refused benefits to be granted under a "most favored nation" clause.[8] The Qing initially hoped to maintain the previous model of regional relations, but was powerless in the face of the fact that "all the diplomats constantly invoked international public law, so we were obliged to use this to manage them."[9] European imperialist international law thus gradually became the basic framework governing regional relations in Northeast Asia. After the Iwakura delegation returned home, the temporary suppression of the "discourse on conquering Korea" *(SeiKan ron)* perhaps resulted from—domestic considerations aside—Japanese concerns that new stipulations of international law would limit their expansionist strategy aimed at Korea and surrounding areas.

What changes took place in the relationship between Japan and the Ryukyus during the course of the Japanese occupation of the Archipelago? The Archipelago consists of the Osumi Islands, the Tokara Islands, the Amami Islands, the Ryukyus Islands, and the Miyako Islands, accounting altogether for 4,500 square kilometers. The Ryukyu tribute relations with the Chinese court can be traced back to the "three mountains period" in 1372, with Chūzan being the first of the islands to pay tribute to Ming China, followed by Nanzan and Hokuzan. In the early fifteenth century the united Ryukyu kingdom took shape, and it continued to pay tribute to China. In 1609 the Japanese Satsuma Han (the Shimazu Clan) took the Ryukyus militarily and the Ryukyu king was forced secretly to submit to Japan vassalage. So although it still regarded China as its legitimate ruler, the kingdom was heavily taxed by Japan for more than 270 years. Dual tribute relations between the Ryukyu kingdom and the Ming on the one hand and between the Ryukyus and Satsuma (and eventually to the Edo Bakufu) on the other thus came into being, although the Ryukyuan king was still enfeoffed by the Chinese court up through the Qing dynasty. When I visited the Ryukyuan royal palace, I saw the gifts—ships in particular—brought back by the tribute missions to the Ming and Qing dynasties, as well as the paintings of the imperial missions sent by China that were on display. The Meiji government reduced the Ryukyus from a kingdom to a feudal clan *(han)* in October 1872, and in March 1879 invaded, establishing Okinawa Prefecture *(ken)*, after which the Ryukyus became part of the Japanese "homeland."[10] The Ryukyus are both poor and small, like the Himalayan kingdoms of Bhutan and Sikkim. Why were these small political entities able to exist among a number of much larger political entities without becoming part of them? And with the advent of the era of the nation-state, why did they gradually turn into special regions of nation-states? What sort of cultural, political, and institutional flexibility was able to provide these small political communities with relative autonomy, and what sort of cultural, political, and formal system ultimately caused them to be included within a formalist concept of sovereignty? These are not problems unique to Japan—many other countries, including China, even without having developed anything like Japanese imperialism, have been part of the same process of transformation and have not been able to isolate themselves from the crises and challenges that have been part of the complicated interchange between what is regarded as internal and what as external.

In the Asian region, especially along China's borders, the relationships among political entities that are now often classified under the concept of the tribute system were totally different from those among nation-states. There is also an inner-outer aspect to tribute relations, but it differs from the inner and outer defined by borders and administrative jurisdiction within those borders, with what is considered close or distant and near or far in the former following a different logic from the inner and outer of the latter. In the tribute system, the distinction among close or distant and near or far allows a significant degree of ambivalence and flexibility between inner and outer, but the distinction in the nation-state system is more rigid. According to the principle of sovereignty, the clear demarcation between inner and outer produces an absolute opposition between independence and unification, with no in-between gray area allowed. The tribute system, however, is more like a system based upon differentiated degrees of kinship and affinity, a relationship flexibly produced by the practice of its participants. Tribute relations, therefore, cannot be equated to the relationships of inner-outer in the nation-state sense. Of course, the difference between tribute relations and treaty relations is a normative and formal difference, with cases of historical overlap. I have conceptualized this overlapping relationship as the dual process of empire-building and state-building in the course of dynastic history, with the relationships between inner and outer under the empire often embodying different models, according to each case; while they are all classified as belonging to the tribute system, they differ in substance.[11] For example, the relationship between Mongolia, Tibet, and the central government differed from that between the Qing and Russia or other European states. The latter resembles modern foreign relations, while the former cannot be understood in that context. The system of "Eight Banners" in Mongolia, the Kashag in Tibet, and hereditary chieftains of Southwest China all differed from one another. Even if they were all relations of vassalage, they varied according to specific historical conditions—the tribute system was not uniform and standardized, but was characterized by more flexible sorts of relationships.

In the era of nationalism, a region either belongs to a given political entity or has sovereign independence—there is no relationship or form that consists of neither unity nor independence, something that signifies the collapse of the traditional mode of relationships. The Japanese colonization of the Ryukyus and its first invasion of Taiwan in 1874 brought significant change to the longtime and effective norms of interaction in Asia. This was not merely a process of one kingdom annexing another, or the waxing and waning of Japanese and Chinese power, but also a sharp transformation of universal norms. The Japanese invasion of Korea, the 1894 Sino-Japanese War, the Russo-Japanese War, the Great East Asia War, and the Pacific War were the sequential embodiments of this normative transformation. Early European international law is actually imperialist international law, and Japan sought to use it to become equal to the European imperialists. In this new era, the legitimacy and legality of the occupation and aggression of one political entity against another relied upon a new set of norms—the old system no longer worked. This is a major event in world history. The source of the Okinawa question emerges from two overlapping processes: endogenous Japanese expansionism and the universalizing of (imperialist) nationalist norms.

The Earliest Use of Imperialist International Law

In 1874, a year after China and Japan exchanged their first treaty, Japan invaded Taiwan on the pretext of a conflict that occurred in November 1871 (in which fifty-four people died) between Taiwanese Aboriginals and Ryukyuan fishermen who had run into a typhoon. Japan initially attempted to open channels with the Qing government through Ryukyuan channels, but later attempted to use this incident as a springboard to attack Taiwan. Prior to the war, in May 1873, the Japanese foreign minister Soejima Taneomi arrived in Beijing requesting an audience with the emperor, then sent his deputy, Yanagiwara Sakimitsu, to question Mao Changxi and Dong Xun of the Ministry of Foreign Affairs, where they asked the Qing government to punish the Taiwanese Aboriginals. Mao Changxi responded: "I've heard that [our] 'vassal' killed the Ryukyuans, but I have heard nothing about your people being hurt. Both islands belong to us, and if residents of each kill one another, it is something completely within our jurisdiction. I am in sympathy with the Ryukyuans and we will deal with the matter ourselves—since this is no concern of yours, why bother yourself to question me?" Obviously, Mao Changxi did not recognize Japanese jurisdiction over the Ryukyus. As he pointed out at the time: "All the murderers are 'savages' *(shengfan)*, so we regard them as beyond the reach of civilizing, and thus difficult to rule properly. The 'Xiayi' in Japan [i.e., the Ainu in Hokkaido] and the 'red savages' [i.e., Native Americans] in the U.S. do not obey the kingly teaching, either—this is something common to all countries."[12] Qing China had a number of legal traditions, for instance, the Qing Code, the Mongol Code, the system of hereditary chieftains in the Southwest, and the Kashag system in Tibet. In Taiwan, the *Shengfan* ("savages") and *Shufan* ("civilized barbarians") were treated differently. This unique system of rule derived from a governing strategy characterized by the principle of "cong yi cong su" (follow local custom and what is appropriate) and enduring political-cultural relations in different regions; it was also related to the "foreign affairs" of the empire.

After the war broke out in 1874, the Ministry of Foreign Affairs sent a note to the Japanese foreign ministry on May 11: "We have taken note that there exist savages in isolated portions of Taiwan, who have yet to be bound by law, so we have not extended the bureaucratic system to those regions. This is based upon the teaching of the *Book of Rites (Li ji)*, 'Do not change their customs and what is appropriate for them,' even though the territory undoubtedly belongs to China. Savages like this also exist in other provinces in China's frontier regions, but they are all within our territory. China allows them to follow their own customs and what is appropriate for them."[13] We may say that this is an institutional model for relationships among peoples that does not posit rigid inner-outer distinctions and allows for diversity. This pluralist legal-political system is still a system of rule and control and has produced different sorts of control and war. Insofar as it enables flexible relationships between pluralism and unity, however, it deserves reconsideration—this does not mean that we should idealize the system, but rather that we should employ a historical horizon to reflect upon the weakness of modern political systems in preserving diversity. We should also ask why such a set of political relationships is so hard to sustain in the era of nationalism, and why the nationalist model so strongly insists upon internal unity, uniformity, and clear-cut relationships between inner and outer.

The inner-outer problem mentioned by the official of the Ministry of Foreign Affairs from the Qing perspective reflected how the Meiji narrative about Taiwan had qualitatively changed. The Qing official's argument that the so-called savages were beyond Qing legal jurisdiction is based upon the unique legal institutions of the Qing. A useful analogy here would be that mainland Chinese law differs from that of Hong Kong, but this difference provides no basis for a separate sovereignty for the region. Japan, however, interpreted the relationship between the Qing Code and local customary law as an inner-outer distinction in the sense of sovereignty. *A Summary of the Expedition to the "Barbarian" Lands in Taiwan*, drafted in February 6, 1874, holds that

> Taiwan's local savage tribes are beyond the authority of the Qing government. . . . It is, therefore, the obligation of the Japanese imperial government to punish them for their crime of having killed people from our vassal of the Ryukyus. This is the primary basis for the general principle behind punishing these savages. . . . If the Qing insists that since the Ryukyus also paid tribute to them, it is also a Qing vassal, we will simply pay them no heed; it will be best to ignore their comments. Our empire has substantial control over the Ryukyus, and we may stop it from its violation of ritual by paying tribute to China after we punish Taiwan, but for the present it is futile to debate with the Qing government.[14]

The Japanese strategy was to differentiate the place they invaded from Taiwan, and on the pretext that these "savages" were "people beyond acculturation" *(huawai zhi min)* and thus without political affiliation, to claim that their attack on the Taiwanese Aboriginals was not an attack on the Qing. This explanation was in direct opposition to the position of the Qing. It is appropriate here to cite the dialogue explaining their respective positions between Li Hongzhang and Yanagiwara Sakimitsu, the new Japanese Minister to China:

> Li: Why do you claim that these savages in Taiwan are not part of Chinese jurisdiction? Yanagiwara: This is a place beyond Chinese politics and education. We also have grounds for our sending of troops. Question: What grounds do you have? (No response) . . . Yanagiwara: The savages in Taiwan are just like people without rulers and have nothing to do with China. Li: How can these savages be considered a state? Yanagiwara: No, they cannot be considered a state, they are merely barbaric *(yeman)*. Li: They reside on our island of Taiwan, so

how can they not be part of China? Yanagiwara: Since China knew that these savages killed many people, why did you not punish them? Li: Investigating and taking action against the leaders takes time and effort, so how do you know that we will not punish them? By the way, the people the savages killed are from the Ryukyus, not Japanese, so why did Japan get involved? Yanagiwara: The Ryukyuan king sent messengers to plead his grievances. Li: The Ryukyuan kingdom is a Chinese vassal state, so why did they not appeal to us? Yanagiwara: Even before there was a treaty between us, our Satsuma feudatory planned to dispatch troops.[15]

Western military intervention in this area and the West's intention to promote its laws formed the background of the Sino-Japanese debate on the status of Taiwan and the Ryukyus. In fact, the Japanese pretext for the invasion of Taiwan imitated the earlier American intruders. In 1853, the American Commodore Matthew Perry's naval fleet knocked open the door to Japan, forcing Japan to sign the Convention of Kanagawa the next year. Between his visits to Japan, Perry invaded Taiwan, and suggested to the U.S. government that it occupy the island: "The geographical position of Taiwan makes it very suitable as a distribution point for American commerce, and from where we can establish trade routes to China, Japan, Okinawa, CochinChina, Cambodia, Siam, the Philippines and all the islands in the surrounding seas."[16] In 1867, the U.S. government sent two warships to attack Taiwan, but fled in the face of strong local resistance. After that the United States adopted the strategy of "using Asians to fight Asians" so as to divide and undermine China, Japan, and Korea. The American Minister to Japan, C. E. De Long, reported to the American Department of State in October 1872: "I have always believed it to be the true policy of the representatives of the Western Powers to encourage Japan in a course of conduct thoroughly committing its government against this doctrine [i.e., the closed door policy and the China-Korea alliance], and by estranging its court from those of China and Corea make it an ally of the Western Powers."[17] Japan's first attack on Taiwan not only adopted the same pretext that the Americans had used in their incursion on Taiwan, but also used the maps and suggestions supplied directly to them by the American consul in Xiamen (Amoy), Charles Le Gendre

(1830–1899), who had undertaken surveys during the American incursion. The Japanese strategy of attacking Taiwan on the pretext that this "barbarian land" was beyond the reach of Chinese political rule and acculturation was, in fact, an American suggestion.

Since the American and Japanese invasions of Taiwan went hand in hand with the extension of the application of Western international law, and because the latter was regarded as advanced knowledge, the aggressors could use it as justification for war. Miyazaki Hachiro, Miyazaki Tōten's elder brother,[18] participated in the Satsuma Rebellion, the 1877 war of great importance in modern Japanese history, as it is taken as an incidence of modern heroism. A bronze statue of Saigo Takamori still stands majestically in Tokyo's Ueno Park—he was not only the key general of the Rebellion, and an early proponent of "the discourse on conquering Korea," but also a clansman of Saigo Tsugumichi, the lead general in the invasion of Taiwan. Is there, then, any shared consciousness between the Rebellion and the 1874 invasion of Taiwan? As Professor Nomura Koichi commented on Miyazaki Hachiro: "The most progressive features of the early Meiji undoubtedly were combined with heroic virtue in the person of Miyazaki Hachiro. Moreover, in different circumstances, these progressive features could suddenly completely reverse themselves into their absolute opposite, a danger that still faces us. We can see this in the opposition between advocacy of liberalism and human rights versus the 'discourse on invading Korea,' and an anti-government movement and the invasion of Taiwan."[19]

As Miyazaki wrote to his father on the question of invading Taiwan: "Japan is involved in few military ventures, so people become mired in convention, leading to lapses in order and discipline. Our recent military victory is thus very much worth celebrating. Last year the Ryukyuan Crown Prince came to pay tribute to Japan, thus determining the position of the Ryukyus as a Japanese vassal state. The Ryukyuan King is accorded the rights of a feudal lord and is counted as part of the Japanese aristocracy. The Taiwanese did harm to Ryukyuans, which is no different than killing Japanese, so our exacting punishment is in accord with international public law."[20] The heroism of the Satsuma Rebellion is thus perhaps intrinsically related to the "international public law" deployed in the attack on Taiwan. Miyazaki also once wrote to Sone Toshitora as the latter was carrying out an important mission in China: "Please tell me of the most recent developments concerning the proliferation of robbers and thieves that you reported on before. We can deliberate on it for a while, then cast everything aside and rush directly to the mainland. As for what happened on the island [Taiwan], there is nothing to say. The only thing I can say is that I'd like to pack my things and look forward to breathing mainland air."[21] From this perspective, the attack on Taiwan and sending troops to the Asian mainland (i.e., China) are interrelated—their common basis is the so-called international public law, that is, international law.

This is the new zeitgeist premised upon the nation-state and its relations between inner and outer. The heroic spirit that overflows in Miyazaki's utterance here indicates that the nationalist mode of knowledge has already taken force as the new basis of political legitimacy. It is this new mode of knowledge that legitimizes the Japanese subjugation of the Ryukyus, Taiwan, and eventually the Asian mainland. This knowledge did not originate in Japan, but was rather a by-product of the competition of the Western powers for regional spheres of influence. The "international public law" mentioned by Miyazaki is most likely based upon the W. A. P. Martin translation of *International Public Law*. This signifies that as a victim of aggression, the Qing was also lured by the Western powers into accepting this form of knowledge—it was often said that the conflicts between the Qing and the Western powers following the Opium War stemmed from Qing ignorance of "international public law."

In other words, the rise of the Ryukyuan, Taiwan, and Korea questions, as well as the subjugation of the mainland, accompanied the legitimization of modern nationalism and the decline of traditional relationships and their values. This constitutes the internal link between nationalist knowledge and imperialism, and it is this link that infused the heroism of Saigo Takamori and Miyazaki and all their officers and men. This heroism is premised on a system of values that legitimizes and renders sublime the self and its actions, but if the result is simply blatant aggression, how can this be called heroism? It must thus be said that the heroism of the early empire is built on the basis of a new kind of knowledge and new rules of legitimacy. The Japanese invasion of Korea follows the same logic—it forced Korea to sign a treaty with Qing China, which by debasing the tribute system provided the premise for imperialist expansion and new colonial rule via a notion of formally equal sovereignty. This transformation of norms treated aggression as liberation and explained the expansionist logic of the traditional struggle for spheres of influence as the new zeitgeist.

The contemporary Okinawan social movement critiques early modern Japanese thought through an analysis of modernization as providing the theoretical justification for Japanese colonial rule. The sense of the appropriateness of modernization still functions as a concept of legitimization: the ideas of formal equality and equal opportunity undergird the legitimacy of relationships of actual inequality in relationships both inside and outside a given country. The premise of nineteenth-century treaties was a formal equality among the agents, but the treaties signed under this premise were not actually equal. In fact, the notion of imperialism first arose from the competition among European powers for resources and colonies, so the idea of formal equality was only appropriate to relations among the metropolitan imperialist states themselves. When treaty relations moved to the realm of ties between imperialist powers and regions that had been colonized or otherwise oppressed, the agents of formal equality could only be established through unequal treaties. In late nineteenth-century Northeast Asia, the enfeoffment relations of the Ryukyus, Korea, and Vietnam with China could only be regarded as inappropriate when seen in the light of the new idea of formal equality and its standards—they could only be taken as relationships of formal inequality. With such a dual standard, imperialist aggression was seen as liberation, because treaty relationships were taken as links between formally equal agents.

Many progressive people in the Meiji era sincerely believed that Japanese domination of the Ryukyus and the invasion of Taiwan embodied the new zeitgeist, something that bespeaks the evident continuity between this belief and the naked hegemony of Western imperialism. The American invasion of Iraq caused a huge number of civilian casualties and encountered the disapproval of world opinion, but it justified itself by claiming not only to be a war on terror, but also a war assisting the Iraqis to bring down a dictator and establish a democracy with human rights. Since this war took place within the framework of the nation-state system, the only issue in need of explanation lay between tyranny and democracy. The difference between this and the nineteenth century lay herein: nationalism had created a new set of relationships and metrics, while in Asia there existed another form of knowledge, as well as other institutions and sets of ritual that maintained relationships among political entities. We see, then, that imperialist aggression at the time directly embodied the clash between two different sorts of international relations. Today, however, with the nation-state system firmly in place, the invasion of Iraq is simply a violation of international law.

An Omen of the Cold War: The Cairo Conference and the Postwar Status of Okinawa

The historical relationship between international law and imperialism does not imply a simple negation of the former. Early international law was merely a set of rules among imperialist states, but with the development of movements for national independence and decolonization, many oppressed nations have become new sovereign states and have used theories of sovereignty from international law to legitimize themselves. The Five Principles of Peaceful Coexistence of the 1955 Bandung Conference synthesized a number of principles and achievements of international law. Since international law is no longer exclusively the tool of superpower manipulation—although it often still is—these powers frequently breach it. The Yugoslav crisis as well as the Kosovo and Iraq wars were all violations of international law. In this sense, the historical critique of international law cannot be equated to its negation, just as attempts to trace traditional models of political relations and interaction do not equal a move to reestablish them. The meaning of all such work lies in establishing a new horizon for reflection and critique, and conceiving of new types of regional-global relationships and the rules for them.

Any discussion on Okinawa's position in the Cold War must inevitably take up the 1943 Cairo Conference. The core of the contemporary Okinawan problem is the American military occupation and the damage caused by it, but this occupation is also part of the overall Cold War configuration of the region. We need to understand the political background of this configuration, and to analyze developments in international relations against this background. In the winter of 2009, I was a visiting scholar at Stanford University and took advantage of the opportunity to check

Chiang Kai-shek's diary in the Hoover Institution and to compare it with American diplomatic papers and Republic of China (ROC) documents, in order to try to determine the nature of the discussion of Okinawa's status at the Cairo Conference. Chiang's diary, entrusted to the Hoover Institution by the Chiang family, runs from 1917 to 1955. The portion covering the 1970s is not yet open to the public, so there is no way to know the nature of U.S. communications with Chiang when it handed Okinawa back to Japan on May 15, 1972. Given the great transformations in Sino-U.S. relations going on at this time, however (Henry Kissinger secretly visited China on July 9, 1971; Richard Nixon paid an official visit beginning February 21, 1972), we can infer the unreliability of the rumor that the United States was once planning to hand the Ryukyus over to Taiwan.

The Cairo Conference was held November 22–26, 1943, with the leaders of three great powers, Roosevelt, Churchill, and Chiang Kai-shek, and their military-civilian officials holding numerous meetings over the course of the event. The conference was of great significance for Chiang. First, China was weak, and after having undergone years of warfare against Japan, to be able to meet with great powers like Britain and the United States to discuss postwar arrangements was uniquely important. Second, the opportunity to engage in collective discussions and negotiations with Roosevelt and Churchill was also something extraordinary for Chiang in his personal life. Over the whole course of the war, there had only been talk of three great powers (the United States, the Soviet Union, and Britain) in opposition to the Axis; there had been no notion of "four powers." Chiang had not been invited to attend the Casablanca conference that had been held earlier in 1943,[22] and during the Cairo Conference when Roosevelt met with Andrey Vyshinsky (1883–1954), the Soviet Vice-Premier and Deputy Commissar for Foreign Affairs, the former still talked only of "three powers."[23] After the Cairo Conference, Roosevelt and Churchill went to Teheran to meet Stalin, with Chiang returning to China by himself, thus maintaining the "three power" structure. The basic framework established by the Cairo Conference, however, had already been confirmed.

The four-power framework of the United States, the Soviet Union, Britain, and China did not actually start at Cairo. On October 21, 1943, the Chinese ambassador to the Soviet Union, Fu Bingchang, signed the

"Four Power Declaration" with V. M. Molotov, the Soviet Foreign Minister, Cordell Hull, the U.S. Secretary of State, and Anthony Eden, the British Foreign Secretary, thus setting the stage for the four-power framework.[24] When it came time to sign the Declaration, however, the Soviet Union opposed China's entry into this "four-power club" on the pretext that China did not send representatives to the Moscow meeting; the British attitude was also quite ambivalent. It was only at the insistence of the United States that this declaration was ultimately published in the name of four powers.[25] Roosevelt had initially intended to hold a four-power conference in Cairo, but since the Soviet Union had yet to declare war on Japan, Chiang deemed "it highly inappropriate that China and the Soviet Union attend the same conference," and sent Song Ziwen (T. V. Soong) to negotiate this point with Roosevelt.[26] The "four-power" framework, which was to have such a powerful influence on the postwar international order, finally came into being at Cairo, via the assistance of Roosevelt and Chinese effort. On November 24, 1943, Chiang Kai-shek ordered Wang Chonghui—at the time Secretary of the National Defense Committee—to send, via Harry Hopkins, a memorandum from the Chinese government to Roosevelt. All four articles of the first section concern the structure the United Nations General Assembly was ultimately to take. China proposed a "four-power" declaration to form a standing committee with the four at its core.[27] With the change in the military situation in 1943, the United States and Britain began to consider the transfer of the locus of the fighting to Southeast and East Asia after the collapse of Nazi Germany, so China took on unprecedented importance. Beyond this, the ultimate goal of Roosevelt's invitation to China to join the "four-power" club was consideration of how to use China to check the Soviet Union and Japan after the war. Military matters aside, the Cairo Conference repeatedly discussed postwar security issues and the status of the American military in the Pacific area, revealing the foresight of the United States and Britain in regard to the future world order,[28] something also consonant with Chiang Kai-shek's struggle for China's international status.

There is a widely circulated notion that the Okinawa issue was not on Chiang's agenda for the Cairo Conference, and that it was brought up by Roosevelt, with Chiang only responding passively: he "refused Okinawa twice" out of fear of the United States and Japan.[29] Consulting Chiang's diary proved this to be incorrect—Chiang was actually well prepared for the meeting, and his responses to Roosevelt had been carefully considered. In his diary entry for Saturday, November 3, Chiang mentioned his preparations for the meeting with Roosevelt and Churchill, and made two points: first, "I will exchange ideas with Roosevelt and Churchill on military, political, economic and other issues open-mindedly, without concern about gains and losses." Second,

> There are three issues to be discussed with Roosevelt. The first includes: 1. Japan should hand over a certain tonnage of naval and commercial ships to China; 2. All Japanese public and private property in China (the regions occupied since the September 18 [1931] incident) should be restored to the Chinese government; 3. At war's end, most remaining Japanese weapons, warships, commercial ships and aircraft should be handed over to China; 4. Hong Kong and Kowloon should be restored to China as free ports; 5. There should be a determination of the relative benefits of a political organization consisting of four powers versus a Far-East committee; 6. There should be a military technology commission of the four powers, to study the future of international military power; 7. There should an organization consisting of the united military staffs of China, Britain and the U.S.[30]

The second item in this statement sets a time limit for the restoration to China of Japanese interests there: September 18, 1931, which would exclude the Ryukyus from the agenda.

As the preparations for the Cairo Conference became more detailed, however, issues from before 1931, including the Ryukyus and Taiwan, inevitably appeared on the agenda. The sixth article of the *Advisory Office of the Military Commission Draft of the Issues to be Raised at the Cairo Conference for Chairman Chiang* specifies as follows: "Article 6, Japan should restore the following items to China: A. Lüshun and Dalian (public property and structures in these two places should be handed over to China without compensation); B. The South Manchuria railway and the Chinese Eastern Railway (restored to China without compensation); C. Taiwan and the Pescadores Islands (public property and structures in both places should be handed over to China without compensation); D. The Ryukyu Archipelago (should be put under international trusteeship, or designated as a de-militarized zone)."[31] The date of this original draft is uncertain, but it must be prior to November 1943, when the Cairo Conference convened. Chiang's first mention of the Ryukyu issue is a diary entry for November 15 (Monday), and it is very likely related to the draft prepared by the Advisory Office of the Military Commission. The entry reads:

> The Ryukyus and Taiwan have different status in our history. As a kingdom, the position of the Ryukyus resembles that of Korea, so we have resolved not to raise the issue, although the independence of Siam is something we should propose. NB: except for issues in which China, Britain [and] the U.S. have a common interest, it would be best for us not to discuss anything with Churchill at the meeting. For example, if the United States raises such issues as Hong Kong/Kowloon, Tibet or the treatment of the overseas Chinese, we had best respond according to established principles and not quarrel with them.[32]

Some of the points here deserve attention: first, Chiang confirmed that the status of the Ryukyus in Chinese history differed from that of Taiwan, Tibet, and Hong Kong/Kowloon; second, he emphasized that the status of the Ryukyus is similar to that of Korea; third, he pointed out that "we should propose" the independence of Siam; fourth, Chiang's judgment that the Ryukyus are "similar" to Korea but "different" from Taiwan was made from the perspective of determining their respective positions in the nation-state system and did not involve the differences in the "similarities" or the similarities in the "differences." Based upon the first point, when Chiang reconsidered his plans for the meeting on November 17, he no longer included the Ryukyu issue on his agenda. The second and third points are relevant to his resolution that China should raise the issue of the independence of Korea and Siam. All these points are closely related to Chiang's understanding of the world order in Chinese history, but his understandings are all in the service of a new historical situation, that is, the postwar international order. The diary entry for November 17 says: "This meeting with Roosevelt and Churchill should focus on the most important issues: A. International political organizations; B. The organization of the Far East Commission; C. The organization of the China,

U.K., U.S. Joint Staff Group; D. Plans for the administration of occupied lands; E. The general plan for the counter offensive in Burma; F. Korea independence; G. The restoration of Manchuria and Taiwan to China."[33] The official memorandum forwarded through Wang Chonghui on November 24, 1943, mentioned such matters as the restoration of the territory occupied by Japan, and the draft of the three-power "joint declaration" mentioned the independence of Korea, but did not bring up the Ryukyus.

Once the meeting had begun, however, the Ryukyu issue was eventually brought up. *The Diary of Chiang Kai-shek* contains the following entry for November 23, 1943:

> I arrived at the dinner hosted by President Roosevelt at 7:30, and we talked straight through past the late hour of 11, when I took my leave, without, however, having finished the discussion. We agreed to resume the discussion the next day, but the main issues brought up in tonight's discussion were: A. The future regime in Japan; B. The talks centered around the matters of communism and imperialism. I very much appreciate Roosevelt's policy toward Russian communism, and we can make use of our success to liberate the oppressed peoples in the world, so as to repay the American contribution to the world war; C. The territorial issue: the four Manchurian provinces as well as Taiwan and the Pescadores Islands should be restored to China. *The Ryukyus, however, can be put under the joint trusteeship of China and the U.S. under an international mandate. I proposed this for the following reasons: 1. I wanted to reassure the U.S., 2. The Ryukyus belonged to Japan even before the 1894–95 Sino-Japanese war and, 3. Joint trusteeship seems more appropriate than giving them exclusively to us;* [emphasis added] D. The Japanese indemnity to China; E. Xinjiang and investments there; F. Russian participation in the anti-Japanese war; G. Korean independence. I laid special emphasis on this point so as to attract his attention and asked him to support my idea; H. A joint general staff meeting of China and the U.S.; I. the Vietnam issue: I strongly suggested that China and the U.S. support its independence after the war and gain the approval of Britain; J. The monitoring of the three Japanese islands by the allied forces after the Japanese surrender. I at first suggested that the U.S. should assume leadership

here and that China can send troops to assist if necessary, but he insisted that China should play the major role—there must be some deeper intent here. On this I did not express any hard and fast opinion. This is everything we discussed tonight.[34]

At 5:00 P.M. on Sunday, November 25, Roosevelt and Chiang met again. According to the account of Elliott Roosevelt, President Roosevelt's son, Chiang and Roosevelt discussed China's unification, "especially the Chinese communists." They also discussed military action in Burma and the Bay of Bengal.[35] While they may have mentioned the Ryukyus at this meeting, there is no record of it in the United States Diplomatic Papers of the Cairo Conference for November 25. Nor do the entries in Chiang's diary for that day, devoted to the meeting and the photos taken with Roosevelt, mention it. At the formal meeting on the afternoon of November 16, aside from discussing military plans for the China-Burma-India theater, Chiang, Roosevelt, and Churchill also touched upon issues that had come up in the preceding days, such as China's economic situation—especially the stability of its currency, the establishment of the Sino-American Economic Commission, the expenses of the American military based in China, the military disposition of the Japanese-occupied islands in the Pacific, the internationalization of the port of Dalian, the achievements of the Moscow meeting of foreign ministers, a general outline of postwar international organization, support for the construction expenses of the Chengdu airport, and the equipping of ninety army divisions. There is no record of the meeting between Chiang and Roosevelt in the November 26 entry of United States Diplomatic Papers, but they contain an "editorial note" saying that Chiang brought up the question of the restoration of Outer Mongolia to China,[36] but since this issue involved the attitude of the Soviet Union, the "joint declaration" by the three countries that followed did not mention it. From the look of the agenda, the Ryukyu issue may well have been discussed, but there is no record in the Papers. Our account must, therefore, limit itself to focusing on the November 23 entries in *The Diary of Chiang Kai-shek* and to analysis of the November 23 records of the Cairo Conference.

In his diary entry for November 23, Chiang Kai-shek reiterated his plan for joint administration of the Ryukyus by China and the United

States without mentioning the status of the Ryukyus in Chinese history. He did, however, bring up three other reasons: "*1. I wanted to reassure the U.S., 2. The Ryukyus belonged to Japan even before the 1894–95 Sino-Japanese war and, 3. Joint trusteeship seems more appropriate than giving them exclusively to us*"[37] [emphasis added]. We can infer from these points, especially the first, either that Chiang was worried that a request to hand over the Ryukyus, Taiwan, and the Pescadores all at once might cause the Americans unease, or that the United States was suspicious of China's attitude toward the Ryukyus. As discussed above, Chiang had differentiated the Ryukyus from Taiwan, the Pescadores Islands, and the four Manchurian provinces from the start, so the wish to "reassure the U.S." clearly refers to American intentions. Thus, his judgment that joint administration "is more appropriate than giving them exclusively to us" did not stem from the "Ryukyus having belonged to Japan even before the 1894–95 Sino-Japanese war," but out of considerations of America's actual objectives. Had Chiang from the Cairo Conference on through the end of the war insisted upon international trusteeship for the Ryukyus or turning the region into a demilitarized zone rather than a zone of U.S. occupation, the fate of the Ryukyus might perhaps have been different, but he evidently had neither the power nor the will to resist the United States.

This point should be looked at in the light of the postwar occupation of Japan that was discussed subsequently: Roosevelt raised the issue of China taking the lead in the military occupation of Japan, but Chiang's statement that "there must be some deeper intent here" clearly indicates that they were testing each other. It is perhaps because of this that the Sunday, November 25, entry in Chiang's diary reads: "Yesterday, November 25, after our photograph at Roosevelt's place, I stayed on and talked with him for half an hour, to tell him the political proposal I presented yesterday was my personal opinion."[38] This entry may not be referring to any particular proposal, but the issues discussed above must certainly have been part of it. The atmosphere of the discussion between Chiang and Roosevelt was good, but the commitments made by the Americans were mostly lip service without real substance. Roosevelt did not even inform Chiang of matters vitally concerned with the War of Resistance against Japan, such as Stalin's promise to join the anti-Japanese war, Churchill's plan to attack the Andaman Islands, and the choice of the Mid-Pacific as the major anti-Japanese battlefront (which reduced the Burmese front to a second priority).[39] A pleasant atmosphere and testing each other out, therefore, are not incompatible notions.

Since Chiang had grouped the Ryukyus and Korea together in his diary entry for November 15, why did he completely neglect to mention Ryukyuan independence when bringing up the independence of Korea, Siam, and Vietnam? This was probably related to his concern "to reassure the U.S.," as Chiang had already realized that because of geopolitical strategic concerns, the United States would not give up military occupation of the Ryukyus after the war, and might not really want to deliver the Ryukyus to the exclusive jurisdiction of China. Just as Li Hongzhang in the late Qing era had been unable to intervene in the Ryukyus, Chiang lacked the strength to resist American will. But this is only one aspect of the problem. From the differentiation Chiang made between the Ryukyus and Chinese territories like Tibet, his position bears upon the Chinese political tradition. According to this worldview, he could not equate traditional tribute (including suzerain) relations to relationships of sovereignty. The relationship of suzerainty between the Ryukyus and China had lasted for five hundred years, but Chinese dynasties rarely intervened in Ryukyuan domestic politics, something quite different from Satsuma's military invasion and its setting up a specially appointed governor to intervene directly in Ryukyuan politics.[40] From Chiang's perspective, Taiwan and the Pescadores differed from the Ryukyus: the former had been under China's direct administrative jurisdiction, with which the latter's tribute or suzerain relationship could not be equated.

Taiwan and the Pescadores, therefore, needed to be restored to Chinese rule, while the Ryukyus could only be subject to an international trusteeship—in rejecting Japan's right to rule the Ryukyus, Chiang indicated that he did not accept Japan's right to the Archipelago dating from the Meiji period. But neither did he use the model of "restoration" to provide a norm for the relationship between China and the islands—what he referred to as joint trusteeship by China and the United States was proposed with a view to postwar international relations and the regional power balance. Chiang's choice here is closely related to the war/Cold War dispensation and affords us a view of the different status of Taiwan and the Ryukyus in the Cold War environment. The kingdoms of Korea,

Siam, Vietnam, the Ryukyus, and Burma were tied up with the tribute system centered on China, and Chiang regarded these relationships as the basis of a moral obligation to them in their struggle for their independence and freedom; he did not see these as relationships of sovereignty. He thus sought to combine the Chinese historical worldview with the values of the Chinese national revolution in an attempt to adapt to the new world order. From this perspective, Chiang's position stands in clear contrast to the British attitude of trying to maintain its colonial system in Asia.

The United States Diplomatic Papers also have a record of the meeting between Roosevelt and Chiang on November 23, although the record was translated into English from notes in Chinese. An "Editorial Note" in the Papers says: "No American official record of this meeting has been discovered, so it is clear that neither party made any preparations. In 1956, in response to a query from our editors, the Chinese ambassador in Washington, Dr. Hollington Tong, confirmed that there is a Chinese language summary of this meeting in the ROC archives." The material on this and its English translation in the American archives was provided by the authorities on Taiwan. The Editorial Note also points out that the Chinese record differs at certain points from Elliott Roosevelt's memoirs and did not touch upon some issues mentioned by the latter, such as the structure of a Chinese coalition government, British interests in Shanghai and Guangdong, future activities of the American rather than the British navy in basing itself in Chinese ports, and the future of the Malay states, Burma, and India.[41] The future status of the Malay states, Burma, and India concerned British colonies and was not referred in the three-power "joint declaration." In fact, in 1943, in response to tensions between the Chinese central government and Tibet, Britain was preparing to give up its recognition of Chinese suzerainty and publicly support Tibetan independence. A Foreign Office report, "Tibet and the Question of Chinese Suzerainty," explicitly stated: "Chinese plans for a post-war settlement in the Far East aim at securing independence from British rule for such territories as India, Burma and Malaya. The real motive, so far as the latter two are concerned, is undoubtedly to clear the ground for Chinese political and economic domination. . . . In order to give effective support to Tibet's claim to complete independence, we should, I submit, abandon our previous willingness to acknowledge China's suzerain rights."[42]

It is noteworthy that Chiang's diary entry for November 15 mentioned that China should propose Siamese independence, but the three-power "joint declaration" only refers to the independence of Korea, something surely related to British attitudes. During the whole course of the Cairo Conference, China and the United States engaged in profound conversation, their attitudes being quite "sincere" (*chengzhi*, Chiang's word). For their part, however, the British quarreled frequently with China, as they did not wish to give up their colonies in Asia. Two items listed in the article as "possible issues to be raised by the British side" in *Advisory Office of the Military Commission Draft of the Issues to Be Raised at the Cairo Conference for Chairman Chiang* were "the Tibet issue" and the "Kowloon, Hong Kong issue." The explanatory note under "the Tibet issue" reads: "In London this past August, Foreign Minister Song discussed this matter with the British Foreign Secretary Eden. The two parties disagreed significantly, so it would seem best to postpone a solution to a later date." The explanatory note under the "Kowloon and Hong Kong issue" reads: "Since Kowloon is a leased territory, there is no doubt whatsoever that it will be restored to China, but from the British perspective, Kowloon and Hong Kong belong to the same category. Since Hong Kong is a ceded territory, with a legal status different from that of Kowloon, it would, therefore, seem best to postpone a solution to a later date."[43] At the meeting between Wang Chonghui and Eden, China and the United Kingdom found it impossible to achieve consensus on the matter of Tibet.

British and American attitudes differed significantly on the issue of colonialism in Asia: the United States hoped that the European metropolitan states of Britain, France, and Holland could follow the American example in the Philippines and allow their colonies to gain independence. The American position was thus in many ways similar to China's, but Britain was trying its best to maintain its imperial rule, even to the point of refusing to recognize China's great power status.[44] In fact, it was not even an easy matter to secure a place for Korean independence in the Cairo Declaration. The contingency plan for the Conference prepared for Chiang by the secretariat of the Supreme Commission for National Defense made a point of singling out Korean independence as a special item and added a detailed "explanation": as for Korean independence, "the

Soviet Union might not wish to offer an opinion because of its current relationship with Japan; Britain may not support it out of concern for its influence on the Indian question, and if the U.S. and Britain cannot reach agreement, the U.S. is bound to be hesitant. Under these circumstances, if China offers unilateral recognition, the world may get the impression that the alliance has developed fractures."[45] During the course of the conference China and Britain held differing opinions and often contended with one another on the wording of articles concerning the return to China of Manchuria, Taiwan, and the Pescadores, as well as on Korean independence.[46] On the pretexts that the British cabinet had yet to discuss the issue and that the Soviet attitude toward the matter needed to be considered, the British Permanent Under-Secretary for Foreign Affairs, Alexander Cadogan, even suggested deleting the section on Korean independence. At the insistence of China and the United States, however, this provision ultimately passed and was included in the joint declaration.[47] After the Conference concluded, Chiang wrote in the section of his diary devoted to "reflections on last week"—he added reflections to his diary every week, month and year—that "the three-power joint declaration included statements by Britain and the U.S. of the restoration to China of the territories of the three Manchurian provinces, Taiwan and the Pescadores, which have been lost to us for between 12 and fifty or more years, as well as recognition of the postwar freedom and independence of Korea, and thus represents unprecedented diplomatic success—these are great events, great proposals and great hopes. If we do not keep up the struggle hereafter, however, this will all be merely worthless paper."[48] Chiang's excitement fairly permeates his text. Considering the struggles and frustrations endured during the course of the negotiations, it is quite understandable how Chiang would regard the inclusion of Korean independence in the Cairo Declaration as a great success.

Chiang Kai-shek's attitude toward the Ryukyus should be analyzed in light of all the questions raised at the Conference. I will at this point set out the meeting between Chiang and Roosevelt as recorded in English in the United States Diplomatic Papers and in Chinese in *A Compilation of Historical Materials on ROC Diplomacy*, while cross-referencing these against Chiang's diary entries. The records of the meeting are as follows:

(1) *On China's International Position*—President Roosevelt expressed his view that China should take her place as one of the Big Four [the United States, China, the Soviet Union, and the United Kingdom] and participate on an equal footing in the machinery of the Big Four Group and in all its decisions. . . .

(2) *On the status of the Japanese Imperial House*—President Roosevelt enquired of Generalissimo Chiang's views as to whether the institution of the Emperor of Japan should be abolished after the war. The Generalissimo said that this would involve the question of the form of government of Japan and should be left for the Japanese people themselves to decide after the war, so as not to precipitate any error which might perpetuate itself in international relations. (The archived Chinese original reads: "it would be best to leave the choice of form of government to enlightened progressives in Japan. . . . It is not the best idea to intervene in another state's structure simply because of having been victorious in war. Moreover, the emperor system has a certain place in the spiritual configuration of the Japanese nation, which Westerners may not comprehend, but we Chinese, as fellow East Asians, understand much better.")[49]

(3) *On Military Occupation of Japan*—President Roosevelt was of the opinion that China should play the leading role in the post-war military occupation of Japan. Generalissimo Chiang believed, however, that China was not equipped to shoulder this considerable responsibility, that the task should be carried out under the leadership of the United States and that China could participate in this task in a supporting capacity should it prove necessary by that time. . . .

(4) *On Reparation in Kind*—Generalissimo Chiang proposed that a part of the reparation Japan was to pay China after the war could be paid in the form of actual properties. . . . Roosevelt expressed his concurrence in this proposal.

(5) *On Restoration of Territories*—Generalissimo Chiang and President Roosevelt agreed that the four Northeastern provinces, Taiwan and the Penghu Islands [*Pescadores*] which Japan had taken from China by force must be restored to China after the war, its being understood that the Liaotung Peninsula and its two ports, Lüshun (Port of Arthur and Dalian) [are] also included. The President then referred to the

question of the Ryukyu Islands and enquired more than once whether China would want the Ryukyus. The Generalissimo replied that China would be agreeable to joint occupation of the Ryukyus by China and the United States and, eventually, joint administration by the two countries under the trusteeship of an international organization. President Roosevelt also raised the question of Hong Kong. The Generalissimo suggested that the President discuss the matter with the British authorities before further deliberation

(6) *On Matters Concerning Military Cooperation*—President Roosevelt proposed that, after the war, China and the United States should effect certain arrangements under which the two countries could come to each other's assistance in the event of foreign aggression and that the United States should maintain adequate military forces on various bases in the Pacific in order that it could effectively share the responsibility of preventing aggression. Generalissimo Chiang expressed his agreement to both proposals. The Generalissimo expressed his hope that the United States would be in a position to provide necessary aid to China for equipping its land, naval and air forces for the purpose of strengthening its national defense and enabling its performance of international obligations. Generalissimo Chiang also proposed that, to achieve mutual security, the two countries should arrange for army and naval bases of each to be available for use by the other and stated that China would be prepared to place Lüshun (Port of Arthur) at the joint disposal of China and the United States. President Roosevelt, on his part, proposed that China and the United States should consult with each other before any decision was to be reached on matters concerning Asia. The Generalissimo indicated agreement.

(7) *On Korea, Indo-China and Thailand*—President Roosevelt advanced the opinion that China and the United States should reach a mutual understanding on the future status of Korea, Indo-China and other colonial areas as well as Thailand. Concurring, Generalissimo Chiang stressed ... the necessity of granting independence to Korea. It was also his view that China and the United States should endeavor together to help Indo-China achieve independence after the war and that independent status should be restored to Thailand. The President expressed his agreement.

(8) *On Economic Aid to China*—Generalissimo Chiang pointed out that China's post-war economic reconstruction would be a tremendously difficult task which would require United States financial aid in the form of loans, etc., and also various types of technical assistance. President Roosevelt indicated that close and practical consideration would be given to the matter.

(9) *On Outer Mongolia and Tannu Tuva*—President Roosevelt enquired especially as to the present status of Tannu-Tuva and its historical relations with its neighbors. Generalissimo Chiang pointed out that the area had been an integral part of China's Outer Mongolia until it was forcibly annexed by Russia. He said that the question of Tannu Tuva, together with that of Outer Mongolia, must be settled in time to come through negotiations with Soviet Russia.[50]

(10) *On Unified Command*—Generalissimo Chiang proposed the formation of a China-U.S. Joint Council of Chiefs-of-Staff, or, as an alternative, China's participation in the existing British-U.S. Council of Chiefs-of-Staff. President Roosevelt agreed to consult the chiefs of staff of the United States in order to reach a decision on the matter.[51]

This memorandum obviously goes into more detail than Chiang's November 23 diary entry, and I will compare the analogous portions of the memorandum and the diary. Aside from the fact that Outer Mongolia and Tannu-Tuva received no mention in the diary, the most important differences are as follows: (1) Chiang's diary mentioned communism and Roosevelt's attitude toward the Soviet Union, while the memorandum is silent on these topics; (2) The diary omits mention of the key question brought up in the memorandum about postwar cooperation between China and the United States in the Asia-Pacific area, including such vital matters as Roosevelt proposing that the United States "should maintain adequate military forces on various bases in the Pacific," that "the two countries could come to each other's assistance in the event of foreign aggression," with both countries arranging for "army and naval bases of each to be available for use by the other," and Chiang's commitment that he "would be prepared to place Lüshun (Port of Arthur) at the joint disposal of China and the United States."

The proposal that the United States maintain adequate military forces in order to prevent aggression was clearly targeted at the Soviet Union. By examining these points, it can be seen that Chiang not only had long recognized the different statuses of the Ryukyus and Taiwan, but also that in the course of the meeting he became aware of American postwar planning for the region, especially its long-term program for a military presence in the Pacific. Judging from Chiang's attitude toward communism and the Soviet Union, he was evidently prepared to actively support the American program.[52] If we analyze this together with the evaluation appended to Chiang's diary entry devoted to Roosevelt's suggestion that "China should play the leading role in the post-war military occupation of Japan," in which the former mentions that "there must be some deeper intent here, [so] on this I did not express any hard and fast opinion," it seems as if Chiang may well have been aware that Roosevelt was testing out China's assumptions about its status in the postwar period.

Considering Chiang's wish that the Japanese form of government should be decided by progressive forces in Japan, it would seem that China and the United States had very different attitudes toward postwar political arrangements there. According to the English summary of the memorandum, Roosevelt did not speak of handing the Ryukyus over to China, but the English wording—"The President then referred to the question of the Ryukyu Islands and enquired more than once whether China would want the Ryukyus"—suggests rather a kind of test. Did Roosevelt's notion of maintaining "adequate military forces on various bases in the Pacific" and of a military presence in the Pacific hint at an American interest in the Ryukyus? If not, why, when asked by Roosevelt whether he "would want" the Ryukyus, would Chiang not only refuse "exclusive" possession, but even say that his proposal for joint trusteeship was to "reassure the U.S.," and then go on to declare that "the task [i.e., the military occupation of Japan] should be carried out under the leadership of the United States and that China could participate in the task"?

The three-power Joint Declaration published at the Cairo Conference does not mention the Ryukyu question, nor does it appear in either the draft or the revised version of the American Communiqué in the United States Diplomatic Papers, nor in the British draft Communiqué. All three versions express the determination found in both American versions that "the islands in the Pacific which have been occupied by the Japanese, many of them powerful military bases, ... will be taken from Japan forever, and the territory they have so treacherously stolen from the Chinese, such as Manchuria and Formosa, will of course be returned to the Republic of China." The fourth paragraph of the revised American version adds: "All of the conquered territory taken by violence and greed by the Japanese will be freed from their clutches."[53] The printed version of the British Communiqué has the words "and the Pescadores" written in fountain pen after the word "Formosa." All three versions mention the liberation and independence of Korea, but neither the Ryukyus, taken in Chiang's diary to be of similar historical status to Korea, nor Siam appears. The final version of the Cairo Declaration reads: "The three great Allies are fighting this war to restrain and punish the aggression of Japan. ... It is their purpose that Japan shall be stripped of all the islands in the Pacific which she has seized or occupied since the beginning of the First World War in 1914, and that all the territories Japan has stolen from the Chinese, such as Manchuria, Formosa, and the Pescadores, shall be restored to the Republic of China. Japan will also be expelled from all other territories which she has taken by violence and greed. The aforesaid three great powers, mindful of the enslavement of the people of Korea, are determined that in due course Korea should become free and independent."[54]

While their historical origins and World War II plights all differed from one another, the postwar fortunes of Outer Mongolia, Thailand, Vietnam, Korea, and the Ryukyus must be understood in the context of the entire history of colonialism as well as the wartime situation, the waxing and waning of the great powers, and, especially, of American strategy and hegemonic intentions in the postwar Asia-Pacific. In other words, the Okinawa problem grew out of the complicated relations with colonialist history, the Pacific conflict, and the Cold War, as well as being the product of the formation of the modern world order. My analysis leads me to the conclusion that the Ryukyus' role in the Cold War had been determined by 1943, when the war had yet to end, but postwar arrangements had already been placed on the Great Power agenda. At present, with the Soviet Union having ceased to exist, the justification for American military bases in Asia has also been correspondingly and dramatically transformed—the Cold War structure has been reengineered. The questions raised by the

Okinawan social movement not only concern its fate and the maintenance of peace in the Asia-Pacific area, but are also related to the rethinking of the modern world order and its future evolution.

The discussions between China on the one hand and Britain and the United States on the other over such issues as the Ryukyus, Thailand, and Korea revealed both the differences and the relationship between the traditional notion of internal-external and the nation-state notion of internal-external shaped by the concept "sovereignty." In political actuality, these two worldviews may overlap, but they cannot define one another. In the Chinese nationalist narrative, the aggression of the Western powers, the rise of Japan, the decline of China, the corruption of the Chinese sociopolitical system, and its technological and military backwardness constitute the basic measures of China's crisis. Since it objectively presents the contestation between different levels of strength—and its consequences—in the era of nationalism, this discourse still has significant explanatory power. It has been unable to fully disclose, however, the great worldwide changes to relationships and norms. Aside from conceiving the path of the rise of the nation-state in an exclusively nationalist framework, the real problem of the nationalist narrative is that it cannot produce new images and norms for international relations—the core of Eurocentrism lies in its having established rules according to the demands of Western interests and then having universalized them. Any critique of Eurocentrism must thus involve the reformulation of those rules themselves. As a result, when discussing matters having to do with the Cold War and nationalism, it must first be asked what point of view we are working under—is it within a nationalist or a pre- or postnationalist perspective? Without first asking ourselves this, we will not be able to break out of the "universal rules" that have held sway since the nineteenth century.

Okinawa's Political Choices

The American occupation and military bases in Okinawa embody some form of recognition of Okinawa's history: there is a difference between stationing troops in the Japanese homeland and in Okinawa—after the war the United States stationed a large number of troops in Japan, but as that country gradually recovered from the war, its struggle for sovereignty became ever more intense. Faced with this pressure from Japanese society, the United States had to move the bulk of its forces to Okinawa, with 75 percent of its troops now based there. The United States did not actually reduce its military presence in Japan—not only has its system of command and control been greatly boosted, but on October 29, 2005, Japan and the United States reached agreement on strengthening the integration of the Japanese Self-Defense Forces and the American military. In 2008, after the conventionally powered aircraft carrier *Kitty Hawk* (stationed at the American base at Yokosuka) was retired from service, it was replaced by the *Nimitz*, a nuclear-powered carrier—the myth of a "nonnuclear" Japanese homeland thus ceased to exist. The deployment of a nuclear-powered aircraft carrier to Yokosuka demonstrates the base's great importance to American global military strategy. Japan and the United States reached an agreement to restore Okinawa's Futenma airfield to Japan, and prior to that time, the United States agreed to transfer 8,000 American troops and 9,000 dependents to Guam, with the Japanese government footing $6.09 billion of the total $10.27 billion cost. In fact, in a time of rapidly advancing military technology, even if the bulk of its military force is transferred to Guam, the American military presence and control in this region will not diminish. Therefore, any critique of American hegemony limited strictly to the domestic or local sphere cannot get at the roots of the issue. The strongest critiques will arise out of an ability to integrate local struggle with global relations.

During the Japanese postwar recovery period, the United States could regard Okinawa as its own base rather than as a base in Japan. Even when it was returned to Japanese jurisdiction, a psychological distinction between the Japanese homeland and Okinawa would continue to exist. The Americans came to the area with their Western perspective, but they were well aware of the internal differences in the region—they appropriated the history of Japanese modern colonialism to insert themselves into a difference that had been created by that colonialism. If we probe more deeply, the great transformation of fundamental international rules in the last century becomes apparent. The pre-nineteenth-century model no longer exists, the Ryukyu kingdom has vanished, and the tribute system has collapsed, but its geohistorical position and its special mechanism of occupation represent particular historical problems for Asia. As a result, the Okinawa question provides a unique perspective to reflect upon the history of modern nationalism and the imperialist mode of knowledge. What are its implications for the Cold War framework, and why, in the post–Cold War era, has the Cold War in Asia not come to a complete end? Pursuing this from the Okinawan perspective also provides a unique perspective from which to understand the Cold War and the post–Cold War order.

The demilitarization of Okinawa would be conducive to regional peace, but on the question of its place in a future regional order, there has been much discussion and disagreement within the Okinawan social movement. I think the source of the fuzziness of this discussion derives from the international relationships we now find ourselves in, where no space is provided to imagine any different sorts of relationships. Relationships of sovereignty do not exist in isolation and cannot be unilaterally put into effect by a single national entity; it is in this sense that the fuzziness of the Okinawa issue is inevitable. My discussion in this essay has involved two different understandings of China: one was produced by revolution, socialism, and internationalism, while the other stems from the political-cultural relations of the pre–nation-state era. Both of these perspectives have faded away today, and even when they are broached now, it is only as part of a nationalist imaginary.

National liberation movements of the twentieth century had clearly defined political goals, which were that "states need to be independent, nations need to be liberated, and people need revolution," three interconnected aspects of a single historical process. Lacking the other two, any one of these goals would end up going in an opposite direction. For example, if in the struggle for independence or living space a country ignores the liberation of other peoples—particularly weaker peoples—the struggle might lead to something like modern Japanese imperialism. If merely nationalist objectives are the central focus, nation-state modernization will become a simple project of self-strengthening that ignores inequality. Lacking demands by ordinary people for reform of existing social relations and their efforts to establish a new order, the imagination of both nation and state can be exploited by a small number of rulers. All three of these factors are thus interconnected parts of political objectives and the political process—they cannot be equated with essentialist definitions of nation, state, or class. Today, none of these three objectives can be simply applied to the Okinawan social movement and its political goals. While no social struggle can do without a specific social identity, if identity politics is simply limited to a politics of nationalism, new distortions will ensue—the social divisions produced by Taiwan's identity politics provide a clear example. Thus, the matter of Okinawa's political subjective agency is worth considering very seriously—such consideration will not only force us to review our historical legacy, but will also lead us to completely new answers to twentieth-century political problems.

6

Weber and the Question of Chinese Modernity

Both Marx and Weber saw the process of social rationalization, or "purposive-instrumental rationality," as becoming ever more dominant: the triumph of rationality did not bring along with it the freedom expected from it, but rather brought about an irrational economic power and the control of the populace via a bureaucratic social order. This insight directly influenced both Max Horkheimer's and Theodor Adorno's theoretical critique of Enlightenment modernity, even as it inspired Jürgen Habermas's "theory of communicative action" and his thinking about modernity. Weber has thus continued to be the source underpinning modern social thought, such that one scholar summed up the principal characteristic of contemporary sociology with the following two phrases: "Marxian Weberianism or Weberian Marxism." The contemporaneity of Weber's theory stems from his having provided a basis for theoretical reflection on modernity and its problems as well as his historical foresight,

---

Translated by Theodore Huters

thus diagnosing the main crises of contemporary society through his reflections on social rationality and rationalization.

In reading Weber's work on Chinese religion, however, *Konfucianismus und Taoismus (The Religion of China)*—a book that has just been translated and published in Chinese—I find it impossible to discover any pessimistic predictions concerning the process of rationalization.[1] In fact, quite to the contrary, rationality and rationalization constitute the basic norms against which he at once described and anatomized the problems of Chinese society. If it is held that modern thought has developed Weber's ideas in two directions—critical theory on the one hand and modernization theory on the other—then it is clear that in the field of Chinese studies, Weber has been applied primarily in the latter. The main purpose of this essay is not to pursue a sociological analysis and explanation of the full Weberian domain, nor even to rectify the many inaccuracies in his accounts of Chinese historical detail, but rather to point out the historical factors lying in the background of Weber's sociological framework and how they limit his ability to analyze and prescribe for Chinese issues. In this, my reflection on modernity is primarily a reflection upon the mind-set of modernity—a mind-set most often appearing as a critique of modernity. What I hope to suggest by this reflection is that any analysis of Chinese "modernity" and its problems must first be placed in the perspective of the study of history and culture, while at the same time attempting to locate a corresponding historical context as the basis for analysis. From this we may move to reflection on the positioning of our social science, and only in this way may we render Chinese the study of matters having to do with China.

Whose Modernity? The Etymology and Evolution of the Term "Modernity"

The etymology of the term "modernity" demonstrates that modernity is a tension-fraught, portmanteau concept that touches upon politics, economics, and culture. Through a historical process that saw the meaning of the term transit from the pejorative to the affirmative, the discourse of modernity reconstructed the relationship people had with the past, the present, and the future. This discourse, created in the Enlightenment, is built upon a recognition of the teleology of an awareness of the irreversibility of time, with "rationality" and "subjective freedom" at its core. The discourse of modernity uses such universal concepts as rationality and subjective freedom, as well as its antireligious posture, to conceal its historical relationship with the Christian culture of Europe.

Modernity (*xiandai xing*) is an internally complicated, much contested Western concept. It contains only one unambiguously clear feature, which is that modernity is principally a conception of time, or, perhaps better to say, a conception of historical time that moves linearly forward and cannot be repeated. It is a view of history that is in absolute opposition to a conceptual framework built upon the notion of repetitive, cyclic, or mythic time. According to Raymond Williams, the term "modern" in English comes directly from the French "moderne" and the late Latin "modernus," both of which originate in the Latin root "modo," meaning nothing more than "now, contemporary, in the sense of something existing now, just now."[2] The notion of modernity, however, departs from conventional wisdom in that, while it is intertwined with the European process of secularization, its roots reveal its origins in medieval Christianity, because implicit in both Jewish and Christian eschatological conceptions of time is the peculiar feature that time cannot be repeated. Owing to the lack of a sense of time in classical Latin thought, it contained no oppositional terminology of "modern/ancient." Our customary contrast between ancient and modern was formed during the Renaissance, becoming specified in the fifteenth century. Matei Calinescu has pointed out the importance of the notion of the "theatrum mundi" in the Middle Ages, something based on an analogy between the theater and human life, in which "humans are actors who unwittingly play the roles assigned to them by divine Providence." In this period, characterized by an "economically and culturally static society dominated by the ideal of stability and even quiescence . . . secular values were considered from an entirely theocentric view of human life."[3] According to Calinescu, it was only later, in the Renaissance, that the periods of antiquity, the Middle Ages, and modernity were distinguished, along with the value judgments accorded to each era, expressed through metaphors of light versus darkness, day versus night, and wakefulness versus sleep. Although the "modern" presaged the passing of the Dark Ages of the medieval period and the advent of a new life, it was only classical antiquity that represented "resplendent light" in itself.

The analogical and historical implications of the modern began to circulate in the sixteenth century, with the terms "modernism," "modernist," and "modernity" coming into widespread use in the seventeenth and eighteenth centuries. It is of particular note that although the sixteenth- and seventeenth-century "debate between the Ancients and the Moderns" brought about the liberation of rationality, and that the work of Montaigne, Bacon, and Descartes all affirm modernity, in the context of comparative terminology all these terms continued to be understood in the pejorative sense. In contrast to the "Ancients," the "Moderns" could be, at best, dwarfs standing on the shoulders of the former, while, in the eyes of Jonathan Swift, modernism was nothing more than the English language as it had been ravaged by the modernists.[4] Beginning in the eighteenth century, "modernize" came to refer to architecture, spelling, and to fashions in dress and behavior.[5] The opposition between "Ancient" and "Modern" went on to produce a whole series of contrary typological labels such as ancient versus gothic, naïve versus sentimental, ancient versus romantic, and the like; modern critical awareness can be said to have been constructed from these particular oppositional propositions.

The negative connotations of modernity and its related concepts underwent a highly evident transformation in the nineteenth, and particularly, the twentieth century, when its implications came to be the equivalent of "improved," "satisfactory," and "efficient." Jürgen Habermas used Hegel's *Lectures on the Philosophy of History* to show how the concept of modernity is an epochal one: the "new age" is the "modern age," which, along with such events as the discovery of the "new world," the Renaissance and the Reformation that took place around 1500 served to demarcate modernity from the Middle Ages. Only after the division of time into Modern, the Middle Ages, and Antiquity, something that is in itself a product of modernity or the new age, had

> lost its merely chronological meaning [did it take] on the oppositional significance of an emphatically "new" age. Whereas in the Christian West the "new world" had meant the still-to-come age of the world of the future... the secular concept of modernity expresses the conviction that the future has already begun: It is the

epoch that lives for the future, that opens itself up to the novelty of the future. In this way, the caesura defined by the new beginning has been shifted into the past, precisely to the start of modern times. Only in the course of the eighteenth century did the epochal threshold around 1500 become conceptualized as this beginning.[6]

Thus did the modern become the anchor point, and did history become historical consciousness of a uniform horizon. "Diagnosis of the new age and analysis of the past corresponded to one another,"[7] modernity became a way station in the progression toward the future and the new age used its relationship with the future to differentiate itself from the past. A historical image of a uniform historical progress was formulated out of this and as part of this historical image the present became a process of perpetual renewal. On the one hand, key terms that continue to circulate even now like revolution, progress, emancipation, development, crisis, and epoch obtain their legitimacy from this particular historical consciousness, while on the other, "modernity can and will no longer borrow the criteria by which it takes its orientation from the models supplied by another epoch; *it has to create its normativity out of itself.*"[8]

Believing modernity to be an integrated and self-sufficient concept, however, is necessarily an oversimplification. In his "Modernity: An Incomplete Project," Habermas sums this up by explaining that Weber

> characterized cultural modernity as the separation of the substantive reason expressed in religion and metaphysics into three autonomous spheres. They are: science, morality and art. They are differentiated because the integrated world-views of religion and metaphysics fell apart. Since the eighteenth century, the problems inherited from these older world-views could be arranged so as to fall under specific aspects of validity: truth, normative rightness, authenticity and beauty. They could then be handled as questions of knowledge, or of justice and morality, or of taste. Scientific discourse, theories of morality, jurisprudence, and the production and criticism of art could in turn be institutionalized. . . . This professionalized treatment of the cultural tradition brings to the fore the intrinsic structures of each of the three dimensions of culture.[9]

The crisis of rationality that Weber refers to is this: each of these rational structures is "under the control of specialists," and, "as a result, the distance grows between the culture of the experts and that of the larger public. What accrues to culture through specialized treatment and reflection does not immediately become the property of everyday praxis."

In fact, from the beginning of the nineteenth century and on into the twentieth, modernity has been a splintered notion, the most important manifestation of which has been the sharp opposition between its serving at once as the conceptualization both for the political and economic modernization of capitalism and for avant-garde modernism in the aesthetic realm. The former function shows itself in such articles of faith as credence to a sense of progress through time, belief in science and technology, veneration for the power of rationality, commitment to subjective freedom, trust in administrative and market institutions and other bourgeois values. On the other hand, in its latter sense, the aesthetics of modernism strongly militate against these very bourgeois values, although this rebellion contains in itself a dependence upon bourgeois modernity for its existence. As far as I know, Daniel Bell's *The Cultural Contradictions of Capitalism* provides the most compelling account of this split, forcefully bringing to our attention how the cultural hegemony of capitalism has been assumed by its most implacable enemy—modernism. Lexically, in the twentieth century, the terms "modernism" and "modernist" refer to the wave of experimental art and writing that was produced between 1890 and 1940, whereas "modern" and "modernist" refer to two mutually differentiated ideas.

In his discussion of Stendhal, Matei Calinescu says that for the former, "the concept of romanticism [which for Calinescu is a virtual synonym for modern] embodies the meanings of change, relativity, and, above all, presentness," while the writer is a "fighter rather than a pleaser," who should "strive to give his contemporaries a pleasure that that they seem unprepared to enjoy and perhaps do not even deserve."[10] As a matter of fact, the aesthetic critique of the bourgeois philistine mentality was always one of the defining characteristics of German romanticism, and in the mid-nineteenth century Marx and Engels transformed this aesthetic critique into an ideological critique and a political tool, drawing a clear and paradigmatic distinction between "revolutionary" and "philistine."

The notion of artistic autonomy and the slogan of "Art for Art's sake" were the "first product[s] of aesthetic modernity's rebellion against the modernity of the philistine."[11] Calinsecu draws special attention to "Baudelaire and the paradoxes of aesthetic modernity," not only because the latter's concept of modernity embodies the paradox of temporality—in other words, the dialectic between the notions of the eternal and the ephemeral—but also because of Baudelaire's efforts "to reveal the poetry hidden behind the most horrifying contrasts of social modernity." For the French poet, modernity is not the reproduction of reality by the artist, but the product of the artist's imagination, which enables him to "penetrate beyond the banality of observable appearances into a world of 'correspondences,' where ephemerality and eternity are one." Baudelaire is "a defender of modernity in aesthetics [and] at the same time an almost perfect example of the modern artist's alienation from the society and official culture of his age."[12] His critique of bourgeois political modernity is built upon a core of abhorrence for natural human instinct, or the state of nature in Rousseau's sense. It is also precisely this distaste that reveals his devotion to urban modernity and civilization.

Raymond Williams appends three related terms to the entry for "modern" in his *Keywords:* "improve," "progress," and "tradition," revealing his view of the correct way to grasp the meaning of the word. "Modern" not only signifies that it is superior to the past, but that it is through a process of differentiation or opposition to the past—"tradition"—that it defines itself: the "tradition/modernity" binary is constructed upon a linear conception of time containing a teleology of "progress." It is particularly worth noting that the early usage of the word "improve" refers to investment in or management of land with financial profit in mind. Even in the eighteenth century, when the connotations of "improve" as "perfection" or "making something better" had been established, these meanings coincided with the sense of profit-oriented economic activity. And because of this, the words most closely associated with "improve" were economic concepts like "development," "exploitation," and "interest," which provided the etymological basis for the concept of "modernization." In its institutional and industrial connotations, "modernize" and "modernization" imply something both absolute and able to invoke admiration; and because the concept of modernization hints at the "local alteration" or improvement of the old order or its institutions, the meaning of this term differs somewhat from that of the word "modern."

Relatively speaking, the terms "progress" and "tradition" are both products of a long process of historical transformation with a number of complicated implications, but in modern thought they are not only responsible for creating an image of a totalized past, but also are in control of our view of modernity itself.[13] The time consciousness with the notion of progress as its content unites a transitory and indefinite present with an eternal future, demanding of people that they commit themselves to "the adventure of the future." As Calinsecu expresses it:

> On the one hand, the future is the only way out of the "nightmare of history," . . . but on the other hand, the future—the begetter of change and *difference*—is suppressed in the very attainment of perfection, which by definition cannot but repeat itself ad infinitum, negating the irreversible concept of time on which the whole of Western culture has been built. If we think that modernity came about as a commitment to otherness and change, and that its entire strategy was shaped by an "antitraditional tradition" based on the idea of *difference*, it should not be difficult to realize why it balks when it is confronted with the perspective of infinite *repetition* and the "boredom of utopia." Modernity and the critique of repetition are synonymous notions. That is why we can speak of the "modern tradition" only in a paradoxical way, as Octavio Paz does when he characterizes it as "A Tradition Against Itself."[14]

The etymology of the term "modernity" explains several things: (1) the concept touches upon the several distinct realms of economics, politics, and culture, but it is holistic, even as it incorporates a number of contradictions and conflicts—at its core lies a conceptualization of history within a temporal framework; (2) the term took shape through a historical process that was shaped by specific political, economic, and cultural factors peculiar to its time. In the process of its transition from having a negative to a positive connotation, the discourse of modernity reconstructed the relationship between people and history and between the self and the future, with the final result producing a self in opposition to its own tradition; (3) via a process of forgetting its specific history, the concept was used in the Enlightenment to delineate a comprehensive history, such that it served merely to label the historical teleology of that period's value-system and ideology.

In his *The Condition of Postmodernity*, David Harvey says:

> Although the term "modern" has a rather more ancient history, what Habermas calls "the *project* of modernity" came into focus during the eighteenth century. That project amounted to an extraordinary intellectual effort on the part of Enlightenment thinkers "to develop objective science, universal morality and law, and autonomous art according to their inner logic." The idea was to use the accumulation of knowledge generated by many individuals working freely and creatively for the pursuit of human emancipation and the enrichment of daily life. The scientific domination of nature promised freedom from scarcity, want, and the arbitrariness of natural calamity. The development of rational forms of social organization and rational modes of thought promised liberation from irrationalities of myth, religion, superstition, release from arbitrary use of power as well as from the dark side of our own human natures. Only through such a project could the universal, eternal, and the immutable qualities of all of humanity be revealed.[15]

Habermas himself takes "subjective freedom" as the hallmark of "the project of modernity": "This was realized in society as the space secured by civil law for the rational pursuit of one's own interests; in the state, as the principle of equal rights to participation in the formation of political will; in the private sphere, as ethical autonomy and self-realization; finally, in the public sphere related to this private realm, as the formative process that takes place by means of the appropriation of a culture that has become reflective."[16]

What Habermas identifies as "subjective freedom" was more commonly thought of as "rationality" in the eighteenth century. As for Enlightenment thought in that period, "All of the various powers of consciousness gathered in one central location of power. The varieties and differences of forms that these took only show the full development of their commonality. When the people of the eighteenth century found a word to describe this power, it was 'rationality.' 'Rationality' became the core and the identity of the eighteenth century, expressing not only the full extent of what was struggled and hoped for in the period, but also that which it achieved."[17] When looked at from the historical perspective, the term "rationality" has long since lost its unitary meaning, but from the perspective of the Enlightenment tradition, the eighteenth century was saturated by credence in the unity and immutability of rationality, namely, that for all thinking subjects, for all peoples, for all times, and for all cultures rationality would be identical. Religion, morality, theoretical propositions, and all aspects of reality could change, but within this variability lay an irreducible unity, that being an essential rationality. Even though there are few who would now subscribe completely to the naïve thinking of the Enlightenment, this language using rationality to denominate different realms of activity is still an important tradition, even if those who employ it have come to doubt the basic Enlightenment project itself.

As far as critical theory is concerned, rationality and subjective freedom are both preconditions for this mode of inquiry, with rationality being premised upon subjective freedom, with freedom having rationality as a condition, with subjectivity depending upon the capacity of rationality to secure its freedom (in terms of epistemology), and with freedom depending upon the emancipation of the subject. In the account that follows I will discuss how Marx, Weber, and Habermas all take reason and its linguistic variants as their theoretical core. Visible through their specific formulation of such concepts as "rationality," "rationalism," and "to rationalize," can be seen the historical unconscious in their linguistic usage. If, for example, we historicize what Habermas refers to as "subjective freedom," then we can see this as a component of Weber's "rationalization process," a process that Weber himself increasingly came to doubt could supply people with subjective freedom. Habermas's thinking about "social rationality and rationalization" originates at least in part from these doubts of Weber's. In the passage on "subjective freedom" quoted above, Habermas failed to bring up another aspect of the concept, that is, in the sphere of international relations, it manifests itself through the formation of the system of European nation-states and the principle of sovereignty at their core—nationalism is a crucial part of "subjective freedom" that cannot be overlooked. The international aspect of "the project of modernity" is something of particular gravity for non-Western countries, since the source of the problem of modernity for these countries is itself international.

Looked at from the perspective of non-European cultures, this issue that Habermas failed to raise is at once a new and an old problem, namely, that prior to evaluating the merits and demerits of "modernity" itself, we must first ask: Just "whose" "project of modernity" is this? Marx analyzed this "project" and its historical relationship with the bourgeoisie from within the ambit of European civilization, but Marx's own historical standpoint is that of the Enlightenment tradition and the Judeo-Christian concept of time contained within it—in short, a modern theoretical system critical of "modernity." Throughout the entire course of the nineteenth and twentieth centuries, the concept of "modernity" refers principally to a secular as opposed to a religious worldview and to a process of secularization that was an emancipation from the religious control of the medieval period. Is not "modern man" a "free-thinker" and a nonbeliever? If, however, "modernity" is analyzed from an etymological perspective, and the term is placed within the context of the religious sources from which it sprang, the relationship between "modernity" and the process of secularization is but a very brief historical phenomenon. In his discussion of the modern theme of the romantic "death of God," Octavio Paz pointed out that "modernity is an exclusively Western concept" that, moreover, cannot be separated from Christianity, because "it could only appear within this conception of irreversible time; and it could appear only as a criticism of Christian eternity."[18] In other words, the myth of the death of God is merely an expression of the negation of the notion of cyclical time within Christian doctrine itself, and the affirmation of linear, irreversible time—the axis of history—because this irreversible time leads to eternal life.

Calinescu not only approves of Paz's formulation; he goes on to critically examine the historicity of the idea of "modernity" from a much wider chronological perspective. In his book *Five Faces of Modernity*, he delineates four distinct historical stages in the use of the concept of "modernity." The first stage is the medieval method of opposing the moderns (*modernus*) against the ancients (*antiquus*), with the moderns as new people and the ancients as those from a past era worthy of respect. As far as the distinction between modernity and antiquity is concerned, antiquity signifies the essential wholism of tradition, the continuity of which did not change even with the coming of Christ. The second stage coincides with the entirety of the Renaissance and the Enlightenment, with its salient feature being the gradual separation of modernity from Christianity. As a result of the Renaissance, even as it retained its highly positive implications, the notion of antiquity underwent an important semantic transformation: it no longer referred to an inseparable past, but now only to a part of it—the non-Christian era and the writers of ancient Greece and Rome. In the beginning the concept of modernity appeared only in such nonreligious contexts as natural philosophy, science, and poetry, with the tradition remaining the foundation of theology. In this period, the concept of modernity underwent a process of changing from the idea that moderns should imitate the ancients to the notion that they should catch up with the ancients, then even to declarations that the moderns were superior to the ancients. Within Christianity there were disputes over the authenticity of the tradition and interpretations of the tradition that were clearly not in accord with orthodoxy, both of these being manifestations of the critical spirit of modernity. "Toward the end of the rationalist and empiricist period of the Enlightenment the idea of modernity had lost much of its previous neutrality. Its conflict with religion finally came out into the open, and to be modern became virtually equivalent to being a 'free thinker' [unbeliever]."[19]

One of the most salient points of the third phase is that in their debates, the German and European romantics in general expanded the notion of modernity "to cover the whole romantic [period], i.e., [the] Christian era in Western history." "The late eighteenth-century religious revival in literature, the new emphasis laid on sentiment and intuition, the cult of originality and imagination, combined with a widespread craze for the gothic and for the whole civilization of the Middle Ages, are part of larger and sometimes confusingly complex reaction against the dry intellectualism of the *siècle des lumières* and its counterpart in aesthetics, neoclassicism." The result was a "romantic identification of the *modern genius* with the *genius of Christianity* and the view that, separated by an unbridgeable gap, there are *two* perfectly autonomous types of beauty, the first pagan, the second Christian." This, in turn, brought about "a truly revolutionary moment in the history of aesthetic modernity. The . . . relativistic Enlightenment philosophy of beauty is now replaced by a fatalistic historicism, which stresses the idea of total discontinuity between cultural cycles. Historical periods are analogous to living individuals, whose existence is ended by death." This suggests that the Christian cycle itself was about to come to an end and that the ideas of a moribund Christianity were able to nurture a whole new range of modern sentiment, even as it "explains why the romantics were the first to conceive the death of God,"[20] a theme that was to be so impressively expanded upon in Nietzsche's work.

The singularity of Calinescu's inventiveness is revealed in his explanation of the fourth phase, which he sees as beginning in the mid-nineteenth century. In his view, the ubiquitous idea of the "death of God" is better seen as marking "a new era of religious quest" rather than as the announcement of a complete break between Christianity and modernity. Modernity, then, "did not succeed in suppressing man's religious needs and imagination; and by diverting them from their traditional course it may even have intensified them . . . in [the domains of] religion proper, in morals, in social and political thinking, and in aesthetics." As Calinescu sums it up: "The crisis of religion [gave] birth to a religion of crisis."[21] He goes on to say that "directly linked to the decline of traditional Christianity's role is the powerful emergence of utopianism, perhaps the single most important event in the modern intellectual history of the West." This enthusiasm for utopia and the myth of revolution "pervades the whole intellectual spectrum of modernity." As Calinescu points out, "the concept of utopia was originally based on a spatial association . . . , but today its temporal implications far outweigh whatever it may have preserved of its strict etymology." Thus, "utopian imagination as it has developed since the eighteenth century is one more proof of the modern devaluation of the past and the growing importance of the future. Utopianism, however, would hardly be conceivable outside the specific time consciousness of the West, as it was shaped by Christianity and subsequently by reason's appropriation of irreversible time. The religious nature of utopianism is recognized by both its adversaries and advocates."[22]

Ernst Bloch, in his early work *The Spirit of Utopia* (*Geist der Utopie*, 1918), expresses the belief that "utopia is not only authentically religious in nature but also the sole legitimate heir of religion after the death of God."²³ As Habermas sums up Bloch's main point: "God is dead, but his locus has survived him. The place into which mankind has imagined God and the gods, after the decay of these hypotheses, remains a hollow space. The measurements-in-depth of this vacuum, indeed atheism finally understood, sketch out the blueprint of a future kingdom of freedom."²⁴ If it can be said that the founders of Marxism sought to transform socialism from an empty utopianism into a scientific reality, then the principal tendency in contemporary Western Marxism is to discard these "scientific" portions of the ideology and restore its "utopian dignity." As discussed above, however, modernism is an entity opposed to its own tradition, and utopian socialism is predicated upon a temporal consciousness of the irreversibility of modernity, even though it is in theoretical opposition to this temporal consciousness. As Calinescu puts it, "arguments previously used against Christian eternity are now turned against the secular eternity envisioned by utopianism."²⁵ In a time when the practice of socialism has run up against extreme difficulties all over the globe, the large-scale critique of utopianism that has accompanied these problems exhibits all the characteristics of the earlier clash between modernism and Christianity, and the voice of the cultural criticism emerging from late capitalist societies is still saturated with overtones of the eternal future of romanticism. The critiques of the present and those of the future each take the other as their point of attack.

The key concepts of modernity were produced from within Christian civilization, so why use them to describe non-Western societies and cultures? I have already addressed the beliefs and strategies of eighteenth-century thinkers: they took such concepts as rationality and subjective freedom that were the products of a particular religious tradition and culture and understood them as truths essential to all times, all societies and all civilizations; the links between these concepts and modernity are self-evident. As a result, we begin to encounter a modernity characterized by intellectual universality. In the final analysis, the intellectual system of modernity manifests deep theoretical contradictions, paradigmatic crises, and elements of self-deconstruction. It would be better to see these as contradictions among the basic constituent ideas that make up modernity's theoretical categories of analysis rather than as problems of theoretical logic or the limitations of the theoreticians themselves: these contradictions reveal themselves in such things as the paradox of the concept of time (and also in such things as contention over the notion of progress), which, in turn, originate in conflicts within Christian doctrine. The contradictions also show up in fissures between the cultural foundations of the categories of analysis and the foundations of the objects to which they refer. By now, we have finally returned to the question that Habermas failed to raise, the answer to which is in the theoretical method of Weber himself: by way of a "rationalized" theoretical explication, Weber located modernity back within the Christian tradition.

Modernity, the Protestant Tradition, and Western Rationalism: The Methods of Studying China

In Weber's theory, the relationship between modernity and Western rationalism is completely clear. By analyzing the process of rationalization, Weber employed a strict theoretical method to place the understanding of the problem of modernity squarely within the Christian tradition, but he also assumed that the problem of modernity was not unique to Europe, but, rather, endemic to world history in general. Modernity in European history is on the one hand a universal factor, while on the other it can only appear via an analysis of non-Western societies that excludes any otherness. The explanation of modernity needs not only to be placed in the context of the relationship between the present and the tradition, but also in the spatial context of the relationship between the West and the non-West. This spatial context, however, is a temporal spatiality.

It is not accidental that Habermas failed to raise the international aspect of "subjective freedom" and "rationalization." In Weber's thinking—one of the sources of Habermas's theories—the methodological expression of modernity is via a series of exclusions, that is, to situate non-Western countries outside the process. In other words, the elucidation of modernity needs not only to be placed in the context of the temporal relationship between the present and the tradition, but also in the context of the spatial relationship between West and non-West, a spatial relationship that is in fact a temporal-spatial relationship. This results from Weber's belief that the process of rationalization that could only take place in the

West is a process of universal development. At the beginning of his essay "Modernity's Consciousness of Time and Its Need for Self-Reassurance," Habermas cites Weber's concept of "rationalization" and links it closely with the notion of modernity: "In his famous introduction to the collection of his studies on the sociology of religion, Max Weber takes up the 'problem of universal history' to which his scholarly life was dedicated, namely, the question why, outside Europe 'the scientific, the artistic, the political or the economic development . . . did not enter the path of rationalization which is peculiar to the Occident?'" Habermas perceptively points out that for Weber "the intrinsic (that is, not merely contingent) relationship between modernity and what he called 'Occidental rationalism' was still self-evident. He described as 'rational' the process of disenchantment which led in Europe to a disintegration of religious world views that issued in a secular culture."[26]

According to Habermas, what "Weber depicted was not only the secularization of Western *culture*, but also and especially the development of modern *societies* from the viewpoint of rationalization,"[27] referring to the process beginning in the eighteenth century by which "rationalization" took place in the various spheres of science, technology, politics, economics, law, the arts, and religion. "Capitalism," a fundamental characteristic of this process of rationalization, is not just an economic and political category, but also one of sociology and culture—in other words, it was the form that most comprehensively encompassed modern civilization. "The new structures of society were marked by the differentiation of the two functionally intermeshing systems that had taken shape around the organizational cores of the capitalist enterprise and the bureaucratic state apparatus. Weber understood this process as the institutionalization of purposive-rational economic and administrative action. To the degree that everyday life was affected by this cultural and societal rationalization, traditional forms of life . . . were dissolved." In discussing this, Habermas draws upon the theorizing of Emile Durkheim and George Herbert Mead to show how "the modernization of the lifeworld is not determined only by the structures of purposive rationality," with this rational lifeworld being characterized by the following traits: by "the reflective treatment of traditions that have lost their quasinatural status; by the universalization of norms of action and the generalization of values, which set communicative action free from narrowly restricted contexts . . . and finally, by patterns of socialization that are oriented to the formation of abstract ego-identities and force the individuation of the growing child." According to Habermas, "this is . . . how the classical social theorists drew the picture of modernity."[28]

It is impossible to fully explain Weber's complicated theoretical system in such a brief passage, but what I am intent upon bringing up here is a question that Habermas raised but did not pursue from the perspective of non-Western civilizations: namely, why is the relationship between the worldwide phenomenon of modernity and Western rationality "self-evident"? The answer to this question has direct implications for the understanding of modernity in non-Western civilizations, including China, and can also allow us to understand why Habermas takes such pains to eliminate the "self-evident" relationship between the non-West and rationality. Let us recall the opening words of Weber's Introduction to his *The Protestant Ethic and the Spirit of Capitalism:* "A product of modern European civilization, studying any problem of universal history, is bound to ask himself to what combination of circumstances the fact should be attributed that in Western civilization, and in Western civilization only, cultural phenomena have appeared which (as we like to think) lie in the line of development having *universal* significance and value."[29] As far as Weber is concerned, the heart of his entire theoretical inquiry turns upon this question, that is, "What social factors brought about rationalization in Western culture?" This question, however, is not one for European history alone, but is rather a matter of world history. This is because, on the one hand, the question of rationalization produced in modern Europe also contains elements that "lie in the line of development having *universal* significance and value," and, on the other, this matter cannot be resolved only within the European context, but can only gain resolution through an analysis of "universal history" that eliminates the notion of otherness. Thus, the question of rationalization in European culture is one that involves a comprehensive historical explanation of modernity, and Weber's main purpose in studying non-Western societies is to disclose the particularly universal characteristics of Western social development.

Our inquiry, however, does not concern itself with what rationalization is, or what brought about European rationalization, or what the factors were that impeded rationalization in China. My question is, rather, how the concept of rationalization has been employed for all societies and for all historical junctures as a conceptual and theoretical principle, how it has organized and regulated our view of social and cultural history, and how it has managed to align all historical data within a seamless theoretical discourse. My way of answering this question will still be to return to Weber's principal theoretical motivations and in accordance with this to penetrate his theoretical logic, without treating him as an expert on either European or Chinese history and thus getting entangled with trying to rectify historical detail.

Proceeding from this, we can apprehend two fundamental questions within Weber's sociology of religion: (1) Can we find something resembling the asceticism of the protestant ethic or a religious worldview comparable to the protestant ethic in the West outside of Western civilization? and (2) How was it possible to develop a common sociology relating religious concepts and economic activity solely via the explication of varying types of religious concept?[30] The answers to these two questions depend upon Weber's analysis of what he called "ideal types," and are also related to the matter of how to understand Chinese modernity.

With respect to the first question, in order to demonstrate the causal relationship between Protestantism and capitalism, one must not only demonstrate that Protestantism is unique to the West, but also that all other aspects of Western and non-Western civilization are exactly the same. Such a conclusion, however, cannot be arrived at by ordinary historical analysis, because we cannot find a historical example of another environment exactly like the West. Weber's method of using the "ideal type"—which "'is formed by the one-sided accentuation of one or more points of view and by the synthesis of a great many diffuse, discrete, more or less present and occasionally absent *concrete individual* phenomena, which are arranged according to those one-sidedly emphasized viewpoints into a unified *analytical* construct."[31]—produces an exceedingly unequivocal result: in his analysis of Chinese civilization, for instance, Weber found that the conditions for the development of a capitalist economic system were all present, with the exception of one essential variable, that being religion. As Raymond Aron pointed out, this analytical method of Weber's needs to demonstrate the following: "The religious view of life and the resultant economic behavior in the West have been one cause of the development of a capitalist economic regime, and outside the Western sphere this factor has been one of those whose absence explains the non-development of a capitalist economic regime."[32]

This thesis directs us toward a way of understanding the second question posed above, that is, if one wants to comprehend a society or a people's lives, one must proceed from a transcendental or religious conceptualization and grasp the implicit logic therein. The existence and mode of living in all societies is related to a predetermined perspective on cosmic order, something that provides the goal for living even as it determines or controls everyday life. According to Weber, other civilizations like China and India do incorporate rational elements within their worldviews—that is to say, the notion of effective work occupies a definite place—and there was a process of rationalization at work in the histories of these civilizations. The rational notions of work and life within their concepts of cosmic order and of customary life, however, contain within themselves neither the rejection of pleasure nor other things essential to capitalism such as the motivation for investment and limitless accumulation that exist only within the material asceticism of Protestantism. For example, rationalization did take place in India, but "in the context of a ritualistic religion and a metaphysic whose central theme was the transmigration of souls," with the latter the only factor enabling faith to exist in a caste society; both of these things together limited the progression of Indian rationalization in the direction of capitalism.[33] The foregoing analysis explains why the "self-evident" link between modernity and Western rationalization cannot be found in ordinary historical work, but requires Weber's particular methodology for it to surface. In other words, this "self-evident" relationship can only appear within the epistemic framework of a "comprehensive history."

The Problem of Rationalization and the Discursive Structure of "Chinese Religion"

Weber's argument in his discussion of Chinese religion and his study of the Protestant ethic are actually the same, but his demonstrations run in diametrically opposite directions, in the former case moving from the perspective of rationalization to explain the reasons why China could not develop capitalism. Weber's research on China is premised upon his categorical analysis of European history, and the materials upon which he based his study were limited by the missionary accounts of China that he was using, limitations that were multidimensional. *The Religion of China* is a theoretical work written as a history and his methodology reveals the interaction of moral and ethical components as well as of the political and economic systems and social behavior; it contains valuable lessons for the study of the question of Chinese modernity even today.

Weber's position on Chinese religion is based upon a unitary principle. *The Religion of China* is but a part of Weber's construction of a cultural history of the world. Its core concern is not the origin of that religion, its development and basic tenets, nor on how capitalism developed in itself (capitalist development in different cultures differs only in external form). As a consequence, neither is it concerned with the material rationality Weber found in Chinese civilization—he thought that in certain respects China had an even greater material rationality than can be found in Protestantism, a paradox, by the way, for the orthodox theory of capitalist development—and its relationship with modernity. The key question, according to Weber, "is rather the origin of this sober bourgeois capitalism with its rational organization of free labour,"[34] or, from the perspective of cultural history, the question is one of the origins and distinguishing features of the Western bourgeoisie. In other words, Weber's discussion of Chinese religion and his study of the Protestant ethic is really the same subject, except that their demonstrations proceed in opposing directions: proceeding via an analysis of the ideal types of Chinese religion, the former inquiry provides an explanation of why the capitalist mode of production could not have originated in China, while the latter attempts to demonstrate the links between the spirit of economic life in the modern West and the asceticism of the Protestant ethic. Here Weber is not concerned with religion in itself, but rather with the "economic ethic" of religion, that is, "the practical impulses for action which are founded in the psychological and pragmatic contexts of religion."[35] Because of this, what Weber's research on the ethical concepts of economics in Chinese religion intends to reveal is the relationship between economic life and Confucianism and Daoism as well as the relationships of these two creeds to their own society and the various social strata within it. His goal is to "find points of comparison with Occidental development. For only in this way is it possible to attempt a critical evaluation of those elements of economic ethics of the Western religions which differentiate them from others." As Weber frankly confessed, his inquiry is thus limited to "the problems which seem important for the understanding of Western culture from *this* view-point."[36]

Owing to this limited goal, as well as to the limitations of his knowledge and the material available to him, the historical observations in *The Religion of China*—as many experts have already pointed out—include numerous omissions and outright errors, as the materials he was working from were confined to accounts of China by early Catholic missionaries (here including both historical records and methodological considerations, as well as their perspectives on China). This point should not, however, prevent us from apprehending the key issue: the purport of Weber's research on China is to employ the notion of "rationalization" to answer the question of why modern capitalism predicated on purely economic considerations failed to appear in China. Since the objects of the study of the sociology of religion are the religious tenets that make up social ethics and the influence of these on people's everyday lives, Weber put "mentality" *(Gesinnung)* at the heart of a method linking social, economic, and political systems with religious doctrine. At the conclusion of the book, he summed up the situation for China: "the basic characteristics of 'mentality,' in this case the practical attitudes toward the world, were deeply co-determined by political and economic destinies. Yet, in view of their autonomous laws, one can hardly fail to ascribe to these attitudes effects strongly counteractive to capitalist development."[37]

The structure of *Religion in China* clearly reveals Weber's method of argument. The book is divided into three sections, with section one devoted to "Sociological Foundations" and sections two and three to "Orthodoxy" (i.e., Confucianism) and "Daoism," respectively. In fact, even these latter two sections are not comprised of pure analyses of the doctrines of Confucianism and Daoism, but rather to the study of the secular manifestations of these doctrines as social ethics, along with their interacting relationships with society, economics, politics, and culture. The entire analysis is carried on as a comparison with Protestant rationalism.

Because economic ethics make themselves manifest in their relationship with any number of socially peripheral phenomena, Weber begins his study with sections on Chinese money, "City and Guild," the system of heredity and bureaucratic politics, religious organization and law, and other such aspects of the Chinese "sociological foundation." All of these topics indicate the extent of the rationalization of economic activity or of the development of rational capitalism.

Weber's discussion of "Chinese sociological foundations" is extremely wide-ranging; the account that follows will clearly show how a historical narrative with "rationalization" as its internal perspective was able to shape the description of Chinese society. For instance, as far as the monetary system is concerned, he allows that "the strong increase of wealth in precious metals led to a stronger development of the money economy, especially in state finance. This, however, did not accompany a shattering of traditionalism. . . . The enormous growth of population . . . was neither stimulated by, nor did it stimulate, capitalist development. Rather it was . . . associated with a stationary form of economy."[38] As far as the city and guilds are concerned, Weber holds that China did have urban organizations that superficially resembled the urban guilds in England, with both having the authority to regulate economic life. Since in Chinese cities clan links had never been severed, however, there was a complete absence of urban political compacts formed by an armed bourgeoisie. It was thus impossible to establish in China a guild system comparable to that of the West in the Middle Ages, with its "fixed, publicly recognized, formal and reliable legal foundations."[39] From the perspective of the development of the state and the bureaucratic system, while ancient Chinese and Western feudalism had their internal differences, they greatly resembled one another in external form. And while the "very schematic state organization under the rational leadership of officials" portrayed by the *Zhou Li* ("the oldest preserved document concerning administrative organization") is difficult to authenticate, in fact it was the "competition of the Warring States [475–221 B.C.E.] for political power [that] caused the princes to initiate rational economic policies."[40]

According to Weber, following upon the establishment of a unified state with centralized power by Qin shihuang in 221 B.C.E., the drive for rationalization that had characterized the period of competition among the feudal princes during the Warring States era came to a halt. Over the course of a long historical period, the hereditary empire set in place and developed a unitary writing system, a uniform system of weights and measures, as well as unified laws and administrative regulations. It set up a merit system of achievement, particularly in the form of an examination for bureaucratic advancement, something that quite evidently contained important elements of rationalization. The extent of this rationalization, however, was far from complete. Not only was the degree of centralization of power in this patrimonial regime exceedingly limited, but power was held by high-ranking local officials only in a formal sense. The force of executive orders from center to locality was perceived as being the product of an ethical relationship, as an authoritative suggestion, or even as merely an expectation. Officials regarded the income they received from the areas they governed as being their official salary, and, in fact, little different from their personal incomes; neither did the state erect a highly rationalized system of tax collection. As far as agriculture was concerned, all rural reform revolved around one concern, that is, with an eye to the struggle between the clans who possessed the land and those with fiscal power who sought to purchase it, while "the patrimonal authorities intervened as moderators out of essentially fiscal interests."[41] The result was that land was divided into ever smaller pieces, something that impeded technological development and the formation of a rationalized agriculture.

Finally, in regard to village autonomy and law, the clan structure that had completely lost its significance in the West during the Middle Ages was in China "preserved in the administration of the smallest political units as well as in the operation of economic associations."[42] In Weber's words, the "city" was a place without autonomy where officials resided, whereas the village was a zone of autonomy that lacked any official presence. Because of the existence of the village temple, both legally and practically the village had the capacity to maneuver as an autonomous entity and it thus became an organization that had the ability to defend the interests of its inhabitants. According to Weber, however, the immense clan power so constituted in order to implement patriarchal regulations had nothing whatsoever in common with "modern" democracy. As a force of traditionalism, what this religious community entailed instead was (1) a further step in the direction of eliminating the feudal hierarchy; (2) the slackening of the patrimonial bureaucratic administration; and (3) the indestructibility and omnipotence of the patriarchal clan. From the perspective of the "patrimonial structure of the law," the result was that "in the patrimonial state, the typical ramifications of administration and judiciary created a realm of unshakable sacred tradition alongside a realm of prerogative and favoritism." As a result, whether in China or elsewhere, since it was "especially sensitive to these political factors, industrial capitalism was impeded by them in its development. Rational and calculable administration and law enforcement, necessary for industrial development, did not exist."[43] What an ethically oriented patrimonial system sought was practical fairness rather than formal law. In sum, there did exist in China a "capitalism" created by agents of the state and of taxation, that is to say, a political capitalism, but China lacked formal legal guarantees and a rational system of administration and judiciary. Beyond that, China was characterized by a "system of prebends" and was additionally "handicapped by the attitude rooted in the Chinese 'ethos' and peculiar to a stratum of officials and aspirants to office," so it was incapable of producing the rationalized entrepreneurial capitalism peculiar to the West.[44]

My purpose in this brief explanation of the "sociological foundations" of China is to explain how Weber used ways of life and worldviews to construct a totality, his intent being to submit all economic, legal, governing, and religious forms—and everything related to them—to an investigation undertaken from the perspective of "rationalization"; it was not to envision society as the direct product of a certain religious ethic. The question, however, is just why "rationalization" has such transparent power to epitomize and thus to categorize all social phenomena? The universalization of the notion of "rationalization" was clearly of great importance to the Enlightenment movement. In Weber's research on Chinese religion, "rationalization" is nothing more than the abstract manifestation of modern European capitalism's political and economic patterns, with the use of this concept resulting in modern European history becoming the universal norm. What Weber wanted to make clear is that an economic ethic is not a simple function of a certain form of economic structure, nor should it be used unequivocally to define the intrinsic qualities of that structure.[45]

It is quite possible that that people's economic dispositions are controlled by their system of beliefs or religious regulations, but this belief and these regulations are also subject to profound influence by the political and economic systems of a particular temporal context made up of geographic, political, social, and national factors. Schemes based on either economic or cultural determinism are incapable of comprehending the peculiar feature of Weber's methodology, since Weber does not separate out an economic base that determines the nature of a cultural superstructure. He regards the two, rather, as being part of an integral process of social and cultural reproduction, although he does not use the Marxist term "reproduction." Weber's study of Chinese religion does not answer the question of why China failed to develop capitalism, but rather the question of why capitalism developed only in the West. As a result, he was obliged to seek out a sole variable, that being religion, thereby centering his discourse on different economic ethics and the modes of life of various social strata, including the rationalized relations within the social, political, and economic structure influenced by them. Weber's discursive method plainly emphasizes the direct link he sees as existing between "rationalization" and the protestant ethic. It is only after grasping Weber's basic motives and methods that we can grasp the two essential characteristics that permeate his at times rather jumbled discussion of the Chinese "orthodox" (i.e, Confucianism) and "heterodox" (i.e., Daoism).

The first point here is that Weber is addressing neither the philosophical Confucius or Laozi, nor the philosophy of Confucianism or of Daoist theorizing, but rather the positions and influence of Confucianism and Daoism in society. Although he gives concise accounts of such Confucian notions as "propriety" *(li)*, "piety" *(xiao)*, and the "cultured man" *(junzi)*, and of the ideas of Daoism and Daoists such as the *Tao (dao)*, "mystic indifference" *(xuwu)*, "quietism" *(wuwei)*, and "techniques for prolonging life" *(changshou shu)*, Weber's stress is on how these concepts operate within the Chinese social framework. In Weber's view, Confucianism ultimately "represented just a tremendous code of political maxims and rules of social propriety for cultured men of the world."[46] This definition touches upon three aspects of Confucianism's role in the overall process of social reproduction: (1) Who takes responsibility for Confucianism? (2) Through what social system is Confucianism propagated? (3) What is the nature of the relationship between Confucianism, the political system of Chinese society, and quotidian social ethics? Thus, the following comprise the three components of the way by which Weber understands Confucianism: (1) the origins, position, and nature of the literati stratum that represented both the determination for cultural unity in China as well as the group who took responsibility for the Chinese political system; (2) the developmental orientation of the educational system—the examination system in particular—that produced the literati who staffed the bureaucracy and also guaranteed the reproduction of society, the political and economic systems, and culture; and (3) the Confucian orientation toward life engendered by Confucian ethics as they worked within this social structure, including attitudes toward politics, economics, and nature, as well as their social consequences.

The second point is that Weber does not discuss Confucianism's position in Chinese society in isolation, but with the constant motive of clarifying the relationship between Confucian rationalism and Protestant rationalism, and in this pursuit uses two metrics that are in many ways closely connected to gauge their respective degrees of rationalism. "One is the degree to which the religion has divested itself of magic; the other is the degree to which it has systematically unified the relation between God and the world and therewith its own ethical relationship to the world."[47] In fact, these two yardsticks are none other than those that he uses to evaluate the essential features of Protestantism in *The Protestant Ethic and the Spirit of Capitalism*. In other words, Weber's point in clarifying the relationship between these two things is to demonstrate that extent of rationalism in Puritanism and its consequent internal relationship with modern capitalism, which, in turn, shows precisely the absolute incompatibility between Confucian rationalism and modern capitalism. All of the key differences between the social systems, cultural habits, and attitudes toward life of Puritanism and Confucianism are also seen as the reasons why China was not able to produce capitalism.

In short, in regard to its disposition toward worldly matters, the Confucian ethic stands in stark contrast to the Puritan ethic—because there was never a transcendent God who set out ethical demands via prophecy, Confucianism had an accommodating attitude toward worldly things, never having developed a tense oppositional posture toward reality. The Puritan ethic, however, stood in a stern posture of tension with the world, and because any religion with an opposition to the world arising out of its rational—ethical—demands would be in a position of tension with whatever was irrational in the world, the degree of tension between its religious ethic and the world was also an index of the degree to which this religious ethic had extricated itself from magic. In Weber's view, the fact that Confucianism lacked this Puritan tension not only proved the link between Confucian ethics and magic, but also produced a whole range of social consequences. In the political realm, Confucian rationalism was of the political order, but the notion that imperial power was divinely ordained and that the cosmic order was equated with that of society fit perfectly with a Chinese imperial power that performed the highest sacrificial offices and combined religious and political authority, thus tallying with the traditionalism of Chinese society. In the educational realm, "education devoted to self-cultivation" had a ritual and ceremonial quality even as it was marked by traditionalism and pervaded by ethics, leaving it without the capacity to produce the kind of education in specialized technologies that would be suitable for a ruling structure characterized by rationality and a modern bureaucracy.

In the legal realm, the Confucian ideal was material equality rather than formal law, and the Confucian social ethic was not based on the sort of natural law of an individual social ethic found in the West, something that had, in fact, been produced by the modern tension between formal law and the notion of material equality. In the scientific realm, the practical nature of Confucian ethics lacked the economic stimulus and pursuit of fame characteristic of the pure rationality that spurred the development of Western science; this practical ethic also caused the bureaucratic stratum to avoid competition, making it impossible to move ordinary technical advancements to the level of experimental science. In the economic realm, the Confucian emphasis on moral quality *(renge)* bound people up in blood and clan relationships, providing no capacity to devote themselves to objective tasks (i.e., the enterprise), even as it made impossible the creation of a professional ethic based on puritanical asceticism, the latter signifying that commercial trust was rooted in an ethical foundation growing out of the trials encountered in one's actual work. In conclusion, Weber's analysis of Confucianism and Daoism and his research on "sociological foundations" are identical; it is merely that the latter explains "the non-existence of political capitalism but it does not explain the non-existence of modern capitalism in China," something that can only be accounted for by the religious variable.

Questioning the Theory of Modernization: The Appointment of Language with History, Cultural Interaction, and Methods of Social History

Weber's pessimism toward the process of rationalization presaged the basic theme of critical theory, but this pessimism is completely absent from his studies of China. Theories of modernization use sociological functionalism to reconstruct this basic thesis of Weber's, their method being to sunder modernity from its internal relationship with the teleology inhering in Enlightenment thought, thus rendering the so-called process of rationalization in Western society a universal social indicator and using it to analyze all societies, including that of China. Modernization theory thus became the essential premise and means of imagining all research on China; this theory, however, was produced through observation of the process of Western rationalization, and is the outcome of this process in the intellectual realm. Building anew the methods and perspectives of the study of culture is a prerequisite to understanding modern Chinese society.

I am departing from the common practice of basing my explication of the relationship between Weber's theory and modernity on *The Protestant Ethic and the Spirit of Capitalism* and *Economy and Society*, not strictly because I am concerned with the problem of Chinese modernity, but more because it is only by understanding his sense of the relationship between Western society and rationalization that we can fully comprehend his attitude toward and standard of judgment of rationality and rationalization. European scholars have labeled Max Weber the "bourgeois Marx" and Raymond Aron, more in the Nietzschean than the liberal camp, uses the vernacular term "pessimistic" to describe the work of the man he calls "our contemporary," because he saw in Weber the influence of Marx and Nietzsche as well as "a vision of universal history leading to a disenchanted world and an enslaved humanity stripped of its highest virtues." For himself, however, "Weber placed above all else not so much success and power as a certain nobility."[48] This profound pessimism is expressed in the core of Weber's thinking when he explains modern Western society—it appears in his attitude toward the rationalization of science, industry, and the bureaucratic system. On the one hand, the capitalist system—that is, market competition between individual ownership of the means of production and the producers themselves—is historically linked with the progression of rationalization. The more rational society becomes, however, the less humankind will be able to escape the alienation described by Marx, so progressive rationalization is the "destiny" of humanity. No social system can escape this fate, because "what threatened human dignity in [Weber's] eyes was the enslavement of individuals to anonymous organizations. The system of efficient production is also a system of man's domination over man."[49]

As a liberal theoretician, Raymond Aron critiqued Weber's explanations of modern society as being too Marxist, as he thought that the latter had failed to see the development of capitalist social productivity and the possibilities that the growth of wealth brought to the solution of social antagonisms; Aron even cites Weber's categorical statement that "there is no way to eliminate socialist convictions and socialist hopes."[50] On the other hand, to explain this from another angle, Weber's pessimism had already touched upon what would later become the central theme of critical theory—that modern society had transformed the relationship between rationality and nonrationality, or, in the words of Herbert Marcuse, "the realm of the irrational becomes the home of the really rational."[51] As a result, the power of a liberated rationality and the subjective freedom thereby produced (that was the Enlightenment promise) came into question and technological progress and the rational organization of society became nothing more than a new form of control over humans and nature. In terms of Weber's intellectual scheme, the expression of the modern tradition of "the self against the self" is the self-contradiction of "rationality."

While Weber's pessimism was produced by the self-contradiction of the notion of rationality, it was also responsible for his complicated attitude toward modern society. We are, however, hard put to find this pessimism in his studies of Chinese religion. Rationality is not only his theoretical baseline; it is also the basic criterion by which he gauges the organization of Chinese society and the ethics of Chinese religion. The discursive structure of the contrast between the Puritan and the Confucian ethics demonstrates that in comparing different societies and cultures, the core constituents of Western modernity, such as science and the deployment of technology, a rational bureaucracy, formal law, and even the moral ethics that correspond to it, not only provide legitimacy for the existence and development of modernity; they also show the internal link between the legitimacy of modern society and Western rationalism. It also shows how this rationalism could only have been produced in the context of Christian culture. Weber considered that the mid-nineteenth-century Taiping Rebellion "may well have been the last opportunity for [the Christian] religion in China," because its ethic was "a peculiar mixture of chiliastic-ecstatic and ascetic elements."[52] This event marks the historical endpoint of the work that Weber completed in 1915. If one were to hold that the 1911 Revolution was too close to the time of writing to have entered into the author's field of vision, does the reform movement of 1898—with its intent being to bring about an agenda of modernization—not qualify as an object of investigation because it is too closely linked to Confucianism? We have no way of knowing. We may, however, continue the inquiry: if, as Habermas maintained, modernization and Western rationalization have a self-evident relationship, and the direct source of the latter is the protestant ethic, then must Chinese social reform be premised upon the Christianization of China? Beyond that, after China lost its "last opportunity" for producing Christianity, how do we explain the historical process and motive power of the formation of the modern Chinese state apparatus, the reorganization of society, the development of a system of industrialization and markets, all of which are grouped within the discourse of "modernity" and "modernization"?

According to the stipulations of Weber's method, the crucial variable in explaining modern Western capitalism can only be religion, because in other respects the social structures of different civilizations and societies all possess, to one degree or another, factors crucial to modernization. Thus, the problem of modernization is not merely a process of adding technologies, but is, rather, a complicated cultural phenomenon. The question we must face is this: Is Chinese modernity characterized by its own integrated cultural properties that correspond to the integrated properties of Western rationalization and its related modernization? Did, in other words, Chinese modernity also have its own set of integrated cultural properties as impetus? Logically, this question leads toward the discussion of how China's modern worldview was constituted: its foundational concepts, its internal propensities, historical evolution, and its correlation with other social environments. The most important question is this: What is the nature of the relationship between rationality, rationalization, and Western rationality and concepts like "public" *(gong)*, "group" *(qun)*, "society," "the individual," "science," and "state," that have been core notions over the course of the formation of the modern Chinese worldview? Can the latter group of ideas be seen as the translation, explication, or manifestation of the former into Chinese? If not, we need to submit these terms and their functions to linguistic and historical analysis and we also need to venture outside the scope of "rationalization" to find an integrated concept of Chinese social and cultural modernity. In other words, any sociological method that bases itself in the process of social rationalization in the West is already incapable of enabling an appropriate analysis of the problem of Chinese modernity, as this method is in itself the product and manifestation of that very process of rationalization.

Weber viewed the modernization and rationalization of society as an integrated historical process. He thus not only points out the importance of how the notion of rationality functions when it comes to the study of social behavior, but also indicates how a religious ethic or a religion (and its language, consciousness, and behavior), with its power to integrate and harmonize various things, could unify disparate individual subjectivities into collective social behavior. In Weber's studies of China, this profound sociological discovery can be extended toward two contradictory conclusions. On the one hand, the relationship between the process of rationalization and a rational Protestant ethic is self-evident, such that the modernity characteristic of this sociocultural process could only be produced in Protestant Europe. On the other hand, even as he demonstrated the basic conflict between Chinese religion and its social foundations and the social process of rationalization, he still attempted to show that cultural phenomena exclusive to Western civilization had universal value and significance and could be found in a whole series of developmental situations. Based on this, he demonstrated his overall plan to solve the social problems arising in general human history via reliance upon the core notion of rationalism. What Weber sought to solve with his analytical method of "ideal types" was precisely rooted in this contradiction between specific and general history. Even if Weber was pessimistic concerning the process of rationalization, his theoretical point of departure proves his deep connection with the concept of modernity created by the Enlightenment. This can be seen in three points Weber has in common with the Enlightenment: (1) he saw rationality as having universal significance and as the motive force behind universal values; (2) based on his notion of universal rationality, he explained the differences among cultures as differences in their degrees of rationalization; (3) with this idea of different levels of rationalization, in analyzing particular cultures, he set up an opposition between traditional and modern societies, and from there transformed spatial relationships among cultures into universal temporal differences.

These features inhering in Weber's theories provided the grounds for later theories of modernization to develop his themes, although this move was carried out in a manner quite opposed to his profound pessimism. "Modernization" began its life as a technical term in the 1950s, with "the mark of [its] theoretical approach that [it] takes up Weber's problem but elaborates it with the tools of socio-scientific functionalism."[53] As Habermas has it, "the theory of modernization performs two abstractions on Weber's concept of modernity. It dissociates 'modernity' from its modern European origins and stylizes it into a spatio-temporally neutral model for processes of social development in general." Beyond that, the theory "breaks the internal connections between modernity and the historical context of Western rationalism, so that processes of modernization can no longer be conceived of as rationalization, as the historical objectification of rational structures."[54] This notion of modernity takes social characteristics produced by an historical process in the West as abstract, universally applicable indices of social development that are part of an interrelated process. Its specific content includes the following: the creation of capital and the mobilization of resources; the development of the forces of production and increased productivity; the setting up of a centralized political authority and the creation of national unity, political participation, the urbanization of life, and popularization of formal education; and the standardization and secularization of values. This concept of modernization that represents the summation of evolutionary theory no longer, however, embodies an integral notion of the teleology of modernity. As Arnold Gehlen's formula claims, "the premises of the Enlightenment are dead; only their consequences continue on." In other words, the process of social modernization has already become separated from the "impulses of cultural modernity . . . ; it only carries out the functional laws of economy and state."[55]

With modernity having been severed from its European and Protestant roots, the theory of modernization has been brought to the study of non-Western regions, with its internal relationship with Western history concealed via a strategy of value neutralization. In *The Modernization of China*, a book edited by Gilbert Rozman, for instance, modernization refers to a huge transformation from an agricultural society in which the average income was very low toward an urbanized and industrialized society that employs considerable science and technology. The main goal of the study of Chinese modernization is to distinguish those things that aid in its furtherance from those that hinder the process, and to evaluate the mode that modernization takes and how fast it comes to pass. Because the theory of modernization has separated the notion of modernity from Western rationalization, the contributors to *The Modernization of China* strive to use the two value-neutral ideas of "successful" and "late-comer" to compare China to other societies. Although the theory of modernization unavoidably treats of an historical process that Weber saw as at once the exclusive product of the West *and* as being of universal significance, this theory turns the historical inquiry into an abstract and ageographical scheme: as soon as modernization is deployed in any part of the world, its influence ineluctably seeps into every corner of the globe, regardless of the actual force behind this influence. In fact, it is precisely because of this supposition that the theory of modernization takes the origins of modernity to be the result of the relationship between the "successful" and the "late-comers," such that the international aspect of modernization becomes the focus of attention. Scholars of modernization believe that the growth of modern knowledge is the motive power of history and the main question they ask concerning premodern societies is this: What is the competence of national leaders with regard to establishing the systems and policies that accept modern knowledge and enable economic growth and the creation of social benefits? In this respect modernization theory recognizes that the process of modernization is something that takes place within a particular country and is a domestic matter. Even more significant, however, is that the particular experiences of China or other "late-comers" come to assist in answering the question of what the norms are for the conditions required for modernization. As modernization theorists point out as they distinguish between their theory and the methodology of Marxism: the level of a country's development can only be gauged by the most easily obtained indicators such as politics, economics and demographics, but cannot be measured by such standards as the ownership of the means of production.[56]

Among the premises of modernization theory there are a large number of inferences that need to be examined from a historical perspective. For example, historically, just who is being referred to when the two neutral terms "successful" and "late-comers" are used? What is their relationship? Just who is it that possesses and uses the increased knowledge that constitutes the motive power of history? What are the historical and international circumstances under which these "domestic transformations" take place? Finally, since modernization theory takes modernization as the goal of history, this teleological narrative not only falls into a tautological mire, but also has no way to pass judgment on the problems created in the process of modernization itself; neither is it capable of setting out standards of evaluation and measures of value that transcend the notion of modernization. Thus, modernization theory distinguishes between modernity and European rationality even as it takes an abstracted European modernity as its norm. Modernization theory generally deals with the question of modernity in non-Western societies, stressing that modernization is a domestic matter in a given country, a function of a society's internal institutions and its value structure. This analysis, however, does not merely grow out of a value-neutral method, but actually takes the cultural values of European modernity as having universal normative force. As a result, there are those who perceive the functionalism of modernization theory as "culturalism," since it employs the terms "modernity" and "tradition" in order to set out the problems of development.[57]

From the perspective of cultural history, we can take a further step in examining the critique of modernization theory in Western historiography by looking at the "world systems" analytical framework of Fernand

Braudel and Immanuel Wallerstein. According to Arif Dirlik, the world systems theory raises doubts about the fundamental suppositions of modernization theory, and represents the best choice to replace modernization theory in explaining development or the lack thereof.[58] In *Civilization and Capitalism, Fifteenth–Eighteenth Centuries*, recently translated into Chinese and first published in English in 1979, the *Annales* scholar Fernand Braudel brings world-systems into his writing of history, exerting a powerful influence on Wallerstein. Braudel used a "three-level hierarchy" to analyze the economic process, placing particular stress on the idea that "there were not one but several economies. The one most frequently written about is the so-called market economy, in other words the mechanisms of production and exchange.... It was on these 'transparent' visible realities, and on the easily observed processes that took place within them that the language of economic science was originally founded. And as a result it was from the start confined within this privileged arena, to the exclusion of any others."[59] What Braudel calls "transparent visible realities and easily observed processes" refers to market economics, and the "non-transparent" level that economic science has excluded refers in the first place to the material civilization that exists beneath the market, which represents semi-economic activity that has yet to take definite shape, or autarkic economies, commodity exchange that takes place at short distances, and the exchange of labor. Second, it also refers to the transnational capitalism that is constructed on top of market economics and controls the European and even certain zones of the world economy from a distance. This second level is co-sanguineous with the East India companies that once existed in many European countries and the legal and factual subsistence of the large and small monopolies that went along with them; these are, in turn, in the same line as current monopoly capital. According to Braudel, absent this "favored domain of capitalism," capitalism itself is unimaginable.[60]

Some economic historians have criticized Braudel for taking seriously only exchange and circulation while paying little attention to production and the relations of production. Exchange and circulation, however, constitute the core of world-systems analysis: it does not seek to explain the emergence of capitalism on the basis of the indigenous development of a particular country nor in the single context of the internal antagonisms of production relations, but rather insists upon understanding and categorizing things—trade, capital flows, and labor exchange—in terms of transnational spatial relationships. The idea of "world systems" "does not refer to the entire world, but only to areas that are more or less autarkic in terms of commodity exchange"; "the relationships between different societies are not merely temporal relations—that is, advanced and backward, developed and undeveloped—but are also spatial relationships." And one of the consequences of positing space as the core argument in analyzing development is to cast doubt upon the teleology of modernization. Because world-systems analysis focuses on the spatial relationships of economic, social, and political units, it interprets the temporal notions of "advanced and backward" and "modern and traditional" characteristic of modernization theory as the spatial relations of the "core" and the "periphery," each of which depends upon the other for its existence: "there is no such thing as a 'modern' and a 'traditional' society. All societies within the world capitalist system are already 'modern,' the only difference between them is that some of them belong to the capitalist core and others belong to the periphery."[61] In contrast to modernization theory, world-systems theory does not treat each country as a self-evident unit of analysis, for these analytical units are decided and transformed by the economic relations among them. In terms of their theoretical scope, however, the differences between world-systems analysis and modernization theory cannot occlude a number of points they have in common, that is, their analyses are both based upon the economic relations of capitalism, omitting attention to historical, cultural, social, and political factors. By discarding the self-explanatory framework of the nation-state, world-systems analysis puts even more emphasis on the structural relationships of world capitalism, thus having an even greater tendency than modernization theory to be plainly economistic, antihistorical, and oblivious to culture.

Frederic Jameson, in a notable article entitled "Third-World Literature in the Era of Multinational Capitalism," brought multinational capitalism into the study of literature and culture. Jameson is extremely attentive to the specific historical traces of the diversity of national and regional cultures among various Third-World areas and peoples, making a special point to announce that the Third-World literature he is discussing is only provisional: "I will be concerned . . . to stress the radical structural difference between the dynamics of third-world culture and those of the first-world cultural tradition in which we ourselves have been formed."[62] Jameson, however, like world-systems theory, stresses structural rather than historical relationships, and the Third-World culture he takes up is that which is engaged in a life-and-death struggle with the culture of First-World capitalism, in other words, the cultural expression of the activity of transnational capitalism. In this scheme, Third-World cultural theory in fact reflects a hope from "the periphery" (the Third World) that "we" (the centers of world capitalism) engage in further reflection and revaluation of "our" perspectives.

Thus the notion of the Third-World literature of "the periphery" is a special rhetoric directed at "us" in the First World, and the significance within the "national allegory" of Third-World texts can only express itself within this structural framework, and, for that matter, can only express the total collectivity of Third-World culture. It is in this context that Jameson maintains that "none of these cultures can be conceived as anthropologically independent or autonomous."[63] The idea of the Third World not only covers over the differences among the national cultures included within the concept—something of which Jameson is aware—but it also takes national cultural subjective agency as a fiction concocted by anthropology, with the result that the real purpose of this theory of the Third World is as self-critique of "our" (the First World, the West, the centers of world capitalism) culture, and not as an interpretation of Chinese, Indian, or African culture. This theory of the Third World refuses to deploy the linguistic category of "Chinese" or any other national language to describe China or any other culture, and what it refers to as the "descriptive nature" of its concept of the Third World cannot help but be an explanatory definition. Jameson barely raises the question of language in the process of cultural transmission even as he fails to raise the issue of whether or not the language of Third-World cultures lacking subjective agency has subjectivity in itself. If, in fact, a national language contains some degree of subjective agency, then one must study cultural questions through the medium of linguistic translation or transfer and historical expression or representation.

Modernization theory and world-systems analysis no longer employ a notion like rationalization to explain matters as did Weber, but the political, economic, and demographic norms they bring to bear are nothing more than the concrete expression of Weber's notion of rationalization. In fact, since the Enlightenment, rationalization has constituted the fundamental starting point and core value of Western theoretical discussion of social and cultural matters. One of the most important tasks in the critical examination of the discourse of modernity and modernization theory is reflection on rationality and the rational, which is why the subtitle of Habermas's book *The Theory of Communicative Action* is "Reason and the Rationalization of Society." Within the scope of social science, people have long been accustomed to taking political, social, and cultural norms as being self-evidently "rational" or "rationalized," with the discussion of rationalization thus having become a series of observations on the specific content of the social relations and religious ethics brought up above. Even within the European context, however, transformations in meaning of the word "rational" have been highly complex, with the meanings of the various words for which it is the root, such as "rationalize, rationality, rationalist, rationalism and rationalization" never immune to change.[64] The self-evident relationship between "rationality" and modernity has been constructed out of the theoretical discourse of the social sciences.

Even more important, however, if one discusses "rationalization" from a non-Western perspective, it becomes instantly clear that although Weber admitted that there were elements of or tendencies toward "rationalization" embedded in such spheres of Chinese life as politics, economics, and education, there was still no concept of the "rational" or "rationalization" in the Chinese language. In such a milieu, we can discern the linguistic basis of such Western ideas as "rational" and "rationalization," which represents the entirely un-self-evident link between the specific content of social life and its expression. It is only through such cultural relations that such positivistic notions as "rational" and "rationalism" become subject to doubt: that is to say, in the event of a lacking practical linguistic referent. This would indicate that the discourse on modernization with "rational" and "rationality" at its heart is merely the application of a basic idea formulated in Western languages. Here, "rational" and "rationality" are the abstract products of the linguistic rules that they represent, and they take themselves as their own object of study, along with their relationship with the things posited to exist within that object of study. In the European context, these concepts and their referents have at least a stipulated historical relationship with one another, but in the Chinese setting even these stipulated relations do not really exist, and the only thing they represent is the linguistic domination of a stronger culture over a weaker one.

If we look even cursorily at Leibniz's seventeenth-century views on China, we will discover that in undertaking similar comparative descriptions of Christian and Chinese culture, Leibniz and Weber have different evaluations of China, with the so-called rational as the crucial variable. Leibniz harbors an admiration toward Chinese astronomy, practical philosophy, and a number of other things that he introduces, with the notion of a "rational life," theretofore thought to be present only in Europe, at the core. Finding this quality in China, however, he as a matter of course labels China "the Europe of the East," with "Europe" here standing as another term for "the rational." The 1697 Latin preface that Leibniz wrote to the *Novissimia Sinica* included the subtitle: "The Latest News from China: Illuminating the History of our Times" and provides a vivid contrast to the way in which Weber used the process of rationalization to interpret Chinese history: their conclusions differ, but the basic yardstick has remained the same, that is to say, the degree of the rational and rationalization.[65] Here, the rational and rationalization provide a constant standard or norm for description. By transforming this norm into its own object of study, and thereby circumscribing the methods by which one may perceive that object, Chinese ways come to be understood only through this language and thus to become structured and encoded. Between these two cultures, the links between conceptualization and the naming of social content thereby become plain, with the process of naming also being a cultural relationship. Chinese and European societies constitute two different discursive worlds, each with different conceptual systems and differing relationships between concepts and their referents. Prior to the modern era, there were hardly even terms to adequately translate ideas from these divergent conceptual systems.

What I am bringing up here is not the "words and things" of Michel Foucault, because to him words are just things like anything else and are thus essentially nontransparent. Hayden White explains that to accept the validity of the mission of language to "represent" the material world is a serious mistake.⁶⁶ Foucault's and White's notions of language represent only part of the question I am addressing here: what is more important to me is that the relatively stable relationships between language and what it signifies grows out of the effective interactions and living history of a linguistic community, and there is simply no practical historical relationship between "rationalization" and its related concepts and Chinese politics, economics, and the content of its culture. Scrutinizing Chinese history from the perspective of rationalization can only be undertaken with the realization that there is no historical linguistic relationship between the signifier and the signified, and that rationalization itself thus becomes the tool of the normalizing description. As a consequence, seeing Chinese history through this lens will, aside from finding a few obvious similarities, only serve to exclude anything other than what has already been anticipated.

In order to establish a new perspective for the study of cultures, the first obligation is to seek out a basic language and framework with which to describe Chinese society and culture, both of which are rooted in a particular linguistic community and social interactions. The second step will be to root this language within the process of its formation and to look carefully at its function, but without presuming it to be a transparent and immutable essence. It must also be taken into account that a linguistic community is not a hermetic entity, which touches upon the transcultural implications for the study of translation and linguistic change. For instance, I will want to study how such key concepts in formulating the modern Chinese worldview as "public" *(gong)*, "community" *(qun)*, "society" *(shehui)*, "country" *(guojia)*, "nation" *(minzu)*, "individual" *(geren)*, "science" *(kexue)*, "progress" *(jinbu)*, and "socialism" *(shehui zhuyi)*, with its "revolutionary" *(geming)* faith, took shape and were structured and transmitted, along with what these terms referred to as well as their social function and values within the specific Chinese linguistic community.

I would take the orientations of historical linguistics and cultural history and attempt to fuse them into a single mode of analysis. From the perspective of this methodology, "public," "individual," "science," and "socialism" and the like can no longer be seen as either self-evident concepts or as simply translations from foreign languages—there are, after all, complicated interactions between these concepts and the lifeworld to which they refer.

On the one hand, via the designation of relevant discursive domains by these concepts a chaotic lifeworld is ordered and made significant even as it manifests a value orientation. On the other, the relationship between concepts and the lifeworld to which they refer is not merely one of arbitrary designation, and as such terms as "public," "individual," "science," and "socialism" took shape and came to be rooted in the historical context, they came themselves to become a part of the lifeworld, and to be vital factors in the process of social and cultural reproduction. It is this latter point that causes me to believe that language and its historically stipulated usages are still of great importance and that these usages and the processes by which they change should be objects of research. Only the analyses of these processes constitute accurate description and are not merely partial explanations of an "externalized" Third World. The real import of the latter sort of explanation exists outside Third-World discourse proper and is nothing other than a self-criticism of "our" Western civilization, or a self-diagnosis of Western modernity and its rationalism. As far as the study of China is concerned, one of the great defects of this theoretical mode is its inability to diagnose the location of the problems inherent to Chinese modernity, merely substituting the crises of Western society and culture for those of China, although, of course, the two are not completely unrelated. In respect to factors relevant to China and to either a West taken as "external" or to other areas, however, what world-systems analysis and Third-World theory have to say about the economic and cultural aspects of transnational capitalism continues to be of great importance.

In seeking to determine a fundamental range of analysis and description from within Chinese society and culture, it must be emphasized that this does not mean that such a field of analysis is only "ours." Quite the contrary; in the context of modern Chinese history, the ideas characteristic of modernity I have been studying like "public," "individual," "society," "science," "socialism," and "revolution" all touch upon cultural translation, transmission, exchange, and contact. In light of this, the problem of Chinese modernity cannot be studied only in the Chinese context, nor can analysis be pursued on a Western model that excludes the Other, because it was a process that included cultural interaction. The theory of communicative action—which, as Habermas points out, provides access to three intertwined topic complexes: first, a concept of communicative rationality that is sufficiently skeptical in its development but is nevertheless resistant to cognitive-instrumental abridgments of reason; second, a two-level concept of society that connects the "lifeworld" and "system" paradigms in more than rhetorical fashion; and, finally, a theory of modernity that explains the type of social pathologies that are today becoming increasingly visible, by way of the assumption that communicatively structured domains of life are being subordinated to the imperatives of autonomous, formally organized systems of action. Thus the theory of communicative action is intended to make possible a conceptualization of social-life context that is tailored to the paradoxes of modernity.[67]

Habermas's theory of communicative action is devoted to explaining the two fundamental questions of "how is social action possible?" and "how is social order possible?" According to Habermas, in order to explain these questions, it is necessary to be able to indicate the conditions under which the behavior of "the other" can connect with that of "the self," a matter that touches upon the many ways in which different subjective behaviors accommodate one another. These would include the conditions under which, when subjectivity manifests itself in behavior, it recognizes interaction and change, the relationship between the interactions of the actor and the external world, the relationship between activity and the transformation of social structure, the complicated mental and physical interactions when activity takes place, and the function of cultural factors in social behavior.[68] By thus bringing into his discourse language and its function in communicative action, Habermas transforms Weber's tendency to divorce himself from language in his researches on human behavior, a tendency that Habermas regards as ultimately arriving at a method of study that serves to isolate the subjective actor from other social subjectivities. It is from such considerations that Habermas put forward his notion of "intersubjectivity."

Habermas's research, however, is still focused on interactive behavior within a particular social or linguistic community, with the result that his basic object of study is the interactions between individuals that constitute social behavior and order, but failing to deal with the interactions among members of different linguistic and social-cultural communities. As far as the problem of Chinese modernity is concerned, from the proposition itself to the manner by which it takes shape to its pathological manifestations, nothing in its ambit is solely a matter internal to Chinese society, nor is anything strictly accountable to transplants from outside. Instead, everything is the product of the interaction among different cultural and linguistic communities. As a result, the study of Chinese "modernity" must concern itself with "interculturality" or "intercultural communicative action."[69] This idea does not deny the passivity that is part of Chinese "modernity," but it also serves to take into account the elements of cultural autonomy that are also part of this "modernity." It is precisely because of this that we need to expand Habermas's theory of communicative action in order to extend his concept of "intersubjectivity" to the study of other cultural and linguistic communities.

Notes

Index

Notes

Introduction

1. Louis Hartz, "Introduction" to Benjamin Schwartz, *In Search of Wealth and Power: Yen Fu and the West* (Cambridge, Mass.: Harvard University Press, 1964), p. vi.

2. Wang Hui, *China's New Order: Society, Politics, and Economy in Transition*, ed. Theodore Huters (Cambridge, Mass.: Harvard University Press, 2003), and *The End of the Revolution: China and the Limits of Modernity* (London and New York: Verso, 2009).

3. It should be noted that in recent years there has been a growing body of American scholarship contesting the appropriateness of purely Western models in taking the measure of Chinese history. Preeminent in this effort has been the so-called Irvine School of historical writing, represented by R. Bin Wong, *China Transformed: Historical Change and the Limits of European Experience* (Ithaca, N.Y.: Cornell University Press, 1997), and Kenneth Pomeranz, *The Great Divergence: China, Europe, and the Making of the Modern World Economy* (Princeton, N.J.: Princeton University Press, 2000). This has, in turn, given rise to work outside the field of Chinese studies following in their footsteps, notably Giovanni Arrighi's *Adam Smith in Beijing: Lineages of the Twenty-first Century* (London and New York: Verso, 2007).

4. Paul Cohen, *Discovering History in China: American Historical Writing on the Recent Chinese Past* (New York: Columbia University Press, 1984).

5. While this work has yet to be translated into English, an extremely good summary of its main points can be found in Zhang Yongle's "The Future of the Past: On Wang Hui's Rise of Modern Chinese Thought," *New Left Review* 62 (March–April 2010), pp. 47–83.

6. Michel Foucault, "Politics and the Study of Discourse," *Ideology and Consciousness* 3 (1978), p. 24, quoted in Robert Young, *White Mythologies: Writing History and the West* (London and New York: Routledge, 1990), p. 71.

7. See, for instance, Nicholas Lardy's *China's Unfinished Economic Revolution* (Washington, D.C.: The Brookings Institution, 1998), a book steadfast on insisting

that the insolvencies that quickly developed in China's banking system in the 1990s would ultimately cause great damage to Chinese economic growth. The obvious irony here in the contrast between the relatively effective way China dealt with this crisis and the more devastating collapse of the Western banking system a few years later hardly needs to be pointed out.

1. The Politics of Imagining Asia

1. Jürgen Habermas, "Why Europe Needs a Constitution," *New Left Review* 11 (2001): 5–26.

2. Nishikyo Bunso, "Looking at Relations among Japan, the US, China and Russia from the Perspective of Twenty-first Century Chinese Strategy," *Seikai Shupo*, February 12, 2002.

3. Takeuchi Yoshimi (Zhunei Hao), *Jindai de chaoke* (Overcoming modernity), ed. and trans. Sun Ge (Beijing: Sanlian shudian, 2005), p. 188.

4. Maruyama Masao (Wanshan Zhennan), *Riben jindai sixiangjia Fuze Yuji* (The modern Japanese thinker, Fukuzawa Yukiiji), trans. Qu Jianying (Beijing: Shijie zhishi chubanshe, 1997), pp. 9–11.

5. Karl Jaspers, *The Origin and Goal of History*, trans. Michael Bullock (London: Routledge and Kegan Paul, 1953), p. 70.

6. A special explanation of Marxian theory needs to be added here. In the preface to *A Contribution to the Critique of Political Economy*, Marx described the Western European historical experience as progressing through "Asiatic, ancient, feudal and modern bourgeois modes of production," these being "epochs marking progress in the economic development of society" (Karl Marx, "Preface," in *A Contribution to the Critique of Political Economy* [Moscow: Progress Publishers, 1977]). (Marxists Internet Archive, http://www.marxists.org/archive/marx/works/1859/critique-pol-economy/preface.htm.) After 1859, however, this preface was never reprinted during Marx's lifetime and he never made mention of this famous progression anywhere else. In 1877, however, the Russian scholar Nicolai K. Mikhailovski used Marxism to argue that Russia should establish capitalism in order to abolish feudalism. Marx commented that his work merely attempted to describe the path that Western capitalism developed from within feudalism, and that one should not "transform his historical sketch of the development of Western European capitalism into a historical-philosophical theory of universal development predetermined by fate for all nations, whatever their historic circumstances in which they find themselves may be. . . . [That view] does me at the same time too much honor and too much insult." Karl Marx, in Saul K. Pandover, ed., *The Letters of Karl Marx* (Englewood Cliffs, N.J.: Prentice-Hall, 1979), p. 321.

7. G. W. F. Hegel, *The Philosophy of History*, trans. J. Sibree (New York: Colonial Press, 1899), p. 60.

8. Adam Smith, *An Inquiry into the Nature and Causes of the Wealth of Nations*, ed. A. S. Skinner, R. H. Campbell, and W. B. Todd (London: Oxford University Press, 1976), pp. 689–692.

9. Ernest Gellner, *Nations and Nationalism* (Oxford: Basil Blackwell, 1983), p. 5.

10. Baron de Montesquieu, "Charles de Secondat," Book 19 in *The Spirit of Laws*, trans. Thomas Nugent (London: Bell and Sons, 1914).

11. Perry Anderson, *Lineages of the Absolutist State* (London: New Left Books, 1974), p. 463.

12. Ibid., p. 397.

13. Ibid., p. 493.

14. Ibid., pp. 400, 412.

15. Montesquieu, *Spirit*, pp. 126–129.

16. Maruyama Masao, *Nihon seiji shiso shi (Riben zhengzhi sixiang shi)* (Modern Japanese political thought) (Tokyo: Tokyo University Press, 1998), p. 8.

17. Ibid., p. 146.

18. Ibid., p. 157.

19. Ibid., p. 160.

20. Pierre Gerbet, *La construction de l'Europe* (Beijing: Chinese Academy of Social Sciences Press, 1989), p. 12.

21. In this context, the issue of the sense in which Maruyama Masao poses the question below becomes a real issue: "If 'shedding Asia and joining Europe' can, in fact, symbolize modern Japan's basic tendency, then can one really employ the phrase to express the history of national Shintoism (or, to use the popular terminology, the Japanese 'national essence' [*kokotai*]), that 'spiritual support of the Great Japanese Empire,' from the full-scale national implementation that took place in the Meiji period to its near-disintegration under the orders of the Allied military following Japan's defeat in WW II?" Maruyama Masao, *Fuze Yuji*, p. 9.

22. V. I. Lenin, "The Awakening of Asia," *Collected Works*, vol. 19 (Moscow: Progress Publishers, 1977). (Marxists Internet Archive, http://www.marxists.org.uk/archive/lenin/works/1913/may/07b.htm.)

23. V. I. Lenin, "Backward Europe and Advanced Asia," *Collected Works*, vol. 19.

24. V. I. Lenin, "Democracy and Narodism in China," *Collected Works*, vol. 18.

25. Ibid.

26. Official statistics from 1889 reveal that the various "dues and obligations" exacted totaled 70 percent of the typical peasant household's net income, and that these "dues and obligations" paid by the peasantry totaled more than twice their net cash income; "the corvée payments due under the system of serfdom were not necessarily this high." Bankrupt peasants, even if they wished to abandon their allotted land, had to pay a special "quit rent" fee on that land. V. I. Lenin, "The Agrarian Question in Russia towards the Close of the Nineteenth Century," *Collected Works*, vol. 15 (Moscow: Progress Publishers, 1973), p. 108.

27. For a discussion of Russian agrarian reform, see Lü Xinyu "Nongye zibenzhuyi yu minzu-guojiade xiandaihua daolu" (Agricultural capitalism and the path to modernization of the nation-state), *Shijie* (Horizon) 13 (2004), pp. 143–215. This article contains a thoroughgoing analysis of what Lenin referred to as the "American path" and the "Prussian path, and my discussion here relies on her research. During the course of revising this article, Professor Lü provided me with a good deal of material, for which I express my gratitude here.

28. V. I. Lenin, "The Agrarian Program of Social-Democracy in the First Russian Revolution, 1905–1907," *Collected Works*, vol. 13. This document was written in November–December 1907 and printed in St. Petersburg in 1908, although not published, as it was seized and destroyed by the Czarist investigative apparatus and only one copy survived, which lacked the conclusion. In September 1917, it was published as a single volume, with Lenin having added a conclusion. In the summer of 1908, however, Lenin, in his capacity as author, responded to the invitation of the Polish Social-Democratic Party and published a summary introduction to the work in the Polish journal *Kritika*. See *Biography of Lenin*, vol. 1, compiled by the Collective of the Marxist-Leninist Academy of the Central Committee of the Soviet Communist Party (Beijing: Sanlian shudian, 1960), p. 204.

29. V. I. Lenin, "The Agrarian Program of Social-Democracy in the First Russian Revolution, 1905–1907," *Collected Works*, vol. 13, pp. 422–425.

30. Ibid., p. 275.

31. Ibid., p. 313.

32. V. I. Lenin, "Democracy and Narodism in China," *Collected Works*, vol. 18.

33. Ibid.

34. V. I. Lenin, "The Right of Nations to Self-Determination," *Collected Works*, vol. 20, p. 313.

35. As far as Lenin is concerned, the problem of Asia is closely related to that of the nation-state. He wrote that in Asia "the conditions for the most complete development of commodity production and the freest, widest and speediest growth of capitalism have been created only in Japan, i. e., only in an independent national state. . . . [The] latter is a bourgeois state, and for that reason has itself begun to oppress other nations and to enslave colonies." V. I. Lenin, "The Right of Nations to Self-Determination," *Collected Works*, vol. 20, p. 312.

36. As early as 1905, Lenin differentiated the "Revolutionary Commune" idea of the "new-*Iskraists*" (i.e., Mensheviks) and the "Revolutionary-Democratic Dictatorship of the Proletariat and the Peasantry," condemning the former as *"revolutionary phrase-mongering"* while grouping the latter with a "provisional revolutionary government," that "even if partial, episodic, etc. . . . will inevitably have to administer . . . *all* the affairs of state." These two political forms have no link. The notion of a "provisional revolutionary government" implies that Lenin was considering a new form of state. See Lenin, "Two Tactics of Social-Democracy in the Democratic Revolution," *Collected Works*, vol. 9, p. 10.

37. *Pravda* 60 (#2991, March 3, 1925), cited in Sheng Yue, *Mosike Zhongshan daxue he Zhongguo geming* (Moscow's Sun Yat-sen University and the Chinese Revolution) (Beijing: Dongfang chubanshe, 2004), p. 16.

38. In 1925 Radek remembered that "in 1918 when both China and Russia were divided among the Czech Legion, the Social Revolutionary Party and Kolchak's forces, Lenin once asked of Chinese workers who had migrated to Russia if they could select a revolutionary to go and make contact with Sun Yat-sen. Now we have successfully established a relationship with the Chinese people, and the mission we have conferred upon the Chinese revolutionaries is to extend the contacts between us and the Chinese millions." Sheng Yue, *Mosike*, p. 16.

39. V. I. Lenin, "The Awakening of Asia," *Collected Works*, vol. 19, pp. 85–86.

40. Russian intellectuals' ideas of Europe and Asia were obviously influenced by political developments in Western Europe and the Enlightenment conception of history. In Lenin's usage, the concept of a despotic Asia and other related notions arose out of modern European historical and political conceptualizations. On the debate between Slavophiles and Westernizers, see Nikolai Berdyaev, *Eluosi sixiang* (Russian thought), trans. Lei Yongsheng and Qiu Shoujuan (Beijing: Sanlian shudian, 1995), pp. 1–70.

41. Wang Ping, *Jindai Ribende Yaxiya zhuyi* (Modern Japanese Asianism) (Beijing: Shangwu yinshuguan, 2004), pp. 65–67.

42. On November 28, 1928, Sun attending a welcoming meeting in Kobe hosted by five organizations, including the Chamber of Commerce, where he presented this speech, which is why it is also known as the "Talk to the Kobe Chamber of Commerce and Other Organizations." See Sun Yat-sen, *Complete Works*, vol. 11 (Beijing: Zhonghua shuju, 1986a), pp. 401–409.

43. Sun Yat-sen, "Talk to the Kobe Chamber," pp. 402–403.

44. In a conversation with journalists in Kobe, Sun said: "'Unification' is the hope of all Chinese citizens. The motive force for this comes completely from the foreigners! The reason is that China and foreign countries have signed unequal treaties, and every foreigner uses those treaties to enjoy special privileges in China. Recently people from the West have not only used these unequal treaties to enjoy special privileges but also to abuse those treaties in outrageous ways." Sun Yat-sen, "Conversation with Japanese Journalists in Kobe," *Complete Works*, vol. 11, pp. 373–374.

45. For instance, he actively participated in the 1898–1900 Revolution in the Philippines, twice arranging to have arms and ammunition sent to the Filipino revolutionaries, believing that the Philippine revolt would spur on the success of the Chinese Revolution. The national revolutionary movements in Indonesia and other nations of Southeast Asia were, in fact, also influenced by Sun's nationalist thought and by the Chinese Revolution, even though they mostly stressed the revolutionary nationalism of his thought at the expense of its socialist features.

46. Sun Yat-sen, "Talk to the Kobe Chamber," pp. 408–409.

47. Ibid.

48. Ibid.

49. Ibid., p. 409.

50. Li Dazhao, "Da Yaxiya zhuyi yu xin Yaxiya zhuyi" (Greater Asianism and New Asianism) *Guomin* (magazine) 1.2 (February 1, 1919).

51. Li Dazhao, "Zai lun xin Yaxiya zhuyi" (New Asianism revisited) *Guomin* (magazine) 2.1 (November 1, 1919).

52. In this sense, Sun's "Greater Asianism" and Li's "New Asianism" are somewhat analogous to what Coudenhove-Kalergi advocated in his 1923 book *Pan-Europe*—the proposal for a "Pan-Europe" premised on the sovereignty of nation-states—and to the Pan-American organizations that had come into existence even earlier. This type of regional concept is not seen as a protectionist

organization, but rather as a regional grouping within a larger world organization. Pierre Gerbet, *La construction de l'Europe*, pp. 28–29.

53. Carl Schmitt, *The Concept of the Political*, trans. George Schwab (Chicago: University of Chicago Press, 1996), pp. 19, 20, 22.

54. Nomura Koichi (Yecun Haoyi), *Jindai Ribende Zhongguo renshi* (Modern Japanese cognizance of China), trans. Zhang Xuefeng (Beijing: Central Translation Press, 1999), pp. 32–37.

55. Wang Ping, *Jindai Ribende Yaxiya zhuyi*, pp. 174–175.

56. Nomura Koichi, *Jindai Ribende Zhongguo renshi*, pp. 68–69.

57. Ibid., pp. 176, 184.

58. Ibid., p. 206.

59. Ibid., p. 117.

60. Ibid., p. 165.

61. Kita Ikki (Weiqi Xiushi), *The Collected Works of Kita Ikki*, vol. 2 (Tokyo: Misuzu shoho, n.d.), p. 292.

62. Ibid., vol. 3, pp. 78–96.

63. Wang Ping, *Jindai Ribende Yaxiya zhuyi*, p. 171.

64. Sebastian Mallaby, "Reluctant Imperialist," *Foreign Affairs* 81 (March–April, 2002), p. 2.

65. Robert Cooper, "Why We Still Need Empires" and "The New Liberal Imperialism," *The Observer*, April 7, 2002.

66. Nishijima Sadao (Xidao Dingshen), "DongYa shijie de xingcheng" (The formation of the East Asian world), in *Riben xuezhe yanjiu Zhongguo shi lunzhu xuanyi* (Selected translations of Japanese scholars' research on Chinese history), vol. 1 (Beijing: Zhonghua shuju, 1993), II:89.

67. Maeda Naonori (Qiantian Zhidian), "Gudai DongYade zhongjie" (The end of antiquity in East Asia), in *Riben xuezhe*, I:135.

68. Miyazaki Ichisada (Gongqi Shiding), "Dongyangde jinshi" (East Asian modernity), in *Riben xuezhe*, I:168, 170.

69. In this same historical thread the rise of the Qing dynasty is seen as the result of an upsurge of Manchu nationalism. See Miyazaki Ichisada, "Dongyangde jinshi" (East Asian modernity), in *Riben xuezhe*, I:211–214. Miyazaki's point of view finds echoes in the work of contemporary scholars; for instance, under the influence of Western studies of imperialism and colonialism, James Hevia, while avoiding the standard distinction between tradition and modernity, nevertheless promotes the idea that post-1793 conflict between Great Britain and the Qing empire resulted from the clash of two expanding empires. Each one had its own particular strategies and interests and each used completely distinctive methods to construct its own sovereignty. See He Weiya [James Hevia], "Cong chaogong tizhi dao zhimin yanjiu" (From the tribute system to studies of colonialism), *Dushu*, August 1998, p. 65.

70. Using this logic, how are we supposed to understand the effect of the Mongolian Yuan dynasty on the process of linking up the Eurasian continent or the relationship between "modernity" and the Manchu Qing dynasty's having essentially demarcated modern China's borders, its institutions and its population? On these points Miyazaki's explanation is not persuasive.

71. Hamashita Takeshi (Binxia Wuzhi), *Jindai Zhongguode guoji qiji: chaogong maoyi tixi yu jindai Yazhou jingji quan* (Modern China's international moment: The Tribute Trade System and the modern Asian economic sphere), trans. Zhu Yingui and Ou Yangfei (Beijing: Zhongguo shehui kexue chubanshe, 1999).

72. Ibid., pp. 35–36.

73. Miyazaki Ichisada "Dongyangde jinshi" (East Asian modernity) in *Riben xuezhe*, I:168, 170.

74. Hamashita Takeshi, "Ziben zhuyi zhimindi tizhide xingcheng yu Yazhou—19 shiji 50 niandai Yingguo yinhang ziben dui Hua shenru de guocheng" (Asia and the formation of the capitalist colonial system: The penetration of British banking capital in the 1850s), in *Riben zhong-qingnian xuezhe lun Zhongguo shi-Song, Yuan, Ming, Qing juan* (Younger Japanese scholars on Chinese history—the Song, Yuan, Ming and Qing dynasties) (Beijing: Zhonghua shuju, 1995), pp. 612–650.

75. Maruyama Masao, "Guanyu 'jindai Zhongguo sixiang shi zhongde lixing wenti' de zhuiji" (Thinking back on "The question of rationality in modern Chinese intellectual history"), in *Riben jindai sixiangjia Fuze Yuji*, p. 160.

76. The quotation is from Xu Baoqiang's Ph.D. dissertation, which has yet to be published. I appreciate Mr. Xu's kindness in allowing me to have a copy of his manuscript.

77. Such unofficial connections between China and Southeast Asia, particularly the Southeast Asian Chinese communities formed through smuggling, trading, and migration and their particular means of connecting with China, supplied an overseas base for the late Qing Chinese Revolution as well as providing the economic modes that link contemporary China and the overseas Chinese. In other words, the unofficial connection between China and Southeast Asia *(Nanyang)* endowed the modern Chinese Revolution with a particular sort of Asian dynamic.

78. Chen Yinke, *Sui Tang zhidu yuanyuan luelun gao* (Sketch of the origins of Sui and Tang institutions), in *Chen Yinke shixue lunwen xuanji* (Selected historical papers of Chen Yinke) (Shanghai: Shanghai guji chubanshe, 1992), p. 515.

79. Owen Lattimore, *Inner Asian Frontiers of China* (Boston: Beacon Press, 1962), p. 55.

80. Karl Marx, "Russian Trade with China" (April 7, 1857), *Marx and Engels Collected Works*, vol. 15 (Moscow: Progress Publishers, 1986), pp. 223–225.

81. Frederic Engels, "Russia's Successes in the Far East" (October 1958), *Marx and Engels Collected Works*, vol. 16 (Moscow: Progress Publishers, 1980), pp. 82–86.

82. Carl Schmitt, "The Theory of the Partisan," trans. A. C. Goodson, *The New Centennial Review* 4(3) (2005), pp. 3, 6, 13–14.

83. For example, the Russian and Qing courts established tribute relations, but for the most part, neither ever placed itself in a hierarchical relationship in which one was lower than the other, with each in a sense regarding the other as its tribute state. Tribute ritual practice is itself the product of interacting forces, and hierarchical ritual encompasses a number of different forms, including varying degrees of reciprocity and the possibility of various interpretations from divergent perspectives. This issue has been addressed in the research on the history of

Chinese relations with Central Asia; see Joseph F. Fletcher, *Studies on Chinese and Islamic Inner Asia* (Aldershot, Hampshire: Variorum, 1995).

84. Wang, Gungwu, "Merchants without Empire," in James Tracy, ed., *The Rise of Merchant Empires: Long Distance Trade in the Early Modern World, 1350–1750* (Cambridge: Cambridge University Press, 1990), pp. 400–421.

85. Miyazaki Ichisada, "Dongyangde jinshi" (East Asian modernity) in *Riben xuezhe*, I:240.

86. Ibid., I:163, 166.

87. Frank points out that that both the European population and European capitalism within the world economy have grown steadily since 1400, and that this process is consistent with the East's decline since around 1800. European countries used the silver they acquired from their colonies in the Americas to buy their way into Asian markets that were expanding at the time. For Europe, the commercial and political mechanisms for this Asian market were unique and effective from the perspective of the worldwide economy. Just as Asia began to decline, Western countries became rising industrial economies through the mechanisms of import and export. In this sense, modern European capitalism resulted from both changes in relations of production within European societies and out of its relationship with Asia. Andre Gunder Frank, *ReOrient: Global Economy in the Asian Age* (Berkeley: University of California Press, 1998).

88. Miyazaki Ichisada, "Dongyangde jinshi" (East Asian modernity) in *Riben xuezhe*, I:236–238.

2. How to Explain "China" and Its "Modernity"

1. Wang Hui, *Xiandai Zhongguo sixiang de xingqi* (The rise of modern Chinese thought), 4 vols. (Beijing: Sanlian shudian, 2004).

2. The translation of *shishi* as "propensity of the times" is from François Julien, *The Propensity of Things: Toward a History of Efficacy in China*, trans. Janet Lloyd (Cambridge, Mass.: MIT Press, 1995).—Ed.

3. Michael Hardt and Antonio Negri, *Empire* (Cambridge, Mass.: Harvard University Press, 2000).

4. S. N. Eisenstadt, *The Political System of Empires* (New York: The Free Press of Glencoe, 1963).

5. *Daotong*: When various Buddhist schools developed in China, each of them claimed that the teachings/doctrines of its founder were uninterruptedly passed from one generation to the next. This was called *daotong*. In his fight against Buddhism, Han Yu of the Tang dynasty proposed a Confucian *daotong*. He argued that the most important *Confucian* teaching/doctrine (*dao*) is benevolence (*ren*), which was passed from Yao, Shun, Yu, Tang, Wen, Wu, and the Duke of Zhou to Confucius and Mencius. This *daotong* ended with Mencius. But Han Yu claimed that he himself was responsible for continuing this *daotong*. Song Neo-Confucians also painted themselves into this picture of the evolution of Confucianism.—Trans.

6. *Tong santong*: *Santong* literally means the orthodoxies of the three dynasties of Xia, Shang, Zhou, ruled by sage kings—that is, the black orthodoxy of Xia,

the white orthodoxy of Shang, and the red orthodoxy of Zhou. The teachings/doctrines of the Gongyang School argue that these three orthodoxies are actually identified with each other. Thus, the literal meaning of *tong santong* is linking with these orthodoxies.—Trans.

7. Isaiah Berlin, *The Age of Enlightenment: The Eighteenth Century Philosophers* (Boston: Houghton Mifflin, 1956), pp. 16–18.—Ed.

3. Local Forms, Vernacular Dialects, and the War of Resistance

1. See Karatani Kojin, "Minzu zhuyi yu shuxie yuyan" (Nationalism and écriture), *Xueren* (The Scholar), vol. 9 (1996), p. 95.

2. Jacob Burkhardt, *The Civilisation of the Renaissance in Italy* (Oxford: Phaidon Press Ltd., 1944), pp. 228–229. Burckhardt goes on to note that "what is more important is the general and undisputed respect for pure language and pronunciation as something precious and sacred. One part of the country after another came to adopt the classical dialect officially."

3. Karatani Kojin, "Minzu zhuyi," p. 94.

4. The term *wenyi*, often translated with the awkward phrase "literature and art," will be translated throughout this essay as "literature," since it almost invariably refers to written work. The term *dazhonghua*, often translated as "popularization" has no real counterpart in English, so the neologism "massification" will be used for it throughout the essay.—Ed.

5. There is some potential confusion here as the term rendered as "nation" or "national" is generally standing for *minzu*, which often has an ethnic rather than a statecraft connotation—Ed.

6. Sakaguchi Naoki, "Guanyu 'minzu xingshi' de lunzheng" (On the "national forms" debate), *Nogusa* (Wild grass) (Japan), April 1974; Sugiki Komio, "Youguan wenyi de 'minzu xingzhi' de lunzheng" (On the "national forms" debate in literature), *Chukoku bungaku kenkyu* (Studies in Chinese literature), December 1977; Li Huoren, "'Minzu xingshi wenyi' lunzheng" (The debate on "national forms in literature"), in *Wenjin* (Literary crossing) (Hong Kong) 1 (April 1973); Liu Tailong, "Guanyu 'minzu xingshi' lunzheng" (On the "national forms" debate), *Xueshu luntan* (Scholarly forum), No. 3 (1980); Liu Tailong, "Shitan minzu xingshi lunzhengde pingjiazhongde jige wenti" (Exploring several questions regarding the evaluation of the national forms debate), *Zhongguo xiandai wenxue yanjiu congkan* (Studies in modern Chinese literature series), No. l (1981); Dai Shaoyao, "'Minzu xingshi' lunzheng zai renshi" (Reconsidering the "national forms" debate), *Chongqing shifan xueyuan xuebao* (Journal of the Chongqing normal university) 2 (1982). In addition, all the more important mainland Chinese histories of modern literature also introduce and research the "national forms" debate. Of particular note is *Wenxuede "minzu xingshi" taolun ziliao* (Documents from the discussion on "national forms" in literature), ed. and comp. Xu Naixiang (Guizhou: Guangxi renmin chubanshe, 1986). It includes many hard-to-come-by documents and indexes of documents, providing many leads for further research. Unfortunately, little new progress has been made on this topic in recent years.

7. Mao Zedong, "Lun xin jieduan" (On the new stage), *Jiefang* (Liberation), No. 57, November 25, 1938. See also "The Role of the Chinese Communist Party in the National War," in *Selected Works*, vol. 2, *1937–1938* (New York: International Publishers, 1954), p. 260.

8. Mao Zedong, *Selected Works*, vol. 2, *1937–1938*, p. 245.

9. Whether the communist movement became a component of the nationalist movement or the nationalist movement became a component of the communist movement is a modern Chinese historical phenomenon worthy of attention. The formation of the European nation-state is closely linked to the development of bourgeois society and so the "nation-state" in Europe for the most part refers to the bourgeois nation-state. The rise of the international communist movement was not only aimed at bourgeois society but also at the bourgeois nation-state, with the slogan "the proletariat has no motherland" as an example related to this. In many Third-World nations, however, including China, the history of communist movements is part of the history of nationalist movements and by gradually freeing themselves from the control of the Comintern, "national autonomy' steadily developed within the communist movement. In this sense, the communist movement itself became a political and cultural force in the construction of the nation-state. That the discussion of "national forms" was produced in the leftist cultural sphere clearly demonstrates the historical connection between Chinese Marxism and nationalism.

10. Ke Zhongping, "Tan 'Zhongguo qipai' " (Talking of "Chinese flavor"), *Xin Zhonghua bao*, February 7, 1939. Nearly all the materials on the discussion of "national forms" in this essay have been collected in Xu Naixiang's *Wenxuede "minzu xingshi" taolun ziliao*, hereafter referred to as *Taolun ziliao*. For the convenience of readers, I include page numbers for those essays that have been collected in this volume. The quote from Ke Zhongping can be found in *Taolun ziliao*, p. 4.

11. Chen Boda, "Guanyu wenyide minzu xingshi wenti zaji" (Notes on the question of national form in literature), *Wenyi zhendi* (Literary battlefront) 3 (April 16, 1939); *Taolun ziliao*, p. 10.

12. Tang Tao and Yan Jiayan, eds., *Zhongguo xiandai wenxue shi* (The History of modern Chinese literature), vol. 3 (Beijing: Renmin wenxue chubanshe, 1980), p. 5.

13. Xiang Linbing, "Guanyu minzu xingshi wenti jingzhi Guo Moruo xiansheng" (Respectfully questioning Mr. Guo Moruo concerning national forms), Chongqing *Da gong bao*, "Zhanxian" (Battlefront) fukan, August 6–21, 1940; *Taolun ziliao*, p. 416.

14. Chang Hong, "Minjian yuyan, minzu xingshide zhenzhengde zhongxin yuanquan" (Folk language, the real source of national forms), *Xin Shu bao*, *Shu dao* (Sichuan roads) fukan, September 14, 1940; *Taolun ziliao*, p. 421.

15. Chen Duxiu, "Wenxue geming lun" (On literary revolution), *Xin Qingnian* (New youth) 2(6) (February 1917).

16. Zhou Zuoren, under the pen name "Zhong Mi," "Pingmin wenxue" (Literature of the common people), *Meizhou pinglun* (The weekly review), January 19, 1919.

17. Lu Xun, "Wenyide dazhonghua" (The massification of literature), *Dazhong wenyi* (Mass literature) 2(3) (March 1930).

18. For example, Hu Feng said, "The 'May Fourth' movement for literary revolution of the mass of the Chinese people led by the petit bourgeois *(shimin)*, was a new stream of the global progressive literary tradition that had been gathering for several hundred years and that came into being only with the emergence of the bourgeoisie." Hu Feng, "Lun minzu xingshi wenti de tichu he zhengdian—duiyu ruogan fan xianshizhuyi qingxiang de piping tiyao, bing yi jinian Lu Xun xiansheng shishi si zhounian" (On the putting forward and debate of the national forms issue: a summary of a number of anti-realism critiques, and in commemoration of the fourth anniversary of Mr. Lu Xun's death), *Zhong-Su wenhua* (Sino-Soviet culture) 7(5) (October 25, 1940); *Taolun ziliao*, p. 461.

19. Guo Moruo, Lao She, Zhang Shenfu, Pan Zinian, Xia Yan, Cang Yuyuan, Yu Dafu, Wu Xiru, and Bei Ou, "Kangzhan yilai wenyide zhanwang" (An overview of literature in the War of Resistance), *Ziyou Zhongguo* (Free China) 1(2) (May 10, 1938). The slogans "Literature of the Trenches" *(zhanhao wenyi)* and "Literature of the Villages" *(xiangcun wenyi)* found here were devised by Pan Zinian; see "San, kangzhan yilai wenyi gongzuozhede renwu" (Three: The task of literary workers since the beginning of the War of Resistance).

20. "The All-China Literary Association to Resist the Enemy" *(Zhonghua quanguo wenyijie kang di xiehui)* was established in Wuhan on March 27, 1938. These slogans were raised at its inaugural meeting.

21. Tian Han, "Kang di yanju duide zucheng jiqi gongzuo" (The organization of resist-the-enemy performance troupes and their work), *Xiju chunqiu* (Annals of drama) 2(2) (July 1942).

22. Wu Xiuru and Hu Feng both took this point of view. See Hu Feng, Gan Nu, Wu Zuxiang, Ouyang Fanhai, Ludi Gen, Ai Qing, Xi Ru, and Chitian Xingzi: "Xuanchuan wenxue jiu xingshide liyong" (On the use of old forms in propaganda literature), *Qiyue* (July) 3(1) (May 1, 1938).

23. Ke Zhongping, "Jieshao 'cha lutiao' bing lun chuangzao xinde minzu xingshi" (Introducing *Checking the Travel Permits*, with a discussion on creating new national forms), *Wenyi tuji* (Literary assault) 1(2) (June 25, 1939); *Taolun ziliao*, pp. 36–44.

24. Xian Xinghai, "Lun Zhongguo yinyuede minzu xingshi" (On national forms in Chinese music), *Wenyi zhendi* (Literary battleground) 1(5) (November 16, 1939).

25. Du Ai, "Minzu xingshi chuangzao zhu wenti" (Various problems in the creation of national forms), Hong Kong *Da gong bao*, "Wenyi" fukan, December 11–12, 1939; *Taolun ziliao*, p. 117.

26. Zong Jue, "Wenyi zhi minzu xingshi wentide zhankai" (The development of the national forms issue in literature), Hong Kong *Da gong bao*, "Wenyi" fukan, December 12–13, 1939; *Taolun ziliao*, pp. 118–126.

27. See Philip A. Kuhn, *Rebellion and Its Enemies in Late Imperial China: Militarization and Social Structure, 1769–1864* (Cambridge, Mass.: Harvard University Press, 1980).

28. Huang Yaomian, "Zhongguohua he dazhonghua" (Sinification and massification), Hong Kong *Da gong bao*, "Wenyi" fukan, December 10, 1939. *Taolun ziliao*, p. 105.

29. Xiang Linbing, "Lun 'minzu xingshi' de zhongxin yuanquan" (On the primary source of "national forms"), Chongqing *Da gong bao*, "Zhanxian" fukan, March 24, 1940. *Taolun ziliao*, p. 194.

30. Ibid., p. 195.

31. Ibid., p. 196.

32. The unification of the spoken and written languages in China was also clearly influenced by Japan. For example, in his 1897 forty-volume *Riben guo zhi* (Annals of Japan), Huang Zunxian (1848–1905) emphasizes understanding the world, foreign events, and the present, also stressing the study of acoustics, optics, chemistry, electronics, and other natural sciences. Just as Japan had solved the problem of mass literacy, he advocated the unification of written and spoken language in China, demanding the creation of a new style of writing that would be "clear, smooth and able to express ideas," "suited to the present, apprehensible to the general" (vol. 33). The key point here in the comparison with Japan is that Chinese intellectuals advocated the creation of a style of writing and not the creation of a script.

33. The *Manyoshu* was compiled into a book probably in the seventh or eighth century; it recorded folk songs and the lyric works of the court and nobility.

34. The *mana* script, that is, Chinese characters, in which the *Manyoshu* is written, stands in antithesis to *kana*, with the latter name referring to its provisionality. *Mana* were also known as "male *kana*" *(otoko kana)*, because only men could be educated in the Chinese classics; women's script *(onna te)* referred to *hiragana*, with the early novel *Tale of Genji* written in *hiragana*.

35. Tokyo languages included the refined, the documentary, and the daily languages. Because the pronunciation of *hiragana* was not at all standardized, Chinese characters, whose special characteristic is that they are not linked to spoken language, were useful as a written language for national communication. It was on this basis that Tokyo pronunciation was proposed.

36. The discussion of the language question in Japan here draws from the relevant sections of the two following works: Ieda Yoshifusa and Kato Michinori et al., eds., *Jōyō kokugo benran* (A brief guide to colloquial national language), 5th ed. (Tokyo: Kunishima Shoten, 1971), pp. 6, 10, 48; and Yamamoto Masahide, *Kindai buntei hassei shi no kenkyu* (A study of the development of modern writing) (3rd printing) (Tokyo: Iwanami Shoten, 1993), pp. 262–298. I thank Ms. Sun Ge for her assistance in locating and reading these materials.

37. Jiang Wanji, *Hanguo jindai shi* (A history of modern Korea) (Beijing: Dongfang chubanshe, 1993), pp. 302–305.

38. Such processes are not confined to the modern era. In the past, too, the process of transcending dialect clearly manifested the political quality of linguistic change and the hierarchical relationship between the center and the periphery, the orthodox *(zhengtong)* and the local, and between the upper and lower classes. In the Confucian *Analects* VII.18, for example, it is written that "What

the Master used the correct pronunciation for: the *Odes*, the *Book of History* and the performance of the rites. In all these he used the correct pronunciation." [Translation of D. C. Lau, *The Analects* (Harmondsworth: Penguin Books, 1979), p. 88.] It is believed today that *"ya"* ("correct") referred to the Xia dynasty (2205–1765 B.C.E.), with the Western Zhou dynasty (ca. 1100–771 B.C.E.) capital of Fenggao believed to be the ancient capital of the Xia. Therefore, "correct pronunciation" and "correct *Odes*" all took the dialect of the Western Zhou capital and the surrounding area both as the "Mandarin" *(guanhua)* of the time and as the standard pronunciation. In his *Lunyu pianzhi* (Superfluous words on the *Analects*), Liu Taigong (1751–1805) says: "The master was born in the state of Lu, so he could not but speak its language. In chanting the *Odes*, in reciting the *History* and performing the observances of ritual *(zhi li)*, however, he had to correct his pronunciation so as to value the teachings of the prior kings and to be prudent about avoiding the errors of mediocre scholarship." His nephew Liu Baonan (1791–1855) said in the eighth *juan* of his *Lunyu zhengyi* (Correct meaning of *The Analects*): "In the western capital of the Zhou dynasty during the rule of King Xuan, they took the pronunciation of the western capital as correct.... Whenever the Master recited the *Book of Changes*, the *Odes*, and the *History* or performed the rituals, he always used correct pronunciation, which enabled him to express himself clearly, and, as Zheng Xuan (127–200 C.E.) commented, enabled a fullness of meaning. Those who followed used the official rhymes *(guanyun)* when writing poetry and had to speak Mandarin—that is, correct pronunciation—when dealing with the populace." This is why *"ya"* speech is called "correct" *(zheng)* speech and *"ya"* pronunciation is called "correct" pronunciation. The *Mao shi xu* (Preface to Mao's [edition] of the *Odes;* the second-century B.C.E. authoritative edition of the *Book of Odes*) has it that *"ya* means correct," and also says, "That which speaks of matters of the realm, and represents the customs of the four quarters is called *Ya*" and "That in which the affairs of the whole state are connected with one person is called *Feng.*" Here, *Feng* refers to the local and to dialect. The second part of the "Annals of Geography" *(Dili zhi, xia)* of the *History of the Han Dynasty (Han shu)* has it that "[o]rdinary people have the five constant virtues [i.e., benevolence, righteousness, propriety, wisdom and fidelity] but they differ in their degrees of strength and weakness, patience and impatience and pronunciation and ways of speaking *(yinsheng)*, all of which result from the local atmosphere *(fengqi)*, and is why we refer to all this as 'customs' *(feng)*. One's likes and dislikes, what one accepts or rejects, whether one is active and outgoing or quiet and withdrawn are not constant, but follow the passions of the ruler, so we refer to them as 'practices'" *(su)*. In the Preface to his *Treatise on Custom (Fengsu tongyi)*, Ying Shao (153–196 C.E.) notes: "'*Feng*' is a matter of the whether the weather is hot or cold, the lie of the land is difficult or easy, the waters and springs are stale or sweet, and whether the gasses are tender or stiff. '*Su*' is a matter of living creatures *(hanxie zhi lei)* resembling one another. Therefore when people talk and sing there are differences among them their dances take different forms, some people are upright and some crooked, some virtuous and some evil." Ying also said: "When the sages were in place everyone wished to make corrections and everything returned to the upright; once the sages were gone, all reverted to their old practices *(su)*." It is written in the "29th Year of Duke Xiang" (i.e., 540 B.C.E.) of the *Zuo Tradition (Zuo zhuan)* that "[t]hey sang to him the minor *ya*," which is glossed as "The Son of Heaven used policy and education to correct *(qizheng)* the realm *(tianxia)*, so when the people narrated his regime, they wanted to refer to it as 'correction,' which is why it was called '*ya*.'" Zheng Xuan has a comment on the "Preface to Mao's *Odes*" to the effect that "*ya* takes its name from 'correction,' so it is said to be an example for future generations." The modern scholar Yu Yingchun states that

> being "correct" *(zheng)* is the same as "governance" *(zheng)*. The "Preface to Mao's *Odes*" glosses "*ya*" as "correct," and explains this as "governance," taking "*ya*" as that which "speaks of why royal government flourishes or decays." While this is an elaboration based on Confucian concepts of governing and education, in a Chinese cultural tradition in which the notion of the kingly way is deeply embedded in political philosophy, it cannot be considered a baseless fabrication. According to the "Explaining the Classics" *(Shi dianyi)* section of Liu Xi's (fl. second century C.E.) encyclopedia *Shiming* (explaining terms), "talking about royal governance is called '*ya*,'" which became the unshakable consensus of generations of scholars and gentry of the Han Dynasty (206 B.C.E.–220 C.E.) and after.

(All of the above discussion draws from Yu Yingchun's "'*Ya*' '*su*' guannian zi xian Qin zhi Han mo yanbian jiqi wenxue yiyi" [The evolution and literary significance of the concepts of "refinement" and "vulgarity" from the pre–Qin dynasty era to the end of the Han], *Wenxue Pinglun* [Literary critique] 3 (1996), pp. 119–120). Concerning the divergence in ancient times between the spoken and written languages and their manifestations in literature, see Guo Shaoyu's "Zhongguo yuyan yu wenzi fenqi zai wenxue shishangde yanbian xianxiang" (The evolution of the divergence between the Chinese spoken and written languages as seen in literary history), in *Zhao ou shi gudian wenxue lunwenji* (Collected essays on classical literature from the corner illumination study) (Shanghai: Shanghai guji chubanshe, 1983), vol. 1.

39. Wang Chong (27–100 C.E.) says in the "Note on Myself" *(Zi ji)* of his *Balanced Discourses (Lun heng)*: "The writing of the classics and the words of the sages are of such weight and elegance *(ya)* that they are difficult to completely comprehend; the ancient meaning is demeaned in the course of the exegesis for the common reader. The talent of the sages was of such grandeur that their language cannot be grasped by the ordinary people." Wang thus already established the opposition between the common and the literary language. In the Preface to his *Treatise on Custom*, Ying Shao says that "vulgar language will lead to mistakes, and matters should be carried out in accord with reason *(yili)*." He also wrote, "Although today's common language is said to be shallow, to use it to communicate between the worthy and the ignorant is still very difficult, like communicating with dogs and horses." This opposition between the vernacular of Ming-Qing *huaben* fiction versus the language of poetry and classical prose clearly

demonstrates the stratification of language and the value orientation attached to that stratification.

40. The "Beijing University Dialect Investigation Society" published books on dialect research; promoted investigation, recording, and research into living languages; designed a set of symbols based on international phonetic symbols for noting sounds; and used them to record fourteen local accents as examples. Zhao Yuanren's (the American-trained linguist known as Y. R. Chao outside China) 1928 *Xiandai Wuyude yanjiu* (Modern Wu dialect research) was the first seminal work to use modern linguistic methodology to research dialect. Zhao, together with Li Fanggui and others, initiated six large-scale dialect investigations carried out by the Institute for History and Language of the Academia Sinica. In the 1920s and 1930s this resulted in the publication of a dozen or so works on dialect. Zhou Zhenhe and You Rujie, *Fangyan yu Zhongguo wenhua* (Dialects and Chinese culture) (Shanghai: Shanghai renmin chubanshe, 1986), pp. 12–13.

41. Starting in 1956, dialect surveys working at the county level were carried out across the whole country. Altogether, 1,849 surveys into individual places were completed, and 1,195 research reports were written, with the formal publication of dialect investigations concerning Jiangsu, Hebei, Anhui, and Sichuan. In addition, many scholarly articles, monographs, and collections of data were published. See Zhou Zhenhe and You Rujie, *Fangyan*, p. 13.

42. In the Sino-Tibetan language family, Chinese is the most important language. It includes seven major dialects, namely, spoken Mandarin, Wu dialect, Jiangxi dialect, Hakka, Hunanese, Hokkienese, and Cantonese. Of these, Mandarin is in use by over 70 percent of the Han Chinese population.

43. Ferdinand de Saussure, *Course in General Linguistics*, trans. Wade Baskin (Glasgow: Fontana/Collins, 1977), pp. 195–196.

44. De Saussure says, "The literary language is not imposed from one day to the next, and a majority of the population is found to be bilingual, speaking both the standard language and the local patois." He cites France and Italy as examples, and circumstances such as these were also very common in China; de Saussure, *Course*, p. 196.

45. The question of phonetics was more closely related to the Romanization issue, as discussed in essays published around "May Fourth" by Qian Xuantong, Fu Sinian, Cai Yuanpei, Li Jinxi, and Zhao Yuanren. The discussions of literary reform and revolution by Hu Shi and Chen Duxiu, however, focused mainly on issues of written language, especially those pertaining to literary written language. Issues concerning phoneticization are discussed below.

46. One of the characteristics of written language is that it breaks from the constraints of dialect, something that has always been true. For example, in his "On the written language" *(Wen yan shuo)* (in *Yanjing shi* 3[2]), Ruan Yuan (1764–1849) says, "It is because they have no dialectal or colloquial expressions mixed in that they (i.e., writings in the classical style) can communicate their ideas and be widely disseminated." Qian Mu (1895–1990) says in his "Reading the *Book of Odes*" *(Du Shijing)*, "In ancient China, there had long been a parting of the ways between written and spoken language; spoken language stuck with the colloquial

(tusu), while writing attained to great refinement. Literary works must rely on the writing of cultivated people as its medium and its tool, and it is simply not the case that literature can be produced directly from spoken language." *Zhongguo xueshu sixiang shi luncong* (Collected essays on the history of Chinese scholarly thought) (Dadong tushu youxian gongsi, 1976), vol. 1. On the division between speech and writing and its connection to the issue of the refined and the vulgar, see Yu Yingchun's "'Ya' 'su' guannian."

47. See Xing, "Wanguo xin yu" (The new universal languages), *Xin shiji* (New century) 6 (July 27, 1907); Wu Zhihui, "Bujiu Zhongguo zhi fangfa ruohe" (What are the methods for curing China?), in *Wu Zhihui xiansheng quanji* (Collected works of Mr. Wu Zhihui), ed. Luo Jialun and Huang Jilu (Taipei: Zhongguo Guomindang zhongyang weiyuanhui, dang shi shiliao bianzhuan weiyuanhui, 1969), vol. 3, p. 23.

48. Qian Xuantong, "Zhongguo jinhou zhi wenzi wenti" (The problem of written Chinese now and in the future), *Xin qingnian* (New youth) 4(2) (April 15, 1918), p. 350.

49. Qian Xuantong, "Hanzi geming" (Revolutionizing Chinese characters), *Guoyu yuekan* (National language monthly) 1(7) (August 20, 1922), pp. 5–25.

50. The *Ma shi wentong*, written by the scholar of foreign affairs and languages Ma Jianzhong (1845–1900) is considered to be the first systemic Chinese grammar, although written under the inspiration of European grammatical analysis. Completed in 1896, it was first published in two volumes in 1898–1899 by the Shanghai Commercial Press *(Shangwu yinshuguan)*; it was later adopted for textbook use.

51. Huang Dekuan and Chen Bingxin, *Hanyu wenzixue shi* (A history of Chinese writing) (Hefei: Anhui jiaoyu chubanshe, 1994), p. 340.

52. As Fang Yizhi (d. 1671) said, "Confusion among characters is due to substitution and borrowing. But supposing that each entity were represented by a separate word, and, as in the distant West sounds were matched to each entity and each sound became a single word, with no overlap or sharing. Would not this be far superior?" *Tong Ya* (Understanding the *Erya*) I.I, p. 18.

53. Chen Wangdao, "Zhongguo pinyin wenzide yanjin: Mingmo yilai Zhongguo yuwende xin chao" (The evolution of the Chinese alphabet: New trends in the Chinese language since the late Ming dynasty), *Chen Wangdao wenji* (The collected writings of Chen Wangdao) (Shanghai: Shanghai renmin chubanshe, 1981), p. 157.

54. Chen Wangdao, *Wenjji*, p. 159.

55. Ni Haishu, *Zhongguo pinyin wenzi yundong shi jianbian* (A concise history of the movement for a Chinese phonetic), 2nd ed. (Shidai chubanshe, 1950); Huang Dekuan and Chen Bingxin, *Hanyu wenzixue*, p. 341. An Amoy dialect edition of the Bible in Roman letters was published in 1850, and sold as many as 40,000 copies by 1926. Of the 146,967 tracts distributed by the South Fujian diocese in 1921, 50,000 were printed in dialect spelled with the Roman alphabet. Between 1891 and 1904, total sales of Roman alphabet Bibles reached 137,870 copies.

56. Wang Zhao, *Guanhua hesheng zimu yuanxu* (Original preface to the Mandarin phonetic alphabet), quoted in Huang Dekuan and Chen Bingxin, *Hanyu wenzixue*, p. 343.

57. Lao Naixuan, "Jian zi conglu, zhi Zhong-wai ribao shu" (A collection of simplified characters: A letter to the *Sino-Foreign Daily*), cited in Huang Dekuan and Chen Bingxin, *Hanyu wenzixue*, p. 343.

58. Huang Dekuan and Chen Bingxin, *Hanyu wenzixue*, p. 344.

59. Huang Dekuan and Chen Bingxin, *Hanyu wenzixue*, pp. 344–345. Wu Zhihui was the chairperson of the "Conference on the Unification of Pronunciation," with Wang Zhao serving as vice-chair. The conference certified the pronunciation of over 6,500 characters, with each character having its initial consonant, rhyming vowel *(sihu)*, tone and final *(yunbu)* tone all clearly indicated. While they were doing this, they also certified more than six hundred slang characters and new characters for academic use. The conference also decided to adopt Zhang Taiyan's "phonetic alphabet" *(jiyin zimu)*, based on a transformed system of "initials" *(niuwen)* and "finals" *(yunwen)*. After revision, this resulted in a formal plan for a "phonetic alphabet" *(zhuyin zimu)* as well as seven methods for its implementation.

60. Hu Shi, "Wenxue gailiang chuyi" (My humble suggestions on literary reform), *Xin qingnian* (New Youth) 2(5) (1917), pp. 1–2.

61. Fu Sinian, "Hanyu gaiyong pinyin wenzide chubu tan" (Preliminary discussion on changing over to a phonetic script for Chinese), *Xin Chao* (New Tide) 1(3) (1919), pp. 393–410. This article was later digested in the special "Hanzi gaige hao" (Chinese character reform) of the *Guoyu yuekan* (National language monthly) 1(7) (August 20, 1922), pp. 187–196.

62. Qian Xuantong, "Hanzi geming," p. 19.

63. On November 9, 1926. the "Preparatory Meeting for National Language Unification" informally announced this plan, and in September of 1928, after the Northern Expedition and under the hard-working guidance of Cai Yuanpei, the Higher Education Board *(daxue yuan)* of the Ministry of Education formulated this plan as "The Second Formula for National Language Alphabetization Lettering" and formally promulgated it. The reaction of society at large to the plan, however, was cool, and it only generated desultory discussion among intellectuals. See Huang Dekuan and Chen Bingxin, *Hanyu wenzixue*, p. 347

64. Huang Dekuan and Chen Bingxin, *Hanyu wenzixue*, p. 347; Ni Haishu, *Zhongguo pinyin*, p. 113.

65. The appearance of the plan for "new Latinized writing" was closely connected with the movement for the elimination of illiteracy in the Soviet Union. Around 1921 while in the Soviet Union, Qu Qiubai first researched the question of spelling Chinese using Latin lettering. In 1928, after a year of research, and together with Wu Yuzhang, Lin Boqu, Xiao San, and the Soviet experts V. S. Kolokolov and A. A. Dragounov, Qu completed the writing of *Zhongguo Ladinghua zimu* (A Chinese Latinized alphabet), in which he established an alphabet and several simple rules for its use. After this, a movement was launched among the workers of the Far East and achieved impressive results. See Huang Dekuan and Chen Bingxin, *Hanyu wenzixue*, p. 348.

66. See Huang Dekuan and Chen Bingxin, *Hanyu wenzixue*, pp. 349–350. According to statistical compilations, between August 1934 and August 1937, there

were over seventy attestable Latinization organizations established in various places throughout the country, with 61 books being published, of which a total of over 120,000 copies were distributed. There were also 36 new serials, and over 40 magazines and newspapers published special issues or articles advocating Latinization; 67 serials adopted the Latin alphabet for titles and 13 plans for Latinizaton were announced. Following the outbreak of the War of Resistance in 1937, in Shanghai alone there appeared 54 books on Latinization between 1937 and 1940, along with 23 new serial publications and six organizations. Well over a hundred refugee classes on the New Writing were set up in 48 refugee centers. In Yan'an alone, the number of "New Writing night schools for farmers" reached 100 in the winter of 1935, and at least 20,000 Red Army soldiers were literate in the New Writing. In November 1940, the Shaanxi–Gansu–Ningxia Border Region New Writing Association was established, with Mao Zedong, Zhu De, Sun Ke and four others as honorary directors of the association, and Lin Boqu, Wu Yuzhang, and 43 others making up the board itself.

67. Huang Dekuan and Chen Bingxin, *Hanyu wenzixue*, p. 350.

68. For example, as early as immediately after the Republican Revolution in 1912, in order to meet the demands of the new situation, the Ministry of Education of the central government gathered educators from all over the country in Beijing and convened a special provisional conference on education; this conference decided to implement a new education system, which included methods to unify the national language. According to "1912: A Diary of the Provisional Conference on Education" (1912 nian wo yi: linshi jiaoyu huiyi riji), "There was a major issue at the conference, which was ways about unifying the national language. There are now people who say it is proper to teach the national language in early primary school *(chudeng xiaoxue)*, but not proper to teach the national writing *(guowen)*, and that if the national language is to be taught, it is first necessary to unify it. The Chinese language, however, is different in each area, and if the language of one particular locality is taken as the standard, other regions will be in opposition. There must be a fairest way to do this, and once the language is unified, we can establish symbols for the sounds." See Zhu Youhuan, *Zhongguo jindai xuezhi shiliao* (Historical materials on the modern Chinese educational system) (Shanghai: Huadong shifan daxue chubanshe, 1990), III.B, p. 9.

69. Pan Zinian, "Lun wenyide minzu xingshi" (On national forms in literature), *Wenxue yuebao* (Literature monthly) 1(2); *Taolun ziliao*, pp. 174–175.

70. Pan Zinian, "Lun wenyide minzu xingshi," pp. 78–79; *Taolun ziliao*, p. 175.

71. Pan Zinian, "Lun wenyide minzu xingshi," pp. 78–79; *Taolun ziliao*, p. 175.

72. Karl Marx and Friedrich Engels, *The German Ideology* (Moscow: Progress Publishers, 1976), p. 451.

73. De Saussure, *Course*, p. 195.

74. Pan Zinian, "Lun wenyide minzu xingshi," p. 176.

75. Huang Sheng, "Minzu xingzhi yu yuyan wenti" (National forms and the language issue), *Da gong bao*, Hong Kong, December 15, 1939, "Wenyi" fukan; *Taolun ziliao*, pp. 127–128.

76. *Taolun ziliao*, p. 129.

77. Ibid., pp. 128–129.
78. Ibid., p. 129.
79. Ibid., pp. 129–130.
80. Ibid.
81. Ibid., p. 130.
82. Ibid., p. 133.
83. Ba Ren, "Minzu xingshi yu dazhong wenxue" (National forms and mass literature), *Wenyi zhendi* (Literary battlefront) 4(6) (January 16, 1940); *Taolun ziliao*, p. 146.
84. Zhou Yang, "Dui jiu xingshi liyong zai wenxueshangde yige kanfa" (One opinion on the use of old forms in literature), *Zhongguo wenhua* (Chinese culture) 1(1) (February 15, 1940); *Taolun ziliao*, p. 169.
85. Hu Feng, "Lun minzu xingshi wentide tichu he zhengdian"; *Taolun ziliao*, p. 439.
86. *Taolun ziliao*, p. 440.
87. Ibid., pp. 440–441.
88. Ibid., p. 441.
89. Ibid.
90. Ibid., pp. 441–442.
91. Ibid., p. 442.

4. The "Tibetan Question" East and West

This essay began as an interview conducted by the reporter Zhang Xiang of the *Twenty-first Century Economic Report (21 shiji jingji baodao)* on April 19, 2008; after more than a month of repeated revising and editing, it took the form of an article entitled "Orientalism, Regional Ethnic Autonomy and the Politics of Dignity" *(Dongfang zhuyi, minzu quyu zizhi yu zunyan zhengzhi)*, published in *Tianya* 4 (2008). Following publication, I received feedback from numerous readers and friends, and after more than a year of research and consideration, in June and July of 2009 I greatly revised and emended my original version.

1. See, for instance, the 1997 collection of conference papers edited by Thierry Dodin and Heinz Raether, *Mythos Tibet: Wahrnehmungen, Projektionen, Phantasien* (Cologne: DuMont, 1997) (the English translation was published as *Imagining Tibet: Realities, Projections, and Fantasies* [Boston: Wisdom Publications, 2001]); and the even more influential book by Donald Lopez Jr., *Prisoners of Shangri-la: Tibetan Buddhism and the West* (Chicago: University of Chicago Press, 1999).
2. The Chinese translation of this book is entitled *Faxian Xizang* (Discovering Tibet), somewhat different than the original title of *Mythos Tibet*. It was translated by Geng Sheng and published in 2006 by the *Zhongguo Zangxue chubanshe* (Chinese Tibet Studies Press).
3. The major works of Ippolito Desideri are included in *Opere Tibetana di Ippoloti Desideri, S.J.* (4 vols.), ed. Giuseppe Toscano (Rome: ISMEO, 1981–1989); other work of Desideri is collected in Luciano Petech, ed., *I Missionari Italiani nel Tibet e nel Nepal* (Rome: Libreria dello Stato, 1954–1957).
4. Johann Gottfried Herder, *Ideen zur Philosophie der Geschicte der Menschheit*, Bd. 1 and 2, ed. Heinz Stolpe (Berlin and Weimar: Aufbau, 1965), book 2, pp. 24ff.

5. Ibid.
6. Ibid.
7. Immanuel Kant, "Toward Perpetual Peace," trans. David L. Colclasure, in Pauline Kleingeld, ed., *Toward Perpetual Peace and Other Writings on Politics, Peace, and History* (New Haven and London: Yale University Press, 2006), p. 82.
8. Ibid., pp. 82–83.
9. Ibid., pp. 83–84.
10. Ibid., p. 83.
11. Ibid., pp. 83–84.
12. Immanuel Kant, "On the Various Races of Mankind" (1775), trans. Holly Wilson and Günter Zöller, in *The Cambridge Edition of the Works of Immanuel Kant: Anthropology, History, and Education* (Cambridge: Cambridge University Press, 2007), pp. 82–97.
13. Immanuel Kant, *Observations on the Feeling of the Beautiful and Sublime* (1764), trans. John T. Goldthwait (Berkeley: University of California Press, 1965), pp. 56–57.
14. Georg Wilhelm Friedrich Hegel, *The Philosophy of Mind*, trans. William Wallace (Oxford: Clarendon Press, 1971), pp. 304–305.
15. Ibid.
16. *Helena Blavatsky*, edited and introduced by Nicholas Goodrick-Clarke, Western Esoteric Masters Series (Berkeley: North Atlantic Books, 2006).
17. Jackson Spielvogel and David Redles, "Hitler's Racial Ideology: Content and Occult Sources," *Simon Wiesenthal Center Annual* 3 (1986), chap. 9.
18. Jean-François Revel and Matthieu Richard, *The Monk and the Philosopher: A Father and Son Discuss the Meaning of Life*, trans. John Canti (New York: Schocken Books, 1999), pp. 4–5.
19. Tsong-kha-pa is the founder of the Tibetan Gelug ("Yellow Hat") School of Tibetan Buddhism, the leading school in that religion since the late sixteenth century.—Trans.
20. Revel and Richard, *The Monk and the Philosopher*, p. 5.
21. Ibid., p. 19.
22. Ibid., p. 8.
23. Ibid., p. 9.
24. Ibid., p. 16.
25. Ibid., pp. 16–18.
26. Edward W. Said, *Orientalism* (New York: Vintage Books, 1979), p. 7.
27. U.K. Foreign Office Archive, 371/35755, "Tibet and the Question of Chinese Suzerainty," April 10, 1943, quoted in Melvyn Goldstein, *A History of Modern Tibet, 1913–1951: The Demise of the Lamaist State* (Berkeley: University of California Press, 1989), pp. 398, 399.
28. U.K. Foreign Office Archive, 371/84454, November 9, 1950, quoted in Goldstein, *A History*, pp. 715–716.
29. Zhwa sgab pa (Shakabpa), Dbang phyug bde ldan, *Bod kyi srid don rgyal rabs*, vol. 2 (Lalimpong, 1976), pp. 417–418; quoted in Goldstein, *A History*, p. 673.

30. Fred Halliday, "Tibet, Palestine and the Politics of Failure," in *Open Democracy* (May 13, 2008), http://opendemocracy.net.

31. In 1942 Zur Khang, the secretary of the Tibetan "Foreign Office," told an American representative, "All the credit for the current independence of Tibet is owed to the British." Indian Affairs archive, L/PS/12/4299, March 14, 1943, letter of the British representative in Lhasa to the political commissioner of Sikkim. Quoted in Goldstein, *A History*, p. 321.

32. Benedict Anderson points out that "print-capitalism gave a new fixity to language, which in the long run helped to build that image of antiquity so central to the subjective idea of the nation" and "the convergence of capitalism and print capitalism on the fatal diversity of human languages created the possibility of a new form of imagined community." Benedict Anderson, *Imagined Communities*, rev. ed. (London and New York: Verso, 1991), pp. 44, 46.

33. Ernest Gellner, *Nations and Nationalism* (Ithaca, N.Y.: Cornell University Press, 1983), p. 1.

34. E. J. Hobsbawm, *Nations and Nationalism since 1780: Programme, Myth, Reality* (Cambridge: Cambridge University Press, 1991), p. 131. Hobsbawm believes that although genocide did not proceed on a grand scale until the 1940s, it had already debuted in Turkey and the southern margins of Europe in the waning days of World War I. He is referring to the extirpation of Armenians from Turkey in 1915 and deportation of 1.3 to 1.5 million Greeks from Turkey following the Greco-Turkish war of 1922. "Subsequently Adolf Hitler, who was in this respect a logical Wilsonian nationalist, arranged to transfer Germans not living on the territory of the fatherland, such as those of Italian South Tyrol, to Germany itself, as he also arranged for the permanent elimination of the Jews" (p. 133).

35. Ibid., p. 136.

36. R. Bin Wong, "Two Kinds of Nation, What Kind of State?" in Timothy Brook and Andre Schmid, eds., *Nation Work: Asian Elites and National Identities* (Ann Arbor: University of Michigan Press, 2000), p. 113.

37. W. J. F. Jenner, *The Tyranny of History: The Roots of China's Crisis* (London: Penguin Press, 1992), pp. 1, 249.

38. Lucian Pye, *The Spirit of Chinese Politics*, new ed. (Cambridge, Mass.: Harvard University Press, 1992 [1968]), p. ix.

39. Wu Fengpei and Zeng Guoqing, *Qingchao zhu Zang dachen zhidu de jianli yu yange* (The installation and transformation of the institution of the Qing commissioner in Tibet) (Beijing: Zhongguo Zangxue chubanshe, 1989), pp. 74–75.

40. James Hart was the younger brother of the Commissioner of the Chinese Maritime Customs, Robert Hart, and was close to the British Government of India. During the course of the negotiations, the two brothers provided the British with the Qing negotiating bottom line.

41. "Sino-British Convention Tibet-India Treaty, 1890, 1893," at MIT Tibet Forum, http://tibetforum.mit.edu.

42. In accordance with the treaty stipulation that "The question of providing increased facilities for trade across the Sikkim-Tibet frontier will hereafter be discussed with a view to a mutually satisfactory arrangement by the High Contracting

Powers," Britain and China began new negotiations in Darjeeling. The three great temples in Tibet, along with numerous monks and commoners, all signed a petition to Shengtai protesting the right of British trade and travel in Tibet and the opening up of trade at Yatung. James Hart, however, in accordance with his brother's telegraphed instructions, threatened Sheng Tai that if he did not accede to British demands, the Government of India would bypass China and deal directly with Tibet. "Zhongguo haiguan yu Miandian wenti" (The Chinese Maritime Customs and the question of Mianmar), in *Diguo zhuyi yu Zhongguo haiguan* (Imperialism and the Chinese Maritime Customs) (Beijing: Zhonghua shuju, 1983), p. 156.

43. Quote from Colonel Francis Younghusband in Tim Coates, *The British Invasion of Tibet: Colonel Younghusband, 1904* (n.p., n.d.), p. 70.

44. As the scholar of Tibet Shi Shuo has said: "The two armed invasions of Tibet after 1888 netted for Britain special economic and even political privileges in Tibet, and moved that region, like China proper, toward semi-colonial status. The two invasions had an additional consequence: they brought about the fermentation in Tibet of a profound estrangement and antagonism between the local Tibetan and the Qing governments. This estrangement and antagonism grew out of the policy of compromise and surrender adopted by the Qing in the face of the two invasions, a policy the Tibetans found hard to accept." See Shi Shuo, *Xizang wenming xiangdong fanzhan shi* (A history of the eastern movement of Tibet civilization) (Chengdu: Sichuan renmin chubanshe, 1994), p. 418. This section of Shi's book contains an analysis of relations between Tibet and the Qing around the time of the 1911 Revolution; see the account in chap. 8, pp. 408–465. The book *Jindai Zhong-Ying Xixang jiaoshe yu Chuan-Xang bianqing—cong Kuoerka zhi yi dao Huashengdun huiyi* (Modern Sino-British negotiations over Tibet and the border between Sichuan and Tibet—from the Gorkha battles to the Washington Conference) (Beijing: National Palace Museum, 1996), by Feng Mingzhu, represents an important contribution to the study of negotiations between Britain and China over Tibet and their relationship with the Sichuan-Tibet border issue.

45. Goldstein, *A History*, p. 46.

46. Deng Ruiling, Chen Qingying, Zhang Yun, and Zhu Qiyuan, *Yuan yilai Xizang difang yu zhongyang zhengfu guanxi yanjiu* (Studies on the relations between the central government and the Tibet region since the Yuan dynasty) (Beijing: Zhongguo Xangxue chubanshe, 2005), pp. 794–803; Goldstein, *A History*, p. 47.

47. Shi Shuo points out that "the reforms that Zhao launched in the Sichuan border region not only were preceded by a bloody military suppression, but also ... were marked by significant expansion of the military role. Therefore, the result of the 'new policies' of the Qing on the Sichuan frontier was directly opposite to their goals: in fact, they vastly aggravated the antagonism between the Han and the Tibetans." Shi Shuo, *Xizang wenming*, p. 426.

48. *Jiaoye chenmeng* (Mundane dreams of distant wilds), a 1936 book by Chen Quzhen, a battalion commander in the army of Zhong Ying (Lhasa: Xizang renmin chubanshe, 1999), recounts the events of the Tibet expedition from a firsthand perspective.

49. Quoted in Ya Hanzhang, *Dalai Lama zhuan* (Biography of the Dalai Lama) (Beijing: renmin wenxue chubanshe, 1984), p. 240. See also Shi Shuo, *Xizang wenming*, chap. 8, pp. 408–465.

50. Quoted in Sir Charles Bell, *Tibet Past and Present* (Oxford: The Clarendon Press, 1924), p. 304 [Bell labels this document the "Alleged Mongol-Tibetan Treaty, 1913; said to have been signed in Urga in January 1913."—Trans.]; see also Shi Shuo, *Xizang wenming*, p. 429.

51. *Xizang wenshi ziliao xuanji* (Collected Tibetan literary and historical materials) (Lhasa: Xizang zizhiqu zhengxie wenshi ziliao yanjiu weiyuanhui, 1985), p. 68.

52. According to the "Convention among China, Great Britain and Tibet" *(Zhong, Ying, Zang shi huiyi)* entry in the "Notes on Significant National Events" *(Guonei dashi ji)* section of *Qingnian zazhi* (Youth magazine [which changed its name to *Xin Qingnian* (New youth) the following year]), I.4 (December 1915), the fifth clause of the 1906 Convention held clearly that "[t]he Tibetan Government *(Xizang dayuan)* agrees to honor *(zun)* the orders of the Beijing Government and wishes to reform Tibetan law so as to conform to international law *(geguo falü),*" with Britain thereupon agreeing to forfeit its rights to extraterritoriality in China. After the founding of the Republic, however, taking as its reason that "the Chinese legal system, especially in Tibet, has yet to be fully reformed, . . . we intend to delay revising the provisions of the Convention for ten years." This provision was thus deleted and the demand was made that the Chinese withdraw from Lhasa. [These quotations from *Qingnian zazhi* are not found in the identical English versions of the 1906 Convention found in Bell, *Tibet,* pp. 287–289, and Goldstein, *A History,* pp. 872–828.—Trans.]

53. Goldstein, *A History,* pp. 381–385, 391–397.

54. At the beginning of 1947, George Merrell, the American chargé in India, wrote a dispatch reminding the State Department of the need to prevent the rise of anti-American political authority in South and Southeast Asia and suggested that the United States be prepared to establish air force and rocket bases in Tibet, and use Tibetan Buddhism as an anticommunist ideological bulwark, the only consideration being matters related to U.S.-China relations. See *Foreign Relations of the United States (FRUS), 1947, VII, Tibet,* "The Chargé in India (Merrell) to the Secretary of State," pp. 589–591. A similar argument over foreign policy ensued in 1949–1950, when there was a significant discussion with the State Department over American policy toward Tibet; owing to concerns about angering Communist China and the Soviet Union, the American government did not accept the view of its ambassador to India, Loy Henderson, that it should support Tibetan independence.

55. *FRUS, 1948, VII, Tibet,* "The Secretary of State to the Leader of the Tibetan Trade Mission (Shakabpa)," pp. 779–780; "Memorandum of Conversation, by the Secretary of State," pp. 775–776; "Memorandum of Conversation, by the Assistant Chief of the Division of Chinese Affairs (Freeman)," pp. 782–783.

56. Cable from the New China News Agency *(Xinhua she)* quoting the Press Trust of India, May 11, 1950, *Xixang difang lishi ziliao xuanji* (Collected historical materials for the Tibetan region), pp. 378–379.

57. Goldstein, *A History*, p. 713.

58. The above discussion of American involvement in Tibetan issues relies on Li Ye and Wang Zhongchun, *Meiguo de Xizang zhengce yu "Xizang wenti" de youlai* (American policies toward Tibet and the origins of the "Tibet question"), *Meiguo yanjiu* (American studies) 2 (1999).

59. John Prados, *Presidents' Secret Wars: CIA and Pentagon Covert Operations since World War II* (New York: William Morrow, 1986), p. 159; Carole McGranahan, "Tibet's Cold War: The CIA and the Chushi Gandru Resistance, 1956–1974," *Journal of Cold War Studies* 8(3) (Summer 2006): 102–130.

60. The occasion for the British invasion was the conflict between Bhutan and Cooch Behar, the latter having sought assistance from the Company.

61. The Panchen's letter forbade him entry into Tibet, since that country is "subject to the Emperor of China, whose order [is] that he shall admit no Moghul, Hindustani, Patan or Fringy [i.e., European]." Clements R. Markham, ed., *Narratives of the Mission of George Bogle to Tibet, and of the Journey of Thomas Manning to Lhasa, edited, with notes, and introduction and lives of Mr Bogle and Mr Manning* (London, 1876. Reprint: New Delhi, Manjusri Pub. House, 1971), p. 45.

62. In July 1775 the Panchen Lama sent a letter to Warren Hastings, the Governor-General of British India, saying: "As this country [Tibet] is under the absolute Sovereignty of the Emperor of China, who maintains an active and unrelaxed control over all its affairs, and as the forming of any connexion of friendship with Foreign Powers is contrary to his pleasure, it will frequently be out [of] my power to dispatch any messengers to you." Tashi Lama to Hastings, received 22 July 1775, in Alastair Lamb, *British India and Tibet*, 2nd ed. (London and New York: Routledge and Kegan Paul, 1986), p. 12. The Sixth Panchen Lama died in 1780 (he had gone to Beijing to congratulate the Qianlong emperor on his seventieth birthday, and died there of smallpox, with Samuel Turner sent from India to Tibet in 1783 to gather intelligence. Owing to the passage of (Pitt's) India Act in 1784, the East India Company was reorganized, Hastings resigned, and activities in Tibet subsided, but Britain did not forfeit its ambitions to open a door to China via Tibet. The British attitude toward Tibet, Nepal, and Bhutan was an organic part of its overall colonial activity. The discussion of Bhutan in this essay, along with its related material, is taken from Gao Hongzhi, *Yingguo yu Zhongguo bianjiang weiji* (The border crisis between England and China) (Harbin: Heilongjiang jiaoyu chubanshe, 1998), pp. 25–31.

63. Prior to this British India had occupied the adjoining native state of Assam in 1826 and thereby gained control of seven passes previously held by Bhutan; in 1910 Bhutan was also forced to sign the Treaty of Punakha.

64. This series of treaties put into effect by Britain paved the way for postindependence India to take up the legacy of British colonialism. In 1949, Bhutan and India signed the "Treaty of Friendship between India and Bhutan." According to the terms of this treaty, the two countries would maintain open borders and free trade, with India naturally becoming Bhutan's largest trading partner, aid donor, and creditor. In the 1980s and 1990s, Bhutan forced some 100,000 Nepalese into exile, whereupon they took refuge in seven refugee camps in East-

ern Nepal administered by the United Nations High Commissioner for Refugees; Bhutan and Nepal have undertaken a series of meetings to negotiate the status of these refugees, but the resettlement work has yet to be completed. These frontier and refugee issues are the direct legacy of British colonialism, but the form they take in the present is of antagonisms between nation-states. The relationship between India and Sikkim is even more peculiar. In 1947 India and Sikkim signed an agreement under which India would continue to send a Chief Administrator. In June 1949 the Indian government sent troops into Sikkim to "prevent chaos and bloodshed," took over the administration of a government that had not been in power even a month, and mandated B. B. Lal as Prime Minister. In December 1950 a peace treaty was signed between India and Sikkim, stipulating the latter as the former's protectorate, India thereby legitimating its control over Sikkim's defense, foreign relations, and economy. In August 1968, anti-Indian demonstrations broke out in Sikkim's capital, Gangtok, demanding the abrogation of the treaty between India and Sikkim; in April 1973 India effected a military occupation of Sikkim. On June 20 of that year, the Sikkim Assembly passed a constitution, drafted by India, that stipulated that the Chief Administrator sent from India would be both head of the government and head of the assembly. That September a bill passed the assembly mandating that Sikkim be an "associate state" of India, and one seat in each chamber of the Indian Parliament was allocated to Sikkim. In 1975 the Indian army disbanded the Chogyal's Palace Guard and put the Chogyal under house arrest, and on April 10 of that year the Sikkim Assembly, through the intercession of the chief minister, who had been suborned by India, passed a resolution abolishing the monarchy and uniting Sikkim with India. On April 14, Sikkim held a national referendum which coincided with a resolution of the Indian Parliament, after which Sikkim became an Indian state. Nepal is the only one of the small Himalayan kingdoms to maintain itself as an independent state, but Indian-Nepalese relations in many ways resemble those between India and Bhutan or between India and Sikkim—the treaty signed between India and Nepal after independence inherited many elements of the British colonial period, and to this day the border and refugee problems in south Nepal that are such an annoyance are prime examples.

65. W. Kirkpatrick, *An Account of the Kingdom of Nepaul, Being the Substance of Observations Made during a Mission to That Country in the Year 1793* (London, 1811), p. 350.

66. "Minzuzhuyi lun" (On nationalism), *Zhejiang chao* (The Zhejiang tide), 1–2, in *Xinhai geming qian shinianjian shilun xuanji* (Collection of topical essays from the pre-revolutionary decade) (Beijing: Sanlian shuju, 1978), vol. 1, pp. 486–488.

67. The Korean scholar Ryu Yong-Tae has made a distinction between the views of Kang and Liang, holding that Kang maintained that the Han and Manchu were one race and offered his critique of the Han-centrism of the revolutionaries on that basis; he considers Liang to be the "progenitor of the idea of national unity in diversity." See Ryu, "Jindai Zhongguode minzu renshi he neimianhuale diguo xing" (Modern Chinese national understanding and the internalized imperial nature), unpublished manuscript, pp. 11–12.

68. Ibid., pp. 12–13.

69. Sun Wen, "Linshi da zongtong xuanyan shu" (Proclamation of the provisional president), *Sun Wen quanshu* (Complete works of Sun Yat-sen), vol. 2 (Beijing: Zhonghua shuju, 1982), p. 2.

70. Jiang Zhongzheng, *Zhongguo zhi mingyun* (China's destiny) (Chongqing: Zhengzhong shuju, 1943), pp. 2, 5.

71. Gu Jiegang, "Bian Zhongguo lishi zhi zhongxin wenti" (On the core questions involved in compiling a history of China), in Gu Hong, ed., *Gu Jiegang xueshu wenhua suibi* (Gu Jiegang's notes on scholarship and culture) (Beijing: Zhongguo qingnian chubanshe, n.d.), p. 3.

72. India Office Files, L/PS/12/4177, letter from the Resident in Sikkim to the government of India dated June 27, 1934.

73. Ryu, "Jindai Zhongguode minzu," p. 2.

74. For a discussion of these terms, see "How to Explain 'China' and Its 'Modernity': Rethinking *The Rise of Modern Chinese Thought*" in this volume.—Trans.

75. *Zhonghua minguo linshi yuefa* (The provisional constitution of the Republic of China); see *Sun Zhongshan quanji* (The complete works of Sun Yat-sen), vol. 2, p. 220.

76. "Suiyuan" was a province set up in the Republican period that is now mostly part of the Inner Mongolian Autonomous Region in north China.—Trans.

77. Quoted from Zhou Enlai's speech "Guanyu Woguo minzu zhengce de jige wenti" (On several matters having to do with our nationalities policy, at the August 4, 1957, conference on nationalities work held at Qingdao); *Zhou Enlai xuanji* (Selected writings of Zhou Enlai), vol. 2 (Beijing: Renmin chubanshe, 1984), pp. 259–260.

78. Zhou Enlai, "Minzu quyu zizhi youliyu minzu tuanjie he gongtong jinbu" (Ethnic regional autonomy is advantageous to national unity and common progress), in *Zhou Enlai tongyi zhanxian wenxuan* (Selected writings of Zhou Enlai on the United Front) (Beijing: Dang'an chubanshe, 1984), pp. 334–346.

79. Prior to the first eastern expedition by the Tibetan military in 1917, the Chamdo region did not belong to the region controlled by the Dalai Lama and the Kashag, but after the occupation of 1918 by the Tibetan military, it established the Chamdo governing authority. After the battle of Chamdo in 1950, it became a liberated region of the Chinese PLA.

80. *1949–1966 Zhonggong Xizang zizhiqu dangshi dashi ji* (Major events in the history of the Chinese Communist Party in Tibet, 1949–1966) (Lhasa: Xizang renmin chuban she, 1990), p. 47. On August 2, 1954, in its "Policy on the Propaganda Relating to Dealing with the Dalai and Panchen Lamas," the central government clearly stated: "The policy of the central government is to gradually create a unified autonomous region in the Tibetan regions, . . to unite the patriotic capacities of the Dalai and Panchen Lamas with other patriotic capacities to establish a unified Tibetan autonomous region." Ibid., pp. 50–51.

81. Quoted from Zhou's speech entitled "Guanyu woguo minzu zhengce de jige wenti" (Addressing several matters concerning our policies on ethnicities), delivered at the Qingdao Working Meeting on Ethnicity on August 4, 1957. In *Zhou Enlai xuanji*, pp. 256–257.

82. Ibid., p. 257.

83. Fei Xiaotong, *Zhonghua minzu de duoyuan yiti geju* (The pattern of unity in diversity of the Chinese people) (Beijing: Zhongguo minzu xueyuan chubanshe, 1989), p. 1.

84. Written over a number of years at the beginning of the first century B.C.E., *The Records of the Grand Historian, or Shiji*, by Sima Qian (146–86 B.C.E.), is the first comprehensive history of China, representing a model of historiography and prose style thereafter.—Trans.

85. Fei Xiaotong, "Guanyu woguode minzu shibie wenti" (On the question of distinguishing ethnicity in China), *Zhongguo shehui kexue* (Chinese social science) 1 (1980).

86. Zeng Weiyi, "Baima Zangzu jiqi yanjiu zongshu" (Summarizing the research on the White-horse Tibetans), in Shi Shuo, ed., *Zang-yi zoulang* (The Tibetan-Yi corridor) (Chengdu: Sichuan renmin chubanshe, 2005), pp. 208–232.

87. The theory of "six macro-regions and three corridors" was developed by Li Shaoming, who based it on the conclusions drawn by Fei Xiaotong in his two essays, "Minzu shehuixue diaocha de changshi" (Experimental investigations in ethnic sociology) and "Tan shenru kaizhan minzu diaocha wenti" (Discussions on developing in-depth investigations of ethnicity), both contained in Fei's *Minzu yanjiu wenji* (Collected studies of ethnicity) (Beijing: Minzu chubanshe, 1988), pp. 268–285, 295–305. See Li Shaoming, "Zang-Yi zoulang yanjiu zhong de jige wenti" (Several questions concerning studies of the Tibetan-Yi corridor) in *Zhonghua wenhua luntan* (Chinese culture forum) 4 (2005): 5–8. On the notion of the Tibetan-Yi corridor, see Li Shaoming's "Fei Xiaotong lun Zang-Yi zoulang" (Fei Xiaotong on the Tibetan-Yi corridor), in *Xi'nan minzu xueyuan xuebao* (Journal of the Southwestern College of Nationalities) (January 2006) 27(1): 1–6.

88. Kang Youwei, "Gongmin zizhi pian" (Citizen self-rule), in *Kang Nanhai Guan zhiyi*, vol. 8 (Shanghai: Guangzhi shuju, 1905).

89. In a communication dated January 6, 2010, Professor Shen Weirong addressed detailed comments to this essay, and in them emphasized the difference between the concept of "Greater Tibet" and the historical geographical divisions of Tibet. My account here has been revised in accordance with his suggestions, and I would like to thank him here.

90. Shi Shuo, *Xizang wenming*, p. 11.

91. Ibid., pp. 72, 102.

92. Ma Rong, "Jingji fazhan zhong de pinfu chaju wenti—quyu chayi, zhiye chayi he zuqun chayi" (The question of wealth difference in economic development—regional disparities, occupational disparities and ethnic disparities), *Beijing daxue xuebao* (Journal of Peking University) (zheshe ban) (humanities and social science edition) 1 (2009): 116–117.

93. Phuntsok Wangyal (Phun tshogs dbang rgyal), "Xiegei Hu Jintao de xin" (A letter written to Hu Jintao), http://www.washeng.net.

94. Ben Hillman, "Money Can't Buy Tibetans' Love," *Far Eastern Economic Review*, April 2008.

95. See *Cultural Genocide and Asian State Peripheries*, ed. Barry Sautman (Gordonsville, Va.: Palgrave-Macmillan, 2006), pp. 165–188.

96. In his "Lijie minzu guanxi de xin silu—shaoshu minzu wenti de 'qu zhengzhihua'" (A new way of understanding inter-ethnic relations—the "depoliticization" of the minority nationality question), *Beijing daxue xuebao* (zhexue shuhuikexue ban) 6 (2004); Ma Rong also uses the term "depoliticization," but in a quite different way than I intend here. He is referring to the phenomenon in which Western nationalist movements take ethnicity as a political unit in seeking political goals. He seeks to synthesize traditional culture and use the unit of the citizen to create a universal politics of citizenship. From this it can be seen that his critique of "politicization" and my critique of "depoliticization" overlap to some extent, but the difference lies in that the "depoliticization" I describe is the denial of or veering away from the process of popular politics, and the latter is precisely that which is the premise for the Chinese nation overcoming ethnic divisions and antagonisms and creating a united political community.

97. Lin Hsiao-ting, "War or Stratagem? Resassessing China's Military Advances toward Tibet, 1942–1943," *China Quarterly* (2006): 446–462.

98. On the subject of "the politics of leaving politics behind," see my *Qu zhengzhihuade zhengzhi: duan ershi shijide zhongjie yu jiushi niandai* (The politics of leaving politics behind: The end of the short twentieth century and the 1990s) (Beijing: Sanlian shudian, 2008). This article has been translated as "Depoliticized Politics, Multiple Components of Hegemony, and the Eclipse of the Sixties" by Chris Connery and appears in *Inter-Asia Cultural Studies* 7(4) (2006): 683–700.

99. Eric J. Hobsbawm, *Nations and Nationalism since 1780: Programme, Myth, Reality* (Cambridge: Cambridge University Press, 1990), p. 20.

100. Luo Kaiyun et al., *Zhongguo shaoshu minzu geming shi* (History of Chinese ethnic minorities in the revolution) (Beijing: Zhongguo shehui kexue chubanshe, 2003), pp. 78–79.

101. Goldstein, *A History*, p. 3.

102. Tom Grunfeld, "Tibet: Myth and Realities," *New China* 1(3) (1975): 17–20, quoted in Goldstein, *A History*, p. 34.

103. According to the narrative contained in the preface to chapter 14 of *Xueshan zhi shu* (Letters from the snowy mountains), which appeared in *Piaoliu ke* (Drifting traveler) 57 (April 2008), edited by Guo Jing, prior to the 1950s, the basic structure of Deqin (bDe chen) Tibetan society was of a "unity between politics and religion." "Within this were two systems, one headed by tribal chieftains *(tusi)* and the other by the monasteries who implemented their control of the villages under them through the Headmen and freemen *(zhenghu)* in the village. Each farmer in a village was required to obtain the agreement of the Headman and the elders as well as permission from the Chieftain and the monastery before being able to have land and become a 'freeman.' In general, the freemen were descended from hereditary residents. Others who lacked such registration were either bankrupt farmers, hired laborers or serfs. . . . The chieftains were in charge of the Headmen, who were in charge of the freemen, who were in charge of tenants and serfs. According to research done in the 1950s, there were 660

households of freeman in the county, along with 2,378 households of tenants and serfs. Twenty-three villages of freemen supported one Lamaist monastery, and they were called 'quri' (that is, people of the monastery), paying a fixed rent to the monastery and supplying corvée labor. The 'quri' could buy and sell land, but only to freemen; when land was sold, it was only possible after going to the monastery to pay the rent, with one-third of the sale price going to the monastery. The monastery would affix its seal to the contract. In the event of minor disputes over land, the monastery would adjudicate as it collected the rent; if the dispute were more substantial, the monastery would adjudicate in association with the Chieftain. In addition to rights of rent collection and corvée labor, the monastery also had political control. Freemen in the other villages were called 'chewa'; they did not contribute to the support of monasteries, but only paid a grain tax and corvée to the Chieftain." http://www.strongwind.com.hk/catalog/80045a6b-3c6c-4df0-9a2d-6aead5705225.aspx.

104. *Gongmeng falü yanjiu zhongxin* (The civic alliance legal research center): "Zangqu 3.14 shijian shehui, jingji chengyin diaocha) (written by Fang Kun, Huang Li and Li Xiangzhi" (An Investigative Report into the Social and Economic Causes of the March 14 Incident in the Tibetan Areas), computer printout, pp. 5–6. This report circulated briefly on the Internet, but was never formally published. For the English version, see http://blog.foolsmountain.com/2009/06/02/an-investigative-report-into-the-social-and-economic-causes-of-the-314-incident-in-tibetan-areas/2/.

105. In 2004 I visited a number of Lamaist monasteries along with Tibetan friends, and in the rooms of the Abbot of almost every one was a picture of Mao Zedong, along with portraits of the Dalai and Panchen Lamas on each side. A Tibetan friend from a Beijing university told me that "we Tibetans are simply superstitious, and Mao has become a Bodhisattva." This phenomenon explains how in the Tibetan world the socialist period carried a bit of the flavor of "religion and politics joined together." In his autobiography the Dalai Lama said that socialism is more suited to Tibet than is capitalism.

106. "An Investigative Report," computer printout, p. 10.

107. Ibid., p. 2.

108. *Dushu* 7 (2004): 167.

109. One must make some distinctions on the language question. As Eric Hobsbawm has said of ideas on language in nineteenth-century Europe, "Once it was accepted that an independent or 'real' nation also had to be a viable nation by the criteria thus accepted, it also followed that some of the smaller nationalities and languages were doomed to disappear as such." He added, however, that "there was nothing chauvinist in such a general attitude." Hobsbawm, *Nations and Nationalism*, pp. 34–35. On the other hand, whether states should adopt appropriate measures to preserve and develop minority languages or not is an important issue.

110. Gu Hongming (1857–1928) was a Malayan Chinese of mixed race with degrees from European universities who after moving to China in 1885 became an extreme cultural conservative, rigidly opposed to Westernization.—Trans.

111. The *hukou*, or household registration system, has been used in China to tie people the localities in which they are officially registered, which has tended to be their parents' birthplace.—Trans.

112. Ma Rong and Danzeng Lunzhu, "Lhasa shi liudong renkou diaocha baogao" (Report on the investigation of the floating population in Lhasa city), *Xibei minzu yanjiu* (Research on ethnicities in the northwest) 4(51) (2006): 168.

113. "An Investigative Report," computer printout, p. 10.

114. Following in the wake of the development of a market economy, cities like Beijing and Shanghai have seen the rise of gender discrimination, with, for example, certain companies hiring only men and not women, or different pay rates for the same work. In minority regions such discrimination also exists among different ethnicities—for instance, in areas inhabited by mixed ethnicities, advertisements for hiring workers have included discriminatory provisions such as "50 yuan per day for Han people, 30 yuan for Tibetans." Such discriminatory practices must be ended.

115. Wang Hui, "Wenhua yu gonggong xing daoyan" (Introduction to *Culture and the public sphere*) (Beijing: Sanlian shudian, 1998). This book is a collection of articles concerned with "cultures," "publicity," and "the politics of recognition," and includes essays by Hannah Arendt, Jürgen Habermas, Charles Taylor, and John Rawls. My use of the term "the politics of recognition" here is borrowed from Charles Taylor, *Multiculturalism*, with commentary by K. Anthony Appiah, Jürgen Habermas, Steven C. Rockefeller, Michael Walzer, and Susan Wolf, edited and introduced by Amy Gutman (Princeton: Princeton University Press, 1994), pp. 25–74.

116. He Longqun, *Zhongguo gongchandang minzu zhengce shilun* (A historical discussion of the policies toward minorities of the Chinese Communist Party) (Beijing: renmin chubanshe, 2005), pp. 136–137.

117. Charles Taylor, "The Politics," in *Multiculturalism*, pp. 25–74.

118. In public intellectual discussion in today's China, there is very little conversation about ethnicity and the relations among ethnicities, a phenomenon that is, I think, closely related to the nature of the Chinese intellectual context. There are numerous minority scholars who know any number of minority languages, but they have a hard time making themselves heard in public discussion; their discourse up to now has been limited to minority areas and the field of ethnic studies, a situation urgently in need of change.

5. Okinawa and Two Dramatic Changes to the Regional Order

1. In the Chinese original, the term used throughout to refer to the territory is "Liuqiu," or "Ryukyu" in its Japanese pronunciation. Since in the post–World War II period the territory is almost invariably referred to as "Okinawa" in English usage, I will use that name to refer to the area for the post–World War II period, with "the Ryukyus" used to refer to the area prior to that time.—Ed.

2. Kemuyama Sentaro, *Seikanron Jissō* (The truth about the discourse on invading Korea) (Tokyo: Waseda Daigaku Shuppanbu, 1909), p. 231. On the visit of

the Iwakura diplomatic delegation, see Xie Xiaodong, "Yancang shituan yu Riben xiandaihua" (The Iwakura Diplomatic Delegation and Japanese Modernization), *Bohai daxue xuebao* (zhexue shehui kexue ban) 2(26) (2006/03): 68–71.

3. Okubo Toshiaki, *Iwakura shisetsu no kenkyū* (A study of the Iwakura diplomatic delegation) (Tokyo: Munetaka Shobō, 1976), pp. 161–162.

4. Kume Kunitake, *Bei ō kairan jikki* (Record of a tour of Europe and America) (Tokyo: Iwanami Shoten, 1981), vol. 3, p. 329.

5. Shinobu Seizaburo, *Nihon gaikō shi* (Diplomatic history of Japan) (Beijing: Shangwu yinshuguan, 1980), vol. 1, p. 143.

6. Wang Yunsheng, ed., *Liushi nian lai Zhongguo yu Riben* (China and Japan over the last sixty years) (Beijing: Sanlian shudian, 2005), vol. 1, p. 38.

7. Zheng Jing, son of the merchant/buccaneer Zheng Chenggong, succeeding his father in basing himself in Taiwan and resisting the new Manchu dynasty on the Chinese mainland.

8. The "most favored nation" (*zui hui guo* in Chinese) refers to the stipulation that any right or privilege given to any other nation must also be accorded to the nation having this clause as part of their treaty.—Trans.

9. Wang Yunsheng, *Liushi nian lai*, pp. 57–58.

10. There is a close connection between the occupation of the Ryukyus and the invasion of Taiwan. In fact, even just after the Opium War, Shimazu Nariakira, the feudal lord of Satsuma, suggested that: "Since Britain and France got the upper hand over the Qing, the activity will move east. . . . Therefore our priority should be to defend ourselves against the barbarians; we may either support the remnants of the Ming dynasty in taking Taiwan and Fuzhou, so as to get rid of the foreign threat to Japan. Our Satsuma forces would be sufficient for this task, but we have no warships and cannot fight for supremacy at sea. The urgent task at hand, therefore, is to prepare our armaments." Wang Yunsheng, *Liushi nian lai*, pp. 63–64.

11. See my *Xiandai Zhongguo sixiangde xingqi* (The rise of modern Chinese thought), Introduction to Vol. 1, Part 1; Volume 1, Part 2, "Diguo yu guojia" (Empire and state) (Beijing: Sanlian shudian, 2004).

12. Wang Yunsheng, *Liushi nian lai*, pp. 64–65.

13. *Tongzhi chao chouban yiwu shimo* (The records of the diplomatic Affairs of the Tongzhi reign), vol. 93, pp. 29–30, quoted in Wang Yunsheng, *Liushi nian lai*, p. 72.

14. "Taiwan 'Ban'chi seibatsu yōryaku" (A summary of the expedition to the "barbarian" lands in Taiwan), in *Tai Shi kaiko roku* (Recollections of China), "A Guide to the Expedition to the Barbarian Land in Taiwan," in *Recollections about China*, pp. 53–54, quoted in Wang Yunsheng, *Liushi nian lai*, pp. 65–66.

15. *Li Wenzhong Gong quanshu-yishu hangao* (The complete works of Li Hongzhang—translated correspondence), vol. 2, pp. 36–39, cited in Wang Yunsheng, *Liushi nian lai*, pp. 78–79.

16. Qing Ruji, *Jiawu zhanzheng yiqian Meiguo qinlue Taiwande ziliao jiyao* (Compilation of materials concerning the American aggression in Taiwan prior to the 1894 War), cited in Wang Yunsheng, *Liushi nian lai*, p. 105.

17. Payson J. Treat, *Diplomatic Relations between the United States and Japan*, vol. 1 (Stanford: Stanford University Press, 1932), p. 477. Quoted in Wang Yunsheng, *Liushi nian lai*, p. 106.

18. Tōten is an alternative name of Miyazaki Torazo. A firm supporter of Sun Yat-sen, he helped Sun contact Chinese residing in Japan, when Sun was taking refuge there. In 1902, he published his autobiography, *Sanjūsan nen no yume* (My thirty-three-year dream), describing his and Sun's revolutionary experiences. This book has become important for research on Sun and the 1911 Revolution as well as on Sino-Japanese relations. Miyazaki later worked for the establishment of the *Tongmenghui*, becoming one of its earliest foreign members.

19. Nomura Koichi, *Jindai Ribende Zhongguo renshi* (The understanding of China in modern Japan) (Beijing: Zhongyang bianyi chubanshe, 1999), p. 119.

20. Araki Seishi, "Miyazaki Hachiro," *Sokoku*, May 1954, p. 182; cited in Wang Yunsheng, *Liushi nian lai*, p. 120.

21. *Miyazaki Tōten zenshū* (The complete works of Miyazaki Tōten) (Tokyo: Heibonsha, 1971–1976), vol. 1, p. 109; cited in Wang Yunsheng, *Liushi nian lai*, p. 120.

22. The thirteenth chapter of General Albert Wedemeyer's memoirs, *Wedemeyer Reports!*, says: "Chiang Kai-shek had not been invited to Casablanca, nor had China's needs been given serious consideration.... Yet, thanks in large part to British influence on our thinking and strategy, China's role and China's claim for voice in Allied counsels were disregarded." Albert C. Wedemeyer, *Wedemeyer Reports!* (New York: Henry Holt, 1958), p. 189. The tenth chapter of General Claire Chennault's 1949 memoir, *Way of a Fighter*, also mentioned that "Generalissimo and Madame Chiang still bitterly resented the decision of the British government (taken when they were most pressed at home) to avoid affront to the Japanese by closing the Burma road"; Claire Lee Chennault, *Way of a Fighter* (New York: G. P. Putnam's Sons, 1949), p. 141.

23. Vyshinsky took up the post of Deputy Foreign Minister of the Soviet Union in 1946, becoming Foreign Minister in 1949. The Sino-Soviet Treaty of Friendship and Alliance, signed on February 14, 1950, was signed by him and the Chinese Premier and Foreign Minister Zhou Enlai.

24. For the full text of the "Four Power Declaration," see *Zhonghua Minguo waijiao shiliao huibian* (Compilation of Republic of China materials on diplomatic history), vol. 12, pp. 5931–5932.

25. *Zhonghua Minguo waijiao shiliao huibian*, pp. 5934–5935.

26. *Zhonghua Minguo waijiao shiliao huibian*, p. 6007.

27. Memoranda by the Chinese Government (Cairo, November 24, 1943), *United States Department of State/Foreign Relations of the United States Diplomatic Papers, The Conferences at Cairo and Tehran, 1943* (1943) (Washington, D.C.: Government Printing Office, 1961), p. 387.

28. A November 23 item in the Hopkins Papers of the "Cairo Conference" volume of the U.S. Diplomatic Papers mentions that Chiang paid considerable attention to the Soviet attitude toward China; he made a point of mentioning the Communist Party, Xinjiang issue, and the independence of Outer Mongolia. *Diplomatic Papers, The Conferences at Cairo and Tehran, 1943*, p. 376.

29. See, for example, an article entitled "Jiang jieshi liangci jujue jieshou Liuqiu" (Chiang Kai-shek twice refused to accept Okinawa), in *Jiefangjun bao*, December 24, 2007. *Huanqiu shibao* also published an article, "Diaoyu tai huogen: erzhan hou Jiang Jieshi liang ju Liuqui huigui" (The roots of the Diaoyu tai discord: Chiang Kai-shek twice refused the restoration of the Ryukyus after World War II), which has circulated widely on the Internet.

30. Chiang Kai-shek, *An Inventory of His Diaries in the Hoover Institution Archives*, 43–10 (November 1943), November 3. Prepared by Lisa H. Nguyen, Hoover Institution, Stanford University, 2006, updated 2007, 2008.

31. *Zhonghua Minguo waijiao shiliao huibian* (12), p. 6015.

32. Chiang Kai-shek, *An Inventory of His Diaries*, 43–10 (November 1943), November 15.

33. Chiang Kai-shek, *An Inventory of His Diaries*, 43–10 (November 1943), November 17.

34. Chiang Kai-shek, *An Inventory of His Diaries*, 43–10 (November 1943), November 17, emphasis added.

35. *Diplomatic Papers, The Conferences at Cairo and Tehran, 1943* (1943), pp. 349–350.

36. *Diplomatic Papers, The Conferences at Cairo and Tehran, 1943* (1943), pp. 366–367.

37. The fourth item under "Articles about truce and peace negotiations" in *Guofang zuigao weiyuanhui mishu ting cheng Jiang Weiyuanzhang guanyu zhunbei zai Kailuo huiyi zhong tichuzhe zhanhou shi junshi hezuo, zhanshi zhengzhi hezuo ji zhanhou Zhong-Mei jingji hezuo deng san'ge fang'an* (Three formulas for proposing at the Cairo Conference military and political cooperation during the war and economic cooperation between China and the U.S. in the postwar period, presented by the Secretariat of the Supreme Council on National Defense to Generalissimo Chiang) (November 1943; the date of the original copy is uncertain) explicitly mentions "restoring all territory taken and occupied since 1894." *Zhonghua Minguo waijiao shiliao huibian* (12), p. 6022.

38. Chiang Kai-shek, *An Inventory of His Diaries*, 43–10 (November 1943), November 25.

39. *Zhonghua Minguo waijiao shiliao huibian* (12), p. 6072.

40. According to findings of historical researchers, after 1624, the Chinese in the Ryukyus never gained decision-making power, and their function was limited to supervising the tribute-paying of the Ryukyuan king. For Japan to use this precedent to claim the right to rule the Ryukyus, therefore, has no basis.

41. *Diplomatic Papers, The Conferences at Cairo and Tehran, 1943* (1943), pp. 322–323.

42. *Foreign Office Papers* 371/35755, letter from R. Peel, India Office, London, to the Foreign Office, London, dated 7 May 1943. Quoted in Melvyn Goldstein, *A History of Modern Tibet, 1913–1951: The Demise of the Lamaist State* (Berkeley: University of California Press, 1989), pp. 398, 399.

43. *Zhonghua Minguo waijiao shiliao huibian* (12), pp. 6016–6017.

44. Luobo-Dalaike (Robert Dallek), *Luosifu yu Meiguo duiwai zhengce* (Franklin D. Roosevelt and American foreign policy, 1932–1945), trans. Chen Qidi et al.

(Beijing: Shangwu yinshuguan, 1984), pp. 474, 556, 612, 474, 556. On the difference between the United States and Britain on their relationship to China and Asian colonies, see Wang Jianlang, *Cong Jiang Jieshi riji kan kangzhan houqide Zhong-Ying-Mei guanxi* (Sino-British-U.S. relations in the late anti-Japanese war period in the diary of Chiang Kai-shek, *Minguo dang'an* (Republican Archives) 4 (2008).

45. *Zhonghua Minguo waijiao shiliao huibian* (12), pp. 6021–6022.

46. For example, Britain opposed wordings like "the four Northeastern four provinces and Taiwan must be restored to China" and "the necessity of granting independence to Korea," advocating it be replaced by "must certainly be given up by Japan" and "leave Japanese rule," out of fear of the associations this might conjure up in its Asian colonies. *Zhonghua Minguo waijiao shiliao huibian* (12), p. 6064.

47. *Zhonghua Minguo waijiao shiliao huibian* (12), p. 6035.

48. *Chiang Kai-shek, An Inventory of His Diaries*, 43–10 (November 1943), November 22–26, 1943. This entry records his reflections following the Cairo Conference.

49. *Zhonghua Minguo waijiao shiliao huibian* (12), p. 6060. It is noteworthy that Jiang mentions here the relationship between state structure and the "spiritual configuration of the nation" as well as compares "we Chinese, as fellow East Asians" to "Westerners" on the question of state structure. This demonstrates how different visions of world order played a definite role in the arrangements for a postwar order.

50. The Tuvas live in the area between the Sayan and the Tannu-ola Mountains. In the Qing period, the area was called "Tannu Uriankhai" and was a special area under the jurisdiction of the Qing military governor at Uliasutiai with a status equal to the four parts of Mongolia that included Kobdo and Kerk. The area was militarily occupied by Russia in 1914 and after the October Revolution, in mid-August 1921, the All-Tuva Constituent Khural declared the establishment of the Tannu-Tuva Ulus Republic and passed its first constitution. In 1944, the year after the Cairo Conference, Tannu-Tuva was unilaterally annexed by the Soviet Union.

51. *Diplomatic Papers, The Conferences at Cairo and Tehran, 1943* (1943), pp. 324–325.

52. Before the Marco Polo Bridge Incident [July 7, 1937, the beginning of the 1937–1945 war between China and Japan], China and the Soviet Union had signed a nonaggression pact and exchanged opinions; the two parties also signed the "Sino-Soviet Non-Aggression Pact" after Japan extended the war to Shanghai on August 13. By 1940, however, the Soviets had cooled to China because they thought China "enthusiastically supported the proposal to expel the Soviet Union from the League of Nations." In 1941, the Soviet Union put much pressure on Chiang after the New Fourth Army Incident and in the same year signed a treaty of neutrality with Japan, expressing in it its recognition of Manchukuo and the People's Republic of Mongolia. In Xinjiang, the Soviet army had invaded Hami in 1933–1934 and supported Sheng Shicai in his expulsion of Ma Zhongying, but it was not until the 1940s that Sheng came into conflict with the Soviets. Five months prior to the Cairo Conference, the Soviets withdrew their air force de-

tachment and geological survey group from Xinjiang, dismantled their aircraft factory, and withdrew their technicians. Sino-Soviet relations had, in other words, run into serious setbacks prior to the Cairo Conference. See *Zhonghua Minguo waijiao shiliao huibian* (12), p. 5818.

53. See *Diplomatic Papers, The Conferences at Cairo and Tehran, 1943* (1943), p. 403. A copy of the printed British document mentioned below can be found on p. 404.

54. *Diplomatic Papers, The Conferences at Cairo and Tehran, 1943* (1943), pp. 448–449.

6. Weber and the Question of Chinese Modernity

1. Weber's *Konfucianismus und Taoismus* has been translated into English by Hans H. Gerth as *The Religion of China: Confucianism and Taoism*, by which title it will be referred to subsequently in this text.

2. Raymond Williams, *Keywords, a Vocabulary of Culture and Society*, rev. ed. (New York: Oxford University Press, 1983), p. 208.

3. Matei Calinescu, *Five Faces of Modernity: Modernism, Avante-Garde, Decadence, Kitsch, Postmodernism* (Durham, N.C.: Duke University Press, 1987), p. 19.

4. Ibid., pp. 23–69.

5. Williams, *Keywords*, p. 208: "Walpole, 1748: 'the rest of the house is all modernized'; Fielding, 1752: 'I have taken the liberty to modernize the language'; Richardson, 1753: 'He scruples not to modernize a little.'"

6. Jürgen Habermas, *The Philosophical Discourse of Modernity: Twelve Lectures* (Cambridge, Mass.: MIT Press, 1987), p. 5.

7. Reinhart Koselleck, "Neuzeit," in *Futures Past: On the Semantics of Historical Time* (Cambridge, Mass.: MIT Press, 1985), p. 241. Quoted in Habermas, *Discourse of Modernity*, p. 6.

8. Habermas, *Discourse of Modernity*, p. 7.

9. Jürgen Habermas, "Modernity: An Incomplete Project," in Hal Foster, ed., *The Anti-Aesthetic: Essays on Postmodern Culture* (Port Townsend, Wash.: Bay Press, 1983), p. 9. In his authoritative *The Theory of Communicative Action*, vol. 1, trans. Thomas McCarthy (Boston: Beacon Press, 1984), pp. 168–185, Habermas provides a more detailed explication of rationality and the division among its three component parts.

10. Calinescu, *Five Faces*, pp. 39–41.

11. Ibid., p. 45.

12. Ibid., pp. 54–55.

13. Williams, *Keywords*, pp. 208–209, 160–161, 242–245, 318–329.

14. Calinescu, *Five Faces*, p. 66.

15. David Harvey, *The Condition of Postmodernity* (Cambridge, Mass.: Basil Blackwell, 1990), p. 12.

16. Habermas, *Discourse of Modernity*, p. 83

17. Ernst Cassirer, *The Philosophy of Enlightenment* (Boston: Beacon Press, 1951), p. 5.

18. Octavio Paz, *Children of the Mire*, trans. Rachel Phillips (Cambridge, Mass.: Harvard University Press, 1974), p. 23; quoted in Calinescu, *Five Faces*, p. 61.

19. Calinescu, *Five Faces*, p. 60.

20. Ibid., pp. 60–61.

21. Ibid., pp. 62–63.

22. Ibid., p. 63.

23. Quoted in ibid., p. 65.

24. Jürgen Habermas, "Ernst Bloch—A Marxist Romantic," *Salmagundi* 10–11 (Fall 1969–Winter 1970): 313; quoted in Calinescu, *Five Faces*, p. 65.

25. Quoted in Calinescu, *Five Faces*, p. 67. The relationship between the Christian concept of time and utopianism is somewhat controversial. I visited the Chinese University of Hong Kong in 1994 and talked with the scholar of Christian theology Liu Xiaofeng. He thinks that Western utopian thought originated in ancient Greece rather than in Christianity—as far as the conceptualization of time is concerned, utopia exists in the future, and people thus move toward it. On the other hand, Christian doctrine holds that Christ approaches us, with God thus moving in our direction.

26. Habermas, *Discourse of Modernity*, p. 1.

27. Ibid., pp. 1–2.

28. Ibid., p. 2.

29. Max Weber, *The Protestant Ethic and the Spirit of Capitalism*, trans. Talcott Parsons (London: Routledge, 1992), p. 13.

30. Raymond Aron, *Main Currents in Sociological Thought*, vol. 2, trans. Richard Howard (New York: Anchor Books, 1970), p. 268.

31. Edward Shils and Henry Finch, eds., *Max Weber on the Methodology of the Social Sciences* (New York: The Free Press, 1949), p. 90, quoted in Lewis A. Coser, *Masters of Sociological Thought: Ideas in Historical Context*, 2nd ed. (New York: Harcourt Brace Jovanovich, 1977), p. 223.

32. Aron, *Main Currents*, p. 269.

33. Ibid., p. 270.

34. Weber, *The Protestant Ethic*, p. 24.

35. Max Weber, *From Max Weber: Essays in Sociology*, trans. and ed. H. H. Gerth and C. Wright Mills (New York: Oxford University Press, 1958), p. 267.

36. Weber, *The Protestant Ethic*, pp. 27–28.

37. Max Weber, *The Religion of China: Confucianism and Taoism*, ed. and trans. Hans H. Gerth (New York: Macmillan, 1964), p. 249.

38. Ibid., p. 12.

39. Ibid., p. 20.

40. Ibid., p. 41.

41. Ibid., p. 81.

42. Ibid., p. 86.

43. Ibid., p. 100.

44. Ibid., p. 104.

45. Hans Norbert Fugen, *Max Weber Mit Selbstzeugnissen und Bilddokumenten* (n.p.: Rowohlt Taschenbuch Verlag, 1985), p. 132.

46. Weber, *The Religion of China*, p. 152.
47. Ibid., p. 226.
48. Aron, *Main Currents*, p. 302.
49. Ibid., p. 300.
50. Ibid.
51. Herbert Marcuse, *One Dimensional Man: Studies in the Ideology of Advanced Industrial Society* (London: Routledge and Kegan Paul, 1968), p. 251.
52. Weber, *The Religion of China*, pp. 222–223.
53. Habermas, *Discourse of Modernity*, p. 2.
54. Ibid.
55. Ibid., p. 3.
56. Gilbert Rozman, ed., *The Modernization of China* (New York: The Free Press, 1982).
57. Arif Dirlik, "Shijie tixi fenxi he quanqiu ziben zhuyi—dui xiandaihua lilun de yizhong jiantao" (An analysis of world systems and global capitalism: A review of modernization theory) *Zhanlue yu guanli* (Strategy and management), *Chuangkan hao* (first issue), p. 51.
58. Ibid., pp. 51–52.
59. Fernand Braudel, *The Structures of Everyday Life: Civilization and Capitalism, Fifteenth–Eighteenth Century*, vol. 1 (New York: Harper and Row, 1985), p. 23.
60. Ibid., p. 24.
61. Dirlik, "Shijie tixi," pp. 52–53.
62. Frederic Jameson, "Third World Literature in the Era of Multinational Capital," *Social Text* (Fall 1986): 71.
63. Ibid., p. 68.
64. Williams, *Keywords*, pp. 252–256.
65. Gottfried Wilhelm Leibniz, *Novissima Sinica*, trans. Daniel J. Cook and Henry Rosemont Jr. (Chicago: Open Court, 1994), p. 1.
66. Hayden White, *Tropics of Discourse—Essays in Cultural Criticism* (Baltimore: Johns Hopkins University Press, 1978), p. 239.
67. Jürgen Habermas, *The Theory of Communicative Action*, vol. 1, trans. Thomas McCarthy (Boston: Beacon Press, 1984), p. xl.
68. See Gao Xuanyang, *Habomasi lun* (On Habermas) (Taibei: Yuanliu chubanshe, 1991) p. 280.
69. The words "intercultural" and "transcultural" have been used in English quite a bit, but the term "wenhua jianxing" I use here can be translated as "interculturality." In his essay "Seeking the Renovation of Research on China," Liu Dong uses this term, but the derivations and explanations of the term differ from one another. Liu's essay can be found in *Xueren* (The scholar), no. 7 (1994).

Credits

Chapter 1, The Politics of Imagining Asia, previously published as "The Politics of Imagining Asia: A Genealogical Analysis," in *Inter-Asia Cultural Studies* 8.1 (March 2007): 1–33.

Chapter 2, How to Explain "China" and Its "Modernity": Rethinking *The Rise of Modern Chinese Thought*, previously published as "The Liberation of the Object and the Interrogation of Modernity: Rethinking the Rise of Modern China," in *Modern China* 34.1 (January 2008): 114–140.

Chapter 3, Local Forms, Vernacular Dialects, and the War of Resistance against Japan: The "National Forms" Debate, previously published as "Local Form, Dialect and the Debate on 'National Form' in the War of Resistance against the Japanese Invasion," in *The UTS Review* (now *Cultural Studies Review*), 4:1 (May 1998): 25–41 (Part I); 4:2 (November 1998): 27–56 (Part II).

Index

Acheson, Dean, 171
Agency, subjective, 195, 263, 300; Chinese Revolution and, 53–54; in political analysis, 3, 34–35, 41; political legitimacy and, 85–86; Tibet and, 204–205
Aggression, as liberation, 241–243
Agrarian revolution, 24–26, 311n26–27
Agriculture, capitalist, 24–26, 311n27
Ai Siqi, 97
All China Literary Association to Resist the Enemy, 104
Anderson, Benedict, 76–77, 329n32
Anderson, Perry, 18
Anglo-Chinese Conventions, 173
"Anti-modern modernity," 91–93
Antiquity, 266, 274–275
Aristotle, 18
Aron, Raymond, 281–282, 291–292
Art, Chinese, 106–107, 208–209
ASEAN, China and, 11–12
Asia, European idea of, 12–22, 58–62
Asian historical narratives, 41–59; "core/periphery" framework and, 45–48, 55; inland relations and, 49–54; maritime Asia and, 46, 48–49, 52–54; networks and, 47–49, 54, 315n77; tribute system and, 45–49, 54–55; wars and revolutions and, 51–54
Asian regional cooperation, 11–12, 59–60
Asian totality, as category, 46, 61

Baihua vernacular, 96, 105. *See also* Modern language movement (China)
Bandung Conference, 243

"Barbarians," expelling, 20–22
Ba Ren, 130–131
Baudelaire, Charles-Pierre, 270
"Beijing University Dialect Investigation Society" (1924), 116, 323n40
Bell, Daniel, 269
Berlin, Isaiah, 89
Bhutan, 172–173, 332n60, 332–333nn63–64,
Bismarck, Otto von, 231
Blavatsky, Helena Petrovna, 147–148
Bloch, Ernst, 276–277
Bodin, Jean, 18
Bön religion in Tibet, 210, 215
Bourdieu, Pierre, 214
Bourgeois values, 269–271
Braudel, Fernand, 297–298
Brauen, Martin, 138
Buddhism, Tibetan, 152–153, 206, 210, 213–215; compared to Indian Buddhism, 141; opposing views of, 139–140
Burkhardt, Jacob, 95, 317n2
Burma, 252

Cadogan, Alexander, 254
Cairo Conference, 243–260; Chiang and Roosevelt at, 248–250, 254–258; Joint Declaration of, 248–249, 252–254, 258–259; Ryukyu issue and, 245–251, 254, 258–259
Calinescu, Matei, 266, 269–270, 271, 277; *Five Faces of Modernity*, 274–276
Capitalism: agriculture and, 24–26, 311n27; Asia and European development of, 57–58, 316n87; in European idea of

Capitalism *(continued)*
 Asia, 15–17, 19, 22, 59–60; Lenin on, 23–26, 27, 34; modernity and, 269, 279–282; modernization theory and, 299; monopoly, 298; print, 329n32; rationalization and, 292; Song dynasty, 57; study of literature and culture and, 299–300; transnational, 298, 300; Weber's views of China and, 283, 287, 289; world system analysis and, 299
Castro, Hector David, 171
Centralized administrative structure, 64–66; compared to ethnic autonomous regions, 179; Kyoto School and, 74–75, 79; Weber's view of, 285–287
Chamdo region, 183, 334n79
Changzhou School, 87
Checking the Travel Permits (troupe), 106–107
Cheefoo Convention, 165
Chen Boda, 97, 101–102
Chen Duxiu, 323n45
Chennault, Claire, 340n22
Chen Wangdao, 120
Chen Yinke, 50, 71
Chiang Kai-shek: at Cairo Conference, 244–251, 253–259; *China's Destiny*, 177–178; diaries of, 244, 246–250, 253–254, 257–259; the three powers and, 244, 340n22
China: banking system of, 309–310n7; as diverse category, 78, 86, 163; economics and, 198–199, 220, 257; Japan and, 232–234; modernity in (*see* Modernity, China and); political tradition of, 251–252, 260 (*see also* Institutional structures; Tribute systems); regions and corridors of, 190, 335n87; rural and urban, 103–104; Soviet Union and, 258, 342–343n52; United States and, 248–250, 254–258; Weber's study of (*see under* Weber, Max). *See also* Ethnic autonomous regions; Language, Chinese; Ming dynasty; "National forms" debate; Qing dynasty; Song dynasty; "Tibetan Question"; Yuan dynasty
China's Destiny (Chiang), 177–178
Chinese characters, reform and, 118–119, 122, 134
Chinese Communist Party, 99, 179, 318n9
"Chinese flavor," 98–101
Chinese nation, 177–179, 188, 200–201

Chinese Revolution (1911): impact of, on socialism, 22–29; inland relations and, 53–54; movements for independence and, 161; nationalist knowledge and, 91; Tibetan response to, 168; Western youth and, 151–152
"Chinese style," 98–101
Christianity, modernity and, 266, 274–282, 293
Churchill, Winston, 244–245, 249
Cinema, Chinese, 208
Clan structure, 286–287
Class: Asian analysis of, 34–37, 97, 99; Chinese language and, 105, 109, 111, 115–116, 119, 123, 127–128, 132; politics, end of, 199; politics, Tibet and, 203, 205
Classical Studies, New Text Confucianism and, 87
Cold War, 251, 259, 262
Collective objectives, 221–222, 224
Collective ownership, 212
Colonialism: British, 165–167, 171–175, 332–333nn60–64; Cairo Conference and, 253, 343n46; conceptualization of Asia and, 12; Tibet and variations on, 155–175
Common language, Chinese, 103, 105, 110–112. *See also* Modern language movement (China)
Common speech (*putonghua*), 109, 116–117, 119, 133
Communalist perspective, 221, 223
Communication: Habermas's theory of, 301, 304–305; significance of, 57
Communist movement, 99, 318n9
"Conference on the Unification of Pronunciation," 121–122, 325n59
Confucian *Analects*, 320–322n38
Confucianism, 13, 163; ethics of, compared to Puritan, 289–290, 293; political legitimacy and, 80–81, 85–88, 316n5; rationalism, 289–290; in Song dynasty, 65–72; Weber on, 283–284, 288–291. *See also* Neo-Confucianism
Consciousness: Chinese, 178; historical, 69–70; language and social, 128–129; political, 35, 134
Continuity, political legitimacy and, 77, 85–87
Convention of Kanagawa, 239
Cooper, Robert, 41–42
Cooperation, ethnic autonomous regions and, 180–181

Index

"Core/periphery" framework: in tribute systems, 45–48, 55, 315–316n83; in world systems analysis, 299–300
Cornwallis, Charles, 173–174
Corridors, of China, 190, 335n87
Court for Managing the External (*Lifan yuan*), 157
"Culturalism," 18, 42, 209
Cultural migration (China), 103–104
Cultural politics. *See* Political culture
Cultural reproduction, 288, 303–304
Cultural Revolution, Tibet and, 203–204, 209
"Cultural sphere," 41–59, 61
Culture, Chinese, 103, 163, 178; linguistic community and, 303–306
Culture, new perspective on study of, 303–306

Dalai Lamas, 167–170, 183, 189, 334n79, 337n105; "Greater Tibet" idea of, 191–194
Dalian, 255
Danzeng Lunzhu, 219
Daoism, Weber on, 283–284, 288–291
Daotong (orthodoxy), 86, 316n5
"Death of God," 276–277
De Long, C. E., 239
Democracy, ethnic communities and, 222, 227
Depoliticization, 41, 199–200, 336n96; Tibetan crisis as, 208–209
Deqin Tibetan region, 212, 216, 336n103
Desideri, Ippolito, 140
"Despotism" concept, 15, 18–19
Developmentalism, logic of, 198, 219, 225, 227
Dialects: Chinese "national forms" debate and, 109–112, 114–130; Japanese and Korean languages and, 112–114; surveys and, 116, 323n41; transcending, 115, 320–322n38
Dirlik, Arif, 298
Discourse of modernity, 6, 265–278
Discourses on Asia, 2, 12–62; Asian historical narratives and, 41–59; critique of, 77–85; European discursive context and, 12–22, 313n40; new "world history" narratives and, 58–62; Russian/Leninist perspective and, 22–29, 33–34; social revolutionary perspective and, 29–41; "starting point" theory in, 15–17. *See also* Empire, concept of; *Nation-state concept*

Discrimination, in China, 195–196, 222
Diversity, 61, 93, 223; unity in, 177–179, 187–194, 197, 227
Dolan, Brooke, 170
Dorzhiev, Agvan, 169–170
Drepung monastery, 203
Du Ai, 108
"Dynasty" concept, 84

East Asia: European discursive context and, 12–22; historical narratives of, 41–59; modern Japanese idea of, 20
"East Asian Cooperative Community," 39
East Asian international order: 19th and 20th century changes in, 228–236; Japanese invasion of Taiwan and, 236–243
"East Asian modern age," 74–75
East India Company, 172–173, 332n62
East is Red (musical), 208
East/West binary: critique of, 2, 4, 64–65, 84, 88; historical narratives and, 12, 42, 44–45, 47, 57, 60; Japan and, 21; modernity and, 78–80; socialism and, 40
Economic ethic, Weber and, 283–285, 287–288
Economic growth of China, 198–199, 220. *See also* Market reforms in China
Economics: autarkic, 298–299; Confucianism and, 290; market, 17, 22, 298
Eden, Anthony, 245, 253
Education system (China), 121, 290, 326n68
Eisenstadt, S. N., 79
Empire, concept of: Chinese *"diguo"* and, 81–82; Chinese modernity and, 72–85; "cooperative," 41–42; critique of, 78–82; in European idea of Asia, 3, 15–19, 59–60; Lenin, capitalism and, 27; Montesquieu's explanation of, 19–20; opposing discourses on, 11–12, 41–42, 78
Empire and State (Wang), 78, 80
Enfeoffment, 65–66, 242
Engels, Friedrich, 51, 269
Enlightenment, 15, 272–275, 313n40
Equality: ethnic autonomous regions and, 195–197; ethnic minority society and, 220–224; formal *versus* actual, 195, 242; material *versus* formal law, 290; struggle for discursive, 8; Tibetan "democratic reform" and, 205
Ethnic autonomous regions, 179–187; concept of "region" and, 190–191; hybrid

Ethnic autonomous regions (continued) nature of, 187–194; institutional structure of, 180; mobility and, 218–220; questions about, 221–224; undermining of, 206. See also by name of region

Ethnicity: changing society and, 226–227; interaction and, 223–224, 338n118; problems in theory of, 189–190; villages and, 188

Ethnic nationalism, 162–165, 329n34; Han Chinese and, 176–177; Tibet and, 169

Ethnic policy: crisis of, 194–199; equality and, 195–197, 221–224; preferential treatment in, 195–196, 222

Eurocentrism, 4, 61–62, 260

Europe: idea of Asia of, 12–22; new system of knowledge in, 15–18; orientalism of, 137–154; reexamining the idea of, 58–59; sinking back into Asia and, 14

European union, 11, 41–42

Exceptionalism, Western, 164

Expansion, colonial, 15; international law and Japanese, 230–236; logic of, 231–232

Explanation for the Dispatching of the Ministers Plenipotentiary (Meiji government), 231

Fang Yizhi, 324n52
Fei Xiaotong, 184, 187, 189–190, 335n87
Feng, 320–322n38
Five Faces of Modernity (Calinescu), 274–276
"Folk forms," 101–106, 110–111
Folk literature, 110–111
"Forced transformation," 104
Formosa, 259
Foucault, Michel, 6, 302–303
"Four Power Declaration," 245
Four-power framework, 244–245, 255
Frank, Andre Gunder, 57–58, 316n87
Freedom. See Subjective freedom
French Revolution, 21–22
Fu Bingchang, 244–245
Fukuzawa Yukichi, 13, 18–21, 35–36
Fu Sinian, 122
Future, modernity and concept of, 268, 271–272, 276–277

Gao Changhong, 104
Gao Hongzhi, 174
Gehlen, Arnold, 296
Gellner, Ernest, 17, 162
General Truth and Anti-General Truth (Wang Hui), 91–92

Genocide, 329n34
Ge Yihong, 97
Globalization, impact of, 41, 196, 212, 214, 221, 224; on linguistic crisis, 215–217
Goldstein, Melvyn, 203, 213
Gongyang learning, 80, 83, 87, 316–317n6
Great Britain. *See* United Kingdom
"Greater Asianism," 30–33; cultural heterogeneity and, 31, 313n44; Pan-Europe proposal and, 313–314n52; socialism and, 40–41; Sun Yat-sen and, 30–33, 313n42
"Greater East Asia" policy (Japan), 29, 32
"Greater Tibet" idea, 191–194
Great Wall, as "center," 50
Greek mysteries, Tibet and, 144–145
Grunfeld, Tom, 203
Guangxi Zhuang Autonomous region, 186
Guerrilla strategy, 52–54
Gu Hongming, 217, 337n110
Gu Jiegang, 178
Guo Moruo, 104
Gu Yanwu, 82

Habermas, Jürgen, 11; "intersubjectivity" of, 305–306; on modernity, 267–268, 277, 343n9; on modernization theory, 295; on subjective freedom, 272–273; *The Theory of Communicative Action*, 301, 304–305; Weber and, 264, 278–280
Halliday, Fred, 160–161, 199
Hamashita Takeshi, 45–49, 55
Han Chinese: chauvinism of, 185–186; ethnic consciousness of, 176–177; ethnicity and, 182, 216–217; Qing dynasty and, 86; Tibetan hostility toward, 168–169
Han Yu, 316n5
Hardt, Michael, 78
Hart, James H., 166, 329n40, 329–330n42
Hartz, Louis, 1
Harvey David, 272
Heavenly Principle worldview, 66–72, 74–75, 77
Hegel, G. W. F., 16–18, 33–34, 44, 70, 146–147
"Hegemonic way, the culture of the," 31–33
Hegemony: U.S. intentions and, 258–259; Western orientalism and, 153
Herder, Johann Gottfried, 140–142
Heroism, Japanese, 240–241
Hevia, James, 314n69

Index

Hilton, James, Shangri-la story of, 149–150
Hiragana writing system, 320nn34–35
Historical change, perceptions of, 67–72, 75; modernity and, 266, 268; "the propensity of the times" and, 69–70
Historical narratives: creation of new "world history" and, 58–62. *See also* Asian historical narratives; Discourses on Asia
Hitler, Adolph, 148, 329n34
Hobsbawm, E. J., 73, 200, 329n34, 337n109
Hong Kong, 253
Hopkins, Harry, 245, 340n28
Huang Sheng, "National Forms and the Language Issue," 126–130
Huang Yaomian, 109–110
Huang Zunxian, 111, 320n32
Hu Feng, 132–134, 319n18
Hukou household registration system, 218, 337n111
Hull, Cordell, 245
Hu Shi, 122, 323n45
Hu Yaobang, 214

Identity: Japan, Korea and national, 114; Tibetan, 204, 206, 213, 215
Identity, Chinese national: creating, 97, 100–101, 208–209; diversity and, 93; "local forms," language and, 107; minority role in, 208–209; politics of universal, 206, 209
Identity politics, 206, 223, 263
Imperialism: aggression and, 241–243; Chinese trade networks and, 48; formal equality and, 242; "Greater Asianism" and, 31–32; international law and, 230–236; logic of, 61–62, 231–232
Independence movements (China), 169–170, 176
India, 170–171, 252, 282, 332–333n64
Indo-China (Vietnam), 252, 256, 259
Industrial Revolution, 58
Inequality, 195–196, 198–199. *See also* Equality
Inner Mongolian Autonomous Region, 184–185
Institutes for Proper Pronunciation, 96
Institutional structure (China): autonomous prefectures and counties and, 184–185, 191; centralized administrative structure and, 64–66, 74–75, 79, 180; clan structure and, 286–287; critique of Weber's view of, 285–287; divinely ordained imperial power as, 290; ethnic autonomous regions as, 179–194; flexible inner-outer distinctions of, 234–235, 237–243; following local custom and, 102, 180, 188, 222, 237–238; spiritual configuration and, 255, 342n49; townships and, 188, 191
"Interculturality," 306, 345n69
Internationalism, 32–33, 35, 98–99
International law: earliest use of imperial, 236–243; impact of, on Asian order, 230–236
International Public Law (Martin), 233
"Intersubjectivity," 305–306
"Investigative Report into the Social and Economic Causes of the March 14 Incident in the Tibetan Areas," 204–205, 337n104
Iraq, invasion of, 242–243
Irvine School of historical writing, 309n3
Iwakura delegation, 231
Iwakura Tomomi, 232

Jameson, Frederic, 299–300
Japan, 20–21, 29, 53, 255; "cultural sphere" idea of, 42–59; language and, 112–113, 320n32; logic of expansion and, 231–232; Meiji government in, 112–113, 231–234. *See also* Okinawa; Ryukyus
Jaspers, Karl, 13–14
Jin dynasty, 87
Joint progress, of ethnic autonomous regions, 185–186

Kana phonetic syllabary, 320n34
Kang Youwei, 90, 177–178, 190–191, 333n67
Kant, Immanuel, 142–145
Karatani Kojin, 95
Kashag. *See* Tibetan Kashag (governing council)
Katakana writing system, 320n34
Katayama Junkichi, 113
Ke Zhongping, 97, 99–100, 106–107
Kido Takayoshi, 232
Kim Dae-jung, 213–214
"Kingly way, the culture of the," 31–33
Kita Ikki, 37, 39
Knowledge: modern, 296–297; nationalist, 3, 86, 88–94, 161, 164, 165
Korea: independence of, 247–248, 251–254, 256, 259; language and, 113–114

Kowloon, 253
Kyoto School, 73–76, 79, 83

Lamaism, 141–142, 149–154. *See also* Dalai Lamas; Panchen Lamas
Land reform, 23–26, 203–205
Language: European and Sanskrit, 15–16; European orientalism and, 145–146; Japanese, 112–113, 320n32; Korean, 113–114; nation-states and written, 95–96; subjective agency and, 300
Language, Chinese, 6–7, 95–135; challenge to classical, 115–116, 125; Chinese characters and, 118–119, 122; class and, 105, 109, 111, 115–116, 119, 123, 127–128, 132; critiques of reform of, 125–130; dialects issue and, 109–130; grammatically complete, 125–126; lifeworld roots of, 303–306; linguistic crisis in Tibet and, 215–217, 337n109; movement, modern, 109–130; National Language (*guoyu*) and, 117–118, 121–123, 3 23–324n46, 325n63; political aspects of, 106, 124, 126; "rational" concept and, 301–303; rural "folk language" and, 104, 106–107; shift to oral, 115–116; social consciousness and, 128–129; urban "common language" and, 103, 105, 110–112; Westernization and, 118–119, 127–128; Western phonetic spelling and, 118–123
Lao Naixuan, 121
Lardy, Nicholas, 309–310n7
"Late comers," in modernization theory, 3, 296–297
Latinization movement, 119, 123–124, 133–134, 325–326nn65–66
Lattimore, Owen, 50
Le Gendre, Charles, 239–240
Legitimacy, political. *See* Political legitimacy
Leibniz, Gottfried Wilhelm, 302
Lenin, V. I.: Chinese Revolution and, 22–29, 312n38; on multinational states, 27, 30; on national self-determination, 27–28, 36–37, 40; problems of state and, 27–28, 312n36
Lhasa, 167–169, 178, 198, 201, 219
Liang Qichao, 91–92, 177, 333n67
Liaotung Peninsula, 255
Liberalism, rights-based, 221, 223
"Liberal revolution," 151–152
Liberation movements, 60, 179; "Greater Asianism" and, 29, 33, 35, 37–39, 41; political goals of, 262–263; Sun Yat-sen and, 32, 313n45
Li Dazhao, 33, 109–110, 313–314n52
Lifeworld, language rooted in, 303–306
Li Hongzhang, 238–239
Linguistic communities, 303–306
Linguistic modernity, 129
Linguistic nationalism, 162, 329n32
Li Shaoming, 335n87
Literary "massification" movement, 96, 110, 132–134, 317n4
Liu Baonan, 320–322n38
Liu Dong, 345n69
Liu Taigong, 320–322n38
Liu Xiaofeng, 344n25
Local custom, following, 102, 180, 188, 222, 237–238
"Local forms," 101–106
Long March, 201–202
Lüshun (Port of Arthur), 255–257
Lü Xinyu, 311n27
Lu Xun, 133

Machiavelli, Nicolò, 18, 35
Macro-regions of China, 190, 335n87
Maeda Naonori, 43
Ma Jianzhong, *Ma's Language Reference*, 118, 125, 324n50
Malay states, 252
Mallaby, Sebastian, 41
Manchuria, 232, 253, 259; Japan invasion of, 240–242; language and, 113–114; Qing dynasty and, 84, 86
Mandarin alphabet, 121
Mandarin (*Guanhua*) language, 96
Manyogana system, 320nn33–34
Mao Zedong, 54, 98–99, 204, 337n105
Marcuse, Herbert, 292
Maritime Asia narrative, 46, 48–49, 52–54
Market economics: in European idea of Asia, 17, 22; in world systems analysis, 298
Market reforms in China, 221; discrimination and, 220, 338n114; income disparity and, 195, 199; religious penetration and, 206, 211–213; social divisions/turbulence and, 198, 206–207; "Tibetan Question" and, 205–207, 211–213, 215–220
Ma Rong, 195–196, 219, 336n96
Marshall, George, 170

Martin, W. A. P., *International Public Law*, 233, 241
Maruyama Masao, 20–21, 35–36, 47, 311n21
Marx, Karl, 23, 26, 51, 292, 310n6; modernity and, 264, 269, 273–274
Marxism: Chinese, 98, 318n9; Western, 277
Ma's Language Reference (Ma), 118, 125, 324n50
Massification of literature, 96, 105–106, 110, 132–134, 317n4
Material asceticism of Protestantism, 282
Material equality *versus* formal law, 290
May Fourth Literary Movement, 7, 97, 105, 117; critiques of, 111–112, 125–130; negation of negation of, 130–135
Media, 225–226
Meiji government: international law and, 231–234, 237–243; language and, 112–113
Merrell, George, 331n54
Middle Ages, 266
Mikhailovski, Nicolai K., 310n6
Militarism, Chinese regional, 108–109
Ming dynasty: Japan and, 232, 234; Tibet and, 156–157
Ministry of Foreign Affairs (China), 236–237
Minorities. *See* Ethnic autonomous regions; Ethnicity; Ethnic policy
Missionaries, 119–120, 139–141, 144
Miyake Yonekichi, 112
Miyazaki Hachiro, 240–241
Miyazaki Ichisada: "East Asia" definition of, 44–46; on Song dynasty, 57–58, 73–74, 83, 314–315nn69–70
Miyazaki Tōten, 37–39, 240, 340n18
Mobility, ethnic regions and, 218–220, 224
Modernity: Asian, 23, 44–45, 49, 51, 57, 62; European and Asian ties and, 57–58; markets and, 58; narrative of, 15, 18, 59; science and, 89; Western mystical response to, 147–154
Modernity, China and, 5–6, 63–94; "anti-modern," 91–93; antithetical concepts and, 63–72; empire and nation-state narratives and, 72–85; future study of, 304–306; linguistic, 129; nationalist knowledge and, 88–94; political legitimacy and, 85–88; Western rationalism and study of, 278–282
Modernity, mind-set of, 264–306; aesthetic, 269–270; Christianity and, 266, 274–282, 293; contradictions within, 269, 271, 277–278; Enlightenment project of, 272–274; etymology and evolution of, 265–278; modernization theory and, 291–306; negative and positive connotations of, 267–268; studying China from within, 278–291. *See also* Rationalism; Rationality; Rationalization
Modernization theory, 291–306; beginning of, 295; Chinese discursive world and, 300–306; premises of, 297; specific content of, 295–296; "success" and "late comers" in, 3, 296–297; world systems analysis and, 297–299
Modern language movement (China), 109–130, 133–134; Chinese characters and, 118–119, 122; class and, 105, 109, 111, 115–116, 119, 123, 127–128, 132; critiques of, 125–130; dialects and, 109–112, 115–116, 320–322n38; history of, 114–119; reconsideration of, 130–135; Western phonetic spelling and, 118–123
Molotov, V. M., 245
Mongolian population, 184–185
Mongolian Yuan dynasty, 44, 87
Montesquieu, Baron de, 18–20
Moslem population, 185
"Most favored nation" clause, 233, 339n8
Multiculturalism, 188, 220
Multinational states/empires, 15, 27, 30
"Mutual frontier," thesis of, 50
"Mutual market" relationship, 55
Mysticism, Western, 147–154

National citizenry, 133–134
"National Forms and the Language Issue" (Huang), 126–130
"National forms" debate, 95–135, 317n6; "Chinese style" and "Chinese flavor" in, 98–101; "local forms" and, 101–106; modern language movement and, 109–130; negation of negation of "May Fourth" and, 130–135; problem of the "local" and the "pan-Chinese" in, 106–109; universal connotation of, 132; war time state building and, 97
Nationalism: Asian, 12, 32, 44, 52; classic model of, 21; constructing national languages and, 124, 326n68; European, 19, 161–165; Kyoto School view of,

Nationalism (continued)
73–74; linguistic, 162, 329n32; modern Chinese, 55, 175–179; "parochial," 225; subjective freedom and, 273–274; suzerainty and, 156; Tibet and, 137, 155–175. See also National self-determination; Nation-state concept

Nationalist knowledge, 3, 86, 165; construction and questioning of, 88–94; Tibetan question and, 161, 164

National Language (guoyu) (Chinese), 117–118, 121–123, 323–324n46, 325n63; Romanization, 122–123, 325n63

National liberation. See Liberation movements

National self-determination: Lenin on, 27–28, 36–37, 40; socialists and, 40; Sun Yat-sen and, 30–33; Third World movements and, 100; Wilson and, 7, 162

Nation-state concept: Chinese modernity and, 72–85; conflict between tribute system order and, 229–263; different political entities and, 79; in European idea of Asia, 3, 15–20, 59–60; European "principle of nationality" and, 161–165; European union and, 11; French Revolution and, 21–22; Japan and, 20–21, 38–41; Lenin and capitalism and, 27–28, 312n35; in post revolution China, 175–179; relationship between inner and outer and, 241–243; rethinking, 78–81; Third World and, 100

Nation-state logic, 3, 7–8; Okinawa and, 229, 233

Negri, Antonio, 78

Nehru, Motilal, 159–160

Neo-Confucianism, 65–67, 70, 74–75

Neoliberalism, 4, 10–11, 41

Nepal, 172–174, 332–333n64

"New Asianism," 33, 313–314n52

"New Empire" concept, 10, 12, 61

New Literature Movement, 96, 102–103

New Text Confucianism, 87

New Writing, 123, 325–326n66

Ngawang Gelek, 198

Ningxia Hui [Moslem] Autonomous Region, 185

Nishijima Sadao, 42, 48

Nomura Koichi, 38–39, 240

Occidental rationalism, 279, 284

October Revolution, 27–28

Okinawa, 8, 228–263; Cairo Conference and postwar status of, 243–260; changes in international rules and, 230–236; Japanese invasion of Taiwan and, 236–243; political choices of, 260–263; "restoration concept" and, 228, 246, 248–249, 251, 341n29; social movements of, 228–229, 242, 260, 262–263; sovereignty, Japan and, 238–243; U.S. military occupation of, 243. See also Ryukyus

Okubo Toshimichi, 231

Olympics, 136–137, 198, 225

Orazio, Francesco, 143, 144–145

Order, East Asian. See East Asian international order

"Ordering Popular Customs" policy, 96

"Orientalism, Regional Ethnic Autonomy and the Politics of Dignity" (Wang), 327 (Chapter 4)

Orientalism, Western, 137–154

Orthodoxy (daotong), 86, 316n5

Ottoman Empire, 18–19

Outer Mongolia, 257, 259

Overseas Chinese, 48, 51–52, 56, 136, 138, 225–226

Ozaki Hotsumi, 39

Pacification Offices, 156–157, 192

Pacific War, as "struggle for living space," 231–232

Panchen Lamas, 176, 183, 194, 203, 332nn61–62

Pan Zinian, 124–126, 319n19

Particularism, 13, 88

Partisans, 52–54

Patois. See Dialects

Patriotism, internationalism and, 98–99

Paz, Octavio, 271, 274

Peasants, Chinese, 24, 26, 29, 53

Perry, Matthew, 239

Pescadores Islands, 246, 248, 250–251, 253, 255, 259

Phonetic alphabet, 121–122, 325n59

Phonetics, 323n45; Western phonetic spelling and, 118–123

Phonocentrism, 95–96

Phuntsok Wangyal, 197

Pingwu County Tibetan Autonomous Region, 189

Pinyin alphabet, 120

Political analysis, 34–41; partisan warfare and, 53–54; versus "state rationality," 35–41

Political consciousness, 35, 134
Political culture, 163–165, 178, 199; minorities in, 208–209; modern states and, 79; political legitimacy and, 86–88; tribute systems as, 55–56, 80. *See also* Chinese nation; Depoliticization
Political legitimacy, 77, 80–81, 83, 85–88; nationalism and, 162; Sino-British conflict and, 174–175; universalism and, 90–91
Political tradition of China, 251–252, 260. *See also* Institutional structure (China); Tribute systems
Politics of dignity, 226
Politics of recognition, 86, 338n115; public association and, 223–224; Tibet and, 155, 160–161, 169, 220–224
Popularization: of literature, 105; of vernacular, 116
Populism, Chinese Revolution and, 22–29
PRC (People's Republic of China), 80, 195, 202
Preferential treatment, 195–196, 222
Prejudice, Chinese, 223–224
Prester John, 139
Private property, theory of, 221
Progress, modernity and, 270–271
"Propensity of the times" (*shishi*), 5, 69–70, 76, 91, 94, 316n2
Protestant tradition, Weber's rationalism and, 278–282
Protest movements, 224–227
Purangir Gosain, 172
Puritan ethic, 289–290, 293
Pye, Lucian, 164

Qian Mu, 71, 323–324n46
Qian Xuantong, 115, 118, 122
Qing dynasty, 51, 54–56, 83–85, 314n69; flexible inner-outer distinctions in, 237–239; Japan and, 231–233, 236–239; Tibet and, 157, 165–168, 171–174, 330n44, 330n47
Qu Qiubai, 325n65

Rab Dgav, 202
Radek, Karl, 28, 312n38
Rationalism: Confucianism and, 289–290; modernity, Protestant tradition and, 278–282, 284, 289, 293; occidental, 279, 284
Rationality: as abstract product of linguistic rules, 301–302; modernity and, 266, 272–273, 277; "self-evident" link of to modernity, 280–282, 301; Weber and, 6, 292, 295; Weber's crisis of, 268–269. *See also* "State rationality"
Rationalization: in China, 281–282, 293–295; Chinese language and, 301; in India, 282; separation of modernity from, 295–296; universalism and, 278–280; Weber's study of China and, 282–291; Weber's theory of, 264–265, 273, 278–280, 291–295, 301–302; world systems analysis and, 300–301
Recognition. *See* Politics of recognition
Records of the Grand Historian, The (Sima), 189, 335n84
Regional order, East Asian. *See* East Asian international order
Regions: as autonomous units, 182–185; concept of, 190–191; six macro, 190, 335n87. *See also* Ethnic autonomous regions
Religion, Tibet and, 199, 202–203, 205–206, 209–215, 336–337n103
Religion, Weber's study of Chinese, 282–291
Religion of China, The (Weber), 265, 283–291
Returning gifts (*hu ci*), 55–56
Revel, Jean-François, 151–152
Revolution: Bolshevik, 29, 162; perspective of social, 12, 29–41, 162. *See also* Chinese Revolution (1911)
"Revolutionary literature" (1930s), 97, 105
Ricard, Mattieu, 150
Ricci, Matteo, 119
Rights, collective and individual, 221
Rise of Modern Chinese Thought (Wang), 5, 63–64, 70, 88–90, 93
Rites/music and institutions, Song Confucians and, 65–72
"Ritual China," 83–85
Romanization movement, 120–123, 324n55, 325n63
Romanticism, modernity and, 269, 275–277
Roosevelt, Elliott, 248–250, 252
Roosevelt, Franklin D., 244–245, 248–250, 254–258
Rozman, Gilbert, 296
Ruan Yuan, 323–324n46
Russia, 24–26, 32–33, 51, 169–170. *See also* Soviet Union

Russian Revolution, 29, 162
Russo-Japanese War (1905), 30, 51
Ryukyus, 230, 338n1; Cairo Conference and, 244–252, 254, 258–259; Chiang's joint trusteeship proposal for, 248, 250–251, 258; Chinese history and status of, 247; Chinese tribute system and, 233–234, 251, 341n40; Japan and, 232–234; Taiwanese aboriginals and, 236–242. *See also* Okinawa
Ryu Yong-Tae, 178, 333n67

Said, Edward, 138–139, 153
Saigo Takamori, 240–241
Saigo Tsugumichi, 240
Sanskrit and European language, 15–16
Satsuma Han, 234, 251, 339n10
Satsuma Rebellion, 240
Saussure, Ferdinand de, 116–117, 126, 323n44
Sautman, Barry, 198
Schmitt, Carl, 36, 52–53
Scientism, 89, 92, 118, 128–129
Secularization, 205–206, 274–275, 279
"Separate establishment," 180–181
Separatism, 180, 182, 183
Serfdom: abolition of Russian, 24; in Tibet, 203–205, 336–337n103
Seventeen-Point Agreement, 171
Shanghai Cooperation Organization (the "Shanghai Six"), 11
Shangri-la, 149–150, 154
Shatra Pal-jor Dorje, 170
"Shedding Asia," theory of, 13–15, 19–20, 311n21
"Shedding Europe," 29
Sheng Tai, 166, 329–330n42
Shen Weirong, 191, 335n89
Shimano Seiichiro, 113
Shi Shuo, 192, 330n44, 330n47
Siam (Thailand), 247, 252
Sikkim, 166, 172–173, 332–333n64
Silk Road, 143–144
Sima Qian, *The Records of the Grand Historian*, 189, 335n84
Simla Conference, 158–159, 170, 193
"Sinification," Tibet and, 213–214, 220
Sino-British treaty, 167
Sino-Japanese treaty, 233
Sino-Japanese War (1894), 53
Sino-Soviet Treaty of Friendship and Alliance, 340n23
Sino-Tibetan language family, 323n42

Smith, Adam, 16–18
Social and cultural reproduction: Confucianism and, 288–289; linguistic community and, 303–304; Weber and, 288
Socialism, 40–41, 205–206, 209; impact of Chinese Revolution on, 22–29; utopian, 277
Social rationalization. *See* Rationalization
Social revolutionary perspective, 12, 29–41
Soejima Taneomi, 236
Song dynasty, 44, 65–76, 79, 83
Song Ziwen, 245, 253
Sovereignty: contrasted with suzerainty, 158, 251; establishing Asian, 60; inner-outer distinctions and, 238–243, 260, 262; oppressed nations and, 243; politics of recognition and, 155, 160–161; Qing state and, 56; Third World and, 100; Tibet and, 155
Soviet Union, China and, 258, 342–343n52
Spatial relationships: colonialism and, 17; Tibet and China and, 192; utopia concept and, 276; Weber and, 278, 295; in world systems analysis, 299
Spring and Autumn Annals, 87
"State rationality": Japan and, 20–21; *versus* political analysis, 35–41
States: diverse political cultures of modern, 79, 81; the state *versus* the political and, 36. *See also* Nation-state concept
'*Su*' (practices), 320–322n38
Subjective agency. *See* Agency, subjective
Subjective freedom, 266, 272–274, 277
Sun Yat-sen: "Chinese nation" and, 177–179; "Greater Asianism" and, 30–33, 313n42, 313n44; land reform of, 23–26; national self-determination and, 40; on overseas Chinese, 51–52
Suzerainty: China and, 158; contrasted with sovereignty, 158, 251; imperial, 155–160; politics of recognition and, 155–161
Swift, Jonathan, 267

Tachibana Shiraki, 38–39
Taiping Rebellion, 293
Taiwan, 239–240, 244, 246–248, 250–251, 253, 255
Taiwan invasion (1874), 84–85, 339n10; imperialist international law and, 236–243

Takeuchi Yoshimi, 12–13
Tang-Song transition, 73–75
Tannu Tuva, 257, 342n50
Taylor, Charles, 223, 338n115
Taylor, Michael, 139, 327n2
Teleology, history and, 70, 76, 78
Thailand (Siam), 247, 252, 259
Theory of Communicative Action, The (Habermas), 301, 304–305
Theosophy, image of Tibet and, 147–149
Third Department of the Political Bureau of the Military Commission of the National Government of China, 104
Third World, 100, 300, 304
Tibet: central China and, 155–157, 174–175, 197, 199–202, 205–207; colonialism and, 158–159, 165–175; corruption in, 214; "democratic reform" in, 205; eastward progression of, 192–194; European excursions into, 139, 165–167; India and, 159–160, 170–171; internal conditions of, 176, 197, 207, 216–218; land reform in, 203–205; linguistic crisis in, 215–217; Ming dynasty and, 156–157, 193; mobility and, 218–220; Mongol rule of, 193; opposing views of, 139–140; population of, 184–185; Qing dynasty and, 157, 165–168, 171–174, 193, 330n44, 330n47; rebellion (1959) in, 200–203; religion and, 202–203, 205–206, 209–215, 336–337n103; response to imperialism of, 201–202; riots (2008) in, 136–137, 195, 198, 208, 211, 214; Russia and, 169–170; serfdom in, 203–205, 336–337n103; "sinification" and, 213–214; transformation (1950s) of, 201–205; United States and, 170–171, 331n54; Yuan dynasty and, 156
Tibetan Autonomous Region, 183–184, 191–194, 334n80
Tibetan Buddhism. *See* Buddhism, Tibetan
Tibetan Communist Movement, 202
Tibetan independence movement, 136, 138, 169–170, 197–198, 212
Tibetan Kashag (governing council), 170–171, 183, 194, 334n79
"Tibetan Question," 7–8, 136–227; Chinese nationalism and, 175–179; colonialism and, 165–175; conflicts between religion and secularization and, 209–215; ethnic autonomous regions and, 179–194; "Greater Tibet" idea and, 191–194; market reforms and, 205–207, 211–213, 215–220; politics of recognition and, 155, 160–161, 220–224; post-revolutionary development and, 194–209; protest movement and, 224–227; relationship with central China and, 199–202; suzerainty and, 155–161; "unity in diversity" and, 187–194; Western orientalism and, 137–154; Western "principle of nationality" and, 161–165
"Tibetan Revolutionary Party," 202
Tibetan-Yi corridor, 190
Tibetan Youth Congress (TYC), 198
Tibet-India Treaty, 166
Tibet-Mongolia Treaty, 169–170, 176
Tibet-Nepal Treaty, 165
Time, Western thought and, 70, 266–271, 273–274, 276–277
Tokugawa Ieyasu, 232
Tolstoy, Ilya, 170
Tong, Hollington, 252
Tong santong, 87, 316–317n6
Tōya, discourses on Asia and, 12–22
Toyotomi Hideyoshi, 232
Trade networks, 48–49, 56, 315n77
"Trans-systemic society," 189
Treaties, unequal, 165–167, 170–175, 242, 329–330n42, 331n52, 332–333nn63–64
Treaty of Friendship between India and Bhutan, 332–333n64
Treaty of Punakha, 332n63
Treaty of Sagauli, 172
Treaty of Sinchula, 173
Treaty systems, in European theory, 54–55
Tribute systems: Asian historical narratives and, 45–49, 51–52; conflict between nation-state logic and, 229–263; "core/periphery" framework of, 45–48, 55, 315–316n83; in European theory, 54–55; flexible inner-outer aspect of, 234–235, 251, 260, 341n40; "Greater Asianism" and, 31–32; Ryukyus and, 8, 233–234, 251, 341n40; Tibet and, 155–157, 174–175; as unique political culture, 55–56, 80
Trigault, Nicolas, 119
Tse-pon Shakabpa, 170
Tsong-kha-pa, 151, 328n19

United Kingdom: Cairo Conference and, 252–254, 258–259, 342n46; colonialism

United Kingdom *(continued)*
   of, 165–167, 171–175, 332–333n60–64; Tibet and, 158–159, 165–167, 174–175, 252–253, 330n44
United States: Cairo Conference and, 248–259; discourses of "empire" and, 41–42; hegemonic intentions of, 258–259; invasion of Iraq by, 242–243; Okinawa and, 243, 260–261; scholarship and western models, 309n3; Taiwan and, 239–240; Tibet and, 170–171, 331n54
"Unity in diversity," 177–179, 187–194, 197, 227
Universalism: Confucian, 90; European, 13, 15; identity and, 206, 209; linguistic logic of, 132; modernization theory and, 295–297; nation-state concept and, 90–91, 260; particularism and, 13, 88; rationalization, modernity and, 278–280, 287; singular, 88; Western exceptionalism and, 164
Universal Principle *(gongli)*, 77–78
Urban culture, common language and, 103, 105, 110–112
Utopianism, 276–277, 344n25

Vernacular language movement. *See* Modern language movement (China)
Vietnam (Indo-China), 252, 256, 259
Vilar, Pierre, 200
Villages, 188, 286
Vyshinsky, Andrey, 244, 340n23

Wang Chong, 322–323n39
Wang Chonghui, 245, 248, 253
Wang Gungwu, 56
Wang Hui: *Empire and State*, 78, 80; *General Truth and Anti-General Truth*, 91–92; introduction to, 1–9; "Orientalism, Regional Ethnic Autonomy and the Politics of Dignity," 327 (Chapter 4); *The Rise of Modern Chinese Thought*, 5, 63–64, 70, 88–90, 93
Wang Zhao, 121, 325n59
War of Resistance: Chinese literature and, 103–109; Latinization movement and, 119, 325–326n66; massification, nationalism and, 105, 133; "national forms" and, 98–99, 101; U.S., Chiang and issues regarding, 250–251

Weber, Max: on modernity, 264–265, 268–269, 273; pessimism of, 291–292; Protestantism, rationalism and, 278–282; *The Religion of China*, 265, 283–287; study of China by, 265, 281–291, 292–294, 302; theory of rationalization of, 6, 264–265, 273, 278–280, 291–294, 301–302
Wei Yuan, 56
Wenchuan earthquake, 227
White, Hayden, 302–303
"White-horse People," 189–190
Williams, Ray, 266, 270
Wilsonism, influence of, 161–162
Wong, R. Bin, 163
World history: creating new narratives for, 4, 58–62; critique of 19th century notion of, 74, 81; rationalization and, 280
World systems analysis, 297–301
World War II. *See* Pacific War; War of Resistance
Wuhan, cultural migration and, 104
Wu Zhihui, 118, 325n59

Xiang Linbing, 97, 104, 110–111
Xian Xinghai, 107–108
Xiao Liangzhong, 182–183
Xinjiang Uygur Autonomous Region, 181
Xu Baoqiang, 48

Ya ("correct"), 320–322n38
Yanagiwara Sakimitsu, 236, 238–239
Yan Fu, 1, 91–92, 121
Ying Shao, 320–323nn38–39
Yoshino Sakuzo, 37–38
Yuan dynasty, 44, 87, 156
Yu Yingchun, 320–322n38

Zaibatsu (Japanese), 37–38
Zeren Dengzhu, 212
Zhang Taiyan, 91–92, 115, 177, 325n59
Zhang Yintang, 167
Zhang Zongxiang, 37–38
Zhao Erfeng, 168, 330n47
Zhao Yuanren, 323n40
Zheng Jing, 232
Zheng Xuan, 320–322n38
Zhong Ying, 168
Zhou Enlai, 181–186, 194, 196, 340n23
Zhou Yang, 97, 131
Zur Khang, 329n31